ENCYCLOPEDIA OF COMPUTER SCIENCE AND TECHNOLOGY

VOLUME 34

INTERNATIONAL EDITORIAL ADVISORY BOARD

ENCYCLOPEDIA OF COMPUTER SCIENCE AND TECHNOLOGY

EXECUTIVE EDITORS

Allen Kent   *James G. Williams*

UNIVERSITY OF PITTSBURGH
PITTSBURGH, PENNSYLVANIA

ADMINISTRATIVE EDITORS

Carolyn M. Hall   *Rosalind Kent*

PITTSBURGH, PENNSYLVANIA

VOLUME 34
SUPPLEMENT 19

MARCEL DEKKER, INC.   NEW YORK • BASEL • HONG KONG

MARCEL DEKKER, INC.
270 Madison Avenue, New York, New York 10016

LIBRARY OF CONGRESS CATALOG CARD NUMBER: 74-29436
ISBN: 0-8247-2287-6

Current Printing (last digit)
10 9 8 7 6 5 4 3 2 1

PRINTED IN UNITED STATES OF AMERICA

CONTENTS OF VOLUME 34

Contributors to Volume 34   *v*

ARTIFICIAL INTELLIGENCE IN EDUCATION
John A. Self   1

COMPUTER PERFORMANCE
Rob J. Pooley   19

CONCEPTUAL STRUCTURES AND CONCEPTUAL GRAPHS
Guy W. Mineau   43

A COOPERATIVE COMPUTER
Anthony A. Clarke   77

DATABASE THEORY: AN INTRODUCTION
Gottfried Vossen   85

A DEEP KNOWLEDGE ACQUISITION TOOL
Rosamaria Morpurgo and Silvano Mussi   129

ELECTRONIC MUSIC
Lloyd Ultan   149

FUZZY LOGIC IN ARTIFICIAL INTELLIGENCE
Erich Peter Klement and Wolfgang Slany   179

FUZZY MODULES AND THEIR BASES
Godfrey C. Muganda   191

HUMAN ERROR BEHAVIOR IN CONCEPTUAL AND
   LOGICAL DATABASE DESIGN
Dinesh Batra   203

HUMAN RESOURCE MANAGEMENT
Dae-Ho Byun   223

iii

MANAGING INFORMATION TECHNOLOGY:
A RESOURCE ENHANCEMENT PERSPECTIVE
Mohan R. Tanniru   247

THE MODULARITY OF FACE RECOGNITION
Gillian Rhodes   261

NONMONOTONIC REASONING
Victor W. Marek and Anil Nerode   281

OPEN SYSTEMS SECURITY STANDARDS
Walter Fumy and Manfred Reitenspiess   301

PARALLEL RENDERING
Thomas W. Crockett   335

AN UNDERGRADUATE COURSE-ADVISING EXPERT
SYSTEM IN INDUSTRIAL ENGINEERING
Luis G. Occeña and Shannon L. Miller   373

CONTRIBUTORS TO VOLUME 34

DINES BATRA, Ph.D.   Department of Decision Sciences and Information Systems, College of Business Administration, Florida International University, Miami, Florida: *Human Error Behavior in Conceptual and Logical Database Design*

DAE-HO BYUN   Management Information Systems Laboratory, Department of Industrial Engineering, Pohang University of Science and Technology, Pohang, South Korea: *Human Resource Management*

ANTHONY A. CLARKE   Department of Computer Studies, Loughborough University of Technology, Loughborough, Leicestershire, England: *A Cooperative Computer*

THOMAS W. CROCKETT   Institute for Computer Applications in Science and Engineering, NASA Langley Research Center, Hampton, Virginia: *Parallel Rendering*

WALTER FUMY, Ph.D.   Corporate Research and Development, Department Systems and Networks, Siemens AG, Munich, Germany: *Open Systems Security Standards*

ERICH PETER KLEMENT, Ph.D.   Professor Mathematics, Fuzzy Logic Laboratory Linz-Hagenburg, Department of Mathematics, Johannes Kepler University Linz, Linz, Austria: *Fuzzy Logic in Artificial Intelligence*

VICTOR W. MAREK   Professor of Computer Science, University of Kentucky, Lexington, Kentucky: *Nonmonotonic Reasoning*

SHANNON L. MILLER   Industrial Engineer, U.S. Postal Service, St. Louis, Missouri: *An Undergraduate Course-Advising Expert System in Industrial Engineering*

GUY W. MINEAU   Department of Computer Science, Université Laral, Quebec City, Quebec, Canada: *Conceptual Structures and Conceptual Graphs*

ROSAMARIA MORPURGO   Full Professor of Computer Science, Dipartimento di Elettronica, Politecnico di Milano, Milan, Italy: *A Deep Knowledge Acquisition Tool*

GODFREY C. MUGANDA   Department of Computer Science, North Central College, Naperville, Illinois: *Fuzzy Modules and Their Bases*

SILVANO MUSSI   Manager of Research Projects, Consorzio Interuniversitario Lombardo per L'Elaborazione Automatica (CILEA), Milan, Italy: *A Deep Knowledge Acquisition Tool*

ANIL NERODE   Goldwin Smith Professor of Mathematics and Director, Mathematical Sciences Institute, Cornell University, Ithaca, New York: *Nonmonotonic Reasoning*

LUIS G. OCCEÑA, Ph.D.   Associate Professor, Department of Industrial Engineering, University of Missouri-Columbia, Columbia, Missouri: *An Undergraduate Course-Advising Expert System in Industrial Engineering*

ROB J. POOLEY   Department of Computer Science, University of Edinburgh, Kings Buildings, Edinburgh, Scotland: *Computer Performance*

MANFRED REITENSPIESS, Ph.D.   System Unit Midrange Systems, Siemens Nixdorf Informationssyteme AG, Munich, Germany: *Open Systems Security Standards*

GILLIAN RHODES, Ph.D.   Department of Psychology, University of Canterbury, Christchurch, New Zealand: *The Modularity of Face Recognition*

JOHN A. SELF   Department of Computing, Lancaster University, Lancaster, England: *Artificial Intelligence in Education*

WOLFGANG SLANY, Ph.D.   Christian Doppler Laboratory for Expert Systems, Information Systems Department, Technical University of Vienna, Vienna, Austria: *Fuzzy Logic in Artificial Intelligence*

MOHAN R. TANNIRU, Ph.D.   Associate Professor, School of Management, Syracuse University, Syracuse, New York: *Managing Information Technology: A Resource Enhancement Perspective*

LLOYD ULTAN, Ph.D.   Professor Emeritus, School of Music, University of Minnesota, Minneapolis, Minnesota: *Electronic Music*

GOTTFRIED VOSSEN   Professor of Computer Science, Institut für Wirthschaftsinformatik, University of Münster, Münster, Germany: *Database Theory: An Introduction*

ENCYCLOPEDIA OF COMPUTER SCIENCE AND TECHNOLOGY

VOLUME 34

ARTIFICIAL INTELLIGENCE IN EDUCATION

INTRODUCTION

Any review of Artificial Intelligence in Education (AI-ED) should logically begin with a discussion of the (educational) problems being addressed before embarking on a survey of how AI might contribute to solutions. The main relevant issues appear to be the following:

1. What is the nature of knowledge?
2. How may knowledge be learned?
3. How are the social and cultural aspects of education taken into account?
4. Should systems instruct, tutor, guide, or train students?
5. How should new technologies be used in education?
6. What are the measures of effectiveness?

Educationalists will debate such issues at great length, but it is not the aim of this article to contribute to that debate except to the extent that it discusses the AI-ED field's views (implicit and explicit) on them. This review focuses on the technical contribution that AI is making and might make to education.

The following six sections consider each of the above issues in turn. Each section illustrates a general discussion about AI-ED's views with exemplar AI-ED systems. The six sections do not attempt to give a comprehensive account of implemented systems (there are now too many for a short review) and those systems referred to are not discussed in detail but only to the extent necessary for the point under discussion. The review ends with a short discussion of the main controversies within the AI-ED field today.

THE NATURE OF KNOWLEDGE

Most AI-ED systems are intended to help their student-users become more knowledgeable in some respect. AI-ED system designers are well aware that education has broader aims — to develop ethical and moral values, to improve attitudes, to nurture better citizens, and so on — but this awareness only indirectly influences their system design. It is rather assumed (or hoped) that the context in which AI-ED systems will be used will convey these broader goals.

Given the focus on the knowledge-to-be-learned, it is natural that AI-ED designers often begin by trying to specify this knowledge as precisely as possible. To achieve this, the full panoply of AI knowledge representation techniques (production systems, frames, semantic networks, predicate logic, etc.) has been applied in AI-ED systems. In so doing, AI-ED designers might be considered as adopting a philosophy of knowledge called *objectivism*, which holds that the world is com-

1

pletely and correctly structured in terms of entities, properties, and relations (1). Thus, an AI representation might be considered to be an attempt to describe this structure and, hence, the aim of an AI-ED system might be to help learners acquire the entities, properties, and relations of this "correct" propositional structure.

The "classical" approach to AI-ED system design is illustrated by SPENGELS (2), a straightforward intelligent tutoring system to help Dutch students learn the conjugation and spelling of English verbs, that is, to be able to use the correct form of verbs (such as "prefer," "begin") in sentences such as "He _____ to work with pen and paper." The first step, as no spelling algorithm already existed, was to represent as a decision tree the morphosyntactic and spelling alternation rules taught in different Dutch textbooks. The decision tree effectively asks a series of questions: Is the verb form finite? Which tense is needed? Is the number singular? and so on, leading to a node of the tree showing the correct conjugation. This algorithm then becomes the basis for teaching the student, for deriving correct answers, for checking student answers, for determining misconceptions the student may have, and so on.

Some of the knowledge we wish students to acquire *is* objective because it is knowledge defined (by us) to be correct — for example, the syntax of programming languages or the allowable operations on an algebraic expression. It is no coincidence that the majority of AI-ED systems are concerned with such topics. For example, GREATERP (3), a beginners' LISP tutor, will comment that "You are within a PROG so you need to use a RETURN" because there is no scope for argument about the correctness of this statement (although there is scope for arguing whether the student needs to be told so in a particular way and at a particular time).

There are many other domains where it seems necessary to adopt an objectivist view, to some extent. For example, a student in a first-aid course must be given the correct way of dealing with a child suspected of being accidentally poisoned. Although this does not necessarily mean that a student must just be told the correct way — one can easily imagine that a student will understand and remember better if he discovers the correct way, in this case, preferably by experimenting with simulated patients, not real ones.

There are also domains where an objectivist view is adopted (temporarily, perhaps) as part of an academic game by students and teachers. For example, the equations for uniform acceleration [$s = (u + v)t/2$; $s = ut + at^2/2$, etc.], although understood to be not always applicable, are adopted as axioms to solve problems. In the case of English verb endings (discussed above), a pedant might point out that these endings are not fixed — they may be different in medieval English and American English — but if the learner's context is "preferred (i.e., U.K.) English," "preferred" is accepted to be correct.

There is, of course, a great debate within AI, and specifically with expert system research, about the extent to which "correct" knowledge can be specified in areas where it does not obviously exist. In the case of English verb endings this seems a reasonable expectation, but in more substantial areas of English use, such an approach would probably not be contemplated. To the extent that "correct" knowledge can be specified, such expert system representations may be used to convey it to students. The prototypical attempt to carry out this program was the adaptation of the MYCIN expert system for medical diagnosis into the GUIDON tutoring system (4,5).

However, even within domains for which objectivism seems reasonable, it soon becomes apparent that the real learning problems lie not in the objective knowledge but in its relation to less objective knowledge. For example, in programming, the focus moves from the syntax of the language to aspects such as programming design or debugging, where there is no definitively "correct" knowledge. For example, in the BRIDGE Pascal tutor (6), the focus is on guiding the student through the stages of planning a program from the initial English-like description through to the Pascal code.

Similarly, in algebra the issue is not so much what the operations are (syntactically) but when they should be applied. Thus, AI-ED algebra systems do not just check the correctness of operations (in fact, they often perform the operations themselves, as that is assumed not to be the student's difficulty) but provide students with an environment in which they can experiment with the operators. For example, ALGEBRALAND (7) displays a problem-solving tree of the student's solution attempt. This is intended to make it easier for students to monitor their on-going solution and to reflect on their solution attempts afterward. ALGEBRALAND itself gives no explicit tutorial support to these aspects — it only checks that an operator is applicable. The hope is that, relieved of the need to worry about the low-level detail of operator application, students will be more likely to engage in the desired metacognitive activities.

Even when a successful expert system can be built, it does not follow that the expertise embedded in it is a suitable basis for an educational interaction. The expert's performance-oriented knowledge may not be based on a conceptual structuring of the domain which a learner will understand (8). To put it another way, many studies have shown expert–novice differences suggest novices may not learn well from experts. This conclusion is explicit in GREATERP, in which the student's solution is not compared to an expert solution but to that of an "ideal student." Thus, the production rules of GREATERP do not summarize expert knowledge but are aimed to correspond to conceptual units that novices can understand.

A view of knowledge that is often presented as opposed to objectivism is that of *constructivism*, which holds that meaning is imposed on the world by us, rather than existing in the world independent of us. Constructivisits therefore emphasize the process of actively structuring the world and contend that there are many meanings or perspectives for any event or concept, rather than there being a single correct meaning toward which a student must be guided.

It does not follow that an AI-ED system which possesses an objective representation of knowledge has to adopt an interaction style which violates all contructivist principles. For example, the Socratic dialogues of WHY (9) do not simply tell students the "correct" conception but try to help them construct one through subtle sequences of counter examples such as, "Do you think that any place with mountains has heavy rainfall?" "Yes." "Does southern California have a lot of rain?"

But the designer of a system which possesses knowledge which is deemed to be correct is sorely tempted to use that knowledge (usually acquired after great effort) in a direct knowledge communication mode: "No, southern California doesn't have a lot of rain." To avoid such temptations, an extreme constructionist might argue that an AI-ED system (assuming that it is still to be deemed an AI-ED system) should possess no such knowledge and simply present an environment for the student to explore. The deceptive word here is "simply," for it is by no means easy to design environments in which knowledge (of any kind, intended or not) can be discovered. The most well-known such system is LOGO (10) which has now been subjected to numerous studies and its constructivist foundation has become rather shaky, as the extent to which LOGO needs to be buttressed by other supports has been documented. Similarly, the recent enthusiasm for developing hypermedia and multimedia systems (11) for students to explore has to be tempered by the fact that unaided students have some difficulty in negotiating the vast search spaces. The technologists' manifestation of constructivism as microworlds and other exploratory environments — often contrasted with the tutoring systems of objectivists — is a rather pale image of the comprehensive philosophy of constructivism, which is "a discursive practice that provides the means through which one can describe the social, political and economic circumstances that surround and give meaning to a given piece of educational technology" (12).

An intermediate, but technically difficult, position is to argue that *both* agents, the AI-ED system and the student, should adopt a constructivist approach. In this case, the system would not contain a priori correct knowledge but would attempt to discover it in a joint endeavor with the student. The PEOPLE-POWER system (13) illustrates this approach. The student and the system are supposed to design experiments to be carried out on a simulated political system in order to determine what makes a system democratic in the sense that seats gained in a parliament are proportional to the votes cast for the corresponding parties. Both the student and the system can make (fallible) suggestions and interpretations. There is no target "correct" knowledge available to the system.

Situationism shares some tenets of constructivism but emphasizes that the constructed knowledge does not exist in memory but rather emerges from interaction with the environment. It is argued that traditional AI, with its emphasis on symbolic knowledge representations, has assumed [sometimes explicitly, as in the classic Newell and Simon studies (14)] that those representations have some psychological reality, that is, they correspond, not literally but functionally, with structures in the learner's memory. Situationists argue that representations are created in the course of activity but are not themselves knowledge, knowledge being a capacity to interact. Thus, both constructivists and situationists deny that knowledge of the world can be defined (correctly) independent of a mind; the former but not the latter might accept that an individual mind creates its own idiosyncratic knowledge structures in memory.

The status of situationism is still a subject of debate (15–17) and there are as yet no AI-ED systems which clearly illustrate its principles. Most discussions of situationism in AI-ED refer to the idea of cognitive apprenticeship (18) but cannot point to any exemplar systems in the way that objectivists might point to GREATERP, and so on. Clancey (19) has, however, listed some principles for designers of such systems, contrasting them with the perceived emphases in objectivism-based AI-ED approaches:

- Participate with users in multidisciplinary design teams
- Adopt a global view of the context in which a computer system will be used
- Be committed to providing cost-effective solutions to real problems
- Aim to facilitate conversations between people
- Realize that transparency and ease of use is a relation between an artifact and a community of practice

- Relate schema models and AI-ED systems to the everyday practice by which they are given meaning and modified
- View the group as a psychological unit

Some commentators (e.g., Ref. 20) have related the situationist view to that of *connectionism*, another view of knowledge which is presented as a contrast to the symbol-processing version of objectivism. Connectionism holds that knowledge is implicitly represented in the weights and links between large numbers of nodes modeled on neural networks. However, although connectionist representations lack the kind of symbolism characteristic of objectivist representations, they are still very much concerned with representations in memory, rather than in the situation. Connectionist methods have been used to develop components of AI-ED systems, as described below, but no AI-ED system follows a wholly connectionist philosophy, presumably because the representations themselves, with only implicit understanding, do not easily support learning interactions.

An interesting question, after reviewing how philosophies of the nature of knowledge relate to students' knowledge, concerns how those philosophies relate to teachers' knowledge (or AI-ED systems' knowledge of how to teach). Some researchers (e.g., Ref. 5) have attempted to apply the expert system paradigm to teaching knowledge and to specify "tutoring rules" to be interpreted by an AI-ED system. This, then, reflects an objectivist view that such knowledge exists and can be specified. Most AI-ED systems, however, do not have explicit knowledge of how to teach: It is implicit in the way they react to certain situations. This might appear to be a situationist approach but, in fact, is not because the knowledge is clearly possessed by the system but not in a form which it is easy for observers to analyze. A few studies (e.g., Ref. 21) have adopted a constructivist view and considered whether an AI-ED system might be able to build an instructional strategy from "experiments" with students interacting with it.

THE NATURE OF LEARNING

Philosophies of knowledge imply philosophies of learning, to some extent. For example, connectionism, with its assumption that knowledge exists in the weighted links between the nodes of large neural networks, implies that learning is a statistical process whereby the weights are adjusted as many examples and nonexamples are encountered. Unfortunately, there is no unequivocal mapping from philosophies of knowledge to philosophies of learning, and it is one of the difficulties of AI-ED research that heated arguments about the nature of knowledge often lead to similar conclusions about the nature of learning and, hence, of teaching and AI-ED system design. For example, an objectivist might not demur from some of the principles derived from situationism listed above, for example, that it is time to move on from 'laboratory studies' to putting more emphasis on "real-world applications."

One of the few attempts to link a theory of learning to that of AI-ED system design is that to relate ACT* (22) to GREATERP and similar systems. The following principles are supposed to follow from ACT*:

- Represent the student as a production system
- Communicate the goal structure underlying the problem solving

- Provide instruction in the problem-solving context
- Promote an abstract understanding of the problem-solving knowledge
- Minimize working memory load
- Provide immediate feedback on errors
- Adjust the grain size of instruction with learning
- Facilitate successive approximations to the target skill

These principles do not follow in the mathematician's sense of being derivable from axioms of the theory but are more like implicit implications. Moreover, the principles do not lead directly to design prescriptions. These weak links make it hard to argue that the success (or otherwise) of the systems implemented can be attributed to the psychological theory.

ACT* is an objectivist theory emphasizing stored schemas in the student's memory. Recently (23), ACT* has been modified to encompass some aspects of situationism, but these modifications have yet to lead to modified principles for AI-ED system design. As they stand, GREATERP and its brothers are remediationist systems based on the assumption that learning is failure-driven.

Many other approaches have the basic idea of failure-driven learning. For example, SOAR (24) is intended to be a comprehensive cognitive architecture based entirely on a process of "impasse-driven learning." An impasse is a situation where the architecture has insufficient knowledge to determine how to proceed. The impasse triggers a heuristic search to create a new operator to overcome it. Similarly, VanLehn's theory (25) is an impasse-driven one, derived from the influential "repair theory" (26) originally developed to explain how students learned "bugs" in subtraction.

The "failure" does not have to be blatant exhibition of lack of success: It could just be some evidence which causes the student to consider whether their current conception is sound. For example, the idea of case-based learning (27), derived from the field of case-based reasoning in AI, is that students learn from stories (cases) presented at the precise point of becoming interested in knowing the information conveyed by the story. For example, DUSTIN is a language-training system with which students enter a multimedia simulated environment in which they interact with (images of) people they will deal with in their work environment. The student attempts authentic tasks, such as checking into a hotel, and on failure, is shown a relevant example before reattempting the task. This approach is, thus, an interesting merger of objectivist methods (there are ostensibly correct representations of how to perform the task) with a constructivist philosophy (with rationales such as "in order to assimilate a case, we must attach it someplace in memory") and a situationist style (with the emphasis on authentic tasks).

The "case" presented to a student may be

- A very short piece of text (as in a counterexample of a WHY dialogue, as above)
- A complex photograph [as in the Sickle Cell Counselor (28), a system designed to teach museum visitors about sickle cell disease]
- A paragraph giving a case history [as in DECIDER (29), which gives summaries of events such as the U.S. invasion of Nicaragua while the student is expressing political beliefs]
- A longish video [as in JASPER (30), where students are presented a story

in which the characters are faced with challenges that the students must solve]

In the last example, the video becomes a motivating way to present complex problems for students to solve. Implicit in this approach (apart from the use of video and the avowed constructivist philosophy, as the emphasis is on students constructing knowledge in realistic situations rather than receiving divorced classroom instruction) is a belief in learning by problem solving, an approach also characteristic of an objectivist philosophy, which would also emphasize that an AI-ED system itself should be able to solve the problems it sets. [In fact, of the systems mentioned in this and the previous paragraph, only DECIDER does not have (or cannot work out) a correct solution].

Thus, a learning by problem-solving approach can be rationalized by many different philosophies and supported by many different styles of AI-ED system; for example:

- GREATERP students solve problems and receive immediate feedback on mistakes (the system being able to monitor each step of a solution).
- LOGO students receive feedback from the system when solutions are executed but no didactic help.
- WEST students (who learn arithmetic skills in the context of a simple board game) are given hints from the system if certain constraints are violated (31).
- JASPER students may receive hints to help them improve their solutions (earlier versions of JASPER had students solving the problems off-line).

So to say that most AI-ED systems reflect a learning by problem-solving philosophy is not very illuminating unless the nature of the problem and the degree of system support are clarified.

A standard scenario is a problem-solving environment in which students perform experiments and are guided by the system in their interpretation. For example, QUEST (32) provides a graphic simulation of circuits to enable students to understand principles governing the behavior of those circuits by performing troubleshooting operations. For such an interaction to be useful to students, the system's interventions must be couched in terms analogous to those of the student: Thus, for novices, the system needs representations of naive qualitative physics. The topic of qualitative reasoning is another broad field of AI whose application to AI-ED has still to be explored in detail, although it was arguably initiated by early AI-ED studies of the SOPHIE system (33).

The tension between extreme objectivist and constructivist/situationist views is well illustrated by discussions about how students might learn the kinds of causal models needed in science. An objectivist might present the standard formulas ($F = ma$, etc.) and require students to apply them to various (textbook) problems; a situationist might expose the student to many real-world instances and hope that generalizations will (implicitly, perhaps) evolve. White (34) argues that causal models of an intermediate degree of abstraction can foster learning provided that they are

- Understandable, that is, they build on intuitive notions of causality and mechanism
- Learnable, that is, they generate explanations of key domain phenomena

- Transferrable, that is, the objects and actions within them are represented in a decontextualized form
- Linkable, that is, they help link different levels of abstraction and different model perspectives
- Usable, that is, they can be used to predict, control, and explain physical phenomena

When students interact with a simulation, it has been found (35,36) that they tend to focus on tweaking the simulation to achieve the desired short-term effect without addressing the mistaken beliefs and conceptions which will continue to cause difficulties in the longer term. Thus, there appears to be a need to engage the student in a dialogue to get at the fundamental misconceptions. This dialogue may be with a human teacher, other students, or a computer-based learning environment; but in any case, it reflects a constructivist view that knowledge is structured by interpreting events, albeit that this interpretation requires the mediation of other agents rather than isolated cogitation. Along these lines, an environment has been described with which students express (and withdraw) commitments during some debate, the system acting as a "referee" using the guidelines of dialogue game theory to determine the validity of moves (37). Such an interface, it is argued, might help students not only clarify their conceptions of the domain under debate but also develop general reasoning skills. Eventually, the nature of such a debate may be sufficiently understood that the system itself may adopt the role of a player as well. This work is derived from many fields of AI (belief revision, agent theory, distributed AI) and elsewhere (in cognitive and social psychology and the language sciences) (38).

The work on self-explanation [i.e., the hypothesis that better students spend more time on explaining examples to themselves (39)] can be interpreted as a theory about the benefits of arguing with oneself. The self-explanation line of research has recently (40) been developed into a general proposed methodology for AI-ED research:

- Collect experimental protocols of learners and divide them into good and poor learners (on the basis of outcome measures)
- Investigate what behaviors and processes were different in the two groups (e.g., self-explanation)
- Develop a cognitive simulation model to account for the identified differences [e.g., the CASCADE system (41)]
- Design appropriate interventions to cause the more effective behavior to occur (e.g., strategically hide information to encourage self-explanation)
- Test the resultant AI-ED system

Overall, then, AI-ED system design reflects a rather eclectic view of the nature of learning, regardless of one's view of the nature of knowledge. Clearly, many different kinds of event and activity can lead to learning and many of them have been supported, to some extent, within AI-ED systems (usually without the dogmatic claims that accompany discussions about the nature of knowledge).

SOCIAL AND CULTURAL ASPECTS

AI-ED research has not taken into account much of the social and cultural settings within which AI-ED systems have to be designed and used. Until recently, the emphasis has been on the technical challenge of constructing interesting systems within research laboratories. However, when such systems are used in classrooms, the effects are not usually as intended (perhaps not surprisingly).

For example, when a geometry tutor (based on the Anderson principles itemized above) was tested in schools, both teachers' and students' behaviors changed in not entirely anticipated ways (42). Although teachers devoted more time to slower students and adopted a more collaborative style and students increased their effort on tasks (all presumably welcome changes), it was also found that the system increased competition among the students. Because students could progress at their own pace (unlike in the normal classroom) and could easily determine the progress of their co-students, a race developed between them — in fact, 40% of the students attributed their greater effort to the increased competition. The self-pacing feature also led to a modification in teachers' grading practices, as it was now less appropriate to mark students on the percentage correct — instead they tended to assess on the effort invested.

These kinds of observation lead naturally to proposals for "socio-technical design" (19), where the emphasis is on designing a system within the social and physical context in which it is intended to be used. Such proposals are often couched in political terms, presenting such an approach as more "democratic" because it involves user groups in the decision making and control of the systems they will use (as opposed to a "dictatorial" approach in which designs are delivered to users).

In particular, user-participatory design, a trend in human-computer interaction and usability research, has recently been applied to AI-ED system design (43). The project involved (1) developing a representational framework for domain content and tutoring strategies that was understandable by educators, (2) implementing a set of knowledge acquisition tools, and (3) involving educators in building the system, through conception, design, implementation, and evaluation. This line of work is part of a broader discussion about the general principles of instructional design theory and knowledge acquisition in AI.

An extreme objectivist might argue that when all the knowledge-to-be-learned and the knowledge-of-how-to-teach-it has been fully specified, the delivery of AI-ED systems to the classroom will not be problematic. The design will take account of all situations and the system will adapt itself accordingly. This assumes that a complete cognitive analysis will subsume the affective dimensions. Most AI-ED systems only indirectly consider issues such as motivation, whereas studies of human tutors, especially for certain classes of learners such as remedial students, show that they devote more time and attention to motivation and affect than to the strictly cognitive content (44). Human tutors' techniques for maintaining or increasing motivation — based on manipulating the goals of confidence, challenge, control, and curiosity — can be seen to be implicitly encoded in some AI-ED systems to the limited extent that some of these techniques seem applicable to such systems.

In any case, situationists would not accept that the goal of explicitly defining all relevant knowledge in deliverable AI-ED systems is a sensible one. It simply does not take account of the fact that the teacher–learner culture is too rich and that the people involved in the use of such systems are able to (indeed, must) contribute to successful design and use of the systems.

Because situationists hold that knowledge does not reside in individual heads, they would also move away from one-to-one tutoring systems (which are caricatured as aiming to transfer knowledge to individuals) and encourage more collaborative learning systems, where understanding is developed by group negotiations (as constructivists would accept). Thus, they have a different image of the context of use than some tutoring system designers. They would tend to play down the role of AI *within* computer-based systems, that is, to provide explicit symbolic reasoning, and argue that AI's role is to mediate the collaborative interactions; they would, therefore, seek bridges to work on computer-supported collaborative work (CSCW) and computer-mediated communication (CMC). This opens up a debate about the nature of educational institutions and students' activities within and without them which would be too broad to pursue in this review.

INSTRUCTION, TUTORING, GUIDING, TRAINING

The view of teacher expertise embedded in present AI-ED systems is, it has to be admitted, rather naive. This is because AI-ED system designers generally do not have substantial teaching expertise themselves nor have access to it. In addition, perhaps surprisingly, the teaching component has often been considered to be of less importance than, for example, the representations of domain knowledge and, hence, has often been added on as an afterthought.

However, the earlier sections have given many examples of the various teaching styles adopted by AI-ED systems. The old distinction between theories of learning as being descriptive and theories of instruction as being prescriptive, with no necessary connection between the two, is rejected by AI-ED research. For example, VanLehn's proposed methodology, given at the end of the section The Nature of Learning, assumes that identifying learning differences will lead directly to prescriptions for instructional interventions.

The criticisms of the styles of present AI-ED systems which are often made are rather misplaced. None of these systems aims to provide a comprehensive coverage of either a significant part of a curriculum or the range of teaching styles. Rather, each system is an investigation of one style applied to one rather circumscribed topic. Thus, we should consider whether the teaching style of a system is appropriate for the limited aims that its designers have.

For example, it is inappropriate to criticize GREATERP for its domineering style of putting students right immediately after they stray off the correct path if this is an effective strategy for bringing large numbers of beginning LISP programmers up to a standard of competence after which more subtle strategies may be needed. Similarly, those systems which have a clear training objective, for example, the Space Shuttle Fuel Cell Tutor (45) and SHERLOCK (46), an avionics troubleshooting tutor, in which it is essential that students master the operation of complex equipment, may quite justifiably adopt an essentially objectivist approach of defining the knowledge-to-be-learned and ensuring that students acquire it as effectively as possible.

For many AI-ED systems, however, the aims are not so clear-cut. Often there is a "surface" objective for the student (to write a program to draw a specific shape, to manipulate parameters to maintain an economic simulation in a stable state, to solve a specific algebraic equation) which masks the real objective (to develop various higher-order skills, such as planning and monitoring solution attempts).

System interventions directed at the former objective (e.g., to point out that a program is incorrect) are irrelevant or harmful if they interfere with the latter objective. Many years ago the designers of the WEST system (31) proposed instructional guidelines such as "do not tutor on two successive moves" which only make sense if it is accepted that the system's aims are more than to ensure that the student obtains the "right answer." With such systems the balance between "guiding," "telling," or "leaving" the student, and hence the whole vexed issue of the balance of control between the learner and the system, is a continuing debate. The specification of precise and general guidelines has proved elusive and the design of the instructional component of AI-ED systems remains more an art than a science, as it does for other educational systems.

NEW TECHNOLOGIES IN EDUCATION

Regardless of philosophy, psychology, or any other academic consideration, it is undoubtedly the case that the new technologies increasingly being applied to education have stimulated some of the trends discussed above. For example, the advent of high-fidelity multimedia and virtual reality systems naturally leads to its enthusiasts arguing for the merits of learning through "immersion in a situation," which is a variation of the situationist's view. Similarly, the availability of high-speed networks permits a degree of distributed, collaborative working which was previously unattainable and this leads to discussions about the intrinsic virtues of "social learning" mediated by technology.

This review is concerned specifically with the role of AI in education; hence, we will not discuss the technical details of new technologies but only the potential relevance of AI to them. At the moment, the current excitement with the new technologies owes nothing to AI. However, as the history of educational innovation shows, new technologies tend not to deliver all that they promise, and it is quite predictable that as the limitations of the new technologies become clearer, AI techniques will be adopted to help overcome them; for example:

- The successful use of multimedia interfaces requires models not only of the media themselves, but of the user, task, and discourse (47), aspects that have long been studied in conventional AI-ED research. No doubt, existing work on, for example, student modeling and discourse management will not be immediately applicable and will need to be adapted, but this is clearly work with an AI orientation.
- The effectiveness of virtual reality as a learning environment depends fundamentally on the relation between learning and social and perceptual experience, a relationship which is central to AI research. Even at the technical level, preliminary experiments have already shown the need for surrogate "co-learners" and other intelligent agents in the environment (48).
- It has been argued (49) that the demand for computer-supported collaborative learning environments for workplace training can best be met by adapting the coached practice environments, such as SHERLOCK (46), originally developed for individual learning. If so, present AI-ED research

can be seen as the basis from which the new theories required for these environments will evolve.

Whatever the future, recent technological advances have radically changed AI-ED systems. A few years ago, a review such as this would be profusely illustrated with screen images to show student–system interactions. Now it is virtually impossible to capture on paper the richness and immediacy of such interactions.

MEASURES OF EFFECTIVENESS

The evaluation of any educational innovation, including AI-ED systems, is inherently difficult (50,51). However, because of the expense of AI-ED system implementation, the demand for successful evaluations is quite reasonably made. It is only recently that AI-ED research has been able to respond to the challenge by carrying out large-scale empirical studies which show the benefits of AI-ED systems in real educational settings; for example, the evaluations of the following:

- The Geometry tutor, as mentioned earlier (42)
- SMITHTOWN, a discovery world that teaches scientific inquiry skills in the context of microeconomics (52)
- SHERLOCK, where 20 hr using the system were judged to be as effective as 2 years "on the job" (53)
- A STATICS tutor, where the instructional design effort per hour of instruction time was about 85 hr, compared to 100–300 hr for traditional CAI (54)
- A VCR tutor (55)
- The Space Shuttle Fuel Cell tutor, where NASA trainers were so convinced of its superiority over alternatives that it was adopted without need for a formal evaluation (45)

These evaluation studies, however, use educational techniques with AI-ED products but do not themselves use AI techniques. More relevant to this review is the possible use of AI for evaluative purposes.

Any AI-ED system is an implementation of a (usually implicit) theory of learning and instruction. If the theory were sufficiently explicit, it could be expressible in executable form and, thus, the outcomes from the AI-ED system could be predicted by running the system with "simulated students." A simulated student might be used to support teaching training, to enable an AI-ED system to act as a collaborative partner, and to permit formative evaluations (56). In the last case, for example, one can imagine using a failure-driven subtraction learning procedure to determine which of the following examples is more likely to promote learning:

$$\begin{array}{cc} 85 & 745 \\ -27 & -127 \end{array}$$

The example on the right might lead to the generalization that borrowing should be from the column immediately to the left; the example on the left might also lead to the generalization that borrowing should be from the leftmost column. Thus, the theory would predict (in contrast to standard teaching) that the example on the right is better because it is potentially less confusing to an impasse-driven learner.

Thus, an AI-ED system itself may be used for formative evaluations before being used with real students. This is, of course, standard practice in other fields of computer use, but its usefulness in AI-ED may be doubted because of our lack of faith in the soundness of the theories of learning concerned. The principle, however, seems sound.

Similarly, we can imagine applying the student modeling component of AI-ED systems to assist with the thorny problem of assessment (57). Most AI-ED systems which are not entirely exploratory environments maintain some kind of student model, that is, some representation of what it is believed the student has understood. This student model may be used for many purposes within an AI-ED system, for example, to determine appropriate problems to set, to provide remediative feedback, and so on. Many techniques have been developed to build student models (58); some are derived from well-known AI techniques such as the following:

- Discriminative concept learning (59), where the aim is to induce the student's problem-solving procedure from observations of his correct and incorrect results.
- Resolution from computational logic (60), where the technique is used to suggest and prove hypotheses about a student's beliefs
- Neural networks (61), where the network is trained to simulate a student's cognitive processes
- Fuzzy logic (62), to provide an approximate diagnosis, recognizing that a student's behavior is not entirely consistent, and induction from it is risky
- Bayesian belief networks (63), also to provide a less precision-oriented approach to student modeling
- Model-based diagnosis (64), to cast the student modeling problem in terms of general diagnosis in AI
- Belief revision (65), to keep the model consistent with observations
- Logic meta-programming (66), to reconstruct hypothetical solution paths to check against constraints associated with correct solutions

The need for, and success of, these methods remains a controversial topic within AI-ED research (67,68). But to the extent that these techniques are successful and so provide a useful evaluation of an individual student (useful in the sense that it may support individualized interactions) they may be used for assessment purposes. Educationalists must argue about the ethics of computer-based assessment and about whether what can be reliably assessed in this way is in fact what should be assessed, but again the principle seems sound: Many AI-ED systems aim to build student models, and to the extent that this is possible it may form a basis for assessment of the student and, hence, an evaluation of the system's effectiveness in helping that student to learn.

ONGOING DEBATES

Education has been a controversial topic for two millenia at least: AI has been equally controversial for a shorter period. AI in Education is bound to provoke debate. After two decades, a body of techniques had been developed which are beginning to be consistently reapplied in new systems. Some early AI-ED concepts are now routinely used in off-the-shelf computer-based learning systems; for example, a $50 typing tutor uses a student model with a bug catalog to generate new practice lessons as needed. Some larger-scale AI-ED systems have been shown to be effective within larger organizations such as the military (as discussed above).

But still there is considerable argument about AI-ED research. Some of the arguments have been touched on earlier. We conclude by mentioning some more general questions:

- Is AI a dangerous metaphor for education? For some critics, AI is seen as supporting a rather behavioristic approach to learning, in that it aims to adapt the learner the conform to the knowledge embedded in the AI system. As we have indicated, this is a simplistic characterization of only a subclass of AI-ED systems.

- Can AI-ED systems support student autonomy and open learning? The more that intelligence is put within AI-ED systems, the more the temptation may be to apply it to control and direct the student's interactions with the system. However, the range of AI-ED systems includes much more than overbearing tutoring systems.

- Will AI-ED systems ever be used in real educational settings? Of course, this depends on what is understood by a "real educational setting." The traditional school classroom is perhaps not a very promising setting for many systems. But the organization of classrooms is changing rapidly and it also seems likely that more learning will occur outside the official classroom as access to computer technology improves and individuals learn at home or at work, for their own interest or career development.

- What will be the impact of educational technologies and what role will AI play within them? At the moment, we are in a phase where the radically different nature of the new technology has sidelined AI. Eventually, however, there will be a merging of the more software-oriented AI focus with the more hardware-oriented new technology focus.

- Will AI-ED research continue to progress through the rather unprincipled implementation of demonstration systems, or will some theoretical basis of AI-ED system design be developed? Currently, only certain components of AI-ED systems are amenable to any kind of theoretical analysis and no comprehensive "theory of AI-ED systems" is likely in the near or medium-term future.

- Do AI-ED systems reflect a reasonable view of the nature of knowledge and learning? This brings us full circle. As we have discussed, there is no consensus within AI-ED research about these issues and we can find examples of systems which reflect many different philosophies. Apart from the perception of AI-ED research as a field oriented toward producing practically useful systems, AI-ED may also a provide a more technical contribution to such fundamental debates.

REFERENCES

1. G. Lakoff, *Women, Fire and Dangerous Things*, University of Chicago Press, Chicago, 1987, p. 159.

2. E. Bos and J. van de Plassche, "A Knowledge-Based English Verb Form Tutor," *J. Artificial Intell. in Educ.*, *5*, 107–129 (1994).

3. J. R. Anderson and B. J. Reiser, "The LISP Tutor," *Byte*, *10*(4), 159–175 (1985).

4. W. J. Clancey, "Transfer of Rule-Based Expertise Through a Tutorial Dialogue," Ph.D. thesis, Stanford University (1979).

5. W. J. Clancey, *Knowledge-Based Tutoring*: *The GUIDON Program*, MIT Press, Cambridge, MA, 1987.

6. J. Bonar and R. Cunningham, "BRIDGE: An Intelligent Tutor for Thinking About Programming," in *Artificial Intelligence and Human Learning*, J. A. Self (ed.), Chapman and Hall, London, 1988.

7. C. L. Foss, "Learning from Errors in AlgebraLand," Technical Report IRL 3, Institute for Research on Learning, Palo Alto, CA (1987).

8. W. J. Clancey, "Methodology for Building an Intelligent Tutoring System," in *Methods and Tactics in Cognitive Science*, W. Kintsch, P. G. Polson and J. R. Miller (eds.), Erlbaum, Hillsdale, NJ, 1984.

9. A. L. Stevens and A. Collins, "The Goal Structure of a Socratic Tutor," *Proc. of the National ACM Conference*, 1977.

10. S. Papert, *Mindstorms: Children, Computers and Powerful Ideas*, Basic Books, New York, 1980.

11. P. Kommers, D. Jonassen, T. Mayes, *Cognitive Tools for Learning*, Springer-Verlag, Berlin, 1992.

12. W. Sack, E. Soloway, and P. Weingrad, "Re: Writing Cartesian Student Models," *J. Artificial Intell. in Educ.*, *3*, 381–400 (1992).

13. P. Dillenbourg and J. A. Self, "A Computational Approach to Socially Distributed Cognition," *Eur. J. Psychol. Educ.*, *7*, 353–372 (1992).

14. A. Newell and H. A. Simon, *Human Problem Solving*, Prentice-Hall, Englewood Cliffs, NJ, 1972.

15. W. J. Clancey, "Representations of Knowing – In Defense of Cognitive Apprenticeship," *J. Artificial Intell. in Educ.*, *3*, 139–168 (1992).

16. J. Sandberg and B. Weilinga, "Situated Cognition: A Paradigm Shift?" *J. Artificial Intell. in Educ.*, *3*, 129–138 (1992).

17. H. U. Hoppe, "Cognitive Apprenticeship – The Emperor's New Method?" *J. Artificial Intell. in Educ.*, *4*, 49–54 (1993).

18. A. Collins, J. S. Brown and S. Newman, "Cognitive Apprenticeship: Teaching the Craft of Reading, Writing and Mathematics," in *Cognition and Instruction*, L. B. Resnick (ed.), Erlbaum, Hillsdale, NJ, 1988.

19. W. J. Clancey, "GUIDON-MANAGE Revisited: A Socio-technical Systems Approach," *J. Artificial Intell. in Educ.*, *4*, 5–34 (1993).

20. B. Bredeweg, "A Report on the Intelligent Tutoring Systems 92 Conference," *J. Artificial Intell. in Educ.*, *3*, 365–372 (1993).

21. T. O'Shea, "A Self-Improving Quadratic Tutor," in *Intelligent Tutoring Systems*, D. H. Sleeman and J. S. Brown (eds.), Academic Press, London, 1982.

22. J. R. Anderson, *The Architecture of Cognition*, Harvard University Press, Cambridge, MA, 1983.

23. J. R. Anderson, *Rules of the Mind*, Erlbaum, Hillsdale, NJ, 1993.

24. J. Laird, P. Rosenbloom, and A. Newell, *Universal Subgoaling and Chunking: The Automatic Generation and Learning of Goal Hierarchies*, Kluwer, Hingham, MA, 1986.

25. K. VanLehn, "Rule Acquisition Events in the Discovery of Problem Solving Strategies," *Cognitive Sci.*, *15*, 1–47 (1991).

26. J. S. Brown, and K. VanLehn, "Repair Theory: A Generative Theory of Bugs in Procedural Skills," *Cognitive Sci.*, *4*, 379–426 (1980).

27. R. C. Schank, "Case-Based Teaching: Four Experiences in Educational Software Design," *Interactive Learning Environ.*, *1*, 231–254 (1990).

28. B. L. Bell and R. Bareiss, "Sickle Cell Counselor: Using a Goal-Based Scenario to Motivate Exploration of Knowledge in a Museum Context," *Proc. of the World Conference on Artificial Intelligence in Education, Edinburgh*, AACE, Charlottesville, VA, 1993.

29. G. Bloch and R. Farrell, "Promoting Creativity Through Argumentation," *Proc. of Intelligent Tutoring Systems 88*, 1988.

30. T. Crews and G. Biswas, "A Tutor for Trip Planning: Combining Planning and Mathematics Problem Solving," *Proc. of the World Conference on Artificial Intelligence in Education, Edinburgh*, AACE, Charlottesville, VA, 1993.

31. R. R. Burton and J. S. Brown, "An Investigation of Computer Coaching for Informal Learning Activities," *Int. J. Man-Machine Studies*, *11*, 5–24 (1979).

32. B. White and J. Frederiksen, "Causal Model Progressions as a Foundation for Intelligent Learning Environments," *Artificial Intell.*, *24*, 99–157 (1990).

33. J. S. Brown, R. R. Burton, and J. de Kleer, "Pedagogical, Natural Language, and Knowledge Engineering Techniques in SOPHIE I, II and III," in *Intelligent Tutoring Systems*, D. H. Sleeman and J. S. Brown (eds.), Academic Press, London, 1982.

34. B. White, "Intermediate Abstractions and Causal Models: A Microworld-Based Approach to Science Education," *Proc. of the World Conference on Artificial Intelligence in Education, Edinburgh*, AACE, Charlottesville, VA, 1993.

35. J. Rochelle, "Designing for Conversations," *AAAI Symposium on Knowledge-Based Environments for Learning and Teaching*, 1990.

36. M. Byard, S. Draper, R. Driver, R. Hartley, S. Henessey, C. Mallen, T. O'Shea, E. Scanlon, F. Spensley and D. Twigger, "Conceptual Change in Science," *Final Report to the Economic and Social Research Council*, 1992.

37. R. M. Pilkington, J. R. Hartley, D. Hintze, and D. Moore, "Learning to Argue and Arguing to Learn," *J. Artificial Intell. in Educ.*, *3*, 275–295 (1993).

38. M. Baker, "A Model for Negotiation in Teaching–Learning Dialogues," *J. Artificial Intell. in Educ.*, *5*, 199–254 (1994).

39. M. T. H. Chi, M. Bassok, M. W. Lewis, P. Reimann, and R. Glaser, "Self-Explanations: How Students Study and Use Examples in Learning to Solve Problems," *Cognitive Sci.*, *13*, 145–182 (1989).

40. K. VanLehn, "Cascade: A Simulation of Human Learning and its Applications," *Proc. of the World Conference on Artificial Intelligence in Education, Edinburgh*, AACE, Charlottesville, VA, 1993.

41. R. Jones and K. VanLehn, "A Fine-Grained Model of Skill Acquisition," *Proc. of 14th Annual Meeting of the Cognitive Science Society*, Erlbaum, Hillsdale, NJ, 1992.

42. J. W. Schofield, D. Evans-Rhodes, and B. R. Huber, "Artificial Intelligence in the Classroom: Impact of a Computer-Based Tutor on Teachers and Students," *Social Sci. Computer Rev.*, *8*, 24–41 (1990).

43. T. Murray and B. P. Woolf, "Tools for Teacher Participation in ITS Design," *Proc. of Intelligent Tutoring Systems 92*, 1992.

44. M. R. Lepper, M. Woolverton, D. L. Mumme, and J-L. Gurtner, "Motivational Techniques of Expert Human Tutors: Lessons for the Design of Computer-Based Tutors," in *Computers as Cognitive Tools*, S. P. Lajoie and S. J. Derry (eds.), Erlbaum, Hillsdale, NJ, 1993.

45. P. C. Duncan, "The Space Shuttle Fuel Cell Tutor: A Simulation-Based Intelligent Tutoring System with Yoked Expert Systems," *J. Artificial Intell. in Educ.*, *3*, 297–313 (1992).

46. A. M. Lesgold, G. Eggan, S. Katz, and G. Rao, "Possibilities for Assessment Using Computer-Based Apprenticeship Environments," in *Cognitive Approaches to Automated Instruction*, W. Regian and V. Shute (eds.), Erlbaum, Hillsdale, NJ, 1992.

47. M. T. Maybury, "Research in Multimedia and Multimodal Parsing and Generation," to appear in *Artificial Intell. Rev.* (1995).
48. V. J. Shute and J. Psotka, "Intelligent Tutoring Systems: Past, Present and Future," in *Handbook of Research on Educational Communications and Technology*, D. Jonassen (ed.), 1994.
49. S. Katz and A. Lesgold, "Extending an Intelligent Tutoring System to Support Collaborative Learning: Towards a Methodology for Computer-Supported Learning Environments," LRDC report, University of Pittsburgh (1994).
50. M. A. Mark and J. E. Greer, "Evaluation Methodologies for Intelligent Tutoring Systems," *J. Artificial Intell. in Educ.*, 4, 129–153 (1993).
51. P. H. Winne, "A Landscape of Issues in Evaluating Adaptive Learning Systems," *J. Artificial Intell. in Educ.*, 4, 309–332 (1993).
52. V. J. Shute and R. Glaser, "A Large-Scale Evaluation of an Intelligent Discovery World: Smithtown," *Interactive Learning Environ.*, 1, 51–78 (1990).
53. P. Nicholls, R. Porkorny, G. Jones, S. P. Gott, W. E. Alley, "Evaluation of an Avionics Troubleshooting Tutoring System," Technical Report, Armstrong Laboratory, Brooks Air Force Base (1993).
54. T. Murray, "Formative Qualitative Evaluation for 'Exploratory' ITS Research," *J. Artificial Intell. in Educ.*, 4, 179–208 (1993).
55. M. A. Mark and J. E. Greer, "The VCR Tutor: Evaluating Instructional Effectiveness," *Proc. of 13th annual Meeting of the Cognitive Science Society*, Erlbaum, Hillsdale, NJ, 1991.
56. K. VanLehn, S. Ohlsson, and R. Nason, "Applications of Simulated Students: An Exploration," *J. Artificial Intell. in Educ.* (1994).
57. J. D. Martin and K. VanLehn, "OLAE: Progress Toward a Multi-activity, Bayesian Student Modeler," *Proc. of the World Conference on Artificial Intelligence in Education*, *Edinburgh*, AACE, Charlottesville, VA, 1993.
58. P. Dillenbourg and J. A. Self, "A Framework for Learner Modelling," *Interactive Learning Environ.*, 2, 111–137 (1992).
59. P. Langley and S. Ohlsson, "Automated Cognitive Modelling," *Proc. of the National Conference on Artificial Intelligence*, 1984.
60. E. Costa, S. Duchenoy, and Y. Kodratoff, "A Resolution Base Method for Discovering Students' Misconceptions," in *Artificial Intelligence and Human Learning*, J. Self (ed.), Chapman and Hall, London, 1988.
61. S. Mengel and W. Lively, "On the Use of Neural Networks in Intelligent Tutoring Systems," *J. Artificial Intell. in Educ.*, 2, 43–56 (1991).
62. S. J. Derry, and L. W. Hawkes, "Local Cognitive Modeling of Problem-Solving Behavior: An Application of Fuzzy Theory," in *Computers as Cognitive Tools*, S. P. Lajoie and S. J. Derry (eds.), Erlbaum, Hillsdale, NJ, 1993.
63. S. Katz, A. Lesgold, G. Eggan, and M. Gordin, "Modelling the Student in SHERLOCK II," *J. Artificial Intell. in Educ.*, 3, 495–518 (1992).
64. J. A. Self, "Model-Based Cognitive Diagnosis," *User Modeling and User-Adapted Interaction*, 3, 89–106 (1993).
65. Y. Kono, M. Ikeda, and R. Mizoguchi, "A Modeling Method for Students with Contradictions," *Proc. of the World Conference on Artificial Intelligence in Education*, *Edinburgh*, AACE, Charlottesville, VA, 1993.
66. S. Beller and H. U. Hoppe, "Deductive Error Reconstruction and Classification in a Logic Programming Framework," *Proc. of the World Conference on Artificial Intelligence in Education*, *Edinburgh*, AACE, Charlottesville, VA, 1993.
67. S. P. Lajoie and S. J. Derry (eds.), *Computers as Cognitive Tools*, Erlbaum, Hillsdale, NJ, 1993.
68. H. Spada, "How the Role of Cognitive Modeling for computerized Instruction is Changing," *Proc. of the World Conference on Artificial Intelligence in Education*, *Edinburgh*, AACE, Charlottesville, VA, 1993.

69. E. Wenger, *Artificial Intelligence and Tutoring Systems*, Morgan Kaufmann, Los Altos, CA, 1988.

BIBLIOGRAPHY

No general book on AI in Education has been published since Wenger's book (69), which reviewed all the significant research up to 1987. Many AI-ED books have been published since then, but nearly all of them are edited collections of papers (with the remainder describing a particular project). Thus, none of the recent books gives a balanced and comprehensive picture of the field. Nonetheless, in addition to the references quoted, the books listed below provide useful further information. Relevant research is also published in the following journals: *Journal of Artificial Intelligence in Education, Journal of the Learning Sciences, Interactive Learning Environments, International Journal of Human–Computer Studies,* and *Instructional Science.*

Bierman, D., J. Breuker, and J. Sandberg (eds.), *Artificial Intelligence and Education: Synthesis and Reflection*, IOS, Springfield, VA, 1989.

Birnbaum, L. (ed.), *Proceedings of the Conference on the Learning Sciences*, AACE, Charlottesville, VA, 1991.

Brna, P., S. Ohlsson, and H. Pain (eds.), *Proceedings of AI-ED 93*, AACE, Charlottesville, VA, 1993.

Clancey, W. J., *Knowledge-Based Tutoring: the GUIDON program*, MIT Press, Cambridge, MA, 1987.

Costa, E. (ed.), *New Directions in Intelligent Tutoring Systems*, Springer-Verlag, Berlin, 1992.

de Corte, E., M. Linn, H. Mandl, and L. Verschaffel (eds.), *Computer-Based Learning Environments and Problem-Solving*, Springer-Verlag, New York, 1991.

Farr, M. J. and J. Psotka (eds.), *Intelligent Instruction by Computer*, Taylor and Francis, Washington, DC, 1992.

Frasson, C. and G. Gauthier (eds.), *Intelligent Tutoring Systems: At the Crossroads of Artificial Intelligence and Education*, Ablex, Norwood, NJ, 1990.

Lajoie, S. and S. Derry (eds.), *Computers as Cognitive Tools*, Lawrence Erlbaum, Hillsdale, NJ, 1993.

Larkin, J., R. Chabay, and C. Sheftic (eds.), *Computer-Assisted Instruction and Intelligent Tutoring Systems: Establishing Communication and Collaboration*, Lawrence Erlbaum, Hillsdale, NJ, 1992.

Mandl, H. and A. Lesgold (eds.), *Learning Issues for Intelligent Tutoring Systems*, Springer-Verlag, New York, 1988.

Polson, M. C. and J. J. Richardson (eds.), *Foundations of Intelligent Tutoring Systems*, Lawrence Erlbaum, Hillsdale, NJ, 1988.

Regian, W. and V. J. Shute (eds.), *Cognitive Approaches to Automated Instruction*, Lawrence Erlbaum, Hillsdale, NJ, 1992.

Self, J. A. (ed.), *Artificial Intelligence and Human Learning*, Chapman and Hall, London, 1988.

Sleeman, D. H. and J. S. Brown (eds.), *Intelligent Tutoring Systems*, Academic Press, New York, 1982.

JOHN A. SELF

distribution of arrivals into the queue, the second letter describes the *distribution of service times* for entities which reach the front of the queue, the first number describes the *number of servers* for the queue, the second number is the *size of the waiting room*, that is, the number of entities which can be present simultaneously in the queue including those currently being served, and the last number describes the *total population* of potential customers. If the last two numbers are omitted, they are assumed to be infinity.

Distributions are identified by code letters, so that M means exponential times (from the name Markovian), D means constant or deterministic times, G means generally distributed (i.e., only the mean is considered significant).

Little's Law

One of the most important results in queueing theory is Little's Law. This was a long-standing rule of thumb in analyzing queueing systems but gets its name from the author of the first paper which proves the relationship formally. It is applicable to the behavior of almost any system of queues as long as they exhibit a steady-state behavior. It relates a system-oriented measure — the mean number of customers in the system — to a customer-oriented measure — the mean time spent in the system by each customer (the mean sojourn time), for a given arrival rate.

Little's Law states

$$m = \lambda w,$$

where m is the expected (mean) number of entities at any time, λ is the arrival rate of new entities, and w is the mean time spent in the system.

Unfortunately, Little's Law only holds for the means (expected values), not for higher moments such as the variance.

Analysis of Single Queues

We give results for the three commonest types of single queue, $M/M/1$, $M/G/1$, and $G/G/1$. There are many other kinds of queues, including those where first in, first out (FIFO) is not assumed, but few yield easily usable analytic results. Details of some of these are given in the textbooks in the Bibliography.

The M/M/1 Queue

We start by considering the simplest of all stochastic queues, the $M/M/1$. This represents a Poisson stream of independent arrivals into a queue whose single server has exponentially distributed service times. The queue is assumed to be unbounded and the population of potential customers to be infinite.

Let λ be the (mean) rate of arrivals and μ be the (mean) rate of service. We derive a measure called traffic intensity ρ as

$$\rho = \frac{\lambda}{\mu}.$$

Using this, we note that the distribution of N, the number of customers present in the queue, including any being served, at any time is geometric for the steady-state condition $\rho < 1$:

$$P(N = n) = \rho^n (1 - \rho), \qquad n = 0, 1, \ldots$$

From this we see that the mean and variance of the number of customers in the queue are

$$E[N] = \frac{\rho}{1 - \rho},$$

$$Var[N] = \frac{\rho}{(1 - \rho)^2}.$$

It also turns out that the sojourn time (time waiting plus time being served) for each customer is exponentially distributed with parameter $\mu - \lambda$. Thus, the mean sojourn time is

$$E[W] = \frac{1}{\mu - \lambda}$$

and its variance is

$$Var[W] = \frac{1}{(\mu - \lambda)^2}.$$

Finally, we note that the utilization, that is, the percentage of the theoretically available time actually used, of the server is given by

$$U = P(N > 0) = \rho.$$

G/G/1 Queues

We gain some insights into more general queues, where we may know the mean and variance, but not the form of the distribution. First, we note that the formula for utilization still holds for general interarrival times and service times, with their means still equal to λ and μ, respectively, that is, the class of $G/G/1$ queues.

M/M/1 Queues

We also hold the arrivals to be Poisson with rate λ but allow the service times to be generally distributed with mean μ and variance V, that is, the class of $M/G/1$ queues.

We define the coefficent of variation, C, as

$$C^2 = \mu^2 V.$$

The formula for the average number of customers in the system, N, is now given by

$$E[N] = \rho + \frac{\rho^2(1 + C^2)}{2(1 - \rho)}.$$

This is known as the "Pollaczek–Khintchine's Formula."

From Little's Law we now compute the average time spent in the system as

$$E[W] = \frac{E[N]}{\lambda}.$$

Again, this assumes the steady-state condition $\rho < 1$.

Queueing Networks

Continuing the examination of analytically tractable models, we look for useful results for networks of queues. These can be divided into two main groups: *product form* and *nonproduct form*.

Product form networks have the property that they can be regarded as independently operating queues, where steady state can be expressed as both a set of global balance equations on customer flow in the whole network and a set of local balance equations on each queue. Local flow balance says that the mean number of customers entering any queue from all others must equal the number leaving it to go to all others, including customers which leave and rejoin the same queue immediately.

Several different ways of identifying this sort of behavior have been proposed, but the name product form comes from Jackson's theorem, which states that the joint probability of the numbers of customers at each queue being a particular combination is the product of their individual probabilities of having that number. We begin by considering Jackson networks and then look at the extension to a more general class of product form networks described by the Baskett, Chandy, Muntz, Palacios-Gomez (BCMP) theorem.

Jackson Networks with Closed-Form Solutions—Open Networks

Consider the case of a network of M queue/server nodes. Customers enter the network at node j in a Poisson stream with rate γ_j. Each node has a single server and service times are distributed exponentially, with mean $1/\mu_j$ ($j = 1, \ldots, M$). When a customer leaves node j, it goes to node k with probability q_{jk}, ($j = 1, \ldots, M$, $k = 1, \ldots, M$). Customers from j leave the network with probability $(1 - q_{j1} + q_{j2} + \cdots + q_{jM})$.

Now let λ_j be the average total arrivals at node j, including those from outside and those from other nodes. If the network is in steady state, λ_j is also the rate of customers leaving j. Overall, we can formulate a set of "flow balance equations" which express these flows:

$$\lambda_j = \gamma_j + \sum_{k=1}^{M} \lambda_k q_{jk}, \qquad j = 1, 2, \ldots.$$

As long as the network is open, that is, at least one γ_j is nonzero, this represents a set of linear simultaneous equations with an obvious solution.

Let traffic intensity at j be, as usual, $\rho_j = \lambda_j/\mu_j$. The joint distribution of the number of customers at each of the M nodes, $N_1, N_2, \ldots, N_M$, can be expressed as

$$P(N_1 = n_1, N_2 = n_2, \ldots, N_M = n_M) = \prod_{j=1}^{M} \rho_j^{n_j}(1 - \rho_j).$$

This is Jackson's theorem. It describes each node as an independent single-server system with Poisson arrivals and exponential service times.

For simplicity from now we write the current state, $N_1 = n_1, N_2 = n_2, \ldots,$ $N_M = n_M$, as **n**. The total average number of customers in the network is

$$E[N_1 + N_2 + \cdots + N_M] = \sum_{j=1}^{M} \frac{\rho_j}{(1 - \rho_j)}.$$

Then from Little's Law, the total time spent by customers in the network is

$$E[W] = \frac{E[N_1 + N_2 + \cdots N_M]}{\gamma_1 + \gamma_2 + \cdots + \gamma_M}.$$

An Example of an Open Network

Let us model a simple time-sharing computer system as an open queueing network. There is a CPU capable of serving jobs at rate 75 per second and an I/O subsystem capable of serving jobs at 10 per second. Jobs arrive at the CPU from outside at 6 per second. When a job finishes processing at the CPU, it either goes to the I/O subsystem, with probability 0.1, or it goes back into the CPU queue for another time slice, with probability 0.8. Thus, a tenth of all jobs leave the system after leaving the CPU. Jobs finishing at the I/O subsystem either go to the CPU queue, with probability 0.8, or leave the system, with probability 0.2.

Let us denote the CPU as node 1 and the disk subsystem as node 2:

$$q_{11} = 0.8, \qquad q_{12} = 0.1, \qquad q_{21} = 0.1, \qquad q_{22} = 0,$$
$$\gamma_1 = 6, \qquad \gamma_2 = 0, \qquad \mu_1 = 75, \qquad \mu_2 = 10.$$

The flow balance equations are

$$\lambda_1 = 6 + 0.8\lambda_1 + 0.8\lambda_2,$$
$$\lambda_2 = 0 + 0.1\lambda_1 + 0.$$

Solving these as simultaneous equations, we get $\lambda_1 = 50$ and $\lambda_2 = 5$. Thus, $\rho_1 = 1/2$, and $\rho_2 = 2/3$. Then,

$$E[N] = \frac{\frac{2}{3}}{\frac{1}{3}} + \frac{\frac{1}{2}}{\frac{1}{2}} = 3, \qquad E[W] = \frac{3}{6} = 0.5.$$

Multiple-Class Open Networks

It is possible to consider networks with different classes of customers, which are treated differently by servers according to their class. Such networks can be broken into a set of *routing chains*, defining the probability that a job in one node and with one class will next move to another particular node and take on another particular class. This leads to the more general formulation of product form below.

BCMP Networks

The fullest categorization of networks which are all guaranteed to be product form is the BCMP theorem, named after the authors of the paper where it was first formulated (F. Baskett, K. M. Chandy, R. R. Muntz and F. Palacios-Gomez). In the BCMP theorem, nodes of the following types are allowed:

FCFS: A single first come first served (or FIFO) queue; all classes of job having the same exponential service distribution. Service rate can be a function of the length of the queue.

Processor sharing: A single queue; all jobs served simultaneously; server shared equally by all jobs. Different classes may have different service time distributions, but these must be Coxian. Service rate may depend on the queue length.

Infinite server: Sometimes called the *server per job* node type. Each job receives service without waiting. The rate may be unaffected by additional jobs or may be a function of the number in the node. Different classes may have different service time distributions, but these must be Coxian.

LCFSPR: *Last come first served with preemptive resume* where a new job arriving displaces any currently in service and the job displaced will resume at the point in its service where it was interrupted after all jobs which arrived after it. Different classes can have different service time distributions, which must be Coxian. Service times can depend on the queue length.

We can now define a set of equations for each routing chain, in a form similar to those for Jackson networks:

$$\sum_{i,r \in C} v_{ir} p_{ir;js} + p_{0;js} = v_{js}, \qquad j, s \in C,$$

Where the routing chain C is a set of node/class pairs for the network such that there is a positive probability for each pair in C that any job in that pair will either reach or have already passed through every other pair in C. $p_{ir;js}$ is then the probability that a job in node i with class r will move to node j and become of class s. Typically jobs arriving from outside are defined by $p_{0;ir}$, the probability that an arriving job enters node i with class r.

As with open Jackson networks, which form a special case of open BCMP networks, there is a simple closed-form algebraic solution. An open network has at least one nonzero $p_{0;js}$ term.

Closed Jackson Networks

If there is no constant additive factor in the definition of at least one of the λ_j terms, the system is closed, representing a situation where no new customers enter the system. Because we are assuming steady state, this can also be expressed as saying that no existing customers leave the system, that is,

$$\sum_{j=1}^{M} q_{ij} = 1, \qquad M > =i > 0.$$

There is now no unique analytic solution to the balance equations of Jackson's theorem alone. They can in theory be solved by noting that the sum of the probabilities in any one of the possible states must equal 1. This allows us to find a *normalization constant* for the balance equations (by convention denoted as G) which satisfies both the balance equations and this total probability constraint. This gives us a unique answer if we use a general solution of the form

$$P(N_1 = n_1, N_2 = n_2, \ldots, N_M = n_M) = P(\mathbf{n}) = G \prod_{j=1}^{M} \rho_j^{nj}, \sum_{\mathbf{n} \in S} P(\mathbf{n}) = 1,$$

where S is the set of all possible states of the network. However, this approach breaks down very quickly, as the number of states can increase exponentially as the network gets bigger. A number of more efficient algorithms have been proposed. The three most commonly used examples are the convolution algorithm, mean value analysis (MVA), and local balance algorithm for normalizing constants (LBANC) and their extension to multiple-class networks.

As an example of the types of approach used, MVA works by iteratively solving the network for each population until the one of interest is reached. It depends on the *arrival theorem*, which notes that a customer entering a queue observes the network's mean state with itself removed.

Nonproduct-Form Networks

There is no guarantee that a particular problem will yield a product-form solution. We may, therefore, need to find some other approach. This usually means some numerical technique. It may, however, be possible to model a good enough approximation analytically.

Approximation Techniques

There are many different approximate techniques for solving non-BCMP networks. Some are quite crude at first sight, such as approximating priorities for classes of customers by reducing the amount of servicing time devoted to those classes with lower priorities in proportion to the time spent on higher-priority customers. A better approximation for priorities is to modify the delay time calculated by the MVA algorithm in a suitable manner. Both can lead to useful estimates.

A second approach is to solve separately the subnetwork containing the most interesting (or most critical) elements by short-circuiting across its connection to the rest of the network and using, in turn, all populations of interest. This approach depends on Norton's theorem, which comes from the analysis of electrical circuits by a similar short-circuit approach. The total network can then be solved substituting the aggregate performance of the subnetwork as a *flow equivalent service center*. (See Figs. 1 and 2.)

It may also be possible to model two approximations which are known to provide a lower and an upper bound on the real behavior of the system. In the crudest of these approaches, *asymptotic bounds* are assumed, such as utilization of 1 at a node. This approach can certainly fix limits on what might be expected. A more refined approach chooses two simplified models, where each approximation is product form. By solving each model, bounds can be placed on the true solution. The approximations are based on establishing the missing local balance properties of nodes in ways which are known to give a better or worse performance in all cases. Once local balance is restored, we are guaranteed to have a product form, because the independence of each node is restored.

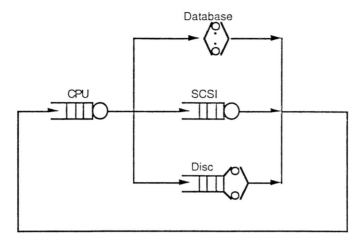

FIGURE 1   Simple queueing network.

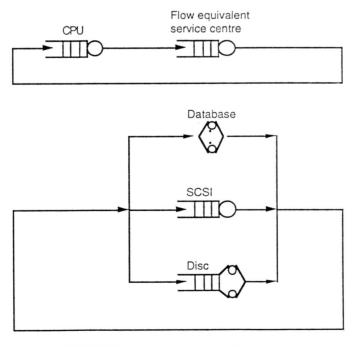

FIGURE 2   Decomposed queueing network.

Numerical Techniques

In some cases the approach is to represent the underlying stochastic model, known as a Markov chain, directly. This involves generating all the states of the system and then manipulating the resulting matrices. It can cause major space and time complexity problems.

The main constraints on product-form networks concern independence (i.e., the Markovian property of the overall network). This makes it impossible to deal with the need for individual customers leaving one server to have to arrive in the same order at another one. Thus, many communication protocols are not able to be represented as product-form networks. Queueing theory also gives only limited insight into transient behavior, as it is usually used under steady-state assumptions.

There are many numerical methods for dealing with queueing networks. These nearly all work on the transition rate matrix of the underlying Markov process. We list several of the major approaches to solution here and refer the reader to the literature for further details.

The stationary distribution of a Markov process is given by the following matrix equation representing the balance equations:

$$\pi^{T} Q = 0^{T}.$$

These are linear in the steady-state probabilities. Thus, they can be solved by the usual techniques for *homogeneous equations*. Alternatively, the equations can be reformulated to allow *eigenvector* approaches.

More widely used are techniques which decompose the network into *nearly completely decomposable subnetworks*. This allows aggregate states representing these subnetworks to be used in a reduced transition matrix, having precomputed the solutions for these. Where the property of *lumpability* exists, this aggregation is exact.

Finally, *matrix geometric* techniques may be possible.

In general, queueing models are useful for simple, quick approximations and for gaining insight into the complications of systems. Very often, we must resort to simulation to find accurate answers to detailed problems.

STOCHASTIC PETRI NETS (SPNs)

As an alternative to queueing networks, the second half of the 1980s saw a growing interest in using Petri nets to model performance. This passed through timed and stochastic variants of Carl Petri's original nets. Their former purpose had been to express and analyze the behavioral properties of systems, particularly those with concurrent events.

A Petri net is essentially an extension of a finite-state automaton that allows, by means of tokens, several concurrent threads of activity to be described in one representation. It is essentially a graphical description, being a directed graph with its edges defining paths for the evolution of a system's behavior and its nodes or vertices being of two sorts, *places* and *transitions*. All incoming edges to a place must come from a transition and vice versa. *Tokens* are held in places and when all the input places to a transition are *marked*, that is, have at least one token, that transition is *enabled* and *fires*, depositing a token in each of its output places.

There are a number of extensions to these simple *place/transition nets*, mostly to increase the ease of describing complex systems. The most widely used is to define *multiplicities* for the edges, which define how many tokens flow down an edge simultaneously. This is shorthand for an equivalent number of edges linking the same pair of vertices.

The use of Petri nets in performance modeling now centers on the Generalized Stochastic Petri Nets (GSPNs) defined by Ajmone Marsan and others. These incorporate the following extensions:

Multiplicities on arcs.

Firing delays (usually restricted to be exponentially distributed) between the enabling of a time transition and its firing.

Other *immediate* transitions, which fire instantly but where a choice of output arcs may be represented, in a similar manner to branching probabilities in queueing networks.

Sometimes *deterministic* firing rates are allowed, usually restricted so that only one such transition is enabled at one time.

In most tools based on this approach, *colored tokens* are used to represent classes of tokens in a similar way to classes in BCMP queueing networks.

GSPNs are useful because they allow many of the structural and behavioral properties of a net to be examined, as well as its performance to be calculated. They are usually solved by numerical techniques or by simulation, but recently Henderson has defined a set of restricted nets with product-form solutions. It is not yet clear how useful this will be.

Methods which allow much larger Markov models to be solved efficiently also offer the prospect of GSPNs becoming more useful.

PERFORMANCE PROCESS ALGEBRAS

Although still the subject of research, process algebras, which evolved to address some of the shortcomings of simple Petri nets for behavioral analysis, are now being extended in a similar way to GSPNs and their use for performance analysis is being tested. As they are inherently compositional, unlike Petri nets, there are some grounds for believing that they may become a very useful tool.

SIMULATION

A simulation is a model where each step in the evolving behavior of a system is matched by a corresponding step in a computer program.

Approaches to Simulation

The earliest simulations were written in general purpose languages and typically used an *next event* approach. In such models, times are generated for the next of each particular class of events, such as arrivals and departures in particular queues.

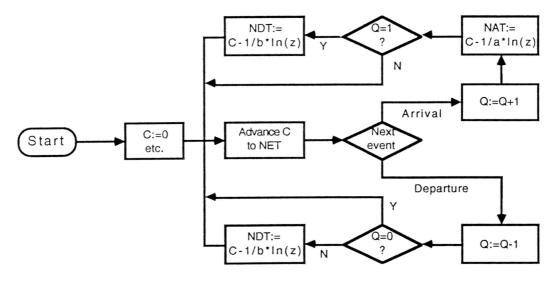

Q = Queue length $\quad$ C = Clock time $\quad$ NET = Next event time

NAT = Next arrival time $\quad$ NDT = Next departure time

FIGURE 3 $\quad$ Next event model of a simple $M/M/1$ queue.

A global *simulation clock* variable is used to record the earliest of these, which is taken as the current simulation time. This selects which event is deemed to have occurred and, as necessary, a new next event time for the class to which the current event belonged and for any dependent events will be generated by adding some delay to the current event time. This cycle is repeated until some stopping condition is achieved, such as the global clock passing some limit or the number of events of a certain type exceeding some limit.

Figure 3 is the flowchart of a simple next event simulation of an $M/M/1$ queue. Such models are only really practical for fairly simple models, unless written in a special purpose language. A number of packages exist to support this, most notably the SIMSCRIPT II.5™ language, marketed by the CACI Corporation. In addition, there are two other widely used approaches: activity scanning and process based. Again, a number of packages exist to support these.

Activity scanning centers on the definition of the activities in a model. Entities are assumed to flow through the model waiting for other entities before engaging in activities in a certain order. Again, a number of languages exist which support this approach. Figure 4 is an example of a model which is defined for the HOCUS™ package, marketed by PE Consultants. In the process view, the model is defined as a set of active components called processes or entities and a set of passive resources which control the activities of the active processes. This is a widely used means of modeling computer systems and networks. The earliest version of this approach was

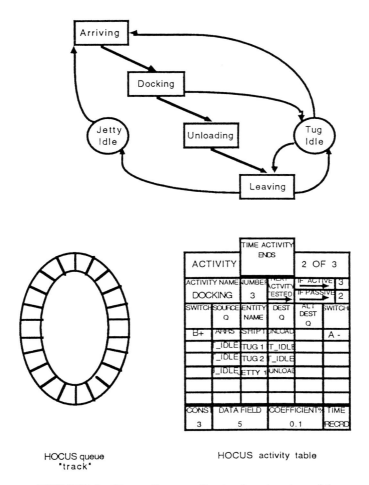

FIGURE 4   Hocus diagram of a simple network model.

the transactions view of GPSS, but the classic implementation is Discrete Event Modeling on SIMULA (DEMOS). (See Fig. 5.)

Random Number Generation

Many models cannot be represented by exact methods. For these we need to introduce some estimate of delays and behaviors. In general we often need to use *stochastic processes* to model parts of the system where we are uncertain of the behavior. A stochastic process is one where one or more of the values involved is defined by a distribution. There are many types of distribution, each of which is useful for approximating a particular form of behavior. This is a summary of some of the commonest and most useful. In each case a DEMOS histogram is included as an illustration of the shape of the distribution. These are produced horizontally rather than vertically. (See examples in text.)

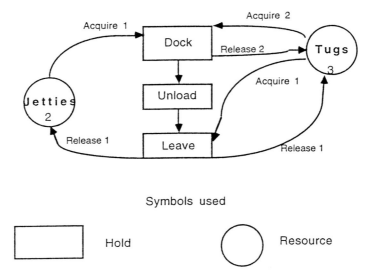

Symbols used

Hold   Resource

FIGURE 5   DEMOS activity diagram of the same simple model.

Poisson

The Poisson distribution models a set of totally independent events as a process, where each event is independent of all others. It is not the same as a uniform distribution. Whereas knowledge of past events does not allow us to predict anything about future ones, except that we know the overall average, the Poisson distribution represents the likelihood of one of a given range of numbers of events occuring within the next time interval.

```
CELL/LOWER LIM/    N/  FREQ/CUM %
                                 I----------------------------
    0 -INFINITY      0  0.00    0.00  I
    1      0.000   530  0.53   53.00  I******************************
    2      1.000   340  0.34   87.00  I******************
    3      2.000   105  0.11   97.50  I******
    4      3.000    19  0.02   99.40  I*
    5      4.000     5  0.01   99.90  I.
    6      5.000     1  0.00  100.00  I.
    7      6.000     0  0.00  100.00  I
                                 I----------------------------
```

(Negative) Exponential

If the Poisson represents the likely number of independent events to occur in the next time period, the negative exponential distribution is its converse. It represents the distribution of interarrival times for the same arrival process. Its mean is an interevent time, but it is often expressed in terms of the arrival rate, which is 1/ interarrival time.

```
CELL/LOWER LIM/      N/  FREQ/CUM %
                                    I----------------------------
     0  -INFINITY       0   0.00    0.00   I
     1      0.000     620   0.62   62.00   I*****************************
     2      1.000     237   0.24   85.70   I***********
     3      2.000      92   0.09   94.90   I****
     4      3.000      36   0.04   98.50   I**
     5      4.000       5   0.01   99.00   I.
     6      5.000       4   0.00   99.40   I.
     7      6.000       5   0.01   99.90   I.
     8      7.000       1   0.00  100.00   I.
     9      8.000       0   0.00  100.00   I
                                    I----------------------------
```

Normal

The normal distribution expresses the distribution of values around a mean when the number of occurrences of values either side of the mean is balanced symmetrically. We use the normal distribution as an *ideal* distribution. As well as a mean, the normal distribution has a variance (sometimes expressed as a standard deviation = $\sqrt{\text{variance}}$). This measures how compressed the distribution is around its mean, that is, how likely values are to lie close to the mean. The tighter the distribution, the smaller the variance and so the more likely values will be close to the mean.

```
CELL/LOWER LIM/      N/  FREQ/CUM %
                                    I----------------------------
     0  -INFINITY       0   0.00    0.00   I
     1      6.000       0   0.00    0.00   I
     2      7.000      17   0.02    1.70   I*
     3      8.000     141   0.14   15.80   I***********
     4      9.000     319   0.32   47.70   I***************************
     5     10.000     356   0.36   83.30   I*****************************
     6     11.000     138   0.14   97.10   I***********
     7     12.000      25   0.03   99.60   I**
     8     13.000       4   0.00  100.00   I.
                                    I----------------------------
```

Uniform

The uniform distribution has equal probability of any of its values occurring. This is not the same as the normal, where we require the values to become more likely as we near the mean, nor the Poisson, where the numbers are the sum of independent events.

Empirical

In many simulation packages, an empirical distribution holds a table corresponding to the histogram of observed (empirically determined) frequencies of a range of values. It returns values with frequencies matching those in the table. It is especially useful for irregular data.

Implementing Random Numbers as Functions

The key problem is to define a function which generates a stream of randomly spread values. This is the basic drawing function which is then used to implement the various distribution functions. When using random number generators it is

important to know how "random" they actually are, that is, how well spread the
values are. Many are far from well spread. Many have very short cycles before they
repeat the same sequence. In using a package, this should be tested if it is not
documented, by using standard statistical tests.

All random number generators for simulation must be psuedorandom, in that
it must be possible to reproduce exactly the same stream on demand. This allows
accurate comparisons of different strategies, by generating the same stream of event
times in different model runs.

A good basic drawing function is the Lehmer, or linear congruential, drawing
function:

$$U_{k+1} = (C_1 U_k + C_2), \qquad \text{mod } M.$$

In many packages, this is implemented with the constant C_2 as zero, giving a more
computationally efficient form known as a multiplicative congruential generator:

$$U_{k+1} = C_1 U_k, \qquad \text{mod } M.$$

This can be used to generate a number in the range 0..1 by dividing the current value
of U by M.

The values of the constants are chosen to give a long period to the cycle of
numbers, that is, until U reaches a value it has had previously.

Generating a Distribution

Using the basic drawing scaled to the range 0..1, we can generate close approximations to our required distributions. In our first event-based model we used the
formula for the negative exponential distribution

$$-\frac{1}{b} \ln z,$$

where z is the scaled random variate. Similar formulas can be found for most useful
distributions.

The initial value of U is called the seed of our distribution. Note that U is
updated each time a new number is sampled.

To ensure that different streams of random numbers are not in phase, we need
to generate well-spread seeds within the same stream, so that each stream occupies a
distinct part of the random drawing cycle. Ohlin's trick of NextSeed ensures this for
the Lehmer generator in DEMOS. This notes that

$$U_{k+n} = A^n U_k, \qquad \text{mod} M,$$

allowing us to move rapidly down the random number stream.

Analyzing Simulation Results

When we are running models, we are conducting experiments. To make sense of the
output, we use the same techniques as in any observational science. Most importantly, we use the techniques of statistics.

A series of measured values for some value of interest provides us with the
basis of statistical analysis. Typically, such series arise within a model either when a

process repeats a cycle or a number of entities engage in the same sequence of activities. Typically, we might measure the length of a queue for a resource or the time spent in a system by an item. We can derive the usual estimates from such streams, that is, the mean and standard deviation. To be meaningful, a mean must refer to a system in *steady state*.

The mean is defined as the estimator for the true value R,

$$R = \overline{X} = \frac{1}{n} \sum_{i=1}^{n} X_i.$$

The standard deviation is

$$\left(\frac{1}{n} \sum_{i=1}^{n} (\overline{X} - X_i)^2 \right)^{1/2},$$

or the square root of the variance.

To avoid storing the individual observations, we can estimate the standard deviation at the end of collection by recording both the sum and the sum of the squares of the observations as we go and use the following estimate:

$$\left(\frac{n \sum_{i=1}^{n} X_i^2 - \sum_{i=1}^{n} X_i}{n(n-1)} \right)^{1/2}.$$

The mean is an estimate for the expected value of the distribution of values being observed. The standard deviation is an estimate for its dispersion or width. Note that these estimates do not depend on the form of the actual distribution. Fitting a distribution to a series of observations requires more sophisticated techniques.

Observations and Accuracy

When we run a simulation model we can obtain an estimate for a set of values of interest within the system being modeled, for a given set of conditions which we set for that execution. From one run we generate a single point in observation space, but we know very little about how accurate this point estimate is. We need some estimate of its accuracy as well. Formally, we need both a point estimate and an interval estimate. The former says what the expected value of the observed quantity is under the given conditions; the latter says what interval we expect the real value to be in around this estimate. We normally call this interval the confidence interval and express it as a percentage probability that the estimated value lies within a certain distance of the correct one compared with the standard deviation of the distribution of observed results.

Estimates Used

To get the desired estimates we have to run our model repeatedly under the same levels of its free variables to obtain a set of independent observations. We would like to use this set to generate a single *unbiased* and *consistent* estimate of the actual value. If we assume a set of observations $\{O_1, O_2, \ldots, O_n\}$ we want to derive an estimate R for the value V, with the following properties: unbiased and consistent.

Unbiased

$$E[R] = V \quad \text{for all } n,$$

where $E[R]$ is the expectation or mean of R. This states that as the size of the sample increases, the expected value of the estimate always equals the actual expected value. (This does *not* say that it will ever be the actual value.)

Consistent

$$P(R = V) \rightarrow 1 \quad \text{as } n \text{ increases.}$$

More useful for the consistency property is

$$P(R - V < w) \rightarrow 1 \quad \text{as } n \rightarrow \infty.$$

This means that the likelihood of R lying within distance w of V increases as we increase the sample size, that is, our confidence in this accuracy of the estimate increases.

The arithmetic mean has both these properties for independent observations and so our task is reduced to ensuring that the observations are indeed independent. This is consistent because

$$\text{Var}(\overline{X}) = \frac{\sum\limits_{i=1}^{n} \text{Var}[X_i]}{n^2} = \frac{\text{Var}[X]}{n}.$$

Independence and Bias

We want to gather a set of n unbiased observations and use their mean as our overall estimate. In practice, this usually means making n runs or breaking one run into n independent subruns. This begs the question of independence and bias.

We might make a single run, observe each process or customer, and measure their times through the system. This could give us a sample of C observations for C customers, but it would be unlikely to be a sample of independent observations, as each customer's presence in the system will interfere with the others. Thus, it would seem that one run can only generate one observation. By running it long enough we can hope that steady state will be reached, and the longer we run it, the more likely that becomes, that is, the mean of the individual customers' delays will approach some constant level. Thus, this mean is unbiased and consistent, but its variance can be hard to estimate.

Instead, we usually make multiple runs, each with the same conditions but a different random number seed, and use the mean over each run as a single observation. The problem is then to define equivalent lengths for each run. If we are using the mean value of something per customer in the system, we should allow the runs to continue until an equal number of customers have passed through. This is called a customer-oriented *stopping condition* for the simulation. If we are measuring something in terms of simulation time, we must have equal simulation time run lengths as our stopping condition. An example might be the number of customers waiting in a queue at any given time. This preserves the unbiased nature of the individual observations. It is a system-oriented stopping condition.

If we use fixed time length runs for the customer-oriented measure, we bias the estimate, as the number of customers in the sample may be different in each run. This is biased because the estimate of the average waiting time of customers is now the ratio of two random variables, the total waiting time and the number of customers, and the expectation of this value is not the same as the ratio of their individual expectations. We must choose an appropriate stopping condition depending on the type of measure we are trying to estimate. Unfortunately, we may want to estimate values of different sorts. In that case we have to accept that some of the estimates will be biased. The only answer in general is longer run times, as the biases are asymptotically zero.

We can sometimes get two values for the price of one in a simulation by using the relationship called Little's Law, which we defined in the section on queueing theory. This is applicable to most queues and queueing systems and it relates a system-oriented measure (the mean number of customers in the system) to a customer-oriented measure [the mean time spent in the system by each customer (the mean sojourn time), for a given arrival rate]. Little's Law was defined earlier when discussing analytical techniques.

CONFIDENCE INTERVALS

For any estimate defined as the mean of some sample of values in our simulation, we have said our unbiased and consistent estimate will be R as defined above. Our confidence interval is defined by two functions $A_1(X)$ and $A_2(X)$ such that

$$P\{A_1(X) < \alpha \leq A_2(X)\} = 1 - \beta, \qquad 0 < \beta < 1.$$

The $1 - \beta$ expression is the probability that in each of a large number of estimates of our confidence interval bounded by A_1 and A_2 we would find the actual value, α.

Essentially, we set up a hypothesis that such a probability applies, with the width of our confidence interval defining a desired accuracy and the probability given above defining the confidence we wish to place in the result. By testing that hypothesis under certain assumptions about the distribution of estimates obtained from our runs, we know whether we have achieved the accuracy we wish with the confidence we wish.

Generating Samples

There are two different types of estimate that require different treatments when generating our set of values to make up a sample. Transient or short-term behavior depends on an initial set of conditions which affect the behavior significantly. To generate a sample of N values this type of model requires N independent runs. The seeds used must be carefully chosen to be independent. This is the method of *independent replications*.

Long-term or steady-state models do not depend on their starting conditions and are assumed to settle into a dynamic equilibrium, that is, the average behavior is stable after some warm-up period, and so the probabilities of values equaling their mean is constant.

This requires much longer runs than the short-term estimates above and it is desirable to be able to discard the warm-up period. This can be estimated by watching the changes in values and noting when they become stable. The warm-up period can be shortened by starting with values near the estimated equilibrium. Values from an initial run may be useful here. Even with this improvement, independent replications are usually very long because of the warm-up phase. To improve this situation, two methods are often employed.

The first method is to divide the run into a series of subperiods and collect the measures over each subrun as a point estimate. This is unreliable because the subperiods are clearly not independent and so are biased. Using longer periods reduces the bias but is more expensive. This is the method of *batched means*. The definition of the duration of a sub-period must be in terms of customer numbers or elapsed time depending on what we are estimating, as for separate runs.

A second method is to define points in a simulation run where the model returns to an exactly equivalent state. These are called regeneration points. Periods between regeneration points are genuinely independent subruns. Unfortunately, not all models have easily defined regeneration states. Even so, the *regeneration method* is often cited as the most accurate.

Simulation of Queues and Petri Nets

It is always possible to simulate queueing networks and Petri nets. The activity scanning approach applies well to both, although it may not be as efficient as purpose-written simulators using other approaches. The entities are the customers in the queueing network or the tokens in the Petri net. The activities are the servers in the queues and the transitions firing in the Petri nets.

BIBLIOGRAPHY

General

Ferrari, D., *Computer Systems Performance Evaluation*, Prentice-Hall, Englewood Cliffs, NJ, 1978.
Smith, C. U., *Performance Engineering of Software Systems*, Addison-Wesley, Reading, MA, 1990.

Measurement

Ferrari, D., G. Serazzi, and A. Zeigner, *Measurement and Tuning of Computer Systems*, Prentice-Hall, Englewood Cliffs, NJ, 1983.

Queueing Theory and Stochastic Modeling

Allen, A. O., *Probability, Statistics and Queueing Theory*, 2nd ed., Academic Press, New York, 1993.
Baskett, F., K. Chandy, R. Muntz, and J. Palacios, "Open, Closed and Mixed Networks with Different Classes of Customers", *J. Assoc. Comput. Machines, 22*, 248–260 (1975).
King, P. J. B., *Computer and Communication Systems Performance Modelling*, Prentice-Hall, Englewood Cliffs, NJ, 1990.
Kleinrock, L., *Queueing Systems: Volumes I and II*, Wiley, New York, 1976.

Stochastic Petri Nets

Coleman, J. L., W. Henderson, and P. G. Taylor, "Product Form Equilibrium Distributions and an Algorithm for Classes of Batch Movement Queueing Networks and Stochastic Petri Nets," Technial Report, University of Adelaide (1992).

Molloy, M. K., "Performance Analysis Using Stochastic Petri Nets," *IEEE Trans. Computers, C-31*(9), 913–917 (1982).

Marsan, M. A., G. Conti, and G. Balbo, "A Class of Generalised Stochastic Petri Nets for the Performance Evaluation of Multiprocessor Systems," *ACM Transactions on Computer Systems, 2*(2), 93–122 (1984).

Process Algebras

Hillston, J. and F. Moller (Eds.), *Proceedings of Workshop on Process Algebras and Performance Modelling*, Technical Report CSR-26-93, Dept. Computer Science, University of Edinburgh (1993).

Simulation

Birtwistle, G. M., *Discrete Event Modelling on SIMULA*, Macmillan, New York, 1979.

Franta, W. R., *The Process View of Simulation*, North-Holland, Amsterdam, 1978.

Fishman, G. S., *Concepts and Methods in Discrete Event Digital Simulation*, Wiley, New York, 1973.

Mitrani, I., *Simulation Techniques for Discrete Event Systems*, Cambridge University Press, Cambridge, 1982.

Ohlin, M., "Next Random — A Method of Fast Access to Any Number in the Random Generator Cycle," *SIMULA Newsletter, 6*(2), 18–20 (1977).

Shannon, R. E., *Systems Simulation: the Art and Science*, Prentice-Hall, Englewood Cliffs, NJ, 1975.

ROB J. POOLEY

CONCEPTUAL STRUCTURES AND CONCEPTUAL GRAPHS

INTRODUCTION

Conceptual structures are models of a perceived reality. In effect, any agent builds a mental model of the world with which it has to interact. This model depends on the actual perception and understanding of this world; this is the reason why it is said to be *conceptual*, that is, a model of the mind. The actual actions that the agent will undertake will be conditioned by this model; so it conveys an extreme importance for the agent who has to efficiently achieve a particular task. Through interactions with the outside world, a learning process refines the conceptual models used by the agent to generate its correct behavior.

Machines also need to build conceptual models of their environment if they are to interact with it in an intelligent manner. Realistically speaking, we can define an intelligent behavior as being consistent with the conceptual models of the world used to generate this behavior and as being efficient with regard to some evaluation parameters related to either the agent or the task to be performed, or both. Furthermore, we should also include in the definition of an intelligent behavior, some learning dimension that would ensure that the agent's behavior improves over time according to the evaluation parameters designated earlier. This definition depicts an intelligent behavior as we commonly acknowledge it.

The recent improvements in computer-based technology led us to foresee machines of the future as being autonomous intelligent agents interacting in our day-to-day life. They could be used for more than repetitive chores, for more than giving support to semiautomatic tasks such as the taking-off and landing of airplanes (as is currently done today), but they could assist and even monitor human activities such as surgery in an operation room unit. Of course, the amount of knowledge and processing required to monitor complex human activities is currently out of reach for most machines today. However, all of this is theoretically possible and lies on the path of future scientific improvements and discoveries, provided that the machine can possess a consistent, valid, and complete model of the reality as perceived by the human agent. In brief, it must represent human knowledge.

Conceptual models are pieces of knowledge that describe the outside world with which interaction will occur. An agent uses this knowledge in different inferential processes in order to produce and control its behavior. The automation of reasoning capabilities within a computer is thus a *sine qua non* condition for the development of autonomous agents. Consequently, knowledge has to be represented in some formalism that allows its processing. It became clear many decades ago that this new type of computerized data, often called *conceptual* or *symbolic* data, would represent complex realities and that the usual ways of representing numerical and textual data were then obsolete.

FIGURE 1   A *cat sits on a mat*, a semantic network representation.

Because knowledge encompasses all sorts of complex relationships between various concrete or abstract entities, the acquisition of any piece of knowledge requires the identification of the objects being put in relationship to one another through semantical relations. For example, the proposition *a cat sits on a mat* refers to some concrete entities, that is, physically perceivable entities, *cat* and *mat*, related through a spatial relationship *on* entailed by a situation verb *sit*. Knowledge representation languages must allow all of this to be represented if the semantics of the proposition is to be correctly represented in a format directly processable by a computer.

It seemed natural thousands of years ago to graphically represent the content of propositions using drawings, as written languages were more graphical and iconic than alphabet based (1). Using some drawings, the previous proposition could be represented as depicted in Figure 1 for instance. It was then thought, and still is, that the mind builds models of entities, also called *concepts*, webbed through semantical relations (2).This view was reinforced by past and recent work on neurophysiology which prompted researchers to consider the replication of neural nets in computers (3–5). Consequently, a conceptual structure as graphically represented in Figure 1 is called a *semantic network*.

Of course, knowledge representation languages must be precise and expressive. Expressiveness is necessary for the complete modelization of the domain to be represented in the computer; precision is necessary to avoid representational ambiguities which might result in an unsound behavior. Precision normally limits the representational alternatives of identical propositions. Ideally, there should be only one way of representing a proposition, aleviating ambiguities, and lessening modelization subjectivity. In effect, the knowledge engineer, in charge of the construction of a computerized model of the application domain, must make certain modelization choices. Once these choices are made, the representation of a proposition should be unique. For example, the knowledge engineer may decide that a state resulting from the application of a situation verb on an agent should be graphically linked to this verb, as shown in Figure 2 with the double-lined arrow from *sit* to *on*.

FIGURE 2   A *cat sits on a mat*, revised version.

FIGURE 3   A *cat sits on a mat*, a conceptual graph version.

Of course, a knowledge representation formalism must exhaustively specify all these syntactical details and must formally define the semantics associated with them. Consequently, these graphical notations may be quite diverse and elaborate.

This article will later introduce the conceptual graph formalism of Sowa (6). Just to informally introduce some of the basic graphical features of this notation, here is the proposition of Figure 1 represented as a conceptual graph (see Fig. 3).* Boxes represent typed variables or individuals; circles represent semantical relations between them. This graph asserts that there exists something which is a cat, some-thing which is a mat, something which is the action of sitting, that the cat is the agent of the situation verb sit, and that the location of the situation verb is the mat.

Semantic networks are still very much alive in artificial intelligence nowadays (7). They provide a graphical representation of conceptual structures which would be otherwise much harder to acquire if based on some linear notation (8). For instance, Figure 4 shows the graph of Figure 3 represented as a well-formed formula in first-order predicate calculus. It is obvious to see that more complex graphs would lead to very complex formulas. The syntactical details of such formulas alone are sufficient to prevent their easy encoding or understanding.

However, semantic network-based formalisms provide more than just a graph-ical interface for the acquisition of conceptual structures; they provide a definitional framework for the modelization of an application domain, along with the corre-sponding graph-based operators which are helpful in the transformation of pre-viously acquired graphs (mainly to infer new graphs). For example, if all cats like milk (as shown by the conceptual graph of Fig. 5), then one might infer that the cat which sits on the mat also likes milk (see Fig. 6) This inference is possible through a join operation applied on the graphs of Figures 3 and 5 over the CAT concept (see the subsection The Vocabulary).

In any case, the pros and cons of using semantic networks fall outside the scope of this article; the interested reader is referred to Ref. 9. The remainder of

$$\exists x \exists y \exists z \, (\, CAT(x) \wedge SIT(y) \wedge MAT(z) \wedge agnt(y,x) \wedge loc(y,z) \,)$$

FIGURE 4   A *cat sits on a mat*, a first-order predicate calculus version.

---

*Of course, this graph follows some arbitrary representational choices made by the knowledge engineer, such as (1) the semantical relations are based on Filmore's case grammar, (2) entities are of type CAT or MAT, and (3) verbs are also represented as entities. Other conventions could have resulted in some other conceptual graph, as we will discuss later.

FIGURE 5   *All cats like milk.*

this article will present (1) the issues that the conceptual graph formalism addresses, that is, some of the major representational problems that semantic network-based research has identified and (2) a subset of the notation.

PROBLEMATIC ISSUES RELATED TO SEMANTIC NETWORKS

Early research in knowledge representation has led to the development of many graphical notations which were classified under the same generic heading of *semantic networks*. Of course, early work showed deficiencies which were late corrected. This section depicts some of the major problems of these earlier systems and pinpoints areas where the conceptual graph theory proposes solutions to these problems.

Huge Nets

In the beginning, semantic networks* were perceived as a *single* net of concepts webbed through all sorts of semantical relations either explicitly represented by direct links between concepts (vertices) or implicitly represented by paths from one concept to the other through a maze of interconnected semantical relations. For instance, the semantic network of Figure 7 asserts that the cat which sits on the mat likes milk through the relation is-one-of. From that path, a direct link could be added and stored as in Figure 8.

There is no evidence that the human brain explicitly stores every single relation that can be inferred. On the contrary, inferential mechanisms suppose that inferential paths are used by humans as they are reasoning (10). This allows for a rationalizing of memory and energy. Because computer resources are scarce with regard to the inferential mechanisms that researchers in artificial intelligence are attempting to implement, these same principles soon became a fundamental requirement of the representation language. Consequently, redundant links, those which can also be

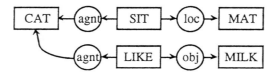

FIGURE 6   A new conceptual graph inferred from known propositions.

---

*The terms *semantic networks* and *semantic nets* are interchangeable.

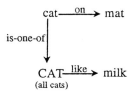

FIGURE 7   A semantic network where a path is used to infer new facts.

expressed by paths, should not be represented. The representation language itself should ensure that knowledge is expressed as minimally as possible. This is the case with the conceptual graph theory, where knowledge is represented as a set of small graphs linked through a partial order of subsumption (see the section The Conceptual Graph Formalism).

Structural and Assertional Knowledge

Furthermore, in earlier systems, all sorts of semantical relations were mixed up in the same net. Some of these relations are used to describe the application domain; some are used to assert facts. This distinction between *structural* and *assertional* knowledge must be made explicit. In effect, both types of knowledge are essential to the inference engine, but the inferences made possible by both are different in nature. In our next example, we chose to represent classes of objects using capital-letter labels. From Figure 9, one could know that a cat is an animal through the *isa* relation which links subclasses to their parent classes (and which is also transitive). This fact depends on the structure of the application domain. One could also know that Morris is orange because it is a cat which is orange, but this is purely factual. It depends on the actual data and not on the structure of the application domain; it could have been otherwise without changing anything from the structure of the application domain.

Having a semantic network which incorporates both types of knowledge is troublesome because it crowds the graphical display with information that is used in different contexts. Also, the structural knowledge about the application domain is said to be of *second order* because it permits reasoning on the structure of the domain itself. For instance, by looking at Figure 9, we know that everything which is true of the class ANIMAL will be true of its subclass CAT. This inheritance

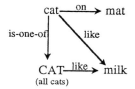

FIGURE 8   An explicit link expressing the same information as in Figure 7.

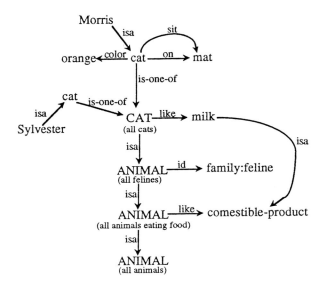

FIGURE 9   A typical semantic network.

property holds between all classes and their proper subclasses. Relations of different order have different purposes, and in order to clean up the semantic net, one could represent the structural and assertional knowledge in different data structures. This subdivision of knowledge is at the heart of a wealth of research on the semantic network (11) and is also present in the conceptual graph formalism.

Quantification

Early semantic nets were not clear about their underlying semantics. For instance, in Figure 9, Sylvester is said to be a cat. Because it is a different cat than Morris, we should use an alternate node labeled *cat*. This necessitates some additional information about the fact that it is one of the cats who like milk, and so on. In brief, it may introduce redundancy. This is yet another reason to divide structural and assertional knowledge. As part of the structural knowledge, we can talk about typical cats, asserting truths which hold for any cat, like the proposition *all cats like milk*. This has nothing to do with the fact that Sylvester and Morris are cats (assertional truths).

In the conceptual graph formalism, one can express truths about all cats, about particular cats, either identified or not, and about typical cats. Basically, the knowledge base is built using assertions about all cats (universal truths), which are represented by universally quantified variables of the type CAT, or about particular cats (existential truths), which are represented by existentially quantified variables of the type CAT or by individuals (constants) of the type CAT. The prototype for CAT, which describes the typical cat, and schemas for CAT, which are plausible and commonsense definitions of the concept CAT in typical situations (graphs), can be used to determine default values for particular descriptive parts of the definition of a cat. These default values and uses of the type CAT do not participate in any inferential process based on the conceptual graph operators because sound inferences must not be done with knowledge which is only partially valid. So, inferences made under the conceptual graph paradigm are soundly grounded on first-order predicate calculus. Consequently, not only inferred knowledge is sound but these inferences are monotonic: What was previously inferred will remain valid forever; that is, no revision is ever needed.

Subsumption

The *isa* links of Figure 9 show that CAT is a subtype of ANIMAL. Often, this information is available and is acquired as such from the knowledge engineer. When a Class C_1 is a superclass of some other class C_2, the former is said to subsume the latter, that is, C_1 subsumes C_2. In our example, the class of all animals, labeled ANIMAL, is said to *subsume* the class of all cats, labeled CAT.

There are different kinds of subsumption relations. For instance, one can think of extensional or intentional subsumption. Extensional subsumption states that a class C_1 subsumes another class C_2 when all individuals of C_2 are also individuals of C_1. Based on set theory, the computation of this subsumption relationship is straightforward but is data dependent. Subsumption holds only for a fixed set of individuals. When this set is altered, subsumption must be recomputed. Furthermore, because it is data dependent, it does not account for all subsumption relations that may exist according to the modelization of the domain. For example, let us suppose that UNICORN is a subclass of HORSE. Because no unicorn exists in our world, its extension set will be empty: There is no individual of type UNICORN. The empty set is included in all other sets. So, UNICORN becomes a subclass of all the other classes, which is most probably not representative of the application domain.

Intentional subsumption states that a class C_1 subsumes another class C_2 when the definition of C_1 is a generalization of the definition of C_2. This is, of course, much harder to compute because definitions need to be compared. When these definitions are represented by a graph-related formalism, their comparison becomes an NP-hard problem. Of course, many heuristics can be applied to reduce the complexity of this task (12–16); the nature of the application domain has also been identified as being a key factor in the complexity figures (17,18). We get a faithful view of the application domain when the different graphs take part in a partial-order relation of subsumption.* Also, validation of subsumption can be achieved. For example, the definition of class FELINE (see Fig. 10) was proven to be at the right

$$\text{ANIMAL} \xrightarrow{\ \text{id}\ } \text{family:feline}$$

FIGURE 10   The definition of the class FELINE.

---

*Naturally, intensional subsumption implies extensional subsumption.

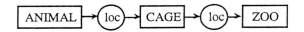

FIGURE 11   The definition of the class ZOO-ANIMAL.

location in the *subsumption hierarchy* of Figure 9 (if all links but the *isa* links are deleted).

Some subsumption relations are obvious and are acquired from the knowledge engineer. They are manually inputted. For instance, adding the FELINE definition to the knowledge base did not need the explicit computation of the subsumption relation with the ANIMAL definition because FELINE is defined in terms of a genus, ANIMAL, and a differentia, the rest of the graph of Figure 10. This is called the *Aristotelian model of type definition*, and it is at the heart of the conceptual graph theory term definition mechanisms (6,19).

However, subsumption relations are not always obvious, and automatic classifier systems do make a claim that the automatic computation of subsumption relations is more thorough and exhaustive than relying on the knowledge engineer to establish those links (20). For example, *cats which like milk* could define a class of objects that should be subsumed by the class of objects defined by the *animals which like comestible products* (see Fig. 9). Because both definitions may not appear as domain classes, only automatic subsumption can relate them to one another. For the same reasons as above, precompiled subsumption links between different graphs are sought because they speed up the query answering process (21,22).

The conceptual graph theory explicitly states that all acquired graphs take part in a partial-order relation of subsumption. Unfortunately, conceptual graphs defining new terms (classes) are not part of this hierarchy. Based on the Aristotelian model of type definition, the subsumption hierarchy is totally acquired from the knowledge engineer who should at least be supported in this activity by some validation tool. But this support is entirely up to the implementors of the system. For example, let us define two classes, ZOO-ANIMAL and CAPTIVE-ANIMAL (shown in Figs. 11 and 12), both with the type ANIMAL as genus. Even though Figure 13 would be the resulting subsumption hierarchy under the present acquisition mechanism, the real subsumption relation that could be computed is shown in Figure 14. The discrepancy between both subsumption hierarchies may create computational problems (at best) or result in an unsound behavior of the inference engine, depending on its implementation (at worst). So the knowledge engineer must make sure that the modelization phase identifies correctly all subsumption relations among all type definitions.

FIGURE 12   The definition of the class CAPTIVE-ANIMAL.

aims at providing a clear semantics to whatever needs to be represented in a particular application domain. Early semantic networks were not that precise in their representation of arbitrary propositions. Some cleaning up needed to be done; subjectivity needed to be minimized. Semantic networks now benefit from a clear definitional semantics.

The ontological primitives of conceptual graph systems are domain oriented. The knowledge engineer has to choose a particular set of terms as its vocabulary. This vocabulary is hierarchically organized: nonprimitive terms are described from primitive terms. Together with graph transforming operations, this freedom of expression seeks representational completeness without sacrificing too much computational power. In fact, as will be presented in the following section, the representational capabilities of the conceptual graph formalism is considerable; it allows great expressiveness.

THE CONCEPTUAL GRAPH FORMALISM

The conceptual graph formalism is much too vast for a full introduction in this article. We will restrict ourselves to conceptual graphs which are mappable to first-order predicate logic, called *first-order conceptual graphs*.* In effect, the theory provides an operator φ, which applied to u, a first-order conceptual graph, produces φu, a well-formed formula in first-order predicate calculus. For example, the graph of Figure 3 was mapped to a well-formed formula through the application of the φ operator, producing φu as shown in Figure 4.

The following subsection deals with representational issues related to concepts and to relations and functions. The subsection The Vocabulary introduces the term definition mechanisms and the transformational operators expand and contract which allow a graph to be transformed according to different levels of representational granularity. The subsection The Canonical Formation Operators presents the canonical formation operators which are used to build new graphs (for instance, to make inferences) from existing graphs. The next subsection presents the canon of the system which is at the heart of every conceptual graph system because it controls the acquisition of assertional knowledge into the system. Finally, the subsection The Acquisition of Assertional Knowledge illustrates how assertional knowledge is acquired; whereas the last subsection briefly introduces some of the more advanced features of the notation.

$$\forall x \, (\, \text{RED-BALL}(x) <=> (\, \text{BALL}(x) \wedge \text{RED}(x) \,) \,)$$

FIGURE 21   The class of red balls.

---

*For a more thorough and formal introduction, the reader is referred to Ref. 6.

Basic Representational Notions

A conceptual graph is a connected, directed bipartite graph. The two types of nodes that can be connected to one another are concepts, either generic or individual, and relations (or functions which were defined as a special type of relations (31)). Concepts are represented by labeled boxes; relations are represented by labeled circles. The following two subsections introduce concepts, relations, and functions, as they are the main components of first-order conceptual graphs.

Concepts

Concepts are represented as labeled boxes. A label has two fields: a concept type and a referent. The referent field may identify an individual, either known (a constant) or unknown (a variable or the * symbol). Unknown individuals are called *generic concepts*. Generic concepts can be either existentially or universally quantified. By default, generic concepts are existentially quantified. For example, the generic concept [CAT:*], with type field CAT and referent field *, also represented as [CAT], means: there exists a cat (some cat) which is not identified for now (but could be after instantiation). So it represents an unknown individual of type CAT. This concept would translate to $\exists x\ CAT(x)$ in first-order predicate logic.

Universally quantified generic concepts are represented as a concept type followed by the ∀ sign. With our previous example it would be [CAT:∀], which means: all cats (any cat). It would translate to $\forall x\ CAT(x)$ in first-order predicate logic.

Individual concepts are instantiated to some constant value and represent individuals. In that case, the referent field of the concept is the identifier of the individual. For instance, Morris the cat would be represented as [CAT: Morris], if Morris is a unique identifier in our system. If not, it would be represented by [CAT: #8339], where the referent field is a unique identifier automatically generated when the individual Morris was created (see the subsection below for the definition of individuals). The referent field can then be seen as a pointer to the individual.

Relations and Functions

Relations are represented as labeled circles. The label stands for the type of semantical link that it represents. These labels (terms) are defined using some term definition construct (see the subsection The Term Definition Operators). Relations connect concepts together. The number and the order of the parameters of each relation are totally arbitrary; they are defined by the knowledge engineer. The example of Figure 5, for instance, shows two relations, agnt and loc, which both have two parameters; they are called binary relations. In each case, the first parameter of the relation is the verb; the other is the concept which is either the agent or the location of the verb. Higher arity relations may exist. The graph of Figure 22 shows a binary relation agnt; the graph of Figure 23 shows the ternary relation between, defined among three physical entities.

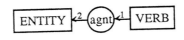

FIGURE 22   An example of a binary relation.

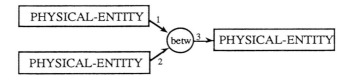

FIGURE 23   An example of a ternary relation.

With *n*-ary relations (where $n \geq 1$), the *n*-1 first parameters are linked to the relation by incoming arcs, with the arrow pointing toward the relation. The last parameter is linked to the relation by an outgoing arc, with the arrow pointing away from the relation. With relations of arity lower than 3, arcs need not be numbered because the direction of the arrows is different. With relations of arity higher than 2, these numbers help the translation of the relation into first-order predicate logic. For instance, the graph of Figure 22 would translate to $\exists x \exists y$ (VERB(x) $\wedge$ ENTITY(y) $\wedge$ agnt(x,y)). The order of the parameters of the predicate agnt is given by the numbers on the arrows. This gives a complete mapping of every relation onto first-order predicates. The graph of Figure 23 would translate to $\exists x \exists y \exists z$ (PHYSICAL-ENTITY(x) $\wedge$ PHYSICAL-ENTITY(y) $\wedge$ PHYSICAL-ENTITY(z) $\wedge$ between (x,y,z)).

Functions are a special type of relation where the last parameter is functionally dependent upon its *n*-1 first parameters. They were orginally missing from the conceptual graph theory. Mineau (31) introduces them. They are graphically represented like relations, except that the outgoing arc is a double-lined arrow, meaning that the last parameter is functionally dependent on the *n*-1 first. The graph of Figure 24 shows the function that exists between a person and his/her age, which is functionally dependent on the former. Functional dependency states that if x_1 (x_2) is connected to y_1 (y_2) through a function f, if y_1 is functionally dependent on x_1, and if $x_1 = x_2$, then $y_1 = y_2$.

The Vocabulary

This section explains how the vocabulary can be constructed; that is, how concept type, relation type, and function type labels can be defined. It then presents the expand and contract operators which are useful in order to allow multiple representations of the same logical content of a graph.

The Term Definition Operators

There are four types of term. A term is either a concept, a relation, a function, or an individual. It must be defined before being used in any other graph. It is defined

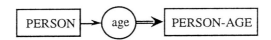

FIGURE 24   An example of a function.

type CAT(x) **is**

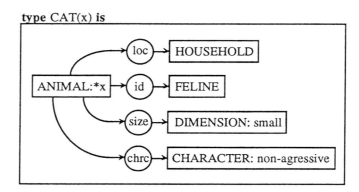

FIGURE 25   The definition of the type CAT.

using a conceptual graph. The components of this *definition graph* must be known before the term is defined. The set of all terms form the vocabulary of the application domain.

There are four different term definition mechanisms, one for each of the four types of terms. They each start with a keyword, either **type, relation, function,** or **individual,** then the label of the term appears, followed by an ordered set of parameters (variables) and the definition graph of the term. The parameters each identify a concept in the definition graph. For example, the concept definition mechanism looks like this: **type** CONCEPT(x) **is** u, where u is the definition graph of the term CONCEPT (which is also called a type or a class, depending on terminology). The graph u contains at least one concept identified with x. This concept is called the genus of the definition of CONCEPT; the rest of the graph is called the differentia. The genus of CONCEPT is the parent of CONCEPT in a type hierarchy, as all terms are hierarchically structured according to this subsumption relation (as explained in the subsection Relations and Functions.)

The relation definition mechanism looks like this: **relation** relation(x_1, x_2, . . . , x_n) **is** u, where $n \geq 1$, u is the definition graph of this relation, and u contains at least n different concepts associated with the n-1 first variables of the parameter list (the input arguments) and with the last variable which identifies the output concept of the relation.

The function definition mechanism looks like this: **function** function(x_1, x_2, . . . , x_n) **is** u, where $n \geq 1$, u is the definition graph of this function and u contains

relation on(x,y) **is**

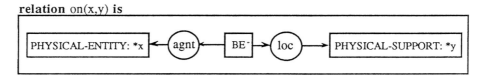

FIGURE 26   The definition of the relation on.

function color(x,y) **is**

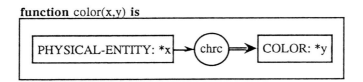

FIGURE 27   The definition of the function color.

at least *n* different concepts associated with the *n*-1 first variables of the parameter list (the input arguments of the relation) and with the last variable which identifies the output concept of the relations, and where this last concept is functionally dependent on the *n*-1 first.

The individual definition mechanism looks like this: **individual** CON-CEPT(referent) **is** *u*, where CONCEPT is a known type, referent is a unique identifier in our system (could be automatically generated from a set of numerical identifiers), and *u* is the definition graph for that individual, called referent. The graph *u* is derived from the definition graph of the type CONCEPT. Figures 25–28 show simple definitions of the concept CAT, of the relation on, of the function color, and of the individual Morris.

The Expand and Contract Operators

Terms can be expanded to their definition. The *type expansion* operation is illustrated in the next two figures. Figure 29 shows the graph of Figure 28 where the CAT concept was expanded to its full definition. Relations and functions can also be expanded. Figure 30 shows the graph of Figure 29 where the relation on and the function color were expanded to their definition.

It is also possible from a type definition encountered in a graph to replace it with its corresponding label. This is called *type contraction*. For example, type contraction on the definition of the function color, the relation on, and the concept CAT would regenerate the graph of Figure 28. Type expansion and contraction imply that types are defined in terms of both necessary and sufficient conditions. Consequently, the terms used in a conceptual graph-based system must be precise.

individual CAT(Morris) **is**

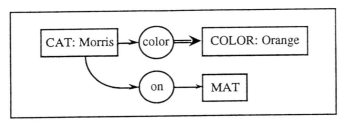

FIGURE 28   The definition of the individual Morris.

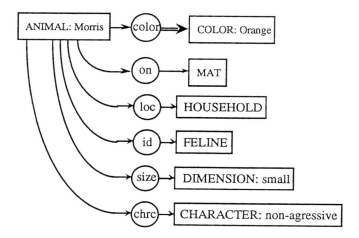

FIGURE 29   The type expansion for the CAT concept in the graph of Figure 28.

No partial definition can be acquired. In regard of certain application domains, this restricts the applicability of the formalism but forces a semantical clarification of these domains, when possible.

Because types are defined in terms of other types, they all take part in a partial order of subsumption. For example, from the definitions given above, CAT is a subclass of ANIMAL, written CAT < ANIMAL. There exist three subsumption hierarchies, one for concepts, one for relations, and another for functions.

These hierarchies are, in fact, lattices. They are topped with the universal concept ⊤, which subsumes every other type; the bottom is the absurd type ⊥, which is subsumed by every other type. The first level of the concept lattice is filled

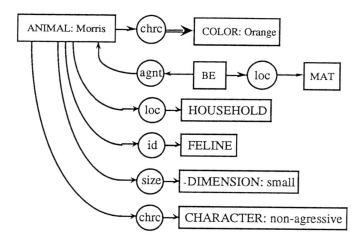

FIGURE 30   The type expansion for the relation on and the function color of Figure 29.

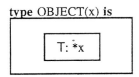

type OBJECT(x) is

T: *x

FIGURE 31   The definition of a primitive concept type OBJECT.

with primitive concept types; that is, types which are not defined in terms of any other type. For example, Figure 31 shows how to define a primitive concept type OBJECT.

Sowa (6) does not formally define the type lattice for relations. Basically, its first level should contain link relations of diverse arity. For instance, in a system where only binary and ternary relations are used, the first level of the type lattice would look like the one shown in Figure 32. Of course, the T and ⊥ types in the type lattice for relations are used only for definitional purposes because relations of different arity cannot be generalized to a common supertype. In fact, there should be as many type lattices for relations as there are relations of different arity, with the proper link relation of the corresponding arity on top of it, and with the absurd relation at the bottom of it (see Fig. 33).

Although Mineau (31) introduces functions in the conceptual graph theory, no type lattice for functions was defined. Intuitively, it should be similar to the type lattice for relations, except that the outgoing arcs of functions are represented as double-lined arrows.

A lattice is defined as a hierarchical organization of some set of elements, where two elements taken randomly have exactly one parent and one child in this hierarchy. This implies that two types will have exactly one supertype and subtype. This unicity property facilitates processing when inferences are being done and when new graphs are created. So, lattices are useful from a computational point of view.

According to these type lattices, every nonprimitive type in a graph can be expanded until every type is primitive. The resulting graph will carry the same logical content as the original graph. The only difference is representational. Do we prefer to encode some semantics using primitive or nonprimitive terms? Nonprimitive terms carry a more specialized meaning; they represent *abstractions* of some

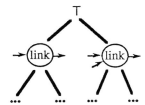

FIGURE 32   The top of the type lattice for relations.

FIGURE 33   The absurd relation of arity 2.

concepts which require whole graphs for their definition. Often abstractions describe the application domain more closely than primitive terms; they carry more
semantics.

These transformational capabilities allow the acquisition of graphs according
to a set of terms which may be different than the one used for processing the graphs.
The modelization of the domain can be done independently of the representational
requirements of the processing tasks: for example, the case grammar-based relations
(27) often encountered in conceptual graph literature (6) allow easy mapping to
natural language. This may be useful to the user who interacts with a conceptual
graph-based knowledge system but may have nothing to do with the inference of
new graphs. Other representational particularities may be required by the inference
engine. Allowing different representations of the same content does not confine the
knowledge engineer or the user to a particular interaction language which may be
far from their reality.

The Canonical Formation Operators

New graphs can be created from existing ones using four formation operators.
These operators are said to be *canonical* because every graph will be derived from
the canon, which is defined in the next subsection.

The first operator is copy, which makes an exact copy of a graph u, producing
another graph v. Naturally, the truth value of v is identical to that of u; the models
which make u true also make v true.

The second operator is restrict, which restricts the set of possible values (individuals) associated to a concept by specializing it. Specialization can occur either
because the type label of the concept is replaced by a subtype or because the generic
referent is replaced by a particular individual. For example, replacing the * symbol
by Morris in the concept [CAT:*], produces [CAT:Morris] only if Morris is an
individual of type CAT (also written CAT::Morris, as explained in the next subsection). If so, it specializes this concept. Replacing the ANIMAL concept type by
CAT in the generic concept [ANIMAL:*], producing [CAT:*], is also a restriction
over this concept. Finally, replacing the ANIMAL concept type by CAT in the
individual concept [ANIMAL:Morris] produces [CAT:Morris] only if Morris is an
individual of type CAT.

The third operator is the join operation (6), which was later redefined as being

FIGURE 34   The first graph to join.

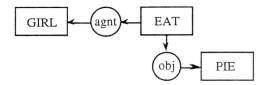

FIGURE 35   The second graph to join.

either external or internal (32). In brief, the external join operation produces a new graph *w* from two graphs *u* and *v*. Identical concepts in *u* and *v* are linked resulting in one single graph *w*. For example, the graph of Figure 6 shows the resulting graph from joining the graphs of Figures 3 and 5 over the CAT concept. In that example, the [CAT:∀] concept was specialized to [CAT] in order to allow the two CAT concepts to become identical. This is possible because if something is true for all cats, then it is also true for some cat ((∀x CAT(x)) ⇒ (∃x CAT(x))). Joins are possible only on identical concepts. Another classic example is illustrated in Figures 34–36.

In this example, the join is done on two concepts: [GIRL:Sue] AND [EAT]. So the [PERSON:Sue] concept of Figure 34 and the [GIRL] concept of Figure 35 were both restricted to [GIRL:Sue], which is possible because GIRL::Sue is true (see the next subsection). Then the two graphs are joined to produce the graph of Figure 36. It is obvious to see that this resulting graph may not be true because nothing proves that the girl who eats a pie is Sue. The restrict and join operations are falsity preserving.

The internal join operator is applied to a graph where two different concepts are to be merged. Figures 37 and 38 show such an operation on the [PIE] and [DESSERT] concepts. Because PIE < DESSERT, the latter will be restricted to PIE. Once again, the graph of Figure 38 is more specialized than the one in Figure 37. In the latter, the desert may be something different than the pie, stating that a girl may also eat something else than the pie, which is nonetheless a dessert. In the former, a girl eats only a pie.

In Ref. 6, the join operation is ill-defined. That is what prompted Chein and Mugnier (32) to redefine it more clearly, also giving related complexity results. Mineau (31) recently provided for a unique definitional framework for both external and internal join operations.

Further, there is the simplify operation, which deletes identical relations (or

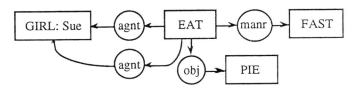

FIGURE 36   The resulting graph, produced from the graphs of Figures 34 and 35.

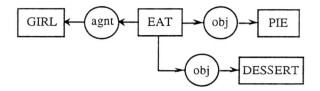

FIGURE 37   A graph where there are two concepts to merge.

functions) between the same concepts. For instance, in Figure 36 there are two relations agnt connected to the exact same pair of concepts, in the same order. Both relations really carry the same logical content. One of the two relations is redundant and could be deleted, producing the graph of Figure 39.

The Canon

The canon represents the grammar of a conceptual graph-based system. It includes the vocabulary structured as type lattices. The three type lattices presented in the subsection The Vocabulary are part of the canon, so is the set of all individuals. There is also a conformity relation :: which relates individuals to types. For instance, CAT::Morris would be true because Morris is an individual of type CAT, so would be ANIMAL::Morris because cats are animals. But MAT::Morris would be false because Morris is in no way an individual of type MAT. The generic referent is of any type, that is, t::* is true for any t, a type label.

Finally, there is a set of basic graphs, called *canonical basis*, which encode some semantical constraints over the application domain. Any other graph in the system must be derived from the canon using the canonical formation operators presented earlier. Consequently, these graphs all obey the semantical constraints of the canonical basis. For example, if only animals can sleep, then the graph of Figure 40 would be introduced into the canonical basis. It represents a *canonical schema* for the relation agnt. Because all graphs are derived from the canonical basis, nothing but animals could be put in relation agnt with the verb SLEEP, if there is only one canonical schema for the relation agnt in the canonical basis.

Different semantical constraints have different ways of being encoded. Multiple semantical constraints may lead to different canonical schemas for the same relation. Sowa (6) only provided for simple overgeneralizations to be avoided. We intend to develop these ideas further. The representation of semantical constraints in conceptual graph theory will be the subject of a forthcoming article.

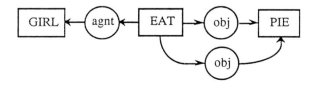

FIGURE 38   After the two concepts were merged.

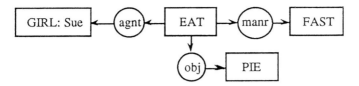

FIGURE 39   After the two concepts were merged.

The Acquisition of Assertional Knowledge

Assertional knowledge is defined as a set of graphs which are canonically derivable from the canon and which are asserted. All of these graphs, called *assertional graphs*, are stored in the knowledge base. Canonical derivation ensures that these graphs obey the semantics of the structural knowledge of the application domain. So, the acquisition of assertional graphs is done through a controlled environment. For instance, the graph of Figure 41, which states that *Morris the cat sleeps on a mat*, is canonically derivable from the canon of the system and is, thus, valid according to the semantics of the application domain. So it can be asserted by adding it to the knowledge base.

For this graph (Fig. 41), the canonical derivation would start with the joining of the canonical schemas associated with the relations agnt and loc, shown in Figures 40 and 42 respectively, after the ⊤ concept of Figure 42 would be restricted to SLEEP. Then the ANIMAL concept would be restricted to CAT:Morris, whereas the PHYSICAL-ENTITY concept would be restricted to MAT. Of course, each term used, either a concept, a relation, a function, or an individual, must be known before the graph is acquired. Furthermore, the restrict operator shows the importance of having all concepts, relations, and functions taking part in the corresponding subsumption hierarchy, as presented in the subsection The Vocabulary.

Because all assertional graphs are canonically derivable from the canon, they themselves take part in a partial order of subsumption, called *generalization hierarchy*. In effect, because it starts from the same building blocks, a partial derivation of a graph will lead to one of its generalizations. For instance, the graph of Figure 43 is a generalization of the graph of Figure 41.

All graphs take part in this generalization hierarchy which represents a partial order of subsumption between graphs. If u is a generalization of v, then it is said that there is a projection πu in v. The π operator projects u onto v. In that case, u is either a subgraph of v, or u' is a subgraph of v, where u' is u with one or more concepts having been restricted. In both cases, u is said to be a generalization of v, written $v < u$. Intuitively, the join operation is performed on graphs which share a common projection. More precisely, the join operation is formally defined on

FIGURE 40   A canonical schema for the relation agnt.

FIGURE 41   *Morris the cat sleeps on a mat.*

compatible projections (6). The reader is referred to Refs. 6 and 31 for formal definitions of compatible projections.

Advanced Features

The original work of Sowa as presented in his book (6) gave a very good and formal introduction to the basics of conceptual graphs, particularly to first-order conceptual graphs. However, his book also included some sketchy ideas which led the international research community on interesting research paths. Some of these ideas are briefly presented below.

Sets

The referent field of a concept could be a set of individuals instead of being a single individual. For example, if Morris and Sylvester are doing the action of sitting on the same mat together, then the graph of Figure 44 can be rewritten as the graph of Figure 45. Figure 45 states that the action of sitting is being done by a *group* of individuals as a whole; Figure 46 states that two cats are sitting on the same mat, individually. *Collective sets* represent sets of individuals who must be connected to some other concept as a whole. There exist a set join operator which would allow the transformation of the graph of Figure 44 into the one of Figure 45.

When individuals of a set are not known, then the generic set {*} is used. By default, this set is collective. Figure 47 shows an example of a generic set. It states that a cat sits on more than one mat. Generic collective sets are used to represent plurals. When the cardinality of the set is known, it can be added to the referent field using the @ symbol followed by an integer. For instance, the graph of Figure 48 states that there is a cat which sits on two mats.*

Also, the graph of Figure 49 could have been produced from the graph of Figure 44. It represents a generalization of the graph of Figure 44. It states that Morris or Sylvester (or both) sit on a mat. The set is said to be *distributive*. When

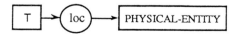

FIGURE 42   The canonical schema for the relation loc.

---

*Numerical quantification could be represented using the qty relation which links a set to an integer which represents its cardinality. This extended referent notation which includes the @ symbol is a measurement contraction, as will be discussed in the subsection Name and Measure Contractions.

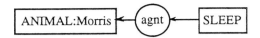

FIGURE 43   *An animal, Morris, sleeps.*

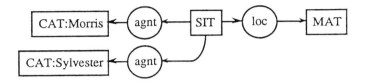

FIGURE 44   A verb with two agents.

FIGURE 45   A collective set as an agent.

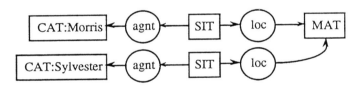

FIGURE 46   The cats as individual agents.

FIGURE 47   Plurals as collective sets.

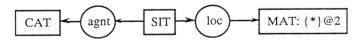

FIGURE 48   Numerically quantified collective sets.

FIGURE 49   A distributive set.

the individuals of a distributive set are not explicitly identified, then the keyword Dist precedes the set. For example, the graph of Figure 50 states that two cats individually sit on a mat.

Finally, there are also *respective sets* which establish correspondence between its elements and the elements of some other set. They are useful for representing propositions like *Bob and Peter are married to Pat and Nancy, respectively*. Respective sets are preceded by the keyword Resp.

Of course, much work still needs to be done in order to integrate the full power of set theory into the conceptual graph formalism. For instance, the impact of numerical quantification over inferential capabilities should be fully assessed. Current research on sets in conceptual graphs cover the extension of the referent field in order to include all sorts of numerical quantifiers, to bound the cardinality of sets using a range, to add explicit pointers to subsets of individuals (as with the memb relation used in Ref. 6), and so on. The reader should refer to Refs. 33–35 for a more complete treatment of sets and extended referents.

Disjunctions

Conceptual graphs are *conjunctive* graphs; that is, they represent some conjunction of predicates. Graphically, the links coming in and out of a single concept are to be interpreted as restricting conditions over this concept. For instance, Figure 25 shows the type definition of the CAT concept. It asserts that cats are identified as felines, *and* that they are of a particular size, *and* that they are characterized by a nonagressive attitude, *and* that they all are located in households.

Consequently, disjunctions are not easily expressed. Internal disjunctions, which are disjunctions of values associated to a single concept, are represented using a disjunctive set referent (as presented in the previous section). External disjunctions, which include at least a relation (or a function), cannot be represented unless disjoint graphs are used, one for each disjunct. For instance, Figure 51 encodes the disjunction: a cat eats a mouse or drinks milk, as two distinct graphs, because no first-order conceptual graph could represent external disjunctions. This introduces a bias: two different cats could exist.

Name and Measure Contractions

In order to provide representational shortcuts for useful syntactical constructs, name and measure contractions were defined. Instead of having some information

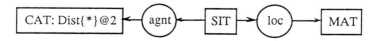

FIGURE 50   A distributive set of unknown individuals.

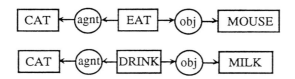

FIGURE 51   An external disjunction as two graphs.

characterizing a concept in the usual way, that is, using relations linked to it, the referent field is somewhat extended to include that information. For example, the proposition: *the person Judy*, represented using the graph of Figure 52, could be abbreviated to [PERSON: Judy #3074]; whereas the proposition *a person, Judy*, represented in Figure 53, could be abbreviated to [PERSON:Judy]* Name contraction results in a referent field where the name of the concept precedes the rest of the referent field.

In addition, measurements could be associated to measurable concepts by extending their referent field. For instance, the graphs of Figure 54 show a name contraction followed by a measurement contraction. The graphs of Figure 55 shows a measurement contraction for a particular reading (#55361) of the current temperature. Measurement contraction results in a referent field where the measurement of the concept ends the referent field. A first example of a measurement contraction was given in the subsection Sets when sets are numerically quantified, instead of explicitly using the qty relation.

Contexts and Coreferents

Contexts represent a set of propositions supposed to be true all together. They are graphically represented as large boxes which contain the conceptual graphs representing the propositions. The truth value of these graphs is asserted only for the context in which they appear. They represent conjunctions of graphs. Consequently, contexts are used to represent situations, states, and worlds. With contexts, tenses and modalities can be represented (36–38). For example, the context of Figure 56 shows the propositions *a man loves a woman* and *a man has a mother*.

Contexts can appear within other contexts. It may be the case that concepts in different contexts represent the same individual, either generic or instantiated. Then coreferent links represented as dashed lines, identify identical concepts. Figure 57 shows an example of this.

FIGURE 52   *The person Judy.*

---

*Please note that names may or may not be unique; that is, two individuals may have the same name; an individual may have more than one name.

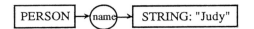

FIGURE 53 A *person, (named) Judy.*

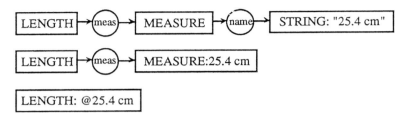

FIGURE 54 Name and measurement contractions.

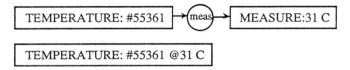

FIGURE 55 Measurement contraction for an individual of type TEMPERATURE.

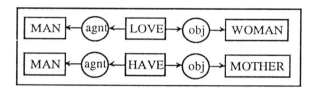

FIGURE 56 A context containing two graphs.

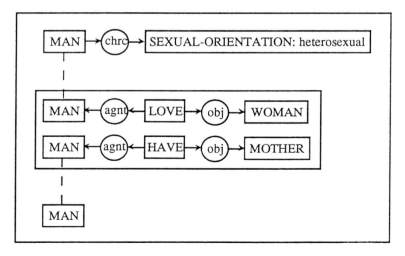

FIGURE 57 A context within a context, embedded contexts.

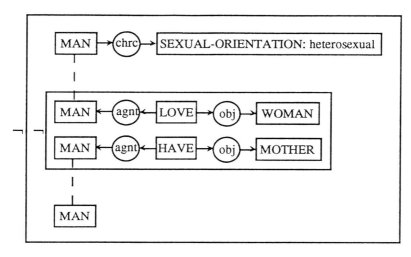

FIGURE 58   Negated contexts and logical implications.

Used in conjunction with negations, logical implications can be represented. For instance, adding the ≥ symbol (the negation symbol) in front of both contexts produces the context of Figure 58, where the interpretation of the outer context now becomes *there is no heterosexual man which does not love a woman*, that is, *every heterosexual man loves a woman*, and *there is no man which does not have a mother*, that is, *every man has a mother*. With the ≥ symbol and the context mechanism, any well-formed formula in first-order predicate logic can be represented.

Actors

Actors are like functions: The output concept is functionally dependent on the input concepts. Furthermore, they are procedural attachments which are triggered when the input concepts are instantiated to some value. Then the output concept is instantiated to the value computed by the actor. They are represented by diamond-shaped boxes to which input concepts are linked by incoming arcs (numbered if more than one) and to which the output concept is linked by an outgoing arc. For instance, Figure 59 shows an actor which computes the age of a person. Unlike Figure 24, this graph states that the actor (procedure) age will compute the age of a person when the input concept PERSON is instantiated. For instance, if we restrict this concept to PERSON:Sue, then the actor will compute the age of Sue and will output this value to the PERSON-AGE concept, restricting it. Basically, the graph of Figure 59 states that such a procedure exists without stating any algorithm. In Figure 24, the age of a person is said to be functionally dependent on that person

FIGURE 59   An actor.

prototype for CAT(x) **is**

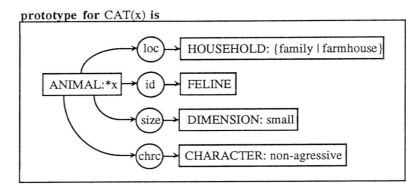

FIGURE 60   A prototype, the definition of a typical individual, for the concept type CAT.

but will not be computed from the input concept PERSON. Unlike here, it would have to be explicitly acquired.

Prototypes and Schemata

Type definitions are graphs built from generic and individual concepts. Often, we can anticipate default values for these generic concepts. If these values exhaustively represent the set of values to which the associated concepts can be instantiated, they must appear in the type definition per se. If they are used only to indicate default values or to loosely validate the acquisition of individuals of that type, then they cannot be part of the type definition. They will take part in the definition of a *typical* individual of that type, called a *prototype.*

Figure 60 shows a prototype for the CAT concept. In that example, we can see that the definition of the prototype is based on the type definition for CAT and that the concept HOUSEHOLD was given a disjunctive set referent which represents typical values (default values) for that concept.

A *schema* for a concept type represents an informal definition of it. In natural language, we would introduce such a definition using the adverb *normally.* For example, normally, cats eat mice (see Fig. 61). Schemas are not necessarily true; they cannot be part of the type definition. So the conceptual graph formalism allows for *plausible* definitions to be acquired. All schemas related to a single concept type

schema for CAT(x) **is**

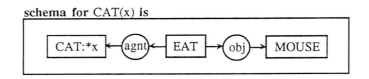

FIGURE 61   A schema for the concept type CAT.

are called *schematic clusters*. Sometimes, prototypes may be inferred from schematic clusters.

CONCLUSION

This article introduced the conceptual graph formalism, which is a semantic network-based knowledge representation language. It first presented some of the main issues which were and still are relevant to semantic network research. It showed how the conceptual graph theory dealt with these issues. Then the main features of the formalism were introduced rather informally. A more thorough and formal introduction to the formalism is given in Ref. 6.

It should be clear to the reader that great efforts were deployed in order to provide a representational language which was very expressive, whose semantics was clear and formally defined, which was sound and complete, which was logically realistic, which was mostly mappable to first-order predicate logic, which provided for representational transformation capabilities, which allowed a close mapping to natural language, which would minimize representational subjectivity as much as possible, which would ease knowledge modelization and acquisition, which provided a controlled environment for knowledge acquisition, which would force the knowledge engineer to be more thorough in his modelization activities, and which could become a standard for first-order-based knowledge representation languages.

For all these reasons, the conceptual graph theory is flourishing. It attracted hundreds of researchers from all over the world, from both industrial and academic backgrounds. Research on conceptual graphs was presented at annual workshops which were mostly held at international events like the National Conference on Artificial Intelligence, sponsored by the American Association for Artificial Intelligence (AAAI), or the International Joint Conference on Artificial Intelligence (IJ-CAI), until they were replaced by international conferences as the interest in conceptual graphs grew stronger. In effect, the theory is now at the center of diverse research efforts in various domains such as knowledge representation, medical data modeling, case-based reasoning, natural language processing, enterprise modeling, knowledge sharing, database modeling, and so on. The diversity of application domains is considerable.

Real-life applications will soon require that large-scale conceptual graph-based shells be available. Current research in that direction are being undertaken (39). The widespread use of the theory is partially linked to the availability of these tools. Along with the refinement of some of the ideas found in the original book of Sowa (6), the theory will mature. We expect its scope to go well beyond first-order logic. It should soon include some of the extensions mentioned in the subsection Prototypes and Schemata. It is also expected that some higher-order features will be added shortly, notably to represent first-order conceptual graphs in terms of higher-order conceptual graphs.

Time has led many researchers on the path of conceptual graphs. Their contribution was highly beneficial to the development of the theory. Basically, the hard core work presented by John Sowa was promising enough to generate interest, and substantial enough so that this interest has not yet fainted and is not about to. The conceptual graph theory has become one of the leading research initiatives in semantic network research today. Its future lies on our individual research agendas, as it will keep us researchers busy for many years to come.

REFERENCES

1. J. F. Sowa, "Current Issues in Semantic Networks," in *Principles of Semantic Networks: Explorations in the Representation of Knowledge*, J. F. Sowa (ed.), Morgan Kaufmann, San Mateo, CA, 1991, pp. 13–44.
2. J. R. Anderson, *The Architecture of Cognition*, Harvard University Press, Cambridge, MA, 1983.
3. E. Davalo and P. Naïm, *Des Réseaux de Neurones*, Eyrolles, Paris, 1989.
4. J. L. J. Martinez and R. P. Kesner, 1991, (eds.), *Learning and Memory, A Biological View*, Academic Press, San Diego, 1991.
5. C. R. Puff, *Memory Organization and Structure*, Academic Press, San Diego, CA, 1979.
6. J. F. Sowa, *Conceptual Structures: Information Processing in Mind and Machine*, Addison-Wesley, Reading, MA, 1984.
7. J. F. Sowa, *Principles of Semantic Networks: Explorations in the Representation of Knowledge*, Morgan Kaufmann, San Mateo, CA, 1991.
8. J. F. Sowa, "Relating Diagrams to Logic," in *Conceptual Graphs for Knowledge Representation*, G. W. Mineau, B. Moulin, and J. F. Sowa (eds.), Springer-Verlag, Berlin, 1993, pp. 1–35.
9. L. Shastri, "Why Semantic Networks?" in *Principles of Semantic Networks: Explorations in the Representation of Knowledge*, J. F. Sowa (ed.), Morgan Kaufmann, San Mateo, CA, 1991, pp. 109–136.
10. J. R. Anderson, "Spread of Activation," in *The Architecture of Cognition*, J. R. Anderson (ed.), Harvard University Press, Cambridge, MA, 1983, pp. 86–125.
11. W. A. Woods, "Understanding Subsumption and Taxonomy: A Framework for Progress," in *Principles of Semantic Networks: Explorations in the Representation of Knowledge*, J. F. Sowa (ed.), Morgan Kaufmann, San Mateo, CA, 1991, pp. 45–94.
12. J. J. McGregor, "Backtrack Search Algorithms and the Maximal Common Subgraph Problem," *Software Pract. Exp., 12*, 23–34 (1982).
13. R. Levinson, "A Self-Organizing Retrieval System for Graphs," in *Proceedings of the AAAI-84*, 1984, pp. 203–206.
14. R. Levinson, "Pattern Associativity and the Retrieval of Semantic Networks," *Computers Math. Appl., 23*, 573–600 (1992).
15. G. Ellis, "Compiled Hierarchical Retrieval," in *Conceptual Structures, Current Research and Practice*, T. E. Nagle, J. A. Nagle, L. L. Gerholz, and P. W. Eklund (eds.), Ellis Horwood, 1992, pp. 271–294.
16. G. W. Mineau, "Induction on Conceptual Graphs: Finding Common Generalizations and Compatible Projections," in *Conceptual Structures: Current Research and Practice*, T. Nagle, J. Nagle, L. Gerholz, and P. Eklund (eds.), Ellis Horwood, 1992, pp. 295–310.
17. G. Mineau, R. Godin, and J. Gecsei, "La Classification Symbolique: Une Approche Non-Subjective," in *Proceedings of the 5ièmes Journées Françaises de l'Apprentissage*, 1990.
18. G. W. Mineau, "Facilitating the Creation of a Multiple Index on Graph-Described Documents by Transforming Their Descriptions," in *Proceedings of the 2nd Int. Conf. on Information and Knowledge Management (CIKM-93)*, B. Bhargava, T. Finin, and Y. Yesha (eds.), 1993, pp. 132–138.

19. G. W. Mineau, "The Term Definitional Mechanisms of the Conceptual Graph Notation and Ontolingua: A Comparison," in *Conceptual Graphs for Knowledge Representation*, G. W. Mineau, B. Moulin, and J. F. Sowa (eds.), Springer-Verlag, Berlin, 1993, pp. 90–105.

20. W. A. Woods and J. G. Schmolze, "The KL-ONE Family," *Computers Math. Appl., 23*, 133–178 (1992).

21. R. McGregor, "The Evolving Technology of Classification-based Knowledge Representation Systems," in *Principles of Semantic Networks: Explorations in the Representation of Knowledge*, J. F. Sowa (ed.), Morgan Kaufmann, San Mateo, CA, 1991, pp. 385–400.

22. R. Levinson and G. Ellis, "Multi-Level Hierarchical Retrieval," in *Proceedings of the 6th Ann. Workshop on Conceptual Graphs*, E. Way (ed.), SUNY at Binghamton, NY, 1991, pp. 67–82.

23. W. A. Woods, "What's in a Link: Foundations for Semantic Networks," in *Representation and Understanding: Studies in Cognitive Science*, D. Bobrow and A. Collins (eds.), Academic Press, New York, 1975.

24. R. J. Brachmann, "On the Epistemological Status of Semantic Networks," in *Readings in Knowledge Representation*, Morgan Kaufmann Publishers, San Mateo, CA, 1985, pp. 191–216.

25. R. C. Schank, *Conceptual Information Processing*, North-Holland, Amsterdam, 1975.

26. R. C. Schank, "Language and Memory," in *Perspectives on Cognitive Science*, D. A. Norman (ed.), Lawrence Erlbaum, Hillsdale, NJ, 1981, pp. 105–146.

27. R. Dirven and G. Radden (eds.). *Fillmore's Case Grammar: A Reader*, J. Groos, Heidelberg, 1987.

28. J. F. Sowa, "Representing Attributes, Roles, and Nondetachable Parts," in *Proceedings of the 1st International Workshop on Formal Ontology in Conceptual Analysis and Knowledge Representation*, N. Guarino and R. Poli (eds.), 1993.

29. R. S. Michalski and R. E. Stepp, "Learning from Observation: Conceptual Clustering," in *Machine Learning: An Artificial Intelligence Approach*, R. S. Michalski, J. G. Carbonell, and T. M. Mitchell (eds.), Morgan Kaufmann, San Mateo, CA, 1983, pp. 331–364.

30. R. E. Stepp and R. S. Michalski, "Conceptual Clustering: Inventing Goal-Oriented Classifications of Structured Objects," in *Machine Learning: An Artificial Intelligence Approach*, R. Michalski, J. Carbonell, and T. Mitchell (eds.), Morgan Kaufmann, Los Altos, CA, 1986, pp. 471–498.

31. G. W. Mineau, "View, Mappings and Functions: Essential Definitions to the Conceptual Graph Theory," in *Proceedings of the 2nd Int. Conf. on Conceptual Structures*, J. Dick (ed.),

32. M. Chein and M. L. Mugnier, "Specialization: Where Do the Difficulties occur?" in *Proceedings of the 7th Ann. Workshop on Conceptual Graphs*, H. Pfeiffer (ed.), New Mexico State University, Las Cruces, NM, 1992, pp. 19–28.

33. D. A. Gardiner, B. S. Tjan, and J. R. Slagle, "Extending Conceptual Structures: Representation Issues and Reasoning Operations," in *Conceptual Structures, Current Research and Practice*, T. E. Nagle, J. A. Nagle, L. L. Gerholz, and P. W. Eklund (eds.), Ellis Horwood, 1992, pp. 67–86.

34. H. D. Pfeiffer and R. T. Hartley, "Additions for SET Representation and Processing to Conceptual Programming," in *Proceedings of the 5th Ann. Workshop on Conceptual Structures*, L. L. Gerholz and P. W. Eklund (eds.), 1990.

35. B. S. Tjan, D. A. Gardiner, and J. R. Slagle, "Representing and Reasoning with Set Referents and Numerical Quantifiers, in *Conceptual Structures, Current research and practice*, T. E. Nagle, J. A. Nagle, L. L. Gerholz, and P. W. Eklund (eds.), Ellis Horwood, 1992, pp. 53–66.

36. B. Moulin, "Modelling Temporal Knowledge in Discourse: A Refined Approach," in

Proceedings of the 7th Ann. Workshop on Conceptual Graphs, H. Pfeiffer (ed.), New Mexico State University, Las Cruces, NM, 1992, pp. 89–98.

37.   B. Moulin and G. W. Mineau, "Factoring Knowledge into Worlds," in *Proceedings of the 7th Ann. Workshop on Conceptual Graphs*, H. Pfeiffer (ed.), New Mexico State University, Las Cruces, NM, 1992, pp. 119–128.

38.   H. van den Berg, "Modal Logics for Conceptual Graphs," in *Conceptual Graphs for Knowledge Representation*, G. W. Mineau, B. Moulin, and J. F. Sowa (eds.), Springer-Verlag, Berlin, 1993, pp. 411–429.

39.   G. Ellis and R. Levinson, "1st. Int. Workshop on PEIRCE: A Conceptual Graphs Workbench," in *Proceedings of the 7th Ann. Workshop on Conceptual Graphs*, H. Pfeiffer (ed.), New Mexico State University, Las Cruces, NM, 1992.

GUY W. MINEAU

A COOPERATIVE COMPUTER

INTRODUCTION

A cooperative computer is a computer which works toward a common goal with a human partner. It is a machine which, by offering the advantages of cooperation, gives the user a new way of solving problems. Most of the work with cooperative computers at the time of writing is still exploratory. The cooperative computers that have been developed so far are used primarily for small-group, task-oriented problem solving, and mainly in the areas of creativity, design, and complex decision making. They have great potential in the increasingly important areas of creativity and emergence.

Cooperative computing is not Computer Supported Cooperative Working (CSCW), group working, or conferencing, and they are not expert systems, although they may be vested with expert knowledge. They are not Decision Support Systems, though they make decisions themselves, and they are not Information Systems, although the processing of information is an important part of their abilities. Like agent-based systems, cooperative computers do perform under direction and they do possess expertise, but they differ in that they are capable of performing the central task, and arriving at acceptable solutions, independently. They represent a separate class of computer application in its own right.

ANTECEDENCE OF THE COOPERATIVE COMPUTER

Hodges (1) quotes Turing:

> . . . the intention in constructing these machines in the first instance is to treat them as slaves, giving them only jobs which have been thought out in detail, jobs such that the user of the machine fully understands in principle what is going on all the time. Up till the present, machines have only been used in this way. . . . There is, however, no reason why the machine should always be used in such a manner: there is nothing in its construction which obliges us to do so. It would be quite possible for the machine to try out variations of behaviour and accept or reject them and I have been hoping to make the machine do this.

Turing wanted to achieve what the constructors of cooperative computers are just beginning to achieve.

Thus, the emergence of cooperative computers is a logical part of the general development in computing, reflecting the changing relationship between them and humans; that is, the computer first as slave, then servant, then agent, and now as a partner.

Cooperation

There have been many definitions of cooperation (2), but one of the most relevant is "working together to a common goal." Before examining the idea of how a machine might work with a human in achieving a common goal, it is useful to look first at some of the advantage, disadvantages, and elements of human–human cooperation.

The advantages have two main dimensions; one is task related and the other is socially oriented. In the task-related dimension, three different levels may be distinguished, namely, **synergy** (where the cooperating partners can together achieve a different order of result from those achievable separately), **possibility** (where the partners can achieve goals not possible for one person to achieve), and **efficiency** (where cooperation minimizes the effort required from the partners in achieving their goal).

Cooperation is also intrinsically rewarding in itself: the partners use the task (such as a friendly game of cards) as a focus of social activity. This forms the social dimension.

The two main disadvantages of cooperation are that (a) there is always an associated energy and/or time overhead, especially in communication, and (b) co-operation can be inappropriate to the task or situation, to the point that the goal is not reached.

There are some elements which must be present in a joint human–human activity for it to be classed as being cooperative. These consist of the following: There must be a goal in common. Two-way communication has to be present (including the potential for metacommunication, i.e., communication about communication). A reward system has to be in place, although the reward can be gained after the goal is achieved. The partners must exhibit goal-directed working, and the behavior and work must conform to norms commonly acceptable to the partners and/or inherent in the task. Part of the observance of norms extends to the playing of roles by each partner; teacher, leaner, expert, and so forth. Finally, processes of distribution, coordination, and timing of responses have to be present.

The context in which these elements operate is important, for cooperation must be voluntary: cooperation and coercion cannot coexist.

MODELING COOPERATION

Cooperation can be modeled, as in Figure 1. The simplest situation is shown, where there are just two partners who are cooperating in achieving the shared or common goal involving a "goal-object." The partners communicate with each other, in a common language, about a number of topics such as the current state of the goal object and the intended state of the goal object (i.e., the intended goal). The partners will also exchange information about themselves, their environments, and the coordination and distribution of responses; that is, the work they are performing on the goal object. The nature and content of communication is also determined by the relative roles being taken up by the partners. The reward system is not visible but may be implicit in doing the task together (a social reward) or in completion of the task.

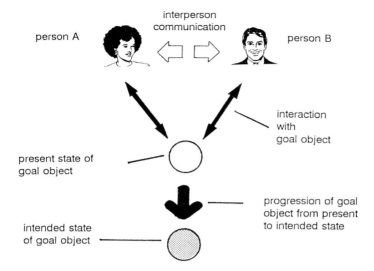

FIGURE 1   A simple model of human–human cooperation.

HUMAN–COMPUTER COOPERATION

Figure 2 shows the situation where there is a computer instead of one of the human partners. (Here, proponents of cooperative computing would put forward a scenario where a lone user is being empowered, rather than where a human is being replaced by a computer.) The same dynamics take place as for the human–human case, that is, the human and the computer are working toward a common goal by

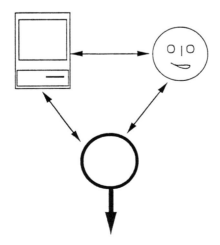

FIGURE 2   Human–computer cooperation.

carrying out various operations on the goal object. They communicate with each other about their view of the state of the common goal object.

TOP-LEVEL SPECIFICATION ELEMENTS OF A COOPERATIVE COMPUTER

Humans are versatile and adaptable, but the computer is bounded and has to be specified. Three top-level elements need to be specified for a cooperative computer, namely, the task, the cooperative behavior, and communication.

Task analysis is critical because the experience of most workers in the field to date suggests that it will not be possible, in the near future at least, to construct a general-purpose cooperative computer. Analyzing the task, both from the point of view of the cooperating human and the computer system designer, calls for understanding of problem analysis and description, the objective, the medium, and the knowledge requirements.

Specifying the cooperative behavior calls for analysis of the behavioral components and associated data flows, especially for goal declaration, the cooperating strategies, and the roles to be played by the partners. Typical decisions here involve setting priorities over each partner, based on perceived criticality, and issues such as the "game turn," that is, when, and in what manner, the computer communicates.

Communication between the partners, whether human–human or human–computer, is the most sensitive factor in cooperation, in that when it fails, cooperation rapidly ceases. (This why metacommunication is so important: the ability to repair communication and the strategies associated with repair are vital.) The design of the human–computer interface is important. Grice's maxims of cooperative conversation are relevant and form a very useful basis for designing the dialogs (at least, until machines learn to tell lies). Some of the problems at this level concern the representation of role and task and the visualization of information. Various ways for the computer to communicate with the human have been tried including voice, "ghosting" (where the human partner draws in solid lines, say, and the computer draws on the same surface using ghosted lines), split screens (i.e., one for the human and one for the computer), and through conventional instruments where the task was one of vehicle control.

THE ARCHITECTURE OF A COOPERATIVE COMPUTER

When the elements of cooperation are considered as processes, the processes can then be expressed in architectural form. A typical architecture is shown in Figure 3.

Goal-Oriented Working

In Figure 3, the cooperating parties work toward the desired goal: Working toward different or conflicting goals will not achieve cooperation. For the human–computer partners to achieve success, there must be agreement, reached via a process of communication, about the goal to be accomplished. In so doing, the parties declare their intent to each other, a necessary precondition for cooperation.

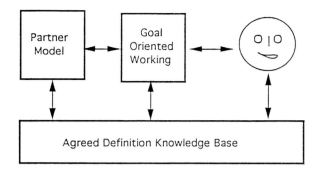

FIGURE 3   The architecture of a cooperative computer.

The Agreed Definition Knowledge Base

Another of the important features of cooperative behavior is the ability of either party to communicate the current state of the interaction. Here it is critical that both the cooperating parties share the same object definitions. This factor is emphasized during human–human cooperation, where a large amount of time is taken up with the mutual identification of, and agreement of, terms of reference to be adopted during the process. The definitions do not have to remain static as long as changes are agreed upon by both parties. (If a cooperative machine is to be fully developed, it must support the interactive updating of the shared knowledge base.)

The Partner Model

The ability of parties to generate alternative solutions within a problem-solving task is an important part of cooperative behavior. To represent this ability in the machine, a mechanism (called in Fig. 3 the Partner Model, PM), accesses a knowledge base common to both the machine and the user (the Agreed Definition Knowledge Base, ADKB). The model consists of domain-specific rules. The model's rules are applied to the goal-related definitions in the ADKB, and the results are then communicated to the user. This process generates viable alternative solutions and, thus, presents a similar behavior observed in human–human cooperation. (The PM is not an embedded user model and does not necessarily reflect the working style of any particular end user.)

The mechanism generates alternative solutions; it also facilitates interaction with the user, who is able to query the rule base.

PERFORMANCE AND TASK REQUIREMENTS OF A COOPERATIVE COMPUTER

Such a machine features the elements of cooperation in the form of mechanisms which enable the cooperative computer to recognize and accept the user's goal or goals when declared, work toward the goal (both independently and in conjunction with the user), and, importantly, offer alternative solutions to the problem represented by the goal.

Just as human–human cooperation is more appropriate for certain tasks than others, so there are tasks which are more appropriate for human–computer cooperation. The tasks which are best suited for the cooperative computer must be achievable; that is, open-ended tasks are not suitable. There must be solutions possible; the goal (or goals) must be identifiable; there must be explicit rules for producing solutions; and the task should be one which can support partial solutions.

APPLICATION OF COOPERATIVE COMPUTING TECHNIQUES

Cooperative techniques can be applied not only to specific types of task but also to functionalities within the computer itself (e.g., the user interface, resource management, knowledge acquisition, or knowledge representation).

POTENTIAL PROBLEMS WITH COOPERATIVE COMPUTING

Some operational problems have been indicated with cooperative computing, including mimicry, "no solution" tasks, and protection or ownership of "the mission."

Consider a situation in which the human and the partner model have the same knowledge. Consider that situation also in a case where the human is unable to reach the declared goal because he or she cannot think of a solution to the problem. There is then a risk that the partner will also be unable to reach the declared goal because it too cannot think of a solution to the problem. Here, two heads are definitely not better than one. Ways to avoid the problem of mimicry include having partners with different but complementary knowledge bases, or making sure that one or other of the knowledge bases are differentially updated.

As far as there being no solution or partial solution possible, Turing noted that ideally one should establish quantitatively how much information is necessary to have on hand at the outset of a search for a solution to ensure that a solution can be found. In a nonideal world, however, people have to come up with answers. Fortunately, humans can operate in circumstances where there is no "optimal solution," but, instead, there exist a set of alternative solutions which satisfice (i.e., solutions which are dependent on a particular metric and a particular viewpoint). So, although the cooperative computer must be able to produce viable solutions, where it proves to be that there are no solutions, the user must be prepared to shift metric and viewpoint.

In the famous story *2001: A Space Odyssey* by Arthur C. Clarke, the space vessel's computer HAL and the crew had the same mission goal, but there was no social dimension in HAL's operation. He, therefore, felt justified in trying to destroy the crew when he suspected that their responses were becoming inadequate. The objection in principle here would be that HAL was not a cooperative computer, as defined. Niceties of definition apart, protection of the mission goal is a problem in the design of cooperative computers.

EXAMPLES OF COOPERATIVE COMPUTERS

Fischer and his colleagues at the University of Colorado have constructed a number of cooperative critiquing systems which support incremental learning. They include ACTIVIST (an active help system for a text editor), LISP-CRITIC (a system which suggests how to improve Lisp code), FRAMER (a knowledge-based design environment for the design of program frameworks), and Janus with MODIFIER (a design environment for creating kitchen designs). These systems are surveyed by Silverman (3).

Banks and Lizza (4) developed Pilot's Associate at the Wright-Patterson Air Force Base. The system is a simulator-based, cooperative airborne pilot's aid. It has a number of roles, including that of mission planner, where it plans and replans missions according to circumstances and orders from control, and weapons operator, where the system sets up the aircraft's passive and active defense systems upon detecting a threat to the aircraft. The pilot has overall control.

At the University of Technology, Loughborough, a number of cooperative systems have also been constructed. They include the exploratory Human–Computer Cooperation (HCC) system by Clarke and Smyth (5), which uses a room-design metaphor for the interface, and the developmental Cooperative Screen Design (COSY) system by Chui (6), for designing computer-interface screens. Currently under construction is a practical system for the selection and implementation of advanced cooperative mechanisms to support designers in the specific domain of industrial knitwear design.

THE FUTURE

Conventional computers have long offered the simplest advantage of cooperation, that is, the saving of effort. More recently, computers have been developed and employed in ways which enable users to achieve the second of the advantages of cooperation, namely, the ability to reach goals otherwise unattainable (e.g., some expert systems and computer control of inherently unstable aerodynamic bodies). None of these systems have necessarily been based on the principles of human–human cooperation (although their acceptance to the users has been markedly improved where they appeared to be). It is the third of the advantages, and also in the social dimension, that the cooperative computer shows the greatest promise. In those cooperative systems where the interaction between computer and users have been evaluated, many users reported the sensation of experiencing a new and different relationship with the computer, "as if it were trying to help me," one remarked. Other users have reported that the process of interacting with the cooperative computer has enabled totally new design solutions to emerge, above and beyond the immediate design goals. This is the exciting area where the development of cooperative computers should take us.

REFERENCES

1. A. Hodges, *The Enigma of Intelligence*, Unwin, Boston, 1987.
2. M. Deutsch, "A Theory of Cooperation and Competition," *Human Relations, 2*, 129–152 (1949).

3. B. G. Silverman, "A Survey of Critiquing Systems: Practical and Theoretical Frontiers," *Commun. ACM, 35*(4), 106–127 (1992).
4. S. B. Banks and C. S. Lizza, "Pilot's Associate: A Cooperative, Knowledge-Based System Application," *IEEE Expert, 6*(3), 18–29 (1991).
5. A. A. Clarke and M. M. G. Smyth, "A Co-operative Computer Based on the Principles of Human Co-operation," *Int. J. Man–Machine Studies, 38*, 3–22 (1993).
6. Y.P. Chui, "Defining the Mechanisms of a Co-operative Computer System Based on Theories of Co-operation," Ph.D. thesis, University of Technology, Loughborough, U.K. (1994).
7. H. P. Grice, "Logic and Conversation," in *Syntax and Semantics, 3*, P. Cole and J. L. Morgan (eds.), Academic Press, London, 1975, pp. 41–58.

BIBLIOGRAPHY

Argyle, M., *Cooperation: The Basis of Sociability*, Routledge, Chapman and Hall. New York, 1991.
Axelrod, R., *The Evolution of Co-operation*, Viking Penguin. New York, 1990.
Bowden, M., *Computer Models of Mind*, Cambridge University Press, New York, 1988.

ANTHONY A. CLARKE

DATABASE THEORY: AN INTRODUCTION

INTRODUCTION

Database systems have become an important tool in many applications over the past 30 years, ranging from traditional ones in business applications to more recent ones in science and technology. In parallel to the development of software systems capable of efficiently managing large amounts of data, the area of databases has seen a tremendous penetration from a theoretical point of view; the goal of this article is to give an introduction to that body of theory.

The practical need for efficient organization, creation, manipulation, and maintenance of large collections of information, together with the recognition that data about the real world, which are manipulated by application programs, should be treated as an integrated resource independent of these programs, has led to the development of database management. A *database system* (DBS) consists of a piece of software, the *database management system* (DBMS), and some number of *databases*. The DBMS basically is a special-purpose program which is stored in a computer's main memory and executed under the control of the operating system. A database is a collection of data which represents information about a specific application from the real world, which due to its size is commonly stored in secondary memory. The DBMS acts as an interface between users and a database: It ensures that users can access their data adequately and efficiently, and that the data are resilient against hardware crashes and software errors and persist over long periods of time independent of programs that access it. Technically, a DBMS is a reentrant program shared by multiple activities, the database transactions.

The distinction between a database, the collection of information, and a database management system, the software that manages the database, implies at least two possibilities for viewing a database system: From a *user's* perspective, a database is commonly viewed at various levels of abstraction, at which different types of data are identified. For example, in the ANSI/SPARC framework (1), *three* abstraction levels are distinguished, which aim at (physical and logical) *data independence*: The (lowest) *internal level* deals with the physical definition and organization of data; the next higher *conceptual level* describes the time-invariant global structure of a database in the conceptual *schema* and in the language of a chosen *data model* which abstracts from the details of physical storage. At the highest *external level*, individual users or user groups can have portions of the conceptual schema configured into an external *schema*, which reflects the way in which they want or are allowed to use the data.

Central to this kind of viewing a database is the conceptual level and its data model. A data model has both a *specification* component, which allows to describe structural aspects of an application and their semantics, and an *operational* component, which allows manipulations of these structures. Consequently, a large body of theoretical investigations has in the past been devoted to the study of data models and their manipulation languages. We will cover highlights of these studies for two prominent types of databases in this survey: for *relational* databases in the second section, and for *object-oriented* databases in the third section.

From an *implementor's* perspective, a DBMS has to provide a variety of capabilities, some of which follow directly from the above exposition of how a database is seen by its users. In principle, we can view the functionality of a DBMS as being organized in four different layers as shown in Figure 1: The *interface layer* manages the interfaces to the various classes of users, including a database administrator, casual users, and application programmers. The *language processing layer* has to process the various forms of requests that can be directed against a database. A query is decomposed into elementary database operations; the resulting sequence is then subject to optimization with the goal of avoiding executions with poor performance. An executable query or program is passed to the *transaction management layer*, which is in charge of controlling concurrent accesses to a shared database ("concurrency control") and at the same time makes the system resilient against possible failures. Finally, the *secondary storage management layer* takes care of the physical data structures (files, pages, indexes) and performs disk accesses.

It turns out that even in this area of database system or implementation technology, theory can help. For example, the issue of query optimization is largely driven by aspects of the underlying data model and the operations it provides. Transaction processing is commonly based on specific synchronization techniques whose correctness require the ability to prove theorems about the underlying mechanisms. We will look into this issue more specifically in the fourth section.

Interface Layer	
Data Model and Query Language	
Host Language Interfaces	
Other Interfaces	
Language Processing Layer	
View Management	Language Compiler
Semantic Integrity Control	Language Interpreter
Authorization	Query Decomposition
Query Optimization	
Access Plan Generation	
Transaction Management Layer	
Access Plan Execution	Transaction Generation
Concurrency Control	
Buffer Management	Recovery
Secondary Storage Management Layer	
Physical Data Structure Management	
Disk Accesses	

FIGURE 1   Functional DBMS layers.

The historical development of databases, their models, and their systems can roughly be divided into three generations. The first generation vastly coincides with the 1970s and is characterized by the introduction of a first distinction between *logical* and *physical* information. Data models were used for the first time to describe physical structures from a logical point of view. In particular, the *hierarchical model* and the *network model* (2) evolved as the basis of *prerelational* systems. Because these data models are not too interesting from a theoretical point of view, we do not consider them further. The second generation, which reached the marketplace in the early 1980s and which is now subsumed under the term "relational systems," was based on a new and simpler approach to data organization, which offered a much clearer distinction between a physical and a logical data model. In particular, relational systems provide a high degree of *physical data independence*, are based on a simple conceptual model (relations), and have more powerful languages available. The first aspect means that physical storage of data is transparent to users and that, in principle, both the physical and the logical side may be changed without the other side being affected. The latter aspect primarily results from *set-oriented* data management and yields nonprocedural or *declarative* languages. In a relational database, a user sees the data as tables. For example, Figure 2 shows a sample relational database for a library application. The tables of a relational database are accessed and manipulated via operators that process them as a whole, without the need to iterate through a relation on a record-by-record basis. As relations are a well-known mathematical concept, it is not surprising that this DBS generation saw an enormous penetration from a theoretical point of view, which started in the early 1970s shortly after the model had been proposed in Ref. 3. On the other hand, relational *systems* rapidly acquired their position in the software market and still continue to do so today.

In the early 1980s, a variety of scientific, engineering, and other applications, in which large collections of data arise, started to discover that treating data as an

Book	*CallNo*	*FirstAuthor*	*AddAuthors*	*Title*	. . .
	123	Date	n	Intro DBS	
	234	Jones	y	Algorithms	
	345	King	n	Operating Syst.	

Reader	*ReaderNo*	*Name*	. . .
	225	Peter	
	347	Laura	

CheckOut	*CallNo*	*ReaderNo*	*RetDate*
	123	225	04-22-94
	234	347	07-31-94

FIGURE 2   A sample relational database.

integrated resource independent of application programs is an idea that might be beneficial for them either. As a result, they started to investigate whether the use of a database system in their specific domain was feasible, and soon recognized that this was not the case for relational systems. Although such systems *are* in use in nonbusiness applications, it has become clear that new solutions are needed for a number of database issues, in order to make such a merger of a new domain with database technology adequate. The requirement that has attracted most of the attention in theoretical developments during the past decade is that of advanced data models (and their operations). After intermediate stages consisting of semantic models and later complex-object models, more recently *object orientation*, a powerful and popular paradigm from the world of programming languages, began to penetrate the database field. Currently, *object-oriented databases* are among the most advanced types of databases, although their theory is less understood than that of relational ones.

A systematic study of theoretical issues underlying databases began with the advent of the relational model, an elegant, well-motivated, and appropriately restricted computational paradigm for database management. As in every other data model, the relational model has a structural component (schemas with dependencies) and an operational one (the relational algebra language). The choice of these basics for specifying semantically meaningful databases and for querying them has been justified through a variety of properties they enjoy. The study of these properties employs a rich body of mathematical machinery, including mathematical logic, graph theory, and algebra, and a considerable apparatus provided by theoretical computer science, including computational complexity, the theory of computability, and even automata theory. It has even shed new light on connections between these fields, in particular the connection between logic and complexity. Using these kinds of tools, typically in various combinations, it could, for example, be shown that relational algebra is equivalent to other natural query paradigms, has low computational complexity, and has a potential for optimization. Although many researchers initially concentrated on studying issues in dependency theory and query languages for the relational model, it was recognized at some point that the relational model was inadequate for dealing with highly structured information. However, the experience gained in studying that model could then be used to study extensions of it, such as nested relations or complex objects.

Database technology as provided by complete systems can be seen as a combination of results from dissimilar areas, namely, data model theory, transaction processing, and access methods. So concurrent with developments in data model theory, other researchers started focussing on the latter two issues. However, once again it turned out that the aforementioned branches of mathematics and theoretical computer science provided a valuable background. The results obtained until today confirm that all areas of database theory have undergone severe investigations in the past and that numerous results could be exploited for building better systems. Today, database theory continues to evolve, although more and more researchers tend to concentrate on development and implementation issues as opposed to basic formal research.

The remainder of this article is organized as follows: the next section discusses important aspects of the theory of relational databases, because database theory has delivered its most interesting facets and deepest results here; in particular, the section treats the syntax and semantics of the relational model, that is, its schemas and its integrity constraints, query languages, their expressiveness and complexity, database logic programming, and sketches how results obtained for the flat model carry over to the nested one. The third section concentrates on the more recent subject of object-oriented databases, for which a theory is not yet as advanced as for relational databases. Nevertheless, important aspects of object models and language design are already understood and go considerably beyond traditional types of databases. The fourth section is a synopsis of the theory of database transactions and concurrency control and deals with classical serializability theory and its extensions. The final section is a short summary.

RELATIONAL DATABASE THEORY

In this section, we will give an overview of important questions, techniques, and results that have been considered, used, and obtained in the context of the relational data model.

The Relational Model

The relational model (3) is based on the mathematical notion of a *relation* and organizes data in the form of *tables*. A table has *attributes* describing properties of data objects (as headline) and *tuples* holding data values (as other rows) as was indicated in Figure 2. A table is, hence, a *set of tuples*, where tuple components can be identified by their associated attributes. This is restricted, for example, from the point of view of *types* in programming languages, as it only allows the application of a tuple *constructor* to attributes and given base domains, followed by the application of a set constructor. On the other hand, the simplicity of the relational model allows an elegant and in-depth formal treatment, sketches of which are given below using formal notations only as far as necessary.

Let $X = \{A_1 \ldots, A_m\}$ be a set of *attributes*, and let each attribute $A \in X$ have a nonempty, finite domain dom(A) of atomic values (integers, strings, etc.). Let $\bigcup_{A \in X}$ dom(A) $=:$ dom(X). A *tuple* over X is an injective mapping $\mu : X \to$ dom(X) satisfying $\mu(A) \in$ dom(A) for each $A \in X$. For given X, let Tup(X) denote the set of all tuples over X. A *relation* r over X is a finite set of tuples over X, that is, $r \subseteq$ Tup(X); the set of all relations over X is denoted by Rel(X).

To associate semantics with a set of attributes, or with several such sets, the relational model allows for a specification of *dependencies*, or *integrity constraints*, where three major types can be distinguished: *Static* dependencies restrict the set of allowable database states; in particular, a dependency over a set X of attributes restricts a given state space Rel(X) to relations which are *meaningful* with respect to the underlying application. For example, the contents of a library database will only be considered valid if for each book stored the call number is unique. A *transitional* dependency restricts the possible state transitions, that is, the ways of getting from one state to the next. Finally, *dynamic* dependencies restrict the possible *sequences* of states which can be observed in a database over time (4).

We will restrict our attention to static dependencies, which have been studied best in the past (5). An important example of static constraints are functional dependencies: Let X be a set of attributes, and let $Y,Z \subseteq X$. A *functional dependency* (FD) $Y \rightarrow Z$ is *valid* in $r \in \text{Rel}(X)$ (or r *satisfies* $Y \rightarrow Z$) if any two tuples from r which agree on Y also agree on Z. An important special case of FDs are *key dependencies*: For given X, $K \subseteq X$ is a *key* for X if $K \rightarrow X$ holds, and no proper subset of K also has this property.

With these preparations, we can say that a *relation schema* has the form $R = (X, F)$; it consists of a name (R), a set of attributes X, and a set F of functional dependencies; this form of a schema suffices for our purposes. It serves as a time-invariant description of the set $\text{Sat}(R)$ of all relations over X that satisfy F. It is said to be in *first normal form* (1NF) if all domains contain atomic values only. If $\mathbf{R} = \{R_1, \ldots, R_k\}$ is a (finite) set of relation schemas, where $R_i = (X_i, F_i)$, $1 \leq i \leq k$, and $X_i \neq X_j$ for $i \neq j$, a (relational) *database* d (over $\mathbf{R}$) is a set of (base) relations, $d = \{r_1, \ldots, r_k\}$, such that $r_i \in \text{Sat}(R_i)$ for $1 \leq i \leq k$. Let $\text{Dat}(\mathbf{R})$ denote the set of all databases over $\mathbf{R}$.

The various relations in a database are often connected via interrelational constraints such as *inclusion dependencies* which state that certain values in one relation have to form a subset of values in another. For example, in the library database it makes sense to require that only books can be checked out which are indeed available in the library, that is, that the set of call numbers appearing in the *CheckOut* relation always is a subset of the call numbers appearing in the *Book* relation. More formally, let $\mathbf{R}$ be a set of relation schemas, $R_i, R_j \in \mathbf{R}$, $R_i \neq R_j$, $R_i = (X_i, F_i)$, $R_j = (X_j, F_j)$. In addition, let $V[W]$ be a sequence of distinct attributes from X_i [X_j]. An *inclusion dependency* (IND) $R_i[V] \subseteq R_j[W]$ is *valid* in $d \in \text{Dat}(\mathbf{R})$ (or *satisfied* by d) if $\{\mu[V] \mid \mu \in r_i\} \subseteq \{\mu[W] \mid \mu \in r_j\}$.

Now let $\mathbf{R}$ be a set of relation schemas, and $\Delta_{\mathbf{R}}$ be a set of inclusion dependencies; again, this will be sufficient for the purposes of this introduction. A (relational) *database schema* is a named pair $\mathbf{D} = (\mathbf{R}, \Delta_{\mathbf{R}})$. It represents a time-invariant (conceptual) description of the set of all *consistent* databases over $\mathbf{R}$ satisfying all the dependencies.

Dependency Theory

The *theory of data dependencies* has been developed around two major themes: implication problems (5) and algorithmic schema design (6). These have been motivated by questions of severe practical importance, which we will try to exemplify in the context of functional dependencies. Consider a relation schema $R = (X, F)$ with attribute set X and FD set F, and let $\text{Sat}(F)$ denote the set of all relations over X satisfying F. From a design point of view, FDs are semantic specifications. From an operational point of view, they are integrity constraints which the DBMS has to maintain at run time, especially if the database undergoes updates. Thus, it seems desirable to have small FD sets available, so that satisfaction can be tested efficiently. To achieve this goal, it is important to understand implication:

Let F be a set of FDs over attribute set X, and let f be an FD with attributes from X. F *implies* f, abbreviated $F \models f$, if $\text{Sat}(F) \subseteq \text{Sat}(\{f\})$ holds, that is, every relation satisfying F also satisfies f. An immediate usage of this notion is a characterization of redundancy of a set of FDs, as well as a characterization of equivalence of two sets of FDs. So studying implication seems appropriate. Because its definition does not suggest an efficient way of testing it, something else is needed in that respect. To this end, let $F^+ := \{f \mid F \models f\}$ denote the *closure* of a given set F of FDs. Then, testing implication means to decide, for given F and f, whether $f \in F^+$ holds, which is called the *membership problem* for functional dependencies. As in many logical theories, a key point now is that the *semantic* notion of implication can be replaced by a *syntactic* notion of derivation. This is due to the fact that FDs can be represented as sentences of the first-order predicate calculus with equality (5). To make derivation precise, a sound and complete axiomatization is needed, which can be based on *Armstrong's axioms* (7):

(A1) $Y \subseteq Z \Rightarrow Z \rightarrow Y$
(A2) $Z \rightarrow Y \wedge Y \rightarrow V \Rightarrow Z \rightarrow V$
(A3) $V \rightarrow Y \wedge Z \subseteq W \Rightarrow VW \rightarrow YZ$

It is easily verified that these axioms are *sound*, that is, every FD obtained through them is indeed implied by the given ones. Formally, derivation can be defined as follows: Let F be a set of FDs (over X), and let $Y \rightarrow Z$ be an FD such that $YZ \subseteq X$. $Y \rightarrow Z$ is *derivable* from F, denoted $F \vdash f$, if there exists a sequence $f_1, \ldots, f_n$ of FDs with the following properties: (i) f_n is of the form $Y \rightarrow Z$ and (ii) for each i, $1 \le i \le n$, either $f_i \in F$ holds, or f_i can be generated from $\{f_1, \ldots, f_{i-1}\}$ using (A1), (A2), and (A3).

The important point now is that the axioms are also *complete*, that is, every FD f implied by some F is also derivable from F, or $F \models f$ iff $F \vdash f$. Thus, to show an implication, it is sufficient to state a derivation. This result can easily be used to design an efficient algorithm for solving the membership problem, which can fruitfully be employed, for example, in algorithmic schema design.

Consider the *Book* schema shown earlier and notice that not only every attribute in this schema is functionally dependent on *CallNo*, if the latter is chosen as the key; but assuming that *Loc* values represent a publisher's main office, there also exists the FD *Publ* $\rightarrow$ *Loc*. Thus, there is a transitive dependence of *Loc* on *CallNo*, which might have the following undesired effect: If a *Book* table has many entries of books from one publisher, the corresponding location information gets repeated redundantly for each. This redundancy can be avoided if attribute *Loc* is dropped from *Book*, and another schema is created with attributes *Publ* (as key) and *Loc*, which would now contain the location information for each publisher exactly once.

The quality measure of reducing or even eliminating redundancy in tuple values of a relation is just one among several others (2). In order to meet them, researchers began to develop a theory of relational database design (8). In this theory, properties that a "good" relational schema has to have can be formalized, and algorithms are available which can be proved to achieve these properties subject to a number of general requirements (2,6). These properties center around various *normal forms* (like *third* normal form which avoids transitivities between certain functionally related attributes). The algorithms, hence, are mostly *normalization procedures*, which transform arbitrary relation schemas into normalized ones.

As the investigation of functional dependencies has produced many fruitful results due to their relationship with logic, and because FDs are unable to capture the entire semantics of a given application, people began to investigate more general types of dependencies and tried to extend the results for FDs to them. However, this work has not only produced positive results, and we will briefly sketch next what has been discovered.

Let us first mention a generalization of FDs: *Multivalued* dependencies (MVDs) intuitively state that in a relation with attribute set $X = U \cup V \cup W$ (where U, V, and W are disjoint), each U value determines a *set* of V values, and does so independent of W values. For example, an employee may have several children, independent of his or her skills. For MVDs, the same program can be gone through as for FDs: Devise a notion of implication, an equivalent notion of derivation via a sound and complete axiomatization, and an efficient solution to the membership problem. In addition, one can investigate how FDs and MVDs interact. More generally, it turns out that the notion of implication is not even restricted to the types of dependencies mentioned so far; if Σ is any set of dependencies, the *general implication-problem* is to decide, for Σ and a single dependency σ, whether σ is implied by Σ, that is, every database satisfying Σ also implies σ (9). The bad news is that in some cases the implication problem is effectively, but not efficiently solvable, and in other cases it is not even effective, that is, it is undecidable (10). Also, there is sometimes a difference between *unrestricted* implication, which takes infinite relations into account, and *finite* implication, which considers finite relations only. Both notions coincide, for example, for FDs and MVDs, which is why these classes of dependencies are also called *finitely controllable*, but they differ for most types of inclusion dependencies and for many mixed sets of dependencies (containing dependencies of distinct types). Moreover, finite controllability is sufficient but not necessary for finite and unrestricted implication being decidable. We finally mention that FDs not only have a close relationship with mathematical logic but also a number of elegant algebraic properties (11). In particular, FD implication can alternatively be characterized in terms of a solution to the generator problem for finitely presented algebras, or in terms of solutions of the uniform word problem for specific semilattices.

Relational Algebra and Calculus

We now turn to the operational part of the relational model and start with six fundamental operations that can be used for introducing a language known as *relational algebra*. The operations are projection, selection, union, difference, natural join, and renaming; a number of additional operations like intersection, semijoin, and division can be defined in terms of these. The formal definitions of these operations are as follows: Let r, $t \in \text{Rel}(X)$, $s \in \text{Rel}(Y)$, and $Y \subseteq X$:

(i)   *Projection* of r onto Y: $\pi_Y(r) := \{\mu[Y] \mid \mu \in r\}$ ($\mu[Y]$ denotes the restriction of μ onto Y).

(ii) *Selection* of r with respect to condition C: $\sigma_C(r) := \{\mu \in r \mid \mu$ satisfies $C\}$. Conditions may either be a term of the form "$A\Theta a$" or "$A\Theta B$," where $A, B \in X$, $a \in \text{dom}(A)$, $\Theta \in \{<, \leq, >, \geq, =, \neq\}$, or several such terms connected by logical $\wedge$, $\vee$, and $\neg$.

(iii) *Union*: $r \cup t := \{\mu \in \text{Tup}(X) \mid \mu \in r \vee \mu \in t\}$.

(iv) *Difference*: $r - t := \{\mu \in r \mid \mu \notin t\}$.

(v)   *Natural Join*: $r \quad s := \{\mu \in \text{Tup}(X \cup Y) \mid \mu[X] \in r \wedge \mu[Y] \in s\}$.

(vi) *Renaming* of $A \in X$ into $B \notin X - \{A\}$ [where $\text{dom}(A) = \text{dom}(B)$]: $\rho_{B \leftarrow A}(r) := \{\mu \in \text{Tup}(X') \mid (\exists \nu \in r) \, \mu(B) = \nu(A) \wedge \mu(X' - \{B\}) = \nu(X - \{A\})\}$, where $X' := (X - \{A\}) \cup \{B\}$.

As an example of the join operation, consider

$$
\begin{array}{ccc}
A\ B\ C & A\ D & C\ D\ E \\
\underline{} & \underline{} & \underline{} \\
1\ \ 1\ \ 1 & 1\ \ 1 & 1\ \ 1\ \ 0 \\
r_1:\ 1\ \ 2\ \ 2 & r_2:\ 0\ \ 1 & r_3:\ 0\ \ 1\ \ 1 \\
2\ \ 0\ \ 2 & 2\ \ 0 & 2\ \ 1\ \ 0 \\
 & & 2\ \ 2\ \ 1
\end{array}
$$

Then

$$
\begin{array}{c}
A\ B\ C\ D \\
\underline{} \\
r_1 \bowtie r_2:\ 1\ \ 1\ \ 1\ \ 1 \\
1\ \ 2\ \ 2\ \ 1 \\
2\ \ 0\ \ 2\ \ 0
\end{array}
$$

$$
\begin{array}{c}
A\ B\ C\ D\ E \\
\underline{} \\
(r_1 \bowtie r_2) \bowtie r_3:\ 1\ \ 1\ \ 1\ \ 1\ \ 0 \\
1\ \ 2\ \ 2\ \ 1\ \ 0
\end{array}
$$

The operations introduced above enjoy a number of properties, such as commutative, associative, and distributive laws (2,6). Also, computing any of these operations takes time at most $O(n \log n)$, where n is the cardinality of the input; thus, they all can be computed efficiently, independent of how the input is stored.

If we write down expressions in which relation names are used as operands, and operands are combined using the operation symbols just described, we obtain the language of relational algebra (RA). Any well-formed RA expression can be represented as a tree, the *parse tree* of its generation, in which each internal node is labeled by an operator and each leaf by the name of a relation schema. The *semantics* (evaluation) of an expression $E \in$ RA can be defined as a function ν_E from $\mathrm{Dat}(\mathbf{R})$ to relations over the "schema" of E (easily determined from E), which can be computed via a bottom-up evaluation of the parse tree of E: For input $d = \{r_1, \ldots, r_k\}$, associate with each leaf labeled R_i relation $r_i \in d$, and with each other node, the result of its label operation applied to the relations associated with its child nodes.

For example, the following algebraic expression E over the library database schema is supposed to return the call number and title of each book checked out by Laura:

$$\pi_{CallNo,\ Title}\,(\sigma_{Name\ =\ \text{``Laura''}}(Reader \quad CheckOut \quad Book)).$$

The result is a relation with attributes *CallNo* and *Title*; when evaluated against the database shown in Figure 2, it only contains the tuple (234, Algorithms).

Relational algebra is a *procedural* language because the user is expected to specify *how* the result is to be obtained. In addition, RA is *closed* because its operators take one or more relations as operands and produce a result relation that may, in turn, be an operand to another operator. Finally, RA expressions can be evaluated efficiently, because, as we mentioned above, all allowed operations have polynomial time complexity.

The library query just shown can alternatively be formulated as the following expression E':

$$\pi_{CallNo, \, Title} \, (\, \pi_{CallNo, \, Title} \, (Book) \quad CheckOut \quad \sigma_{Name \, = \, \text{``Laura''}} \, (Reader)).$$

This expression, when evaluated over the same database as the above, would yield the same result. In other words, the expressions E and E' are *equivalent*, commonly written $E \approx E'$, in the following sense: For each database d, $\nu_E(d) = \nu_{E'}(d)$. One way to prove equivalence is by just referring to the laws of relational algebra and to schema information. For example, if $R_1 = (AB, \, \cdot)$ and $R_2 = (CD, \, \cdot)$, then $E = \pi_{AB}(\sigma_{A=5}(R_1 \quad R_2)) \approx E' = \sigma_{A=5}(R_1)$; so the number of join operations could be reduced. In the library example, a projection and a selection could be moved toward the operands in order to perform them earlier. The latter is reasonable because selections and projections generally reduce (intermediate) results (with respect to the number of tuples or the number of attributes). The aspect illustrated in these examples is one facet of *query optimization*, which when performed at the schema level attempts to cut the evaluation or response time down *without* knowing the internal data structures of the relations involved. In terms of parse trees, the above observations can be cast into *transformation rules* stating, for example, under which conditions projections and selections may be pushed toward the leaves.

The next question we consider is whether RA is a good choice for a query language. For one thing, it is of low computational complexity; in fact, it can be shown that RA belongs to the complexity class NC (11,12) of problems solvable in polylogarithmic parallel time with polynomially many processors, so it can be implemented efficiently. Moreover, if a user is not good at "programming" in RA, a system can easily handle that via optimization as indicated above. We will see next that alternative language paradigms also enjoy these properties.

It was observed in Ref. 3 that RA has a *declarative* counterpart, *relational calculus* (RC), which is based on the insight that a relation schema R with n attributes and a relation symbol R in logic with arity n are similar concepts. Thus, a set of relation schemata $\{ R_1, \ldots, R_k \}$ occurring in a database schema can be considered as a vocabulary of relation symbols; additionally, *variables* are needed which can range over tuples (*tuple calculus*, RTC) or, alternatively, domain elements (*domain calculus*, RDC).

Both RC languages have a solid theoretical foundation because they are based on first-order predicate logic. Semantics is given to formulas by interpreting them as assertions on a given database. For example, an RTC expression for projecting a relation whose schema R has attributes A, B, C, and D onto the first two would be written as

$$\{ t \mid (\exists u)(R(u) \wedge t[A] = u[A] \wedge t[B] = u[B]) \}$$

and read as "find all tuples t for which there exists a tuple u in the relation over R agreeing with t on A and B." Similarly, an RDC expression for the same query would be written as

$$\{ ab \mid (\exists c)(\exists d) \, R(a, b, c, d) \}.$$

We are not presenting the formal details of the RC languages here; these can be found, for example, in Refs. 6, 9, 11, and 13. Instead, we only mention some important results in this context. First, RC is more powerful than RA, because it easily allows one to state queries with infinite answers (e.g., "show all tuples *not* in a given relation"). However, this additional power is rather irrelevant in practice, so it is natural to restrict RC in such a way that infinite answers do not occur any more. Because the finiteness of an answer depends on the choice of domains for attributes, the straightforward approach is to make RC *domain independent*. Unfortunately, this notion is a semantic one and undecidable. So syntactic restrictions are commonly used, which either take the form of *safety conditions* (14,15) or explicit *range declarations* for variables (9).

It can then be shown (3) that every RA expression can be translated in time polynomial in its size into an equivalent safe RC expression and vice versa. Hence, the procedural and the declarative approach to query language design coincide for the relational model. However, the same is not immediately true for RC with range declarations (RC–RD); to achieve equivalence, a union operation needs to be added. This is the reason why the most popular commercial language for relational databases, SQL (16), has a union construct, although it is otherwise based on RC–RD. The consequences of these results are the following: First, a measure of completeness for relational query languages is available. Indeed, RA, RDC, and RTC are frequently called *Codd-complete*, and other languages are termed "complete" if their expressive power coincides with that of, say, RA. Second, the efficiency of RA expression evaluation carries over to the other languages, because each expression transformation also takes at most polynomial time.

What we have just sketched has been the initial approach to "measuring" the expressive power of some query language: establish another language (based on another paradigm) and show its equivalence to the first. This approach takes its attractiveness from the fact that it can be extended, for example, to languages over *nested* relations or over complex objects, which will be discussed later. A different approach to characterizing the expressive power of RA is independent of other languages and looks at the relations that, given a database instance, can be obtained as a result of an RA expression. In this context, the interest is *not* in the queries that can be expressed in RA but in what can be extracted from a database. It turns out that RA expressions can construct all relations that contain only information already in the database instance, and nothing else. Hence, RA is unable to "invent" values, or to include in a query result values that are passed as parameters. The key to this result is a proof that a relation can be the result of an RA expression iff this relation is left invariant under specific automorphisms on the database, details of which can be found in Refs. 9, 17, and 18. The technical tool to investigate the resulting notion of completeness is the *cogroup* of a relation or a database.

Another aspect to be mentioned in the context of query languages is that languages used in practical applications need more than query capabilities; indeed, they must also allow for applying *update operations* to a database. Updating a relational database means inserting new tuples or deleting or modifying existing tuples in its relations, which can formally be described as mappings from the set of all databases over a given schema to itself. Clearly, the interest is not in separate languages for queries and updates but in languages which integrate both aspects of database manipulation. To this end, general database transformations encompassing both updates and queries are studied in Ref. 19. A survey of this subject is provided in Ref. 20. Finally, we mention that most commercial relational products actually do not implement sets (of tuples), but *bags*, that is, sets in which duplicate elements are allowed. The formal study of algebras for bag data has not received too much interest in the past but has regained popularity in connection with the nested relational model (to be discussed later).

Database Logic Programs

Before we embark on the issue of extending first-order or algebraic languages, we introduce a third paradigm for designing database query languages, namely, *logic programming* (21,22). In the area of programming languages, this paradigm was influenced by artificial intelligence and automated theorem proving, and brought about the language Prolog that emphasizes a declarative style of programming. The confluence of logic programming and the area of databases has been driven by the identification of several common features. First, logic programming systems manage small "databases" which are single user, kept in main memory, and consist of fact information and deduction rules. Database systems, on the other hand, deal with large, shared data collections kept in secondary memory and support efficient update and retrieval, reliability, and persistence. Second, a "query" ("goal") in logic programming is answered through a chain of deductions built to prove or disprove some initial statement. A database query is processed by devising an efficient execution plan for extracting the desired information from the database. Third, dependencies specify which database states are considered correct, and a database system is expected to enforce them. In logic programming, constraints are rules that are activated whenever the "database" is modified.

Considering these commonalities and the fact that declarative languages are natural query languages, especially in the relational model, it seems reasonable to combine logic programming with databases. The result, a *logic-oriented* or *deductive* database, is capable of describing facts, rules, queries, and constraints uniformly as sets of formulas in first-order logic, so that the notion of *logical implication* can be used as a basis for defining the semantics of a declarative language. The most prominent example for the use of logic programming in the context of databases is Datalog (14,23,24). This language has a syntax similar to that of (pure) Prolog, but unlike Prolog, is set-oriented, insensitive to orderings of retrieval predicates or of the data, and has neither function symbols nor special-purpose predicates (for controlling the execution of a program). The basic idea behind Datalog and its application in querying a relational database is to define new (derived or *intensional*) relations in terms of the (*extensional*) relations in a given database *and* the new relations themselves, and to do so by providing a set of Horn clauses briefly described next.

An *atom* in Datalog is an expression of the form $P(x_1, \ldots, x_n)$, where predicate P denotes a (base or derived) relation, and the x_i symbols are variables or constants. A *literal* is either an atom (*positive* literal) or a negated atom (*negative* literal); a *clause* is a disjunction of literals. A *Horn clause* is a clause with at most one positive literal, and a Datalog *program* is a finite set of Horn clauses. The restriction to Horn clauses instead of general first-order formulas is again motivated by results from complexity theory: whereas the general satisfiability problem (even for expressions from propositional logic) is well known to be NP-complete (12), the satisfiability problem for conjunctions of Horn clauses can be solved in polynomial time.

Compared to RA, a Datalog program has the obvious new feature that it allows *recursion*. Indeed, in the following sample Datalog program, predicates T and R denote binary relations. Then $\neg R(x, y) \vee T(x, y)$ and $\neg R(x, z) \vee \neg T(z,y) \vee T(x, y)$ are Horn clauses, which are commonly written in program form as

$$T(x, y) \text{ :- } R(x, y).$$

$T(x, y) :- R(x, z), T(z, y).$

The meaning of this program is as follows: We interpret R as the encoding of a directed graph, where the first attribute represents the starting, and the second the end point of an edge. Let all attribute values be integers; then the tuples currently associated with R tell exactly which directed edges exist between what nodes. With this intuition, it should be clear that the above program computes in T the *transitive closure* of the graph stored in R; indeed, the first line says that all of the original graph appears in its transitive closure, whereas the second says that if there is an edge from x to z and one from z to y, then the transitive closure also has an edge from x to y. As an aside we mention that this is an operation which cannot be expressed in RA, a fact that we will return to later.

Informally, the semantics of a Horn clause of the form "$A :- B_1, \ldots B_n.$" is as follows: "For each assignment of each variable, if B_1 is true and B_2 is true and . . . and B_n is true, then A is true." The following terms are common in this context: If $B :- A_1, A_2, \ldots, A_n.$ is a clause occurring in a program, then B is the *head* of the clause, and $A_1, \ldots, A_n$ form its *body*. According to the definition of a Horn clause, three special cases can occur. (1) The clause consists of exactly one positive literal, and nothing else; then it is called a *fact*. Facts are used to describe the contents of a database in a Datalog program. (2) The clause has no positive literal; then it is an *integrity constraint*. (3) The clause is a *rule*, that is, it consists of one positive literal and one or more negative ones.

More formally, a Datalog program, that is, a set C of Horn clauses, can now be given a semantics as follows: If R is a predicate occurring in C, a *relation r* for R is a set of *ground* atoms, that is, atoms without variables (but with constants only). The *input* to C consists of a relation for each predicate that does not appear in the head of any rule. The *output* computed by C basically consists of a relation for each predicate that occurs in the head of some rule; this computation proceeds as follows: The contents of a database is specified as ground atoms (facts) in C. A rule states that if certain facts are known, others can be deduced from them. Newly deduced facts become ground atoms in the output and are at the same time considered to become available as (further) input, so that the rules can be applied again to deduce additional new facts. More precisely, a rule is used to deduce a new fact by *instantiating* its variables with constants, that is, substituting a constant for each occurrence of a variable. If, under such an instantiation, each atom in the body of the rule in question becomes a ground atom, the instantiated head of the rule is added to the output.

It can be shown (14,23) that the procedure just sketched, in logical terms, describes a *least fixpoint* computation, whose result (for Datalog programs without negation in rule bodies) alternatively is the (uniquely determined) *minimal model* of the program in a *model-theoretic* sense, or the set of all facts deducible from the given database in a *proof-theoretic* sense. Furthermore, there is a way to describe it as a (view-defining) *equation* of relational algebra which, for transitive closure, has the form

$$T(x, y) = R(x, y) \cup \pi_{x,y}(R(x, z) \quad T(z, y)).$$

Note that, due to the recursion involved, the meaning of this expression is not obtainable by an ordinary RA expression.

With respect to the expressive power of Datalog as a relational query language, it turns out that Datalog and RA are incomparable with respect to set inclusion: (1) They have a nonempty intersection, consisting of nonrecursive Datalog programs or, equivalently, relational algebra without the difference operator. (2) Recursive queries (like transitive closure) are not RA expressible. (3) RA expressions involving difference are not Datalog expressible. The latter is due to the fact that Datalog programs are *monotone*, that is, enlarging the input *d* to a Datalog program cannot yield a smaller result than on *d* itself, but difference is not a monotone operation.

So far we have excluded negation in the rule bodies of Datalog programs; clearly, an extension in that direction increases the expressive power of the language. However, rule evaluation now becomes nondeterministic in general. One way around this problem is to control the use of negation by *stratification*. Informally, a Datalog program is *stratified* if the following holds: If a negative literal $\neg P$ is used in the body of a rule, then P must have been computed completely at this point. In other words, the program can be divided into *strata* (layers) which are evaluated sequentially. An example is the *complement* of transitive closure, which cannot be computed by an ordinary Datalog program; however, the following Datalog$^{\neg}$ program does it:

$$T(x, y) :\text{-} R(x, y).$$
$$T(x, y) :\text{-} R(x, z), T(z, y).$$
$$C(x, y) :\text{-} \neg T(x, y).$$

The first two lines represent Layer 1 of the stratification and compute the transitive closure (of *R* in *T*) as before. The third line, Layer 2, uses this result for computing the complement. The idea henceforth is to have Layer 1 processed completely before Layer 2 is entered (and to continue in the same way in the presence of more than two layers). More information on this and other extensions of Datalog can be found in Refs. 11, 23, and 25–29. Datalog has been sketched here as a paradigm for defining intensional relations as a whole. Users of a database will often only be interested in a subset of such relations, which can be captured by introducing *goals* into Datalog programs. A goal might be written as "?-literal" and expresses an ad hoc query against a view defined in the program. For both the evaluation of goals and the computation of intensional relations, a variety of methods are described in the literature which exhibit various degrees of efficiency (23,24,30,31).

Computability and Complexity Theory of Queries

We now return to the study of RA and RC as basic query languages for relational databases. In particular, we will discuss extensions that are related to what is made available by Datalog; in addition, we will indicate that there is a close connection between the expressive power of a language and its complexity, and even more generally between logic and complexity classes.

The first observation in that direction is that RA and RC have polynomial time complexities; however, there is a price to pay for this; namely, a *limited* expressive power in the sense that not every reasonable query to a database can be expressed in any of these languages. To this end, it was shown in Ref. 32 that there is no RA expression involving a binary relation whose evaluation yields the transitive closure of that relation, where the latter, for a relation *r* with attributes *A* and *B*, is defined as

$$r^+ := \{\mu \in \mathrm{Tup}(X) \mid (\exists \mu_1, \ldots, \mu_n \in r, n \geq 1) \, \mu(A)$$
$$= \mu_1(A) \wedge (\forall i, 1 \leq i \leq n - 1) \, \mu_i(B) = \mu_{i+1}(A) \wedge \mu_n(B) = \mu(B)\}.$$

The reason for this basically is that, speaking in graph-theoretic terms, RA can compute all paths in a given graph (encoded as a binary relation) of some *fixed* lengths, but not all paths of arbitrary length. This result motivated the question of how RA can be extended so that more database queries can be formulated. A theoretically appealing approach is to extend RA (or one of the RC languages) with constructs (like one for computing transitive closures) that yield additional power. Clearly, the question remains whether some such constructs, and if so which ones, are sufficient to express *all* queries. The study of this question was initiated by Chandra and Harel (33,34), who introduced the notion of a *computable* query. A computable query is a partial recursive function, which, given a database as input, produces as output a relation over the domain of the database and satisfies a *consistency criterion* basically stating that the query output should be independent of the internal representation of the database. This criterion, also known as *C-genericity*, captures the intuition that a query uses only information available at the conceptual level of the database under consideration, so that distinct values can only be treated differently if they can be distinguished via conceptual-level information, or if they appear explicitly in the query. More formally, if C is a finite set of values taken from a universe U, and if $q : D \rightarrow R$ is a query mapping an instance d of database schema D to a relation over schema R, then q is *C-generic* if for every permutation ρ over U such that $\rho(x) = x$ for each $x \in C$, it is true that $\rho(q(d)) = q(\rho(d))$.

First, it is easy to see that RA queries are indeed computable queries, but they form a strict subset of the latter because transitive closure is also a computable query; the same holds for RC. This raises the question of how a language must look like which can express all computable queries. Numerous proposals have been made in that respect; most of them converge toward two central classes of queries in the sense that they turn out to be equivalent to these two (33,34). We denote these languages here by RA + while and RC + fixpoint. The first generalizes relational algebra into a programming language by introducing variables (that take relations as values), assignment statements, and a while-loop as control structure; the while-construct allows the iteration of a program while some (first-order) condition holds. The second is constructed using relational calculus together with a fixpoint operator, which binds a predicate symbol R that is free and appears only positively in the given formula; the formula is iterated until a fixpoint is reached. Both RA + while and RC + fixpoint are not complete, however, because they cannot express, for example, the *even* query (that returns "true" if the cardinality of the operand relation is even).

In the process of increasing the expressive power of relational languages, a new problem was soon observed, namely, that the complexity of query evaluation may also increase considerably. For obvious practical reasons, the interest is in languages whose queries can be computed efficiently, that is, in time polynomial in the size of the underlying database. In other words, the problem (or goal) of language design is to find a good balance between expressiveness and complexity. With respect to the latter, it is obvious, especially with respect to query computations by Turing machines and database encodings as Turing-machine inputs, that queries should by polynomial-time computable, so that language design boils down to finding something intermediate between RA and the class of all polynomially computable queries (35). Various proposals in this direction have been made over the years, including the above-mentioned RA + while, RC + fixpoint, or Datalog extensions. More recently, the addition of *reflection* to RA was proposed in Ref. 36, where reflection is achieved by storing and manipulating RA programs as relations, and by adding a special evaluation operation to the algebra. Surveys of the expressive power of relational query languages can be found in Refs. 11, 37, and 38.

To be more concrete, for queries in the language RC + fixpoint, results of iterations are accumulated, so convergence toward the fixpoint is guaranteed in polynomial time; hence, RC + fixpoint $\subseteq$ PTIME [the class of all queries q such that there is a Turing machine which, given as input a standard encoding enc(d) of a database d, produces as output an encoding of $q(d)$ in time polynomial in $|enc(d)|$]. However, in a while-loop, each iteration is destructive, and while queries may not even converge; hence, RA + while $\subseteq$ PSPACE (the class of all queries computable with a consumption of space polynomial in the length of the input encoding). The *even* query, on the other hand, requires exponential space, so *even* cannot be computable by an RA + while program.

The last remark carries over to an interesting observation that has recently been made: There is a fundamental mismatch between the hardness of some database queries and their ordinary Turing complexity. As we just mentioned, *even* is apparently a hard query, but it has a low Turing complexity. The reason can be seen in the fact that database computations, as mentioned earlier, are required to be generic. Thus, if we want to determine whether a given set has an even cardinality, a generic computation needs to treat all elements of the set uniformly, which rules out the straightforward solution of repeatedly extracting an arbitrary element from the set until it is empty, while keeping a binary counter. This changes radically if the database is assumed to be *ordered*. Roughly, imposing order on a database implies that everything, from the elements in domains to the attributes in a schema and to the tuples in a relation, is ordered, so that it is clear, for example, what the first or the second tuple in a relation is. As shown in Refs. 35 and 39, RC + fixpoint expresses *exactly* PTIME, and RA + while expresses *exactly* PSPACE on ordered databases; in other words, they turn out to be complete. This result was confirmed in Ref. 36 using a different proof technique.

These results in particular show that PTIME equals PSPACE iff RA + while and RC + fixpoint are equivalent over ordered structures; however, because databases are *sets* and hence unordered in general, it remains to investigate whether that connection can be generalized to unordered structures. On the other hand, these results continue a line of discoveries started by Fagin in 1974 (for a recent account, see Ref. 12), which establish a connection between *computational* and *descriptive* complexity. In brief, the computational complexity of a problem is the amount of resources (typically time or space) consumed by a machine that solves the problem. The descriptive complexity of problems is the complexity of describing problems in some logical formalism (40). For example, the complexity class NP coincides with the class of properties expressible in existential second-order logic. The characterizations of PTIME and PSPACE mentioned above hence establish further evidence of the intimate relationship between computational and descriptive complexity.

However, a fundamental difference between the two areas remains. Indeed, a computational device such as a Turing machine works on an *encoding* of a problem, whereas logic is applied directly to the underlying mathematical structures. As a result, machines are able to enumerate objects which are logically unordered. For example, the set of nodes of a graph gets ordered when it is encoded on the tape of a Turing machine. It turns out that the reason for this "mismatch" is also responsible for what we discussed earlier in connection with the *even* query, namely, the discrepancy between the hardness of some database queries and their Turing complexities. The mismatch is due to the generic nature of a database computation, or the distinction between a conceptual and an internal database level, or the general database goal of providing data independence. At the conceptual level, a logical, abstract view of data is provided, chosen purposely to be independent of the internal representation. As a consequence, queries use only information provided by that abstract interface to the database; the internal level, however, has more information available, for example, due to the fact that conceptually unordered objects need to be stored in sequential order on disk. To overcome this mismatch, a new computational device called a *relational machine* was recently introduced in Ref. 41; in brief, a relational machine is a Turing machine augmented with a relational store which can hold a finite set of fixed-arity relations. This store can be viewed as an associative memory supporting the generic part of a database computation, whereas the standard part is carried out on the Turing tape. Designated relations contain initially the input to a query, and other relations hold the output at the end of the execution of the query. While the Turing machine works, it can modify the store through first-order queries. It turns out that relational machines give rise to a new complexity measure ("relational complexity," intuitively the amount of information the machine can extract from an input), under which PTIME equals RC + fixpoint, and PSPACE equals RA + while, both *without* an order assumption (42). In addition, both language classes coincide iff PTIME = PSPACE, even in the absence of order, and several other new results can be obtained on the relationship between logic and complexity, or among various complexity classes (43). Although a relational machine, like every Turing machine, computes some *fixed* query, a reflective extension described in Ref. 44 can even generate queries dynamically.

As the above exposition demonstrates, the use of classical results from theoretical computer science or mathematical logic has a long tradition in database theory and has been extremely fruitful. However, databases turn out not to be just another application of this machinery but do have particular and individual aspects that strongly motivate adoptions and, in a sense, corrections to classical concepts in such a way that the specific database character is properly reflected. It seems that an in-depth understanding of this has only just begun.

The Nested Relational Model

An important aspect of the relational data model is its simplicity, which is largely due to the basic assumption that data are represented as flat tables (in 1NF). A price to pay for this is the inability of the model to directly represent hierarchical structures. To see that these are sometimes more adequate than flat ones, we briefly reconsider the library example and note that a book can have a *set* of authors, or that a publisher can have offices in several locations. This suggests a representation of information oriented on what is commonly available in the type systems of high-level programming languages. Speaking in programming language terms, the only data structure available in the relational model is the *relation*, which is a *set of tuples* such that tuples are aggregations of attributes with their domains. Thus, there are two *constructors*, tuple and set, which can be applied once in the order first tuple, then set. A first generalization is obtained by allowing multiple applications of these constructors, but still in a strictly alternating fashion. The result are relational structures in which the values of attributes can themselves be relations; such structures are called *nested* relations. A second generalization is obtained by dropping the rule that constructor application has to be alternating, and adding more constructors (e.g., list, bags); the result are *complex objects* which will be discussed in the next section.

The proposal to generalize the relational model beyond 1NF tables was originally made in Ref. 45. As an example, the nested relation shown in Figure 3 has two tuples, some components of which are themselves relations.

Many researchers have investigated the nested relational model, in particular issues like algebras (46–48), calculi (49,50), or language completeness (51). Of particular relevance to algebraic languages are the two operations *nest* and *unnest* first proposed in Ref. 46, which have no counterpart in RA. Extensions of RC for nested structures can be provided, which are again more powerful than the nested algebra but which coincide with the algebra if domain independence or safety is imposed. On the other hand, the nested algebra, just like RA, is of limited expressive power, as it can still not compute a transitive closure. The reason for this is that the nested algebra, restricted to flat relations, is equivalent to the flat algebra (52). However, the nested algebra exhibits new possibilities for extending its expressive power. In particular, a *powerset* operator can be added, which is capable of constructing the set of all subsets of a given relation. The resulting *powerset algebra* can compute a transitive closure and has the other interesting properties (e.g., the nest operation is redundant, and it is equivalent to a nested algebra extended by for-loops); for details, see Refs. 53 and 54. As for the flat algebra, the cogroup of a relation can be used to measure the expressive power of query languages for nested relations; even in this context, the powerset algebra is superior to the nested algebra, because it can be used to compute the representation of the cogroup of a relation in a way independent of the actual instance of that relation (55), which the nested algebra cannot. We finally mention that the study of bag data has regained attention

| Book | CallNo | Authors | Title | Publisher | | | ... |
| | | Author | | Name | Location | | |
					City	Country	
	234	Jones	Algorithms	Add-Wes	Bonn	Germ	
		Clark			Reading	MA	
	456	Smith	Computing	Prentice	Englewood	NJ	
		Theo			Norwood	CA	
		Wilkins					

FIGURE 3   A nested book relation.

recently in the context of the nested relational model; see Ref. 56 for results obtained so far.

THEORY OF OBJECT-ORIENTED DATABASES

As we indicated at the end of the previous section, the investigation of data models has meanwhile gone a considerable step forward from the flat relational model to models which are capable of describing highly structured information. This development has followed at least three directions: The first focused on so-called *complex objects*, which are typed objects recursively constructed from atomic objects using constructors for tuples, sets, or other data structures. Although this has been instructive, because, for example, results on query languages could be generalized to this new setting (57,58), it was soon recognized that complex structures alone are not sufficient. Indeed, there has been an increasing interest in modeling *behavioral* aspects of objects as well, and in *encapsulating* object structure and object behavior. This paved the way for including *object-oriented* features in databases, which, in turn, gave rise to the other two directions: One focused on so-called *pure objects*, in which basically everything in a database is considered as an abstract object that has a unique *identity*. The schema of a database can then be considered as a directed graph, whose nodes are class names and whose edges represent single-valued or multivalued attributes. A database instance becomes another directed graph, whose nodes represent objects and whose edges are references between these objects (i.e., attribute values). Although such a model is theoretically appealing, it appears too sophisticated for many real-world applications; the third and currently most active direction therefore is to distinguish between *objects* and their *values*, and to let only the former have an identity. The exposition in this section will mostly center around a corresponding data model.

The Paradigm

Object orientation has been recognized as an important new paradigm in the area of programming languages ever since the arrival of the language Simula. It is roughly based on the following five fundamental principles (59):

1. Each entity of the real world is modeled as an *object* which has an existence of its own, manifested in terms of a unique *identifier* (distinct from its value).
2. Each object has *encapsulated* into it a *structure* and a *behavior*. The former is described in terms of attributes (*instance variables*), where attribute values, which together represent the state of the object, can be other objects so that complex objects can be defined via aggregation. The latter consists of a set of *methods*, that is, procedures that can be executed on the object.
3. The state of an object can be accessed or modified exclusively by sending *messages* to the object, which causes it to invoke a corresponding method.
4. Objects sharing the same structure and behavior are grouped into *classes*, where a class represents a "template" for a set of similar objects. Each object is an instance of some class.

5. A class can be defined as a specialization of one or more other classes. A class defined as a specialization forms a *subclass* and *inherits* both structure and behavior (i.e., attributes and methods) from its *superclasses*.

In the area of programming languages and also in software engineering, the introduction of these principles marked a radical departure from the conventional view (found in languages like Fortran and Algol) that *active functions operate on passive (data) objects*. Instead, the goal now is to have *active objects react to messages from other objects*. It was recognized that this feature is crucial for achieving *data abstraction* and *information hiding*, and for supporting *modularity*, *reusability*, and *extensibility* in program designs. Considering the success of the object-oriented paradigm in these areas, it is not surprising that a merger of object-orientation and database technology got on researchers' agendas. Although initially there has been a lot of confusion about what an *object-oriented database system* (OODBS) actually is, a working definition was established in Ref. 60: An OODBS is characterized by *modeling*, *language*, and *system* properties, which roughly capture the following features. First, the modeling capabilities of an OODBS must support complex objects, each of which has a unique identity, a (data) type, and belongs to a class that is positioned in an inheritance hierarchy. Second, the language features support encapsulation of object behavior (into the corresponding class) and reusability in the form that message names may be *overloaded* or can be *overridden* in specializations (implying that *late binding* of methods to message names, i.e., at run time, is necessary). New types can be defined from existing ones by using given constructors, and the language of the system combines ad hoc query capabilities with the expressive power of a programming language. Finally, an OODBS should be a database system, meaning that it supports persistence, secondary storage management, concurrency control, and recovery.

It is clear that these characteristics create many new research challenges, including data models for objects, operations on objects (e.g., algebraic and calculus like languages), query processing and optimization, transactions processing, or storage organization. We will restrict our attention to models and languages in what follows.

Toward Formal Object Models

We next sketch the basics of a formal model for object-oriented databases, and we do so by distinguishing structural from behavioral aspects. The model we are about to describe can be considered as a framework which can be extended in several ways and which can serve as a foundation for further studies. We will indicate in which directions such studies have been undertaken in recent past. Because any model for object-oriented databases needs to treat structure and behavior separately, we generally consider *schemas*, the central notion of a conceptual database description, to be pairs of the form

$$S = (S_{\text{struct}}, S_{\text{behav}}).$$

Regarding the modeling of structure, complex data types are all that is basically needed, because they serve as descriptions for domains of complex values. One way to introduce such types, that is, to define a *type system T*, is the following:

(i)   integer, string, float, boolean $\subseteq$ T.
(ii) if A_i are distinct attributes and $t_i \in T$, $1 \leq i \leq n$, then $[A_1 : t_1, \ldots, A_n : t_n] \in T$ ("tuple type").
(iii) If $t \in T$, then $\{t\} \in T$ ("set type").
(iv) If $t \in T$, then $< t > \in T$ ("list type").

In other words, a type system is made up of *base types*, from which complex types may be derived using (eventually attributes and) *constructors*; note that constructor application is now arbitrary, that is, not restricted by any rules. Note also that type construction requires nothing additional but the availability of attribute names. Clearly, other base types as well as additional or alternative constructors could straightforwardly be included.

Next, the notion of a domain as a "reservoir" of possible values can be defined as follows; it just has to obey constructor applications:

(a) dom (integer) is the set of all integers; dom is analogously defined for string, float, boolean.
(b) dom $([A_1 : t_1, \ldots, A_n : t_n]) := \{[A_1 : v_1, \ldots, A_n : v_n] \mid (\forall i, 1 \leq i \leq n) v_i \in \text{dom}(t_i)\}$.
(c) dom($\{t\}$) := $\{\{v_1, \ldots, v_n\} \mid (\forall i, 1 \leq i \leq n) v_i \in \text{dom}(t)\}$.
(d) dom($< t >$) := $\{ < v_1, \ldots, v_n > \mid (\forall i, 1 \leq i \leq n) v_i \in \text{dom}(t)\}$.

In a structurally *object-oriented* context, the first thing that needs to be introduced beyond complex types and domains as defined above is the possibility of sharing pieces of information between distinct types, or of *aggregating* objects from simpler ones. At the level of type declarations, an easy way to model this is the introduction of another reservoir of names, this time called *class names*, which are additionally allowed as types. In other words, *object types* are complex types as above with the following new condition:

(v) $C \subseteq T$, where C is a finite set of class names.

This states nothing but the fact that class *names* are allowed as types (later we will complement this with the requirement that classes themselves *have* types). The intuition behind this new condition is that objects from the underlying application all are distinguished by their identity, get collected into classes, and can reference other objects (share subobjects). To provide for this at the level of domains, let us first assume the availability of a finite set *OID* of *object identifiers* which includes the special identifier nil (to capture "empty" references); next, *object domains*, that is, sets of possible values for objects are complex values as above with the following additional condition:

(e)   dom(c) = *OID* for each $c \in C$.

Thus, classes are assumed to be instantiated by objects (class-name types take object identifiers as values, in the same way as, say, the int type takes integer numbers as values). At the level of class instances, conditions will later be imposed which make sure that inclusions or exclusions holds as appropriate from the point of view of the underlying application.

As a simple example, consider a company database in which personnel information is gathered. In terms of the above, this could be described as follows: Let C

= {*Person, Address, Company*}. Because both persons and companies have an address, and because, for example, a person's children are themselves persons, types can be associated with these class names in the following way:

1. Type of class *Person*:
    [name: [first: string, last: string],
    age: integer, married: boolean,
    address: Address,
    children: <Person>,
    works_for: {[company: Company, percentage: integer]}]
2. Type of class *Address*:
    [street: string, city: string, zip: integer]
3. Type of class *Company*:
    [name: string, location: Address]

Domains for these types then provide object identifiers wherever classes are referenced; nil would be used to express, e.g., that children might not yet work.

The object-oriented paradigm has another dimension for organizing information besides aggregation, which is inheritance, or the possibility of defining a class as a specialization of one or more other classes. To this end, a *subtyping relation* is needed through which it can be expressed that a subclass *inherits* the structure of a superclass. Such a relation can be defined in various ways (syntactically or semantically); a syntactical one is the following: Let T be a set of object types. A subtyping relation $\leq \subseteq T \times T$ is defined as follows:

(i) $t \leq t$ for each $t \in T$
(ii) $[A_1 : t_1, \ldots, A_n : t_n] \leq [A'_1 : t'_1, \ldots, A'_m : t'_m]$ if
      (a) $(\forall A'_j, 1 \leq j \leq m)(\exists A_i, 1 \leq i \leq n) A_i = A'_j \wedge t_i \leq t'_j$
      (b) $n \geq m$
(iii) $\{t\} \leq \{t'\}$ if $t \leq t'$
(iv) $<t> \leq <t'>$ if $t \leq t'$

With these preparations, we arrive at the following definition for objectbase schemas that can describe structure of arbitrary complexity: A *structural schema* is a named quadruple of the form $S_{struc} = (C, T, \text{type}, \text{isa})$, where C is a (finite) set of class names, T is a (finite) set of types which uses as class names only elements from C, type : $C \to T$ is a total function associating a type with each class name, isa $\subseteq$ $C \times C$ is a partial order on C which is consistent with respect to subtyping, that is, c isa $c' \Rightarrow \text{type}(c) \leq \text{type}(c')$ for all $c, c' \in C$.

This definition resembles what can be found in a variety of models proposed in the literature (61–63). Note that it still leaves several aspects open, like single versus multiple inheritance; if the latter is desired, a condition needs to be added stating how conflicts should be resolved. Also, implementations typically add a number of additional features not included above.

The second important aspect of an object-oriented database is that it is intended to capture behavior. To this end, the relevant intuition is that classes have attached to them a set of messages, which are specified in the schema via signatures and which are implemented as methods. In addition, behavior can be inherited by subclasses, and message names can be overloaded, that is, reused in various contexts. So a *behavioral schema* is a named 5-tuple of the form $S_{behav} = (C, M, P,$

messg, impl), where C is a (finite) set of class names as above and M is a (finite) set of *message names*, where each $m \in M$ has associated with it a nonempty set $\text{sign}(m) = \{s_1, \ldots, s_l\}$, $l \geq 1$, of signatures; each s_h, $1 \leq h \leq l$, has the form $s_h : c \times t_1 \times \cdots \times t_p \rightarrow t$ for $c \in C$, $t_1, \ldots, t_p, t \in T$ (each signature has the receiver of the message as its first component), P is a (finite) set of methods or programs, messg : $C \rightarrow 2^M$ s.t. for each $c \in C$ and for each $m \in \text{messg}(c)$ there is an $s \in \text{sign}(m)$ such that $s[1] = c$, impl: $\{(m, c) \mid m \in \text{messg }(c)\} \rightarrow P$ is a partial function.

In combining structural and behavioral schemas, we finally obtain the following: An *objectbase schema* has the form $S = (C, (T, \text{type}, \text{isa}), (M, P, \text{isa}, \text{messg}, \text{impl}))$. S is called *consistent* if the following conditions are satisfied:

(i) c isa $c' \Rightarrow \text{messg}(c') \subseteq \text{messg}(c)$ for all $c, c' \in C$.

(ii)   if c isa c' and $s, s' \in \text{sign}(m)$ for $m \in M$ such that $s : c \times t_1 \times \cdots \times t_n \rightarrow t$, $s' : c' \times t'_1 \times \cdots \times t'_n \rightarrow t'$, then $t_i \leq t'_i$ for each i, $1 \leq i \leq n$, and $t \leq t'$.

(iii) $(\forall m \in \text{messg }(c))(\exists c' \in C)\, c$ isa $c' \wedge \text{impl }(m, c')$ is defined.

Condition (i) just says that subclasses inherit the behavior of their superclasses. Condition (ii) says that message-name overloading is done with compatible signatures [called the *covariance condition* (59); it differs from the *contravariance* condition frequently imposed in the context of programming languages]. Finally, condition (iii) states that for each message associated with a class, its implementation must at least be available in some superclass.

It is interesting to note that various natural conditions can be imposed on the programs that are used as implementations of messages. We now sketch one of them, which is based on the view that programs are functions on domains (64). Formally, if $m \in M$ and $s : c \times t_1 \times \cdots \times t_n \rightarrow t \in \text{sign}(m)$, then $\text{impl}(m, c)$, if defined, is a program $p \in P$ of the form $p : \text{dom}(c) \times \text{dom}(t_1) \times \cdots \times \text{dom}(t_n) \rightarrow \text{dom}(t)$. The condition in question informally states that if message overloading appears in isa-related classes (so that the corresponding signatures satisfy the covariance condition), then the associated programs coincide (as functions) on the subclass. More formally, we have the following: If $|\text{sign}(m)| > 1$ for some $m \in M$, then the following holds: If $s, s' \in \text{sign}(m)$ such that $s : c \times t_1 \times \cdots \times t_n \rightarrow t$, $s' : c' \times t'_1 \times \cdots \times t'_n \rightarrow t'$, c isa c', $t_i \leq t'_i$ for each i, $1 \leq i \leq n$, $t \leq t'$, and $\text{impl}(m, c) = p$, $\text{impl}(m, c') = p'$, then p and p' agree on $\text{dom}(c) \times \text{dom}(t_1) \times \cdots \times \text{dom}(t_n)$.

A variety of formal investigations for behavioral schemata in the sense defined above can already be found in the literature, which investigate questions including termination of method executions, limited depth of method-call nestings (an issue related to precompilation of method executions), well-definedness of method calls, that is, consistency as well as reachability considerations (issues related to type inference and schema evolution), expressiveness of method implementation languages (relative to some notion of completeness), complexity of method executions, and potential parallelism of method evaluations. To investigate such issues, our general notion of schema is made precise in various ways. For example, Ref. 65 fixes a simple imperative language for implementing methods as *retrieval programs*, contrasts them with *update programs*, and shows undecidability results for the latter. Several sources introduce distinct notions of a *method schema* to study behavioral issues of OODBS; for example, Ref. 66 investigates implications of the covariance condition using the formalism of program schemas, whereas Ref. 67 looks at tractability guarantees corresponding to those known for relational query languages.

We conclude this section with a brief indication of how *object databases*, that is, sets of class instances or extensions, can be defined over a given schema: For a given objectbase schema S, an *objectbase* over S is a triple $d(S) = (O, \text{inst}, \text{val})$ s.t.

(i) $O \subseteq OID$ is a finite set of object identifiers.
(ii)   inst: $C \to 2^o$ is a total function satisfying the following conditions:
   (a) If c, $c' \in C$ are not (direct or indirect) subclasses of each other, then $\text{inst}(c) \cap \text{inst}(c') = \emptyset$.
   (b) If c isa c', then $\text{inst}(c) \subseteq \text{inst}(c')$.
(iii) val: $O \to V$ is a function s.t. $(\forall c \in C)(\forall o \in \text{inst}(c))\text{val}(o) \in \text{dom}(\text{type}(c))$.

Figure 4 summarizes the central aspects of the object model we have just described, and which, as we said, can be found in this way or a closely related one in many such models.

Theory of Languages for Object-Oriented Databases

In this section, we sketch the theory of languages for object-oriented databases and try to indicate how research on this topic relates to and extends on earlier research conducted in the context of relational languages and their extensions.

It should not come as a surprise that languages for object-oriented databases can be classified into *algebraic* languages, *rule-based* ones, and SQL extensions. Although the latter category is the one that system developers concentrate on, the former two have led to considerable research, which has brought along a great variety of novel results. For concrete proposals, we refer the reader, for example, to the following references: Refs. 63 and 68–70 describe *object algebras*, whereas Refs. 71–76 represent important approaches to designing rule-based languages, central issues of which are the treatment of sets and negation, the simulation of nest and unnest operations, and evaluation techniques.

We mentioned in the second section that the notion of a query has been generalized in Ref. 19 to *database transformations*, which even encompass updates. The language proposed there for expressing (deterministic) transformations had the novel feature of being able to *invent* values, that is, to introduce new domain

class		*has*		**type**
	C	$\overrightarrow{\text{type}}$	T	
contains	$\downarrow$ inst		dom $\downarrow$	*describes*
	O	$\overrightarrow{\text{val}}$	V	
object		*has*		**value**

FIGURE 4   The central ingredients of an object model.

elements (in intermediate results of a computation). In object-oriented terms, value invention means object *creation*, and it soon turned out that object-oriented databases need the capability to create new objects not only in intermediate but also in final results. Next, we briefly sketch the concept of a database transformation, as it applies to object-oriented databases.

If D is a set of constants and O is a set of object identifiers, a *DO-isomorphism* is an isomorphism on $D \cup O$ mapping D to D and O to O; similarly, an *O-isomorphism* is a *DO*-isomorphism h such that $h(d) = d$ for each $d \in D$. *DO*-isomorphisms on instances like the ones defined earlier in this section can then be understood as binary relations, so that it is even possible to consider *nondeterministic* queries. In particular, a binary relation γ on instances is called a *database transformation* if the following conditions are satisfied:

* $(\exists S, S')\, \gamma \subseteq \mathrm{inst}(S) \times \mathrm{inst}(S')$, i.e., γ is well typed.
* γ is recursively enumerable (effective).
* $(I, J) \in \gamma$ implies $(h(I), h(J)) \in \gamma$ for each *DO*-isomorphism h, that is, γ is generic.
* $(I, J_1), (I, J_2) \in \gamma$ implies that there is an *O*-isomorphism h' such that $h'(J_1) = J_2$, that is, the output is allowed to contain new object identifiers.

The fourth property makes a transformation *determinate* (76). Although it is nondeterministic, the possible results of the transformation applied to a given input are equal up to renaming of new domain elements. In other words, object creation happens almost deterministically, where a commonly made restriction is that the *O*-isomorphism is the identical mapping on the constants involved. A generalization of this condition is *semideterminism* (77), where the *O*-isomorphism is required to leave the input invariant, that is, is a *DO*-automorphism. A nontrivial problem in this context is that of *copy elimination*; indeed, the language described in Ref. 76 is in a sense complete, but only up to copies. It is important to note that copies have nothing to do with *duplicate* elements in query results, which can occur because due to object identity, different objects especially in a set may represent the same value. A proposal for solving the copy elimination problem are the *constructive* queries introduced in Ref. 78. Further results on the expressive power of languages allowing queries like the ones just described can be found in Refs. 79–81. An excellent and comprehensive investigation of the impact of object identity on database manipulation is Ref. 82 (which among other things even establishes a connection between copies and duplicates).

TRANSACTIONS AND CONCURRENCY CONTROL THEORY

We now switch to a completely different database issue—in terms of the ANSI model, we now move from the conceptual to the internal level, in which once again lots of theoretical investigations have been undertaken with many fruitful results, this time directly for implementation purposes. The abstractions used to model the issues under consideration here are remarkably different from what we have discussed so far; in fact, they are even much simpler. Nevertheless, they turn out to be adequate in this context, and the theory which can be built on them is again a very rich one, and employs a number of mathematical techniques, for example, from logic or graph theory.

As was mentioned in the Introduction, a core DBMS functionality is to allow users shared access to a common database, and simultaneously to provide a certain degree of fault tolerance. For both purposes, a DBMS knows the concept of a *transaction* (83). The basic idea underlying the transaction concept is to consider a given program that wants to operate on a database as a logical unit, to process it as if the database was at its exclusive disposal, to require that it leaves the consistency of the database invariant, and to make sure that program effects survive later failures. This results in at least two problems that have to be solved: The *concurrency control problem* is to provide synchronization mechanisms which allow an efficient and correct access of multiple transactions to a shared database; the *recovery problem* is to provide mechanisms that can react to certain types of failures in an automated way.

To design such mechanisms, it is necessary to come up with a suitable *model* of transactions and their *executions*, to establish a notion of *correctness* of executions, and to devise *protocols* which achieve that. Although the basic problem is not new for computer systems in general, the database context has its special requirements, namely, to preserve the consistency of a given database and to provide each database program with a consistent view of the data even in the presence of failures, so that specific solutions are needed. One general paradigm here is *serializability theory*, which is based on a computational model in which (at least) the following "system components" are represented:

1. A *database*, that is, a set of objects on which certain operations can be executed
2. *Transactions*, considered as programs under execution and described as (finite) sequences of operations
3. *Schedules* for describing interleaved executions of distinct programs that operate on the same database
4. A notion of *conflict* for operations from distinct transactions occurring in a schedule

In what follows we will first make this program more precise in terms of the *read-write model* of (flat) transactions. As will then be indicated, various approaches to realizing that program can follow a uniform methodology. However, a number of issues will not be taken into account by that model, which motivates the search for others that at least for certain database applications seem more appropriate.

The Read–Write Model of Transactions

The most prominent transaction model (for centralized systems) considers transactions as *sequences of read and write operations*, thereby abstracting from all kinds of computations that a user program might execute in main memory or in its buffer. This model is justified by the fact that database programs, when executed, are treated by the underlying operating system like any other program; hence, they reside in main memory, are subject to execution scheduling, and are assigned a buffer space to manipulate data and to create results. However, transactions frequently access *secondary* memory via read and write operations, and as multiple transactions may access identical locations in that memory, it is the read and write operations that need to be synchronized.

Therefore, in the read–write model of transactions, the underlying database is considered as a countably infinite set $D = \{x, y, z, \ldots\}$ of objects, which (like pages) can be read or written in one step and atomically be transferred back and forth between primary and secondary memory. A *transaction* has the form $t = a_1$, $\cdots a_n$, where each a_i is of the form $r(x)$ ("read x") or $w(x)$ ("write x") for some $x \in D$. A *complete schedule* for transactions $t_1, \ldots, t_n$ is an ordering of all operations of these transactions, which respects the order of operations specified by the individual transactions and additionally contains a pseudostep for each transaction following its last operation that states whether this transactions finally *commits* (i.e., ends successfully) or *aborts* (i.e., is canceled prior to successful termination). If t_i appears in the schedule, a commit [abort] is indicated by c_i [a_i]. A *schedule* is a prefix of a complete schedule. A complete schedule is *serial* if for any two distinct transactions t_i and t_j appearing in it, either all of t_i precedes all of t_j or vice versa. Finally, two steps from distinct transactions are *in conflict* in a given schedule if they operate on the same database object and at least one of them is a write operation.

The following is an example of a complete schedule for four transactions, in which t_0, t_2, and t_3 are committed and t_1 is aborted:

$$s_1 = w_0(x)r_1(x)w_0(z)r_1(z)r_2(x)w_0(y)c_0r_3(z)w_3(z)w_2(y)c_2w_1(x)w_3(y)a_1c_3.$$

If T is a subset of the set of all transactions occurring in a schedule s, the *projection* of s onto T is obtained by erasing from s all steps from transactions not in T. For example, the projection of s_1 onto its committed transactions is the schedule

$$w_0(x)w_0(z)r_2(x)w_0(y)c_0r_3(z)w_3(z)w_2(y)c_2w_3(y)c_3.$$

A serial schedule for the original four transactions would be $s_2 = t_0t_2t_1t_3$. Note that, in general, there always exist $n!$ serial schedules for n transactions.

An important observation is that so far both transactions and schedules are purely *syntactic* objects, describing only the sequencing of data accesses performed by a database program, how these are interleaved, and what eventually happens to each transaction. A common assumption in traditional concurrency control theory is that the *semantics* of transactions are not known. On the other hand, a *pseudosemantics* can be associated with given transactions as follows. It is assumed that the (new) value of an object x written by some step $w(x)$ of a given transaction t depends on *all* values of objects that were previously read by t. The value of x read by some step $r(x)$ of t depends on the last $w(x)$ that occurred before $r(x)$ in t, or on the "initial" value of x if no such $w(x)$ exists. This can be extended to schedules in the obvious way, with the additional condition that transactions which are aborted in the schedule are ignored. For example, in the schedule s_1 above, t_1 reads x and z from t_0, but the value produced by $w_1(x)$ will not appear in the database. A formalization of this intuition can be given using tools from logic, where similar situations (i.e., the need to give a semantics to syntactic objects) occur; indeed, the *Herbrand semantics* of a schedule is formally defined, for example, in Ref. 84.

Note that the distinction between a complete schedule and a schedule correctly captures a dynamic situation, in which transactions arrive at a scheduling device step by step, and the device has to decide on the spot whether or not to execute a given step. For various reasons it might happen that the device at some point discovers that a transaction cannot be completed successfully, so that it has to output an abort operation for this transaction. We do not consider here how aborts (and also commits) are processed internally, but turn to the issue of schedule *correctness* next.

Serializability Notions and Recoverability

Because a serial schedule is always (complete and) correct in the sense that it preserves the consistency of the underlying database (assuming that the transactions it contains are consistency preserving), it makes sense to establish a correctness criterion for nonserial schedules on the basis of a relationship to serial ones. The common way to achieve this is by first introducing an appropriate notion of *equivalence* for schedules and then defining *serializability* via equivalence to a serial schedule. In fact, *all* notions of serializability described in the literature are obtained in this way, including *final-state* as well as *view serializability* (85,86). The former notion simply refers to the Herbrand semantics of schedules: Two schedules are final-state *equivalent* if they have the same pseudosemantics; a schedule is final-state *serializable* if there exists a serial schedule for the given transactions which is final-state equivalent to the schedule under consideration. The notion of view serializability seems intuitively more realistic, because it emphasizes the fact that equivalent schedules should have the same view on the database. We here restrict the attention to a notion of serializability which, although restricted when compared to the two just mentioned, enjoys a number of interesting properties: Unlike final-state or view serializability, which have an NP-complete decision problem, it can be tested in time linear in the number of unaborted transactions. It enjoys closure properties that are relevant for correctness in a dynamic setting, it allows to design simple protocols that can be implemented economically, and it can even be generalized in a variety of ways.

The *conflict relation* conf(s) of a schedule s consists of all pairs of steps (a, b) from distinct, unaborted transactions which are in conflict in s, and for which a occurs before b. If s and s' are two schedules for the same set of transactions, s and s' are *conflict equivalent*, denoted $s \approx_c s'$, if conf(s) = conf(s'). Finally, a complete schedule s is *conflict serializable* if there exists a serial schedule s' for the same set of transactions such that $s \approx_c s'$. Let CSR denote the class of all (complete and) conflict serializable schedules.

For example, it is easily verified for the schedule s_1 above that conf(s_1) = conf($t_0 t_2 t_3$). As the latter schedule, which ignores the aborted transaction t_1, is serial, $s_1 \in$ CSR. Another easy test whether a complete schedule s is in CSR is the following: First, construct the *conflict graph* $G(s) = (V, E)$ of s, whose set V of nodes consists of those transactions from s which are not aborted and which contains an edge of the form (t_i, t_j) in E if some step from t_i is in conflict with a subsequent step from t_j. Second, test this graph for acyclicity; indeed, as shown in Ref. 87, a schedule s is in CSR iff $G(s)$ is acyclic.

As is discussed, for example, in Ref. 84, serializability alone is not sufficient as a correctness criterion for schedules if transactions or the system may fail. There are two basic reasons for that: First, because any uncommitted transaction may abort or a system failure may cause all of them to abort, a correctness criterion must concern the committed ones only. Second, because a system failure may occur at any time during a transaction execution, if a schedule is correct, so must be each of its prefixes. Reference 84 formalizes these intuitions as *closure properties* of schedule properties, in particular closure under commit operations and under taking prefixes, and proves, for instance, that membership in the class CSR is a prefix commit-closed (pcc) property; that is, for each schedule $s \in$ CSR, the projection of any prefix of s onto the transactions committed therein is also in CSR. A schedule is *commit serializable* if the committed projection of any of its prefixes is serializable; that is, in a correct schedule the committed transactions have been executed in a serializable fashion at any point in time. Hence, a schedule must be commit serializable to ensure that the concurrent execution of transactions will not cause inconsistencies. A consequence is that CSR equals the class of all complete and commit conflict-serializable schedules. To ensure that a failure of transactions cannot cause the semantics of committed transactions to change, a schedule must additionally be *recoverable* in the following sense: If, in a schedule s, transaction t_i reads a value written by t_j and t_i is committed in s, then t_j is also committed and does so prior to t_i. In other words, at no time has a committed transaction read a value written by an uncommitted one. Ultimately, a *correct* schedule is one that is both commit serializable *and* recoverable. The latter, which is another pcc property, can be restricted in various ways, for example so that *cascading aborts* are avoided (where the abort of one transaction causes others to abort as well); details are in Ref. 84.

Designing Concurrency Control Protocols

Once a notion of schedule correctness is available, what remains to be done is to design a protocol capable of enforcing that. In the literature, numerous such protocols have been proposed (88,89); they all aim at the dynamic generation of conflict-serializable schedules and differ, for example, in their underlying philosophy: A *pessimistic* protocol is based on the assumption that conflicts between concurrent transactions are likely, so that provisions need to be taken to handle them. Known protocols in this class include *two-phase locking*, *time stamping*, and *serialization graph testing*. On the other hand, an *optimistic* protocol is based on the assumption that conflicts are rare. As a consequence, it is possible to schedule operations arbitrarily, and just make sure from time to time that the schedule generated was correct. Protocols based on this idea are known as *validation protocols*. Detailed descriptions of the protocols just mentioned and of many of their variations can be found in the cited references; here, we sketch the idea behind locking schedulers only, as these are most widely used in commercial systems, and also allow a theory that is interesting in its own right.

The basic idea underlying any locking scheduler is to require that accesses to database objects by distinct transactions are executed in a mutually exclusive way. In particular, a transaction cannot modify (write) an object as long as another transaction is still operating on it (reading or writing it). The central paradigm to implement this idea is the use of *locks*, which are set by the scheduler on behalf of a transaction before the latter reads or writes and which are removed after the access has been executed. For read and write operations, two types of lock operations are basically sufficient: If a transaction wants to read [write] an object, it requests a read lock [write lock] (or locks the object in *shared* [*exclusive*] mode). A read lock indicates to other transactions which want to write that the object in question is currently available for reading only; a write lock indicates that the object is currently not available.

Two locks from distinct transactions are in *conflict* if both refer to the same object and (at least) one of them is exclusive. In this case, only one of the requests can be granted because the requests are *incompatible*. A scheduler operates according to a *locking protocol* if in every schedule generated by it all simultaneously held locks are compatible; it operates according to a *two-phase locking* protocol (2PL) if, additionally, no transaction sets a new lock after it has released one. The most popular variant of 2PL is to hold all locks of a transaction until this transaction terminates (*strict* 2PL). A straightforward motivation for its use is that a point in time at which a scheduler can be sure that a transaction will not request any further locks is the end of the transaction.

It is easy to verify that 2PL is a *safe* protocol; that is, that every schedule generated by 2PL is conflict serializable. In addition, its strict variant even generates a subset of the recoverable schedules. Although this protocol is easy to implement, outperforms other protocols, and can easily be generalized to distributed systems, it also has its shortcomings. For example, it is not free of *deadlocks*, so that additional means need to be taken to discover and resolve these. Other protocols avoid deadlocks but do so at the expense of other restrictions.

From a theoretical point of view, an interesting observation is that 2PL is unable to generate *every* schedule in the class CSR. This raises the question of characterizing the exact power of locking. For this and related questions, a *geometrical interpretation* for locked transactions is described in Refs. 89–92, which for the case of two transactions is roughly as follows. For each transaction, its sequence of steps is represented as a sequence of equidistant integer points on one of the axes spanning the Euclidian plane. Thus, the two transactions define a rectangular *grid* in the plane. Grid points representing a pair of conflicting steps from the two transactions are *conflict points*, which fall into a *forbidden region* of the plane (when locking is used for synchronization) that is defined by the corresponding lock and unlock steps (points). A *schedule* becomes a monotone *curve* through the grid starting at point $(0, 0)$. *Legal* schedules are the ones that avoid forbidden regions, as any point within such a region represents a state in which the two transactions hold conflicting locks on the same object. However, legal schedules may not be serializable, but a legal schedule is serializable iff its curve does not *separate* two forbidden regions. To test whether a schedule is legal or whether it is serializable, it is now possible to employ techniques from computational geometry, which establishes an interesting connection between otherwise unrelated areas of computer science.

Generalizations of the Basic Theory

What we have described so far is the core of concurrency control theory, which centers around the read–write model and (conflict-based) serializability. We now survey a number of extensions and generalizations that have been investigated in recent years. A remarkable point to observe in this context is that, although the fundamentals of transaction theory date back to the late 1970s, even in the 1990s considerable contributions continue to be made even for basic issues.

As we said earlier, central to any model for concurrency control are three ingredients: a model for the underlying database, a model for transactions and schedules, and a notion of correctness for the latter. Basically, all extensions and generalizations of what we have described so far can be classified according to what modifications they make to any of these ingredients and whether these modifications touch one issue in isolation or a combination of them. We describe the major directions of such research in the remainder of this section.

The first major category of investigations has concentrated on schedule correctness in the classical setting (untyped databases, read–write transactions). For example, Refs. 93 and 94 exhibit various similarities between different serializability notions and propose unified frameworks. More promising from a practical viewpoint seems tackling the fact that *correct* schedules need to be both serializable and, say, recoverable. Instead of requiring that a schedule has both properties, it seems near at hand to investigate whether there is a *single* property of schedules ensuring correctness. Two important proposals in this direction are the notions of *commitment ordering* (95) and of *rigorousness* (96), which are relevant even in the context of heterogeneous databases (see below). More recently, a unifying framework was developed in Refs. 97 and 98, which seems to provide a theoretical underpinning for observations like the one made in Ref. 99 that concurrency control and recovery cannot be treated in isolation, but influence each other.

A first generalization that is based on an alternative database model is the assumption that database objects are not updated in place, but any write operation creates a new *version* of the object in question. The result, a *multiversion* database, has a number of nice applications; for example, concurrency control protocols can be relaxed, and recovery mechanisms can be made more flexible. A transaction on a multiversion database needs to be assigned a specific version when it wants to read some database object, and the proper assignment of versions is the major correctness issue in this context. The theory of multiversion concurrency control goes back to Refs. 100 and 101 and was further developed in Refs. 102 and 103; however, it was discovered only recently that the number of versions which can be distinguished in a database has a serious impact on schedule correctness (104). Other modifications of the database model assume that the database is no longer centralized, but *distributed*. This requires a modified transaction model, in which transactions (and hence schedules) are *partial orders* of steps; details are, for instance, in Ref. 105. A special case of a distributed database is that data objects are *replicated* in several locations; a formal study of this case was begun in Ref. 106. More recently, the database community has taken interest in *heterogeneous* distributed databases, which roughly are connections of several autonomous databases; a survey of concurrency control theory in this context is given in Ref. 107.

The second major category of investigations has departed from the classical transaction model. Again, there are several ways of doing this, including adding new operations to the read–write model, considering different types of operations, or giving up the idea that transactions are *flat* objects. Of particular interest nowadays are operations on *typed* databases, which, for example, are based on an object model or, more generally, contain instances of abstract data types (ADTs). The foundations of a concurrency control theory for ADTs go back to Ref. 108. Although analogons to classical correctness notions like serializability can still be established, more appropriate are new notions which take the properties of ADT transactions and especially the state of the underlying database into account (109). Along similar lines is the proposal made in Ref. 110, where user-level operations form the building blocks of transactions; an adequate notion of schedule correctness for the resulting transactions appears in Ref. 111.

Although most proposals of correctness criteria that depart from serializability rely on a transaction model other than the read–write one, even in this model various alternatives can be stated. For example, Ref. 112 proposes *predicatewise serializability* (PWSR), the idea of which is that if the database consistency constraint is in conjunctive normal form, it can be maintained by enforcing serializability only with respect to data items which share a disjunctive clause. For example, in a database with two objects x and y, consistency might be defined by two conjuncts, one of which is over x, the other over y. Now consider the following schedule:

$$s = r_1(x)w_1(x)r_2(x)r_2(y)w_2(y)r_1(y)w_1(y)c_1c_2.$$

Obviously, $s \notin$ CSR, but s is PWSR because it can be decomposed into the two schedules $s_1 = r_1(x)w_1(x)c_1r_2(x)c_2$ and $s_2 = r_2(y)w_2(y)c_2r_1(y)w_1(y)c_1$, each of which is even serial. The PWSR notion is actually more general and can be applied in a variety of other contexts as well. Another interesting correctness criterion called *orderability* was recently proposed in Ref. 113.

The final generalization we describe departs from the flatness of transactions. Such a departure is motivated, for example, by the fact that it has become common to organize a database management system as a hierarchy of functional layers and/ or layers of abstraction as described in the Introduction. A natural question to be asked then is why not make a transaction concept available at distinct layers of this hierarchy instead of just at the lowest one. Another observation is that sometimes complex activities cannot be modeled adequately with standard flat transactions. For example, consider a travel reservation activity consisting of flight reservations, car rentals, and hotel bookings. Although a trip can be made safely only if all reservations have been made successfully, there is no reason why they cannot be made in parallel, and it even makes sense to consider each as a subtransaction of the entire reservation transaction. This renders it possible to abort individual ones, for example, if a flight is fully booked and a switch to another needs to be made.

A more flexible interaction with a database is generally achievable if *flat* transactions are replaced by *nested* ones. As indicated by the reservation example, the basic idea is to allow transactions to contain other transactions as *subtransactions*, thereby giving transactions a tree structure whose leaves are elementary operations, but whose other nodes all represent transactions. If a subtransaction appears atomic to its parent, it can be reset without causing the parent to abort too. Furthermore, if subtransactions are isolated from each other, they can execute in parallel. Two prominent special cases of nested transactions are *closed* ones, in which subtransactions have to delay their commit until the end of their root transaction, and *open* ones in which subtransactions are allowed to commit autonomously. If all leaves in a transaction tree are of the same height, *multilevel* transactions result, in which the generation of subtransactions can be driven by the functional layers of the underlying system. The theory of nested transactions, initiated in Ref. 114 has been developed in a number of recent papers, including Refs. 115–117.

CONCLUSIONS

In this article, we have given an introduction to database theory, its historical development, and its major subjects of study. Although we have certainly not covered every aspect of database theory, we hopefully could convey to the reader that this theory has been and still is a vivid area, in which general techniques from mathematics and theoretical computer science continue to be applied, and the dedicated solutions this has produced continue to evolve. More importantly, database theory has never been a field that is just interesting in its own right, but it has had, and continues to have, a considerable impact on the development of database *systems*. Indeed, the database field is an area in which applications have very often triggered novel questions, which then led to theoretical investigations, whose result could, in turn, help to build better application software. For these reasons, database theory can serve as a good example of an area where computer *science* meets computer *engineering*; the former is interested in the underlying foundations, whereas the latter is concerned with building systems. In the database field, the two have always had strong impacts on each other, so that there is even a good reason for *teaching* database theory. It is our hope that this survey could demonstrate why these things are so and that it will motivate readers to look into database theory in more depth.

REFERENCES

1. D. Tsichritzis and A. Klug, "The ANSI/X3/SPARC DBMS Framework Report of the Study Group on Database Management Systems," *Inform. Syst., 3*, 173–191 (1978).
2. G. Vossen, *Data Models, Database Languages, and Database Management Systems*, Addison-Wesley, Wokingham, UK, 1991.
3. E. F. Codd, "A Relational Model of Data for Large Shared Data Banks," *Commun. ACM, 13*, 377–387 (1970).
4. U. Lipeck and G. Saake, "Monitoring Dynamic Integrity Constraints Based on Temporal Logic," *Inform. Syst., 12*, 255–269 (1987).
5. M. Y. Vardi, "Fundamentals of Dependency Theory," In E. Börger (ed.), *Trends in Theoretical Computer Science*, Computer Science Press, Rockville, MD, 1988, pp. 171–224.
6. D. Maier, *The Theory of Relational Databases*, Computer Science Press, Rockville, MD, 1983.
7. W. W. Armstrong, "Dependency Structures of Data Base Relationships," in *Proc. IFIP Congress*, 1974, pp. 580–583.
8. Y. E. Lien, "Relational Database Design," in S. B. Yao (ed.), *Principles of Database Design*, Vol. 1: *Logical Organizations*, Prentice-Hall, Englewood Cliffs, NJ, 1985, pp. 211–254.
9. P. Atzeni and V. De Antonellis, *Relational Database Theory*. Benjamin-Cummings, Redwood City, CA, 1993.
10. H. Mannila and K. J. Räihä, *The Design of Relational Databases*. Addison-Wesley, Wokingham, U.K., 1992.

11. P. C. Kanellakis, "Elements of Relational Database Theory," in J. Van Leeuwen (ed.), *Handbook of Theoretical Computer Science, Vol. B: Formal Models and Semantics*, North-Holland, Amsterdam, 1990, pp. 1073–1156.

12. C. H. Papadimitriou, *Computational Complexity*, Addison-Wesley, Reading, MA, 1994.

13. J. Paredaens, P. De Bra, M. Gyssens, and D. Van Gucht, *The Structure of the Relational Database Model*, EATCS Monographs on Theoretical Computer Science 17, Springer-Verlag, Berlin, 1989.

14. J. D. Ullman, *Principles of Database and Knowledge-Base Systems*, Vol. I, Computer Science Press, Rockville, MD, 1988.

15. R. Demolombe, "Syntactical Characterization of a Subset of Domain-Independent Formulas," *J. ACM, 39*, 71–94 (1992).

16. J. Melton and A. R. Simon, *Understanding the New SQL: A Complete Guide*, Morgan-Kaufmann, San Francisco, CA, 1993.

17. F. Bancilhon, "On the Completeness of Query Languages for Relational Databases," in *Proc. Mathematical Foundations of Computer Science*, Springer-Verlag, Berlin, 1978, pp. 112–124.

18. J. Paredaens, "On the Expressive Power of the Relational Algebra," *Inform. Processing Lett., 7*, 107–111 (1978).

19. S. Abiteboul and V. Vianu, "Procedural Languages for Database Queries and Update," *J. Computer Syst. Sci., 41*, 181–229 (1990).

20. S. Abiteboul, "Updates, A New Frontier," in *Proc. 2nd International Conference on Database Theory (ICDT)*, Springer-Verlag, Berlin, 1988, pp. 1–18.

21. K. R. Apt and M. H. Van Emden, "Contributions to the Theory of Logic Programming," *J. ACM, 29*, 841–862 (1982).

22. M. H. Van Emden and R. A. Kowalski, "The Semantics of Predicate Logic as a Programming Language," *J. ACM, 23*, 733–742 (1976).

23. S. Ceri, G. Gottlob, and L. Tanca, *Logic Programming and Databases*, Springer-Verlag, Berlin, 1990.

24. J. D. Ullman, *Principles of Database and Knowledge-Base Systems*, Vol. II, Computer Science Press, Rockville, MD, 1989.

25. S. Abiteboul and V. Vianu, "Datalog Extensions for Database Queries and Updates," *J. Computer Syst. Sci., 43*, 62–124 (1991).

26. N. Bidoit, "Negation in Rule-Based Database Languages: A Survey," *Theoret. Computer Sci., 78*, 3–83 (1991).

27. S. Naqvi and S. Tsur, *A Logical Language for Data and Knowledge Bases*. Computer Science Press, New York, 1989.

28. J. D. Ullman, "The Interface Between Language Theory and Database Theory," in *Theoretical Studies in Computer Science*, J. D. Ullman (ed.), Academic Press, Boston, MA, 1992, pp. 133–151.

29. M. Y. Vardi, "Automata Theory for Database Theoreticians," in *Theoretical Studies in Computer Science*, J. D. Ullman (ed.), Academic Press, Boston, MA, 1992, pp. 153–180.

30. F. Bancilhon and R. Ramakrishnan, "An Amateur's Introduction to Recursive Query Processing Strategies," in *Proc. ACM SIGMOD International Conference on Management of Data*, ACM Press, New York, 1986, pp. 16–52.

31. F. Bry, "Query Evaluation in Recursive Databases: Bottom-Up and Top-Down Reconciled," *Data Knowledge Eng., 5*, 289–312 (1990).

32. A. V. Aho and J. D. Ullman, "Universality of Data Retrieval Languages," in *Proc. 6th ACM Symposium on Principles of Programming Languages*, ACM Press, New York, 1979, pp. 110–120.

33. A. K. Chandra and D. Harel, "Computable Queries for Relational Data Bases," *J. Computer Syst. Sci., 21*, 156–178 (1980).

34. A. K. Chandra and D. Harel, "Structure and Complexity of Relational Queries," *J. Computer Syst. Sci., 25*, 99–128 (1982).

35. N. Immermann, "Relational Queries Computable in Polynomial Time," *Inform. Control, 68*, 86–104 (1986).

36. J. Van den Bussche, D. Van Gucht, and G. Vossen, "Reflective Programming in the Relational Algebra," in *Proc. 12th ACM SIGACT–SIGMOD–SIGART Symposium on Principles of Database Systems*, ACM Press, New York, 1993, pp. 17–25.

37. S. Abiteboul and V. Vianu, "Expressive Power of Query Languages," in *Theoretical Studies in Computer Science*, J. D. Ullman (ed.), Academic Press, Boston, 1992, pp. 207–251.

38. A. K. Chandra, "Theory of Database Queries," in *Proc. 7th ACM SIGACT–SIG-MOD–SIGART Symposium on Principles of Database Systems*, ACM Press, New York, 1988, pp. 1–9.

39. M. Y. Vardi, "The Complexity of Relational Query Languages," in *Proc. 14th ACM Symposium on Theory of Computing*, ACM Press, New York, 1982, pp. 137–146.

40. N. Immermann, "Languages That Capture Complexity Classes," *SIAM J. Comput., 16*, 760–778 (1987).

41. S. Abiteboul and V. Vianu, "Generic Computation and Its Complexity," in *Proc. 23rd ACM Symposium on Theory of Computing*, ACM Press, New York, 1991, pp. 209–219.

42. S. Abiteboul and V. Vianu, "Computing with First-Order Logic," *J. Computer Syst. Sci.* (1995).

43. S. Abiteboul, M. Y. Vardi, and V. Vianu, "Fixpoint Logics, Relational Machines, and Computational Complexity," in *Proc. 7th Annual IEEE Conference on Structure in Complexity Theory*. IEEE Computer Society Press, Los Alamitos, CA, 1992.

44. S. Abiteboul, C. H. Papadimitriou, and V. Vianu, "The Power of Reflective Relational Machines," in *Proc. 9th Annual IEEE Symposium on Logic in Computer Science*, IEEE Computer Society Press, Los Alamitos, CA, 1994.

45. A. Makinouchi, "A Consideration on Normal Form of Not-Necessarily-Normalized Relation in the Relational Data Model," in *Proc. 3rd International Conference on Very Large Data Bases*, 1977, pp. 447–453.

46. G. Jäschke and H. J. Schek, "Remarks on the Algebra of Non First Normal Form Relations," in *Proc. 1st ACM SIGACT–SIGMOD Symposium on Principles of Database Systems*, ACM Press, New York, 1982, pp. 124–138.

47. H. J. Schek and M. H. Scholl, "The Relational Model with Relation-Valued Attributes," *Inform. Syst., 11*, 137–147 (1986).

48. S. J. Thomas and P. C. Fischer, "Nested Relational Structures," in *Advances in Computing Research, Vol. 3: The Theory of Databases*, P. C. Kanellakis and F. P. Preparata (eds.), JAI Press, Greenwich, CT, 1986, pp. 269–307.

49. M. A. Roth, H. F. Korth, and A. Silberschatz, "Extended Algebra and Calculus for Nested Relational Databases," *ACM Trans. Database Syst., 13*, 389–417 (1988).

50. A. U. Tansel and L. Garnett, "On Roth, Korth, and Silberschatz's Extended Algebra and Calculus for Nested Relational Databases," *ACM Trans. Database Syst., 17*, 374–383 (1992).

51. S. Abiteboul, P. C. Fischer, H. J. Schek (eds.), *Nested Relations and Complex Objects in Databases*, Springer-Verlag, Berlin, 1989.

52. J. Paredaens and D. Van Gucht, "Converting Nested Algebra Expressions into Flat Algebra Expressions," *ACM Trans. Database Syst., 17*, 65–93 (1992).

53. M. Gyssens and D. Van Gucht, "A Comparison Between Algebraic Query Languages for Flat and Nested Databases," *Theoret. Computer Sci., 87*, 263–286 (1991).

54. M. Gyssens and D. Van Gucht, "The Powerset Algebra as a Natural Tool to Handle Nested Database Relations," *J. Computer Syst. Sci., 45*, 76–103 (1992).

55. S. Abiteboul, M. Gyssens, and D. Van Gucht, "An Alternative Way to Represent the

Cogroup of a Relation in the Context of Nested Databases," *Inform. Processing Lett., 32*, 317–324 (1989).

56. S. Grumbach and T. Milo, "Towards Tractable Algebras for Bags," in *Proc. 12th ACM SIGACT–SIGMOD–SIGART Symposium on Principles of Database Systems*, ACM Press, New York, 1993, pp. 49–58.

57. F. Bancilhon and S. Khoshafian, "A Calculus for Complex Objects," *J. Computer Syst. Sci., 38*, 326–340 (1989).

58. R. Hull, "A Survey of Theoretical Research on Typed Complex Database Objects," in *Databases*, J. Paredaens (ed.), Academic Press, London, 1987, pp. 193–256.

59. E. Bertino and L. Martino, *Object-Oriented Database Systems*. Addison-Wesley, Wokingham, U.K., 1993.

60. M. Atkinson, F. Bancilhon, D. DeWitt, K. Dittrich, D. Maier, and S. Zdonik, "The Object-Oriented Database System Manifesto," in *Proc. 1st International Conference on Deductive and Object-Oriented Databases*, 1989, pp. 40–57.

61. A. Kemper and G. Moerkotte, *Object-Oriented Database Management — Applications in Engineering and Computer Science*, Prentice-Hall, Englewood Cliffs, NJ, 1994.

62. F. Bancilhon, C. Delobel, and P. Kanellakis, *Building an Object-Oriented Database System — The Story of O_2*, Morgan-Kaufmann, San Francisco, CA, 1992.

63. D. D. Straube and M. T. Özsu, "Queries and Query Processing in Object-Oriented Database Systems," *ACM Trans. Office Inform. Syst., 8*, 387–430 (1990).

64. C. Lecluse and P. Richard "Foundations of the O_2 Database System," *IEEE Data Eng. Bull., 14*(2), 28–32 (1991).

65. R. Hull, K. Tanaka, and M. Yoshikawa, "Behavior Analysis of Object-Oriented Databases: Method Structure, Execution Trees, and Reachability," in *Proc. 3rd FODO Conference*, Springer-Verlag, Berlin, 1989, pp. 372–388.

66. S. Abiteboul, P. C. Kanellakis, and E. Waller, "Method Schemas," in *Proc. 9th ACM SIGACT–SIGMOD–SIGART Symposium on Principles of Database Systems*, ACM Press, New York, 1990, pp. 16–27.

67. K. Denninghoff and V. Vianu, "The Power of Methods with Parallel Semantics," UCSD Technical Report No. CS91-184, University of California, San Diego (February 1991); extended abstract in *Proc. 17th International Conference on Very Large Data Bases*, pp. 221–232.

68. S. Cluet, C. Delobel, C. Lecluse, and P. Richard, "RELOOP, An Algebra Based Query Language for an Object-Oriented Database System," *Data Knowledge Eng., 5*, 333–352 (1990).

69. J. C. Freytag, D. Maier, G. Vossen (eds.), *Query Processing for Advanced Database Systems*, Morgan-Kaufmann, San Francisco, CA, 1994.

70. S. L. Vandenberg and D. J. DeWitt, "Algebraic Support for Complex Objects with Arrays, Identity, and Inheritance," in *Proc. ACM SIGMOD International Conference on Management of Data*, ACM Press, New York, 1991, pp. 158–167.

71. S. Abiteboul, G. Lausen, H. Uphoff, and E. Waller, "Methods and Rules," in *Proc. ACM SIGMOD International Conference on Management of Data*, ACM Press, New York, 1991, pp. 32–41.

72. S. Brass and U. Lipeck, "Semantics of Inheritance in Logical Object Specifications," in *Proc. 2nd International Conference on Deductive and Object-Oriented Databases*, Springer-Verlag, Berlin, 1991, pp. 411–430.

73. R. Hull and M. Yoshikawa, "ILOG: Declarative Creation and Manipulation of Object Identifiers," in *Proc. 16th International Conference on Very Large Data Bases*, Morgan-Kaufmann, San Francisco, CA, 1990, pp. 455–468.

74. M. Kifer and G. Lausen, "F-logic: A Higher-Order Language for Reasoning About Objects, Inheritance, and Scheme," in *Proc. ACM SIGMOD International Conference on Management of Data*, ACM Press, New York, 1989, pp. 134–146.

75. M. Kifer, G. Lausen, and J. Wu, "Logical Foundations of Object-Oriented and Frame-Based Languages," Technical Report 93/06, Department of Computer Science, SUNY, Stony Brook, New York (1993) to appear in *J. ACM.*

76. S. Abiteboul and P. C. Kanellakis, "Object Identity as a Query Language Primitive," in *Proc. ACM SIGMOD International Conference on Management of Data*, ACM Press, New York, 1989, pp. 159–173.

77. J. Van den Bussche and D. Van Gucht, "Semi-determinism," in *Proc. 11th ACM SIGACT–SIGMOD–SIGART Symposium on Principles of Database Systems*, ACM Press, New York, 1992, pp. 191–201.

78. J. Van den Bussche, D. Van Gucht, M. Andries, and M. Gyssens, "On the Completeness of Object-Creating Query Languages," in *Proc. 33rd Annual IEEE Symposium on Foundations of Computer Science*, IEEE Computer Society Press, Los Alamitos, CA, 1992, pp. 372–379.

79. S. Grumbach and V. Vianu, "Tractable Query Languages for Complex Object Databases," in *Proc. 10th ACM SIGACT–SIGMOD–SIGART Symposium on Principles of Database Systems*, ACM Press, New York, 1991, pp. 315–327.

80. R. Hull and J. Su, "On the Expressive Power of Database Queries with Intermediate Types," *J. Computer Syst. Sci., 43*, 219–267 (1991).

81. R. Hull and J. Su, "Algebraic and Calculus Query Languages for Recursively Typed Complex Objects," *J. Computer Syst. Sci., 47*, 121–156 (1993).

82. J. Van den Bussche, "Formal Aspects of Object Identity in Database Manipulation," dissertation, University of Antwerp, Belgium (1993).

83. J. Gray, "Notes on Data Base Operating Systems," in *Operating Systems—An Advanced Course*, R. Bayer, M. R. Graham, G. Seegmüller (eds.), Springer-Verlag, Berlin, 1978, pp. 393–481.

84. V. Hadzilacos, "A Theory of Reliability in Database Systems," *J. ACM, 35*, 121–145 (1988).

85. C. H. Papadimitriou, "The Serializability of Concurrent Database Updates," *J. ACM, 26*, 631–653 (1979).

86. M. Yannakakis, "Serializability by Locking," *J. ACM, 31*, 227–244 (1984).

87. K. P. Eswaran, J. N. Gray, R. A. Lorie, and I. L. Traiger, "The Notions of Consistency and Predicate Locks in a Database System," *Commun. ACM, 19*, 624–633 (1976).

88. P. A. Bernstein, V. Hadzilacos, and N. Goodman, *Concurrency Control and Recovery in Database Systems*, Addison-Wesley, Reading, MA, 1987.

89. C. H. Papadimitriou, *The Theory of Database Concurrency Control*, Computer Science Press, Rockville, MD, 1986.

90. C. H. Papadimitriou, "A Theorem in Database Concurrency Control," *J. ACM, 29*, 998–1006 (1982).

91. C. H. Papadimitriou, "Concurrency Control by Locking," *SIAM J. Comput., 12*, 215–226 (1983).

92. G. Lausen, E. Soisalon-Soininen, and P. Widmayer, "On the Power of Safe Locking," *J. Computer Syst. Sci., 40*, 269–288 (1990).

93. K. Vidyasankar, "Generalized Theory of Serializability," *Acta Inform., 24*, 105–119 (1987).

94. K. Vidyasankar, "Unified Theory of Database Serializability," *Fund. Inform., XIV*, 147–183 (1991).

95. Y. Raz, "The Principle of Commitment Ordering, or Guaranteeing Serializability in a Heterogeneous Environment of Multiple Autonomous Resource Managers Using Atomic Commitment," in *Proc. 18th International Conference on Very Large Data Bases*, Morgan-Kaufmann, San Francisco, CA, 1992, pp. 292–312.

96. Y. Breitbart, D. Georgakopoulos, M. Rusinkiewicz, and A. Silberschatz, "On Rigorous Transaction Scheduling," *IEEE Trans. Software Eng., 17*, 954–960 (1991).

97. H. J. Schek, G. Weikum, and H. Ye, "Towards a Unified Theory of Concurrency

Control and Recovery," in *Proc. 12th ACM SIGACT–SIGMOD–SIGART Symposium on Principles of Database Systems*, ACM Press, New York, 1993, pp. 300–311.

98. G. Alonso, R. Vingralek, D. Agrawal, Y. Breitbart, A. El Abbadi, H. J. Schek, and G. Weikum, "A Unified Approach to Concurrency Control and Transaction Recovery," in *Proc. 4th International Conference on Extending Database Technology*, Springer-Verlag, Berlin, 1994, pp. 123–130.

99. W. Weihl, "The Impact of Recovery on Concurrency Control," *J. Computer Syst. Sci., 47*, 157–184 (1993).

100. P. A. Bernstein and N. Goodman, "Multiversion Concurrency Control — Theory and Algorithms," *ACM Trans. Database Syst., 8*, 465–483 (1983).

101. G. Lausen, "Formal Aspects of Optimistic Concurrency Control in a Multiple Version Database System," *Inform. Syst., 8*, 291–301 (1983).

102. C. H. Papadimitriou and P. C. Kanellakis, "On Concurrency Control by Multiple Versions," *ACM Trans. Database Syst., 9*, 89–99 (1984).

103. T. Hadzilacos and C. H. Papadimitriou, "Algorithmic Aspects of Multiversion Concurrency Control," *J. Computer Syst. Sci., 33*, 297–310 (1986).

104. T. Morzy, "The Correctness of Concurrency Control for Multiversion Database Systems with Limited Number of Versions," in *Proc. 9th IEEE International Conference on Data Engineering*, IEEE Computer Society Press, Los Alamitos, CA, 1993, pp. 595–604.

105. W. Cellary, E. Gelenbe, and T. Morzy, *Concurrency Control in Distributed Database Systems*, North-Holland, Amsterdam, 1988.

106. P. A. Bernstein and N. Goodman, "Serializability Theory for Replicated Databases," *J. Computer Syst. Sci., 31*, 355–374 (1985).

107. Y. Breitbart, H. Garcia-Molina, and A. Silberschatz, "Overview of Multidatabase Transaction Management," *VLDB J., 1*, 181–239 (1992).

108. P. M. Schwarz and A. Z. Spector, "Synchronizing Shared Abstract Types," *ACM Trans. Computer Syst., 2*, 223–250 (1984).

109. W. Weihl, "Local Atomicity Properties: Modular Concurrency Control for Abstract Data Types," *ACM Trans. Program. Languages Syst., 11*, 249–282 (1989).

110. V. Vianu and G. Vossen, "Conceptual Level Concurrency Control for Relational Update Transactions," *Theoret. Computer Sci., 95*, 1–42 (1992).

111. V. Vianu and G. Vossen, "Static and Dynamic Aspects of Goal-Oriented Concurrency Control," *Ann. Math. Artif. Intell., 7*, 257–287 (1993).

112. R. Rastogi, S. Mehrotra, Y. Breitbart, H. F. Korth, and A. Silberschatz, "On Correctness of Non-serializable Executions," in *Proc. 12th ACM SIGACT-SIGMOD-SIGART Symposium on Principles of Database Systems*, ACM Press, New York, 1993, pp. 97–108.

113. D. Agrawal, A. El Abbadi, and A. K. Singh, "Consistency and Orderability: Semantics-Based Correctness Criteria for Databases," *ACM Trans. Database Syst., 18*, 460–486 (1993).

114. J. E. B. Moss, *Nested Transactions: An Approach to Reliable Distributed Computing*, MIT Press, Cambridge, MA, 1985.

115. G. Weikum, "Principles and Realization Strategies of Multilevel Transaction Management," *ACM Trans. Database Syst., 16*, 132–180 (1991).

116. N. Lynch and M. Merritt, "Introduction to the Theory of Nested Transactions," *Theoret. Computer Sci., 62*, 123–185 (1988).

117. N. Lynch, M. Merritt, W. Weihl, and A. Fekete, *Atomic Transactions*, Morgan-Kaufmann, San Francisco, CA, 1994.

BIBLIOGRAPHY

The following is a bibliography containing further references on the topics covered in this article, including dependency theory, nested relations, or object-oriented databases and their query languages. In addition, the bibliography has listings for a number of issues not covered in this article but for which a considerable body of theory has been developed; these include formal properties of relational database schemas, normalization and algorithmic schema design, null values in database relations, the universal relation data model, and database updating. It also contains several additional survey papers on the subject of database theory.

Abiteboul, S., R. Hull, and V. Vianu, *Foundations of Databases*. Addison-Wesley, Reading, MA (1995).

Abiteboul, S., M. Y. Vardi, and V. Vianu, "Computing with Infinitary Logic," in *Proc. 4th International Conference on Database Theory*, Springer-Verlag, Berlin, 1992, pp. 113–123.

Atzeni, P. and E. P. F. Chan, "Efficient and Optimal Query Answering on Independent Schemes," *Theoret. Computer Sci., 77*, 291–308 (1990).

Atzeni, P. and R. Torlone, "Updating Relational Databases Through Weak Instance Interfaces," *ACM Trans. Database Syst., 17*, 718–745 (1992).

Beeri, C., "On the Membership Problem for Functional and Multivalued Dependencies in Relational Databases," *ACM Trans. Database Syst., 5*, 241–259 (1980).

Beeri, C., "Formal Models for Object Oriented Databases," in *Proc. 1st International Conference on Deductive and Object-Oriented Databases* (1989), pp. 370–395.

Beeri, C. and P. A. Bernstein, "Computational Problems Related to the Design of Normal Form Relational Schemas," *ACM Trans. Database Syst., 4*, 30–59 (1979).

Beeri, C. and M. Kifer, "An Integrated Approach to Logical Design of Relational Database Schemes," *ACM Trans. Database Syst., 11*, 134–158 (1986).

Beeri, C., R. Fagin, and J. H. Howard, "A Complete Axiomatization for Functional and Multivalued Dependencies," in *Proc. ACM SIGMOD International Conference on Management of Data, ACM Press*, New York, 1977, pp. 47–61.

Beeri, C., P. A. Bernstein, and N. Goodman, "A Sophisticate's Introduction to Database Normalization Theory," in *Proc. 4th International Conference on Very Large Data Bases* (1978), pp. 113–124.

Beeri, C., M. Dowd, R. Fagin, and R. Stratman, "On the Structure of Armstrong Relations for Functional Dependencies," *J. ACM, 31*, 30–46 (1984).

Beeri, C. and Y. Kornatzky, "Algebraic Optimization of Object-Oriented Query Languages," in *Proc. 3rd International Conference on Database Theory*, Springer-Verlag, Berlin, 1990, pp. 72–88.

Bernstein, P. A., "Synthesizing Third Normal Form Relations from Functional Dependencies," *ACM Trans. Database Syst., 1*, 272–298 (1976).

Bernstein, P. A. and N. Goodman, "What Does Boyce–Codd Normal Form Do?" in *Proc. 6th International Conference on Very Large Data Bases* (1980), pp. 245–259.

Bertino, E., M. Negri, G. Pelagatti, and L. Sbattella, "Object-Oriented Query Languages: The Notion and the Issues," *IEEE Trans. Knowledge Data Eng., 4*, pp. 223–237 (1992).

Biskup, J., "On the Complementation Rule for Multivalued Dependencies in Database Relations," *Acta Inform., 10*, 297–305 (1978).

Biskup, J., "A Formal Approach to Null Values in Database Relations," in *Advances in Database Theory*, Vol. 1, H. Gallaire, J. Minker, and J. M. Nicolas, (eds.), Plenum Press, New York, 1981, pp. 299–341.

Biskup, J., "A Foundation of Codd's Relational Maybe-Operations," *ACM Trans. Database Syst., 8*, 608–636 (1983).

Biskup, J., "Boyce-Codd Normal Form and Object Normal Forms," *Inform. Processing Lett., 32*, 29–33 (1989).

Biskup, J. and H. H. Brüggemann, "Universal Relation Views: A Pragmatic Approach," in *Proc. 9th International Conference on Very Large Data Bases* (1983), pp. 172–185.

Biskup, J. and B. Convent, "A Formal View Integration Method," in *Proc. ACM SIGMOD International Conference on Management of Data*, ACM Press, New York, 1986, pp. 398–407.

Biskup, J., J. Demetrovics, L. O. Libkin, and I. B. Muchnik, "On Relational Database Schemes Having Unique Minimal Key," *J. Inform. Processing and Cybern., 27*, 217–225 (1991).

Biskup, J. and P. Dublish, "Objects in Relational Database Schemes with Functional, Inclusion and Exclusion Dependencies," *Theoret. Inform. and Applic., 27*, 183–219 (1993).

Biskup, J. and R. Meyer, "Design of Relational Database Schemes by Deleting Attributes in the Canonical Decomposition," *J. Computer Syst. Sci., 35*, 1–22 (1987).

Biskup, J., U. Dayal, and P. A. Bernstein, "Synthesizing Independent Database Schemas," in *Proc. ACM SIGMOD International Conference on Management of Data*, ACM Press, New York, 1979.

Biskup, J., H. H. Brüggemann, M. Kramer, and L. Schnetgöke, "One-flavor Assumption and γ-Acyclicity for Universal Relation Views," in *Proc. 5th ACM SIGACT–SIGMOD Symposium on Principles of Database Systems*, ACM Press, New York, 1986, pp. 148–159.

Brosda, V. and G. Vossen, "Update and Retrieval in a Relational Database Through a Universal Schema Interface," *ACM Trans. Database Syst., 13*, 449–485 (1988).

Casanova, M. A., R. Fagin, and C. H. Papadimitriou, "Inclusion Dependencies and Their Interaction with Functional Dependencies," *J. Computer Syst. Sci., 28*, 29–59 (1984).

Chakravarthy, U. S., J. Grant, and J. Minker, "Logic-Based Approach to Semantic Query Optimization," *ACM Trans. Database Syst., 15*, 162–207 (1990).

Codd, E. F., "Further Normalization of the Data Base Relational Model," in *Data Base Systems*, R. Rustin (ed.), Prentice-Hall, Englewood Cliffs, NJ, 1971, pp. 33–64.

Convent, B., "Unsolvable Problems Related to the View Integration Approach," in *Proc. 1st International Conference on Database Theory*, Springer-Verlag, Berlin, 1986, pp. 141–156.

Cosmadakis, S. S., P. C. Kanellakis, and M. Y. Vardi, "Polynomial-Time Implication Problems for Unary Inclusion Dependencies," *J. ACM, 37*, 15–46 (1990).

Date, C. J. and R. Fagin, "Simple Conditions for Guaranteeing Higher Normal Forms in Relational Databases," *ACM Trans. Database Syst., 17*, 465–476 (1992).

Delobel, C. and R. G. Casey, "Decomposition of a Data Base and the Theory of Boolean Switching Functions," *IBM J. Res. Dev., 17*, 374–386 (1973).

Fagin, R., "The Decomposition Versus the Synthetic Approach to Relational Database Design," in *Proc. 3rd International Conference on Very Large Data Bases* (1977), pp. 441–446.

Fagin, R., "Multivalued Dependencies and a New Normal Form for Relational Databases," *ACM Trans. Database Syst., 2*, 262–278 (1977).

Fagin, R., "Functional Dependencies in a Relational Database and Propositional Logic," *IBM J. Res. Dev., 21*, 534–544 (1977).

Fagin, R., "Normal Forms and Relational Database Operators," in *Proc. ACM SIGMOD International Conference on Management of Data*, ACM Press, New York, 1979, pp. 153–160.

Fagin, R., "A Normal Form for Relational Databases That Is Based on Domains and Keys," *ACM Trans. Database Syst., 6*, 387–415 (1981).

Fagin, R., "Horn Clauses and Database Dependencies," *J. ACM, 29*, 952–985 (1982).

Fagin, R., "Degrees of Acyclicity for Hypergraphs and Relational Database Schemes," *J. ACM, 30*, 514–550 (1983).

Fagin, R., "Finite Model Theory: A Personal Perspective," *Theoret. Computer Sci., 116*, 3–31 (1993).

Fagin, R. and M. Y. Vardi, "The Theory of Data Dependencies—An Overview," in *Proc. 11th International Colloquium on Automata, Languages, and Programming (ICALP)*, Springer-Verlag, Berlin, 1984, pp. 1–22.

Fischer, P. C., L. V. Saxton, S. J. Thomas, and D. Van Gucht, "Interactions Between Dependencies and Nested Relational Structures," *J. Computer Syst. Sci., 31*, 343–354 (1985).

Goodman, N, O. Shmueli, and Y. C. Tay, "GYO Reductions, Canonical Connections, Tree and Cyclic Schemas, and Tree Projections," *J. Computer Syst. Sci., 29*, 338–358 (1984).

Grumbach, S., "A Paradox in Database Theory," in *Proc. 4th International Conference on Database Theory*, Springer-Verlag, Berlin, 1992, pp. 312–325.

Grumbach, S. and C. Tollu, "Query Languages with Counters," in *Proc. 4th International Conference on Database Theory*, Springer-Verlag, Berlin, 1992, pp. 124–139.

Gurevich, Y., "Logic and the Challenge of Computer Science," in E. Börger (ed.), *Trends in Theoretical Computer Science*, Computer Science Press, Rockville, MD, 1988, pp. 1–57.

Gyssens, M., J. Paredaens, and D. Van Gucht, "A Uniform Approach Toward Handling Atomic and Structured Information in the Nested Relational Database Model," *J. ACM, 36*, 790–825 (1989).

Hull, R. and R. King, "Semantic Database Modeling: Survey, Applications, and Research Issues," *ACM Comput. Surveys, 19*, 201–260 (1987).

Immermann, N., "Descriptive and Computational Complexity," in J. Hartmanis (ed.), *Computational Complexity Theory*, American Mathematical Society, Providence, RI, 1989, pp. 75–91.

Jou, J. H. and P. C. Fischer, "The Complexity of Recognizing 3NF Relation Schemes," *Inform. Processing Lett., 14*, 187–190 (1982).

Katona, G. O. H., "Combinatorial and Algebraic Results for Database Relations," in *Proc. 4th International Conference on Database Theory*, Springer-Verlag, Berlin, 1992, pp. 1–20.

Kolaitis, P. G. and C. H. Papadimitriou, "Why Not Negation by Fixpoint?" *J. Computer Syst. Sci., 43*, 125–144 (1991).

Korth, H. F., G. M. Kuper, J. Feigenbaum, A. Van Gelder, and J. D. Ullman, "System/U: A Database System Based on the Universal Relation Assumption," *ACM Trans. Database Syst., 9*, 331–347 (1984).

Laurent, D., V. Phan Luong, and N. Spyratos, "Database Updating Revisited," in *Proc. 3rd International Conference on Deductive and Object-Oriented Databases*, Springer-Verlag, Berlin, 1993, pp. 296–309.

Laurent, D., V. Phan Luong, and N. Spyratos, "The Use of Deleted Tuples in Database Querying and Updating," submitted for publication (1994).

Lecluse, C. and N. Spyratos, "Implementing Queries and Updates on Universal Scheme Interfaces," in *Proc. 14th International Conference on Very Large Data Bases*, Morgan-Kaufmann, San Francisco, CA, 1988, pp. 62–75.

Lipeck, U., "Transformation of Dynamic Integrity Constraints into Transaction Specifications," *Theoret. Computer Sci., 76*, 115–142 (1990).

Maier, D., "Minimum Covers in the Relational Database Model," *J. ACM, 27*, 664–674 (1980).

Maier, D. and J. D. Ullman, "Connections in Acyclic Hypergraphs," *Theoret. Computer Sci., 32*, 185–199 (1984).

Maier, D., J. D. Ullman, and M. Y. Vardi, "On the Foundations of the Universal Relation Model," *ACM Trans. Database Syst., 9*, 283–308 (1984).

Maier, D., D. Rozenshtein, and D. S. Warren, "Window Functions," in *Advances in Computing Research, Vol. 3: The Theory of Databases*, P. C. Kanellakis and F. P. Preparata (eds.), JAI Press, Greenwich, CT, 1986, pp. 213–246.

Majster-Cederbaum, M. E., "Ensuring the Existence of a BCNF Decomposition That Preserves Functional Dependencies in $O(N^2)$ Time," *Inform. Processing Lett., 43*, 95–100 (1992).

Mannila, H. and K. J. Räihä, "On the Relationship of Minimum and Optimum Covers for a Set of Functional Dependencies," *Acta Inform., 20*, 143–158 (1983).

Mannila, H. and K. J. Räihä, "Inclusion Dependencies in Database Design," in *Proc. 2nd IEEE International Conference on Data Engineering*, IEEE Computer Society Press, Los Alamitos, CA, 1986, pp. 713–718.

Mannila, H. and K. J. Räihä, "Design by Example: An Application of Armstrong Relations," *J. Computer Syst. Sci., 33*, 126–141 (1986).

Mannila, H. and K. J. Räihä, "Practical Algorithms for Finding Prime Attributes and Testing Normal Forms," in *Proc. 8th ACM SIGACT–SIGMOD–SIGART Symposium on Principles of Database Systems*, ACM Press, New York, 1989, pp. 128–133.

Mitchell, J. C., "Inference Rules for Functional and Inclusion Dependencies," *Proc. 2nd ACM SIGACT–SIGMOD Symposium on Principles of Database Systems*, ACM Press, New York, 1983, pp. 58–69.

Özsoyoglu, Z. M. and L. Y. Yuan, "A New Normal Form for Nested Relations," *ACM Trans. Database Syst., 12*, 111–136 (1987).

Rissanen, J., "Independent Components of Relations," *ACM Trans. Database Syst., 2*, 317–325 (1977).

Rissanen, J., "Theory of Relations for Databases — A Tutorial Survey," in *Proc. 7th Symposium on Mathematical Foundations of Computer Science*, Springer-Verlag, Berlin, 1978, pp. 537–551.

Roth, M. A. and H. F. Korth, "The Design of ¬1NF Relational Databases into Nested Normal Form," in *Proc. ACM SIGMOD International Conference on Management of Data*, ACM Press, New York, 1987, pp. 143–157.

Sagiv, Y., "An Algorithm for Inferring Multivalued Dependencies with an Application to Propositional Logic," *J. ACM, 27*, 250–262 (1980).

Sagiv, Y., "Can We Use the Universal Instance Assumption Without Using Nulls?" in *Proc. ACM SIGMOD International Conference on Management of Data*, ACM Press, New York, 1981, pp. 108–120.

Sagiv, Y., "A Characterization of Globally Consistent Databases and Their Correct Access Paths," *ACM Trans. Database Syst., 8*, 266–286 (1983).

Sagiv, Y., "Evaluation of Queries in Independent Database Schemes," *J. ACM, 38*, 120–161 (1991).

Sagiv, Y., C. Delobel, D. S. Parker, and R. Fagin, "An Equivalence Between Relational Database Dependencies and a Fragment of Propositional Logic," *J. ACM, 28*, 435–453 (1981).

Schäuble, P. and B. Wüthrich, "On the Expressive Power of Query Languages," *ACM Trans. Inform. Syst., 12*, 69–91 (1994).

Spyratos, N., "The Partition Model — A Deductive Database Model," *ACM Trans. Database Syst., 12*, 1–37 (1987).

Thalheim, B., *Dependencies in Relational Databases*, Teubner-Verlag, Leipzig, 1991.

Ullman, J. D., "Database Theory: Past and Future," in *Proc. 6th ACM SIGACT–SIGMOD–SIGART Symposium on Principles of Database Systems*, ACM Press, New York, 1987, pp. 1–10.

Unland, R. and G. Schlageter, "Object-Oriented Database Systems: State of the Art and Research Problems," in *Expert Database Systems*, K. Jeffrey (ed.), Academic Press, San Diego, 1992, pp. 117–222.

Van Gelder, A., K. A. Ross, and J. S. Schlipf, "The Well-Founded Semantics for General Logic Programs," *J. ACM, 38*, 620–650 (1991).

Vianu, V., "Dynamic Functional Dependencies and Database Aging," *J. ACM, 34*, 28–59 (1987).

Vossen, G., "A New Characterization of FD Implication with an Application to Update Anomalies," *Inform. Processing Lett., 29*, 131–135 (1988).

Vossen, G., "Databases and Database Management," in *Handbooks in Operations Research and Management Science, Vol. 3: Computing*, E. G. Coffman, J. K. Lenstra, and A. H. G. Rinnooy Kan (eds.), North-Holland, Amsterdam, 1992, pp. 133–193.

Vossen, G., "Bibliography on Object-Oriented Database Management (3rd and final edition)," Bericht Nr. 9301, Arbeitsgruppe Informatik, Universität Gießen (available from the author; e-mail to vossen@uni-muenster.de).

Wang, K. and M. H. Graham, "Constant-Time Maintainability: A Generalization of Independence," *ACM Trans. Database Syst., 17*, 210–246 (1992).

Yang, C. C., *Relational Databases*, Prentice-Hall, Englewood Cliffs, NJ, 1986.

Yang, C. C., G. Li, and P. A. B. Ng, "An Improved Algorithm Based on Subset Closures for Synthesizing a Relational Database Scheme," *IEEE Trans. Software Eng., 14*, 1731–1738 (1988).

Yannakakis, M., "Algorithms for Acyclic Database Schemes," in *Proc. 7th International Conference on Very Large Data Bases* (1981), pp. 82–94.

Yannakakis, M., "Graph-Theoretic Methods in Database Theory," in *Proc. 9th ACM SIGACT–SIGMOD–SIGART Symposium on Principles of Database Systems*, ACM Press, New York, 1990, pp. 230–242.

Yannakakis, M. and C. H. Papadimitriou, "Algebraic Dependencies," *J. Computer Syst. Sci., 25*, 2–41 (1982).

Yuan, L. Y. and Z. M. Özsoyoglu, "Design of Desirable Relational Database Schemes," *J. Computer Syst. Sci., 45*, 435–470 (1992).

GOTTFRIED VOSSEN

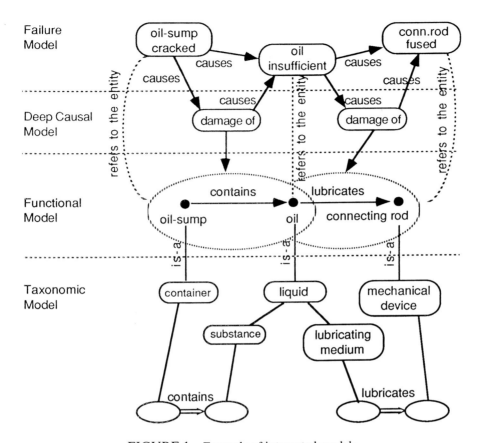

FIGURE 1 Example of integrated models.

and given the functional fact "E1 FUNC E2" which is damaged by F1(E1), the relation:

"if F1(E1) occurs then 'E1 FUNC E2' is damaged and, as a consequence, F2(E2) occurs"

is called *deep causal relation* (DCR) related to CR. For example, if CR is

"if 'oil-sump cracked' then 'oil insufficient,'"

the related DCR is:

"if 'oil-sump cracked' then 'oil-sump contains oil' is damaged, and as a consequence, 'oil insufficient' occurs."

The set of the DCRs related to a physical system S is called the *deep causal model* of S. The graphical representation of this model is a network whose links connect two types of nodes: one type denotes a failure and the other denotes a FF. An example of this semantic network is also shown in Figure 1.

Taxonomic Model

For each functional fact EA FUNC ER, a corresponding *functional metafact* might be defined. This is also a triplet, MEA MFUNC MER, where MEA and MER are *classes* to which EA and ER, respectively, belong (in a semantic network this corresponds to "is-a" links between EA and MEA and ER and MER) and MFUNC = FUNC.

For example the functional metafact related to the FF
    "oil sump contains oil"
might be
    "container contains liquid."

The metafacts, together with the FFs, related to a physical system S will be called the *taxonomic model* of S.

The internal representation of this model is a network organized on three levels:

- The *instance level*, the most basic one, containing instances of the components of S. This level consists of a single layer of entities, connected among themselves through functional links (the FFs).
- The *class level*, containing a network composed by classes (C-classes) which denote successively more abstract classifications of the entities mentioned at the instance level. These entities are, therefore, linked to the C-classes by "is-a" links, providing the basic inheritance mechanism.
- The *function level*, containing classes (F-classes) whose only purpose is to define each function mentioned in the system description. These definitions will be inherited by all the connected nodes at the class level.

The function level consists of disjoint elements in the form node–arc–node, such as

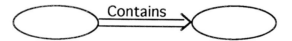

The nodes correspond to *hidden classes*, with the only purpose, stating a property which is common to all the connected classes. The three elements composing the triplet are the *function agent*, the *function*, and the *function receiver*. All the C-classes connected to the function agent (receiver) inherit the property of being agents (receivers) of the function denoted in the triplet.

The class level will be hierarchically structured according to the following principle. To each F-class there corresponds one C-class which carries out (or receives) only one function, the others are subclasses which inherit two or more functions, either as agents or receivers, from the (sub)classes to which they are linked. So a C-class at the top of the hierarchy (i.e., directly connected to an F-class) acts as the most general unifier of the more specific connected C-classes.

In the example given in Figure 2, "container" is one of these classes, whereas "container–conductor" is a more specific C-class (it is the agent of two functions) as is "contained–conducted" (the receiver of two functions). Some C-classes are both agent and receiver of different functions: This is the situation of subclass "contained–conducted–cooler" in Figure 2.

The instance level consists of instances of classes. We can have instances of any C-class, depending on the set of functions that we want to be inherited by the instance. The instance level constitutes the intersection between the functional and the taxonomic models (more precisely, the functional model is part of the taxo-

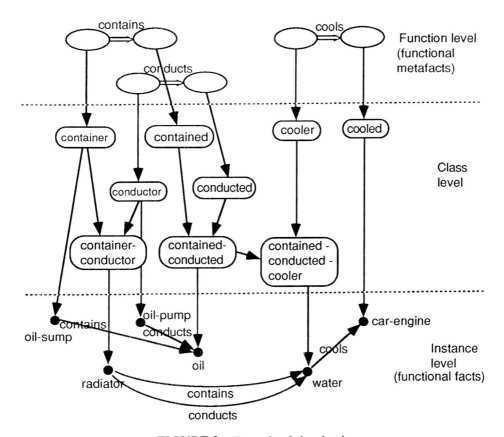

FIGURE 2 Example of class levels.

nomic one). The F-classes are progressively acquired along with the failures mentioned in the failure model and the acquisition of FFs (see the subsection Acquisition of the Taxonomic Model).

The C-classes are hidden, due to the combinatorial explosion of their number. Their set potentially coincides with the power set of the set of functions. In any case a network parser conceals the net implementation from the experts, allowing them to perform only the correct accessing functions. The creation of the C-classes is described in the subsection Acquisition of the Taxonomic Model.

A point we want to stress here is that the C-classes are uniquely identified by the functions attached to them. It is possible to attach names to them, just to ease the interaction with the expert during the acquisition process and to update the meaning of each identifier dynamically, because the semantics of each identifier are uniquely determined by the set of functions characterizing the class it denotes.

In Figure 2, for example, it is possible to denote the classes "contained" and "conducted" with the usual names "substance" and "fluid." Also the classes "contained–conducted" and "contained–conducted–cooler" might be denoted by simpler names such as "liquid" and "cooling medium." A vague name as "cooled" might be substituted by "engine," and so on.

Let us now consider some examples of metafacts. In Figure 2 (updated with simpler names attached to the C-classes), the functional metafact related to the FF "oil pump conducts oil" is "conductor conducts liquid," whereas the one related to the FF "radiator contains water" is "container–conductor contains cooling medium."

Note now how the three deep models are linked to the failure model:

- Each CR is attached to a FF or to a path of FFs.
- Each CR is attached to a DCR or to a path of DCRs.
- Each entity is linked, by an "is-a" relation, to a class of the taxonomic model.

This is made clear in Figure 1.

Note that DK seems mostly independent of any specific goal or intended purpose for which the related models are constructed, whereas the (obvious) goal of the shallow model, that is, the failure tree, is to provide an appropriate KB for diagnosis. (The description of the failure model presented here is not complete; other features of this model, which are described in Ref. 36 make the diagnostic process development easier.) In any case, the three DMs might be (and sometimes should be) used for specific purposes like the ones now described.

The deep causal model is usable by the final expert system in order to provide the user with deep explanations of the cause–effect relations of the failure model. Moreover, during its acquisition, it enriches the shallow model with new failures and CRs.

As pointed out in Ref. 22, although it is hard to find out absolute definitions of "deep" or "shallow," we can assert that a model is deep or shallow with respect to some other model which is respectively shallower or deeper. So, a model of a physical system is deep with respect to a shallow model of the same system, if it is based on more fine-grained elementary causal relationships in such a way that it can provide a justification or an explanation of the shallow model. A causal relation $A \rightarrow B$ at the shallow level (which can be used to deal with questions such as "what if A?" or "why B?") is unfolded at the deep level through the path of deep causal relations: $A \rightarrow A_1, A_1 \rightarrow A_2, \ldots, A_k \rightarrow B$. Thus, the question "why B?" which cannot be answered within the shallow model, can find an appropriate answer in the deep model: "because $A \rightarrow A_1, A_1 \rightarrow A_2, \ldots, A_k \rightarrow B$."

We need the functional model for obtaining the deep causal model (as will be described in the next section), but it can also be used for other purposes. Being a description of the functioning system, it enriches the knowledge about the system itself (through the FFs that denote the reciprocal influences among the entities) and so it can be consulted by the user in order to obtain information about the system behavior.

Finally, the taxonomic model which is automatically created while acquiring the functional model (see the next section) identifies the generalized entities (classes) to which the entities of the physical system belong. This model can be used for tutorial purposes: Because it aggregates entities into classes on the basis of the functions they perform (or receive), it can provide the list of all the entities of the physical system that carry out (or receive) the same set of functions. It might also be used to establish a correspondence among the type of failures and the instances of a particular class (i.e., it might establish which are the failures shared by all the instances of a particular class).

ACQUISITION OF DMs

Let us now describe how the process of acquiring deep knowledge is carried out by D-KAT.

Acquisition of the Functional and the Deep Causal Models

The acquisition of the deep causal relations, being integrated into the failure model acquisition process, produces two important side effects:

1. The enrichment of the functional model
2. The enrichment of the failure model itself

During the acquisition of the failure model, whenever the expert enters a CR "if F1(E1) then F2(E2)," D-KAT asks which one of the functions performed by E1 and damaged by F1 causes F2. The answer is provided by the expert by means of a functional fact. So, if the above CR is entered, the expert is asked to fill in the following structure:

"F1(E1) damages the fact: 'E1 carries out the function . . . upon the entity . . . ,' damage which causes (directly or indirectly) F2(E2)."

The expert fills in the sentence, specifying the function (say FUNC) and the receiver entity which may be either E2 or another entity (say E3). After the acquisition of the expert answers, D-KAT creates a functional fact in which the agent role is played by E1 and the receiver role is played by the entered entity name. So the functional fact might be either E1 FUNC E2 (case a) or E1 FUNC E3 (case b).

It should be noted that the way the expert is asked to fill in the sentence aims at obtaining an integration of the functional and the deep causal model with the failure model, as described in the subsection Taxonomic Model.

Case a

The CR is "if F1(E1) then F2(E2)" and the corresponding FF created by D-KAT is E1 FUNC E2.

D-KAT notices that the receiver entity (E2) in the functional fact is the entity (E2) of the effect–failure of the causal relation entered by the expert. In this case, the acquisition of the deep causal relation ends.

The system functional model has been enriched by adding the functional fact E1 FUNC E2 and the deep causal model has been enriched by adding the DCR:

"if F1(E1) then 'E1 FUNC E2' becomes damaged, and as a consequence, F2(E2) occurs."

Let us consider the following example. The expert enters the CR:

"if water insufficient then car engine overheats."

D-KAT asks the expert to fill in the sentence:

"'water insufficient' damages the fact

'water carries out the function . . . upon the entity . . . ,' damage which causes (directly or indirectly) 'car-engine overheats.'"

The expert answers "cools" for the function specification and "car engine" for the entity specification.

D-KAT creates both the functional fact
"water cools car-engine"
and the DCR
"if 'water insufficient' then 'water cools car engine' becomes damaged, and as a consequence, 'car engine overheats' occurs."

Case b

The CR entered is "if F1(E1) then F3(E3)" and the corresponding FF created by D-KAT is E1 FUNC E3.

In this case D-KAT notices that E3 is different from the entity E2 to which the effect failure of CR refers.

The knowledge acquisition proceeds as described in the following steps.

1. D-KAT asks the expert to fill in the sentence:
    "if 'E1 FUNC E3' is damaged the failure related to E3: . . . occurs and, as a consequence, F2(E2) occurs."
2. The answer, say F3, produces a new CR:
    "if F1(E1) then F3(E3)"
    and D-KAT creates the corresponding DCR:
    "if F1(E1) then 'E1 FUNC E3' becomes damaged' and, as a consequence F3(E3) occurs."
3. Now D-KAT asks the name of the function carried out by E3 that becomes damaged by F3. The answer (say FUNC' related to the entity E') produces the creation of the FF "E3 FUNC' E'."
4. If the name (E') of the receiving entity in the FF just created is different from the entity E2 to which the initial CR refers, the process resumes from step 1. Otherwise, after the creation of the CR "if F3(E3) then F2(E2)" and of the corresponding DCR "if F3(E3) then 'F3 FUNC' E2' becomes damaged and, as a consequence, F2(E2) occurs," the process ends.

At the end of this process, the failure model has been enriched by replacing the initial CR with a path of at least two other CRs. So, new failures and causal relations between them are added to this model.

The functional model has been enriched by adding a sequence of entities functionally related to the one that starts from E1 — the entity mentioned in the premise of the shallow rule (CR) originally entered — and ends in E2, the instance mentioned in its conclusion.

Also, the deep causal model has been enriched by adding a sequence of two or more DCRs that starts from F1(E1) and ends in F2(E2).

Let us consider the following example. The expert, after entering the CR
"if oil sump cracked then connecting rod fused,"
asserts that the corresponding damaged function is "contains" and the receiving entity is "oil."

D-KAT, after the creation of the FF
"oil-sump contains oil,"

notices that "oil" is different from the entity "connecting rod" to which the effect failure of CR refers. Hence, it asks the expert to fill in the sentence

"if 'oil sump contains oil' is damaged, the failure related to 'oil': . . . occurs and, as a consequence, 'connecting rod fused' occurs."

Let us suppose that the answer is "insufficient." So, D-KAT creates a new CR

"if oil sump cracked then oil insufficient"

and the corresponding DCR

"if 'oil sump cracked' then 'oil sump contains oil' becomes damaged, and, as a consequence, 'oil insufficient' occurs."

Now D-KAT asks the expert which function becomes damaged by the failure 'oil insufficient.' If the answer is "lubricates" related to the entity "connecting rod," the new FF

"oil lubricates connecting rod"

is created.

"Connecting rod" being the entity of the effect failure to which the initial CR refers, the process ends after the creation of the CR

"if oil insufficient then connecting rod fused"

and the related DCR

"if 'oil insufficient' then 'oil lubricates connecting rod' becomes damaged and, as a consequence, 'connecting rod fused' occurs."

The failure model has been so enriched by adding a new failure ("oil insufficient") and the two CRs just created. The functional and the deep causal models have been enriched by adding respectively the path of the two FFs and the two DCRs created by D-KAT (see Fig. 1).

Acquisition of the Taxonomic Model

The multilevel hierarchy which constitutes the taxonomic model is autonomously built on the basis of the shallow rules (i.e., the CRs) entered by the expert describing the system to be diagnosed.

Suppose the expert enters "if radiator has a hole then car engine overheats." In the premise of the rule, the instance "radiator" is mentioned. As shown in the previous section, D-KAT asks questions in order to determine the function downgraded by the fault mentioned. Having identified it in "contains," the triplet at the function level is created. The immediate descendant of the agent and of the receiver are created and "radiator" is defined as an instance of the first of them. [Remember that, although the C-classes are hidden (see the subsection Taxonomic Model), it is possible to conceive a network parser which asks the experts to attach a name to a class as soon as it is created.] Having also identified the instance of the receiver of the action of containing (explicitly asking the expert, as described in the previous section, and receiving the answer "water"), D-KAT appends it to the appropriate class.

The expert is then asked which function of "water" is hindered by this leakage, with respect to the fault "car engine overheating." This is determined to be "cooling," so a second triplet at the function level and its immediate descendants are created.

The interesting situation we meet here is that "water" cannot be directly connected as an instance of the class of the agents of cooling, because it has already been defined as a receiver of the action of containing. It is, therefore, connected to the class of objects (autonomously created) identified by these two functions, one as an agent and one as a receiver. The acquisition process is then iterated until the object "car engine" is mentioned as a receiver of a function.

As a remark, we point out that the introduction of a FF does not always imply the generation of a metafact: The function denoted in the FF could be that of a functional metafact already present in the taxonomic model. Consider the introduction of the FF

"radiator contains water"

that generates the metafact

"container contains liquid."

If the FF

"oil sump contains oil"

is now entered, D-KAT notices that the corresponding metafact is already present, so its classes are connected by an "is-a" relation to "oil" and "oil sump."

We might also discover that an entity E, already present in the taxonomic model and connected to a class C_1, becomes the agent (the receiver) of a new function. In this case, a new class C_2 (a subclass of C_1) is created and the "is-a" connection between E and C_1 is replaced by an "is-a" connection between E and C_2. For example, after entering the CR

"if radiator is obstructed then car engine overheats"

"radiator," which is already present in the network as the agent of containing, becomes the agent of the new function "conduct" (the correspondent damaged FF being "radiator conducts water"). In this case, the new class "container–conductor" is created as a subclass of "container" and "radiator" becomes its instance (see also Fig. 2).

AN APPLICATION

Let us consider the following example.

The expert enters the CR:

"if 'water thermostat inactive' then 'radiator does not cool'" (see Fig. 3).

We shall show how the dialog between D-KAT and the expert evolves.

D-KAT: you should fill in the following sentence:

"'water thermostat inactive' damages the fact

'water thermostat carries out the function . . . upon the entity . . .',

damage which causes (directly or indirectly) 'radiator does not cool.'"

Please, specify the function . . .

Expert: switches-on/off

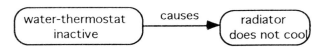

FIGURE 3   Before eliciting the explanation.

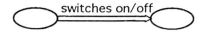

[Now the triplet at the function level of the taxonomic model is created. Also the C-classes respectively agent and receiver of "switches on/off" and whose names "thermostat" and "electric_device" are asked of the expert (see subsection Acquisition of the Taxonomic Model) are created.]

D-KAT: Please, specify the entity . . .

Expert: electric-fan

(Now the FF "water_thermostat switches on/off electric_fan" is created: "water-_thermostat" and "electric_fan" are connected by is_a relation respectively to the C-classes "thermostat" and "electric_device," as shown in Figure 4).

D-KAT: you should fill in the following sentence:

 "if 'water-thermostat switches-on/off electric-fan'

 is damaged, the failure related to 'electric-fan' . . . occurs and,

 as a consequence, 'radiator does not cool' occurs"

Please, specify the failure . . . of 'electric-fan.'

Expert: does not turn

(Now the DCR: "if 'water_thermostat inactive' then 'water_thermostat switches on/off electric_fan' becomes damaged and, as a consequence, 'electric_fan does not turn' occurs" is created. See Figure 4.)

D-KAT: you should fill in the following sentence:

 "'electric-fan does not turn' damages the fact

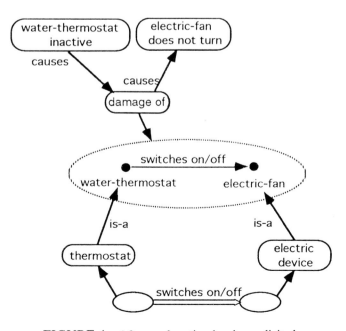

FIGURE 4   After explanation has been elicited.

'electric-fan carries out the function . . . upon the entity . . .',
damage which causes (directly or indirectly) 'radiator does not cool'"
Please, specify the function . . .
Expert: cools

[Now the triplet is created. The C-classes respectively agent and receiver of "cools" and whose names "cooling device" and "conductor" are provided by the expert are also created.]
D-KAT: Please, specify the entity . . .
Expert: radiator
(Now the FF "electric_fan cools radiator" is created and "radiator" is connected to the C-class "conductor." "Electric_fan," being an agent of "cools" and a receiver of "switches on/off," produces the creation of the C-class "electric_cooler" (a subclass of "electric_device" and "cooling_device") to which it is connected. See Figure 5).
At last, after the creation of the DCR "if 'electric_fan does not turn' then 'electric-_fan cools radiator' is damaged and, as a consequence, 'radiator does not cool' occurs," the process ends.

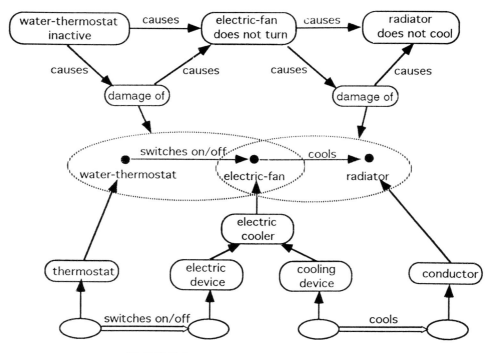

FIGURE 5   Enrichment of the whole model.

The enrichment of the whole model is shown in Figure 5.

CONCLUSIONS

A tool for acquiring multiple models representing knowledge for diagnostic expert systems has been presented. These models denote both the shallow knowledge (represented by a failure model) and the deep knowledge (represented by a functional, a taxonomic, and a deep causal model) to be used by expert systems.

The acquisition of deep knowledge proceeds along with the acquisition of shallow knowledge. A qualifying feature of the tool presented here is that while acquiring the shallow knowledge, the tool elicits deep knowledge which, in turn, is used to improve the whole process (knowledge-based knowledge acquisition). As a consequence, the interview becomes more intelligent as the acquired deep knowledge increases.

The integration between the deep causal model and the failure model aims to provide deep explanations of the shallow knowledge to the end user. In order to provide other types of deep explanations we aim, in future research, to find an effective dialogue between the user and all the models. Another goal for future research is a further exploitation of the knowledge represented by the taxonomic model; for example, for automatically inferring new shallow knowledge.

ACKNOWLEDGMENT

We sincerely thank Dr. Andrew Basden, University of Salford, UK, for his helpful suggestions.

REFERENCES

1. T. Gruber, "Acquiring Strategic Knowledge from Experts," *Int. J. Man–Machine Studies, 29*, 579–597 (1988).
2. J. Pearl, "Embracing Causality in Default Reasoning," in *Readings in Uncertain Reasoning*, Morgan-Kaufman, San Mateo, CA, 1988, pp. 735–741.
3. S. Mussi, "A Method for Putting Strategic Common Sense into Expert Systems," *IEEE Trans. Data Knowledge Eng., DKE-5*, 369–385 (1993).
4. E. A. Feigenbaum and P. McCorduck, *The Fifth Generation*, Addison-Wesley, Reading, MA, 1983.
5. E. H. Shortliffe, *Computer-Based Medical Consultations: MYCIN,* Elsevier Publishing Company, New York, 1976.
6. K. M. Ford and J. Bradshaw, "Introduction: Knowledge Acquisition as Modeling," *Int. J. Intell. Syst., 8,* 1–7 (1993).
7. J. H. Boose, "A Knowledge Acquisition Program for Expert Systems Based on Personal Construct Psychology," *Int. J. Man–Machine Studies, 23,* 495–525 (1985).
8. J. Diederich, I. Ruhmann, and M. May, "KRITON: A Knowledge Acquisition Tool for Expert Systems," *Int. J. Man–Machine Studies, 26,* 29–40 (1987).
9. M. Linster, "Towards a Second Generation Knowledge Acquisition Tool," *Knowledge Acquisition, 1*, 163–183 (1989).

10. K. Morik, *Sloppy Modeling, Knowledge Representation and ORganization in Machine Learning*, Springer-Verlag, Heidelberg, 1989, pp. 107–133.

11. K. M. Ford, J. M. Bradshaw, J. M. Adams-Webber, and N. M. Agnew, "Knowledge Acquisition as a Constructive Modeling Activity," *Int. J. Intell. Syst., 8*, 9–32 (1993).

12. L. A. Cox, "Knowledge Acquisition for Model Building," *Int. J. Intell. Syst., 8*, 91–103 (1993).

13. M. Linster, "Explicit and Operational Models as a Basis for Second Generation Knowledge Acquisition Tools," in *Second Generation Experts Systems*, Springer-Verlag, Berlin, 1992, pp. 477–506.

14. W. J. Clancey, "The Knowledge Level Reinterpreted: Modeling How Systems Interact," *Machine Learning, 4*, 285–292 (1989).

15. B. R. Gaines, "Modeling Practical Reasoning," *Int. J. Intell. Syst., 8*, 51–70 (1993).

16. D. C. Berry, "The Problem of Implicit Knowledge," *Expert Syst.: Int. J. Knowledge Eng., 4*, 144–151 (1987).

17. J. R. Olson and H. H. Reuter, "Extracting Expertise from Experts: Methods for Knowledge Acquisition," *Expert Syst. Int. J. Knowledge Eng., 4*, 152–168 (1987).

18. H. Akkermans, F. van Harmelen, G. Schreiber, and B. Wielinga, "A Formalization of Knowledge-Level Models for Knowledge Acquisition," *Int. J. Intell. Syst., 8*, 169–208 (1993).

19. M. Linster, "Closing the Gap Between Modeling to Make Sense and Modeling to Implement Systems," *Int. J. Intell. Syst., 8*, 209–230 (1993).

20. L. Chitarro, C. Costantini, G. Guida, C. Torasso, and E. Toppano, "Diagnosis Based on Cooperation of Multiple Knowledge Sources," *Proc. 9th Workshop on Expert Systems and their Applications* (1989).

21. P. Fink, J. Lusth, and J. Duran, "A General Expert System Design for Diagnostic Problem Solving," *IEEE Trans. Pattern Anal. Machine Intell., PAMI-7*(5), 553–560 (1985).

22. G. Guida, "Reasoning About Physical Systems: Shallow Versus Deep Models," in *Expert Systems and Optimization in Process Control*, Technical Press, Aldershot, UK, 1986, pp. 135–159.

23. P. E. Hart, "Directions for AI in the Eighties," *ACM-SIGART Newslett., 79*, 11–16 (1982).

24. D. Michie, "High-Road and Low-Road Programs," *AI Mag., 3*, 21–22 (1982).

25. B. Chandrasekaran and S. Mittal, "Deep Versus Compiled Knowledge Approaches to Diagnostic Problem Solving," in *Proc. AAAI-82* (1982), pp. 349–354.

26. J. De Kleer, "How Circuits Work," *Artif. Intell., 24*, 205–280 (1984).

27. B. Chandrasekaran and R. Milne, "Reasoning About Structure, Behaviour and Function," *ACM-SIGART Newslett., 93*, 4–55 (1985).

28. J. H. Boose and C. M. Kitto, "A Survey of Knowledge Acquisition Techniques and Tools," *Int. J. Man-Machine Studies, 31*, 149–160 (1989).

29. L. Eshelman, D. Ehret, J. McDermott, and M. Tan, "MOLE: A Tenacious Knowledge Acquisition Tool," *INt. J. Man-Machine Studies, 26*, 41–54 (1987).

30. G. Kahn, A. Kepner, and J. Pepper, "TEST: A Model-Driven Application Shell," in *Proc. AAAI* (1987).

31. S. Marcus, J. McDermott, and T. Wang, "Knowledge Acquisition for Constructive Systems," in *Proc. of the 9th IJCAI* (1985), pp. 637–639.

32. G. Klinker, J. Bentolila, S. Generet, M. Grimes, and J. McDermott, "KNACK Report-Driven Knowledge Acquisition," *Int. J. Man-Machine Studies, 26*, 65–79 (1987).

33. M. A. Musen, L. M. Fagan, D. M. Combs, and E. H. Shortliffe, "Use of a Domain Model to Drive an Interactive Knowledge Editing Tool," *Int. J. Man-Machine Studies, 26*, 105–121 (1987).

34. G. Gini, R. Morpurgo, S. Mussi, P. Sassaroli, and M. Somalvico, "KAM: A Methodol-

ogy for Knowledge Acquisition in an Inferential Diagnosis System," in *Proc. Computer Factory Automation* (1988).

35. G. Gini, R. Morpurgo, S. Mussi, and P. Sassaroli, "An Integrated Tool for Diagnosis," in *Proc. Congress AI*IA-89* (1989).
36. S. Mussi and R. Morpurgo, "Acquiring and Representing Strategic Knowledge in the Diagnosis Domain," *Expert Syst. Int. J. Knowledge Eng., 7,* 157–165 (1990).
37. W. R. Swartout and S. W. Similar, *Explanation: A Source of Guidance for Knowledge Representation,* Springer-Verlag, Berlin, 1989, pp. 1–16.

ROSAMARIA MORPURGO

SILVANO MUSSI

ELECTRONIC MUSIC

HISTORICAL PERSPECTIVE: BACKGROUND

The technology that led to the development of and continues to enrich electronic music can fairly be said to have begun in the 14th century (~ 1359–1361), and in more primitive form, in the 13th century. ". . . as early as the thirteenth century, some organs were already given the present arrangement with the levers projecting and directly worked by the fingers" (1). Although so early a date may sound impossible or inappropriate for music that depends on electricity to exist, a phenomenon that was not discovered until hundreds of years later, it was approximately during the middle of the 14th century that the first keyboard in the configuration we know today came into being. The keyboard, with its seven white and five black key pattern (at times those colors were reversed), is the principal controller employed in the production of electronic music. An early example of this type of keyboard is depicted in Michael Praetorius' *Syntagma Musicum*, plate no. XXIV (2).

Using that plate as a reference, Figure 1 demonstrates the shapes of the principal ("white") keys and the chromatic ("black") keys which, although different in shape from current keys, were played in essentially the same way and were laid out in roughly the same pattern [although the "black" keys were placed above the right half of the principal "white" key with which they were associated as a raised (sharped) version of the principal]. These were the shapes employed for the Halberstadt Organ (~ 1359–1361), which may be one of the first to use this 7 + 5 configuration.

Also, we are prone to think of electronic music as freeing our tuning system, permitting us to employ pitches that "fall in the cracks" of our trusty piano. Surprising as it may seem, there are early historical precedents for differing numbers of pitches in each octave, dating at least as far back as the middle of the 16th century (~ 1555) when Don Nicolo Vicentino developed one (possibly the most important one) of a number of such "enharmonic keyboards," that is, a microtonal keyboard arrangement using split keys to produce a 31-tone scale—31 pitches per octave, the *Archicembalo*, (3). These pitches were "equally" spaced (logarithmically), equivalent in concept to our 12-tone equal tempered scale. Different tunings also have been employed over the centuries that demonstrate composers' awareness of extremely fine distinctions between pitches and differing preferences for the intervallic relationships that resulted (e.g., Mean-tone temperament and Just intonation). Each tuning had its period of primary interest and each has its own inherent limitations (including equal temperament, the one to which we have greatest indebtedness for the literature in our Western musical heritage). Microtonal keyboards continued to develop with ". . . the most radical instrument . . . developed is Koenig's *Tonametric*, which could divide four octaves into 670 equal parts, or approximately 167 steps per octave" (4).

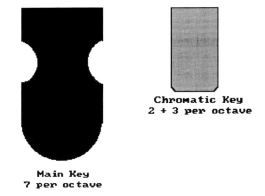

Chromatic Key
2 + 3 per octave

Main Key
7 per octave

FIGURE 1   Halberstadt organ keys (~ 1359–1361).

A vitally important development in the understanding of sound that opened up many areas of continuing sound exploration and was of critical importance to electronic music was the formulation in its entirety of the overtone series by Joseph Sauveur, in 1701 (5). Sauveur's work had implications on understanding pitch relationships and was central to gaining understanding of timbre which, in large part, is dependent on the harmonic spectrum of a sound and the relative amplitudes of the members of that series.

The earliest known efforts to employ electricity for sound production with the ultimate goal of applying it toward musical ends comes with the *electric harpsichord* developed by Jean Baptiste de Laborde in 1759 (6). This device was dependent on static electricity derived from moving one's hand over a glass globe. The impulse activated small metal rods which, in striking each other, produced a bell-like sound that would continue as long as the key was depressed. The only resemblance the instrument had to a harpsichord was the use of a small keyboard controller. It was never used as a functional performing instrument but offers a remarkably early example of an effort to apply electricity to the development of a musical instrument.

Several developments in the 19th century, each in its own distinctive way, contributed toward the ultimate arrival at that which we today recognize generically as electronic music. Possibly the single most important of these was the work of Hermann Helmhotz, *Sensations of Tone*, published in 1863, a book that had profound influence on much of the work in acoustics that followed and had a direct impact on several of the instruments that were subsequently developed. Developments during this period, some of which were influenced by Helmholtz's work, included the following: the invention, by C. C. Page, of an electric tuning fork, in 1837, a device used to produce a stable, continuous pitch that could be adjusted for tuning purposes; the transmission of the voice over wire by Alexander Graham Bell in 1876; Thomas Edison's invention of the phonograph in 1878 (with a stereo, two-horned, version in 1899); Thaddeus Cahill's development, in 1897, of the *Sounding Staves*, an instrument that providing timbre variation, based on Helmholtz's theories, by means of controlling the upper partials, a precursor of his 1906 monster 30-ton instrument, the *Dynamaphone*; Vladimir Poulen's development of a

magnetic recording machine, the *Telagraphone* (the earliest version of a wire recorder); and the first totally electronic instrument, the *Singing Arc*, developed by
William Duddell in 1899. Many other accomplishments in the application of electricity to musical and nonmusical uses took place during this century, a great many
of which can directly or indirectly be viewed as contributions to the eventual emergence of electronic music as a discernible entity unto itself.

HISTORICAL PERSPECTIVE: ELECTRONIC MUSIC

The history of electronic music can be loosely divided into four periods (not including the extended time period during which the stage was set for the emergence of
this medium — the centuries of activity before the 20th century). Such a division, as
in all such efforts, is an attempt to focus and clarify stages in the development of a
complex medium of human expression. This preliminary exercise in identifying
some logical defining time periods in the evolution of this art form must be understood to be at a very early stage of its own delineation. Inevitably, these early
judgments will themselves be modified as some of these periods will be seen on a
broader time spectrum to coalesce. For the present, however, it is believed that such
a time compartmentalization, arbitrary as it may seem, is useful for the purposes of
this introduction.

Most of the principal requirements for the existence of a music that could be
produced and reproduced electronically had been developed by the turn of the 20th
century with the exception of adequate amplification, and that need was quickly
fulfilled by Lee de Forrest who developed the triode vacuum tube in 1906. That
single development opened up all of the possibilities that were subsequently to be
found in the recording, broadcasting, and, ultimately, electronic music industries.
Consequently, the First Period of Electronic Music can fairly be spoken of as
beginning 1906 with both de Forrest's triode and Thaddeus Cahill's Dynamaphone.
The latter, as noted earlier, was a 30-ton device that sat on railroad cars and was a
first major effort to produce music electronically for commercial purposes. The
massive collection of components were played by a team of workers producing
synthesized sounds and transmitting the results over telephone lines to subscribers.
Without adequate amplification, however, the venture was destined to fail, but it
remains a significant first effort toward these ends. Interesting comments of the day
are quoted in an essay by Otto Luening in a small booklet brought out by he and
fellow composer and collaborator Vladimir Ussachevsky. He said,

> I read in 1917 . . . of an invention of Dr. Thaddeus Cahill, the *Dynama phone*, in
> Mount Holyoke in 1906. *McClure's Magazine* of 1906 reported this event in an article
> entitled: *New Music for an Old World. Dr. Thaddeus Cahill's **Dynamaphone** An
> Extraordinary Electronic Invention for Producing Scientifically Perfect Music*, by Ray
> Stannard Baker. Excerpts from the article indicate with what fascination the Dynama-
> phone was received: "Largest musical instrument ever built . . . instead of bringing the
> people to the music, the new method sends the new music to the people . . . by opening
> a switch we may 'turn on' the music . . . Dr. Cahill's instrument gives us a hint of what
> the music of the future may be like . . . A HUNDRED INSTRUMENTS IN ONE . . .
> Electrically Used to Produce Music . . . the musician uses his keys and stops to build
> up the voices of flute or clarinet; as the artist uses his brushes for mixing color to

obtain a certain hue . . . the workmen in the shop speak of 'electric music' . . . we welcome the new with eagerness; it has a great place to fill; it may revolutionize our musical art; but, in accepting the new, we will not give up the old" (7)

This first historical period in the history of electronic music comes to an end in 1929, the year A. Givelet and E. Compleaux developed the first device that could be considered to be a prototype of a modern synthesizer—a set of four oscillators and punched paper rolls (as used in a player piano). During this roughly 25-year period, Leon Theramin developed the instrument that bears his name, the *Theramin* (formally introduced by the inventor on August 5, 1920). This instrument was constructed with two oscillators tuned above the audible range and played by passing one's hands next to the antennas that protruded from them—not touching the unit physically. The *Ondes Martinot* was developed by Maurice Martinot, in 1928, and was used by a number of prominent composers (e.g., Hindemith). The *Hammond Organ*, developed by Laurens Hammond, appeared 1 year later, in 1929. All of the last three instruments have enjoyed some degree of popularity and both artistic and public use since their introduction.

The second historical period for electronic music can be viewed as approximately 1930 to 1950. Activity accelerated in the 1930s with an increased concern for recording sound. A technique for scratching film strips for sound reproduction, "Drawn Sound," was developed by Norman McLaren in 1930 and was used for a short period of time by the movie industry. At approximately the same time, the first practical wire recorder was marketed. The first stereo recording was done in the winter of 1932, by Bell Labs at the Academy of Music in Philadelphia, with Leopold Stokowski conducting the Philadelphia Orchestra. The technology was offered to Radio Corporation of America (RCA) for marketing but was turned down on the basis that the Depression was not a good environment to introduce such a product. The *magnetophone* (developed by Duchamp, in 1935) was the first tape recorder. The instrument was significantly refined in the mid-1940s in Germany and proved to be of the greatest importance contributing to the rapid further development of compositional techniques for a variety of types of electronic music. The first compositions to benefit from this technology were those that became known as *musique concrète*—music created using natural sounds, that is, sounds from everyday life. These recorded sounds were manipulated (spliced, speed changed, played in reverse, and other such techniques) to provide the sound materials for a composition.

Also invented during this second period were the electronic pickup for the Hawaiian lap steel guitar (1931), and the introduction of the "Broadcaster," the first solid-body electric guitar marketed by Leo Fender, in 1948.

Electronic music's third historical period loosely covers the years from 1950 to 1980 and took us from the period of tape recorder music (*musique concrète*) through the early stages of the application of the computer to music. The acceleration of activity witnessed earlier gains greater momentum through these years as an enormous surge of creative activity brought forth some of the works now recognized as classics of electronic music, for example, *Gesange der Jünglinge* (Stockhausen), *Poème electronique* (Varese), *Composition for Synthesizer* (Babbitt), *The Wild Bull* (Subotnick), and many others that deserve equal mention. The period began with the early compositions of the team Vladimir Ussachevsky and Otto Luening, who presented the first concert of their works (both individual and collaboratively created) in 1952, saw vigorous and prolific compositional activity over the three decades, and witnessed the development of the first significant synthesizers reflecting different philosophies and technologies. Although considerable research and creative work was being done in a variety of locations, for example, Cologne, Milan, and other centers, the first major synthesizer developed by Harry Olson and Herbert Belar, the RCA Mark II Synthesizer, was installed in 1955 at what became known as the Columbia–Princeton Center for Electronic Music in New York City (at Columbia University). This synthesizer worked through the use of punch cards which appeared in early efforts at computer development such as the *Holorith Machine* used in Germany in the early 1930s (8).

The first high-speed digital tape recorder (~ 100 inches per second) that was eventually required for the processing of the vast amounts of data produced in sound generation, appeared soon after, around 1956. During 1956–1957, Max Mathews, working at Bell Labs, developed the first computer music program (MUSIC-1). Mathews has stated that only one "terrible" piece of music was composed using this language (9). He, and subsequently others, developed MUSIC-2, -3, -4, -5, and derivatives of these. The principles involved in Mathews' contribution essentially became the bases for all music programming that was to follow.

Although some of the early computer programs, for example, the one used for the *Illiac Suite*, were designed to produce a score for acoustic realization of the resulting piece, programs were being developed that, by use of a digital-to-analog converter, the computer was able to generate the sounds itself as dictated by the parameter controls exercised by the program design (e.g., pitch, envelope contour, and amplitude). The first computer-generated sound was produced in 1957 at Bell Labs, in New Jersey, where Max Mathews (sometimes affectionately referred to as "the father of computer music") was director of the Behavioral Research Lab, where this work was done. This manner of producing computer-generated sound has continued to the present as one of the two primary directions in recent electronic music: computer-generated sound and computer-controlled synthesizer-generated sound.

Possibly the biggest and most significant revolution in terms of placing the required hardware resources for electronic music in the hands of the "average composer" and educator came with Robert Moog's introduction of a modular voltage-controlled synthesizer in 1964–1965. This instrument and several other competitors that quickly appeared on the market (e.g., the Arp and Buchla synthesizers) were priced at a level that schools and individuals could acquire them without an inordinate strain on budgets. Being modular, they were flexible by design, permitting one to order only the modules desired and allowing for expansion and configuration according to personal preferences. The instruments were quickly adopted by the pop world of music and interest in electronic music exploded as a result.

We are currently living in the fourth historical period of electronic music which could be spoken of as having started in 1981 when IBM first introduced the personal computer. Although, as noted, interest in the application of the computer to music began in the mid-1950s (one of the earliest works being the *Illiac Suite for String Quartet*, created by Hiller and Isaacson at the University of Illinois), the introduction of the personal computer (PC) led to a burgeoning of that interest and it has dominated electronic music ever since.

Central to virtually all digital electronic music since it was devised in 1983, the

MIDI (Musical Instrument Digital Interface) code has probably become the most widely used resource available to this medium. This computer code was designed to permit all appropriately designed and equipped instruments to "speak" to each other; that is, the principal parameters that were universal to music production were incorporated into the code (e.g., note on, note off, volume, and velocity) and were adopted as a universal standard by the music instrument manufacturers. One principal musical element, timbre, was left to the proprietary judgment of each manufacturer. This agreement led to an explosion of low-priced synthesizers, samplers, and a wide array of supporting and modifying equipment and software, flooding the market. Every home could have a decent quality electronic music system for far less than an equivalent quality piano, once the principal form of home entertainment.

Finally (for now), amid a storm of controversy, the Digital Audio Tape recorder (DAT) was introduced in 1987. This extremely high-quality and versatile piece of equipment led to long debate in the U.S. Congress as a result of the ease it provided for inexpensively and quickly reproducing high-quality commercial recordings at the same high quality by any individual, seriously threatening the copyright protection otherwise enjoyed by composers and recording companies. The copyright issues resolved, this latest technology is rapidly becoming commonplace in even modest studios of individuals and institutions.

The most advanced sound producing and processing technology known to this author at this time is the IRCAM Signal Processing Workstation, an internal computer card that provides for a very high level of performer/electronics interfacing. Working with the Max program developed at IRCAM in 1986, it provides object-oriented control in real time of the most subtle interaction between performer and the electronic sound producing equipment. Some have characterized this development as being "as far as we can go with technological development—now it's all making music." Although probably more a reflection of optimist enthusiasm and wishful thinking than of reality, the fact remains that, in performance, this equipment/software combination does represent an extremely sophisticated level of technological achievement with enormous musical potential.

THE LITERATURE

The reason for an article on the subject of electronic music appearing in this volume derives from there being a worthy body of music literature that has been created through the resources and techniques provided by the development of an electronic technology that meets the requirements composers have to produce art. Without this result, interest in an article devoted to this subject could reflect little more than interest in novelty or simply a fascination with the diverse possibilities of electronic technology for its own sake. In fact, a very large body of electronic music literature has been produced over a period of approximately 50 years. Included are works that reflect little more than laboratory experiments, others that reveal imaginative original compositions reflecting a variety of stylistic biases, many electronic renditions of traditional literature, "scores" for movies, and an enormous amount of music in a wide spectrum of "pop" styles. In the way of an introduction to some of this literature, a variety of composers and samples of their work will be succinctly discussed in the paragraphs that follow, with no intent of suggesting that more than a token exposure to this vast literature will have been provided. In offering such a sampling, it is inevitable that a point of view will have guided the choices. The interested reader is encouraged to explore the literature using the items presented here only as a point of departure and with an awareness that any two people selecting compositions for such a discussion would probably choose different works with or without some overlap.

Although there are some examples of works that include some electronic dimension (e.g., the use of the theramin prior to 1948, the first exclusively electronic works were presented in that year by Pierre Schaeffer, in France. These compositions and others produced soon after by Pierre Henry were tape recorder compositions, that is, works for which the tape recorder (with microphones) was the only instrument employed in their composition. More commonly referred to as *musique concrète* (music derived from natural sounds), they were the first in a long list of compositions that were generated exclusively or in part employing the process of recording the sounds of everyday life (e.g., traffic noises, a whistle, birds singing, or even the sounds of an acoustic instrument), manipulating those sounds through a variety of tape techniques (e.g., splicing, reverse playback, and speed adjustments), and through these means constructing (composing) a musically designed mix of sounds.

This technique was explored also by Vladimir Ussachevsky and Otto Luening in the early 1950s both as individual composers and in a rare collaborative effort on a number of works. They expanded their "palette" somewhat through the use of other equipment and techniques that contributed toward enriching their compositional and sound alternatives. In a revealing little book, the two men went to some length to explain their problems, solutions, and some of the compositional procedures they followed. One excerpt may assist the reader in understanding their approach and the issues they addressed.

> Between late fall of 1951 and March of 1952 I kept accumulating reels of material. One evening, wandering into Columbia Radio Station WKCR where Peter Mauzey was a student-engineer, I found him playing feedback effects to another member of the station staff. He asked me what I thought of it and my reaction was, 'Great, how do you do it?' . . . And so ensued more urgent borrowing of equipment; and then the hundreds of decisions on how and where to edit, to tie together, how to "mix" it all, to cut tape (often bravely!) (10).

Their early works were first presented in concert at Columbia University, May 5, 1952, and included the three works for which scores are provided in the little book mentioned above, *Fantasy in Space*, *Incantations*, and *Sonic Contours*, pieces employing and manipulating the sounds of a flute, piano, or voice. Some of the techniques they employed in these works included feedback, tape speed alterations at a ratio of 1×2, mixing of multiple tracks derived from the synchronization of multiple (as many as six) single-track tape recorders, and tape splicing.

A novel little piece constructed entirely from a single drop of water, *Dripsody* (1955), by Canadian composer Hugh Le Caine, demonstrates how a tiny sound source can be expanded into a piece of music with thousands of events, all taken from that single source. Using a variable-speed tape recorder, tape loops, and 25 splices, Le Caine was able to create this delightful minute-and-a-half piece of music (11). It is a particularly clear and memorable example of *musique concrète*.

An entirely different area of electronic music exploration was pursued by Karlheinz Stockhausen, working in Cologne, Germany. His initial work was with oscillators generating sine waves and the possibilities that were offered by both additive and subtractive synthesis. In the former, waves were added to each other according to a pattern designed by the composer to produce a variety of timbres. In the latter, white noise (a random distribution of the total audible spectrum sounding together) was used as the source, and bands of sound of differing widths were extracted from it for the same purpose, to produce a variety of timbres. The pair of works Stockhausen produced that demonstrate the application of these techniques are *Studie I* (1953), employing additive synthesis and *Studie II* (1954), constructed by means of subtractive synthesis. Aside from the techniques employed, it also is of interest to note the similar sound qualities that pervade the two pieces.

Stockhausen's long and prolific creative career reflects a continuing commitment to explore a variety of electronic music procedures and includes an array of very different but noteworthy works. Examples of his output that reflect different interests, in addition to the two studies mentioned above, are *Gesange der Jünglinge* (1958) which employs electronically generated and modified sounds combined with recorded natural sounds (young male voices) also electronically modified, with a text taken from the *Book of Daniel, Chapter 3*; *Microphonie I* (1964) composed for tam-tam (a gonglike instrument), microphones (used as performing instruments), two filters, and potentiometers, a work designed for live performance; and *Microphonie II* (1965) composed for chorus, Hammond Organ, and ring modulators, the work seeks to mix the sounds of the live performers through ring modulators to produce a feedback circle that is played through loudspeakers at the same time the live performers are heard (12).

One of the most widely recognized and influential electronic music composers, Milton Babbitt, was one of the four founding codirectors of the Columbia–Princeton Center for Electronic Music (founded in 1959), together with colleague Roger Sessions from Princeton and Ussachevsky and Luening from Columbia. His electronic work was done entirely on the RCA Mark II synthesizer, at Columbia University. The results of his work together with that of others from various parts of the world who were working at the center were first presented in a concert at Columbia University's McMillin Theater, on May 9–10, 1961. His contribution to the program, *Composition for Synthesizer*, is a purely electronic work. It was created entirely on the Mark II Synthesizer and its output was not subjected to any further mutations or modifications" (13). Babbitt subsequently produced a number of works on the Mark II, among which is *Occasional Variations* (1971) which was commissioned for the opening of the first national park for the performing arts, Wolf Trap Farm Park, in Vienna, Virginia. This unique and forward looking commission took electronic music from the confines of recordings or small concert settings to the broadest possible mass audience and was premiered at Wolf Trap, an outdoor concert facility designed to accommodate about 6500 people, on August 6, 1971, during the first season at the park. Another work by Babbitt that provides an interesting look at the composer's compositional views as revealed in acoustic versus electronic music, one of very few such examples, is his piece, *Phonemena* (1974), which he created in two versions: voice and piano, and voice and tape. The coloristic qualities of the tape version may be comparable to the difference that might exist between a traditional piano work and an orchestrated version of that piece. An entirely new spectrum of sound is available and the resultant piece can take on a completely different character.

Although Edgar Varese was not a very prolific composer, he certainly provided us with one of the early classics of the literature, *Poème electronique* (1958). This work was composed for the Brussels Worlds Fair of that year and was designed to accompany a light-and-slide show in a specially designed pavilion, the Phillips Pavilion, by architect Le Corbusier and composer/architect Iannis Xenakis. The composition, like Stockhausen's *Gesange der Jünglinge* 2 years earlier, employed both electronically produced sound and those derived from recording natural sounds (e.g., an airplane and a baby crying). The sound was transmitted from a large number of loudspeakers (published figures range from approximately 350 to 450 such speakers) placed throughout the pavilion, and the composer had about 180 controls designed into the performance that directed the sounds to various combinations of speakers throughout the performance. Varese was notable as being one of the first to bemoan the limited resources that existed in the realm of acoustic instruments and the need for a more flexible medium. He felt so strongly about this limitation that he actually stopped composing for an extended period of time approaching 20 years. When he returned to the compositional scene, it was with a work for orchestra and tape, *Déserts* (1954), in which the two forces do not appear together but are alternated through seven movements.

Quite decisively, a representative of the *musique concrète* mode of composition is Steve Reich's piece, *Come Out* (1966), which was constructed entirely from a young black man's statement after being brought to a police station, "I'm going to open the bruise up and let the bruise blood come out to show them." After several statements of the complete sentence, the words "come out to show them" become the material for the balance of the work, which consists of a seemingly endless repetition of the phrase while the tape recorders on which the tracks were recorded continue to go out of phase with each other. That process continues until the words become indistinguishable and the resulting out-of-phase timbre becomes the center of attention until it fades out to end. Another work designed for voice alone which has been presented in live performance but seems initially to have been conceived for tape alone, is Luciano Berio's *Thema* (1959), a piece that uses an excerpt from James Joyce's *Ulysses* as its text. It opens with a short reading of the text (unaltered), and then the sounds of the voice are fragmented and manipulated electronically to produce a nonpitch-oriented composition of approximately 8 minutes in length.

The first use of electronic sound as an integral part of opera appeared in Karl Blomdahl's *Aniara* (1957), an opera providing an early fantasy of space travel and the evacuation of a planet that was destined for destruction. Similar to this use of electronics in opera, an early example of the incorporation of electronics into the orchestra in which they are an integral part of the unfolding texture and dramatic character of the work is Roberto Gerhard's *Collage: Symphony No. 3* (1960).

The first electronic composition to win the prestigious Pulitzer Prize was Charles Wuorinen's *Time's Encomium* (1968). This extended work (about 45 minutes in length) is designed in two large sections. It was composed on the RCA Mark II Synthesizer at Columbia University. In the same year, one of a series of electronic compositions that were commissioned by Nonesuch Records from Morton Subotnick appeared, *The Wild Bull*. The work was composed on a modular voltage-controlled Buchla Synthesizer, the development of which benefited from Subotnick's participation with inventor Donald Buchla. The piece is a quasi-tone poem based on a story line coming from an ancient poem of the same name. Highly programmatic, it is almost Romantic in character — quite different from most of the other works considered in this discussion.

By the time the mid-1970s arrived, a new force, computer music of various kinds, was beginning to assert its influence and many of the works that attracted attention from that point on were the result of the use of computers in composition. Interest in the use of the computer for musical purposes began in the mid-1950s, and compositions were generated through the use of this new technology as early as 1957. Such a work, the *Illiac Suite for String Quartet* (1957), resulted from a computer program designed by Lajaren Hiller and Leonard Isaacson that produced a musical score. The resulting piece was actually an acoustic work to be performed by a string quartet but was "composed" by the computer following the instructions provided in Hiller and Isaacson's program. Computer-generated or computer-controlled works were few and far between in the earlier stages of development but, since the introduction of the personal computer in 1981, have become the primary tool for almost all aspects of electronic music: whether acoustic works the scores for which were produced on computers; computer-generated and computer-produced works; or compositions for which the computer is the primary development and controlling tool but the sound for which comes from separate synthesizers (which, of course, are themselves dedicated computers). An extremely large literature has resulted from these approaches; some examples follow. To suggest that any one of these (or others not mentioned) has gained a significant position in history is certainly premature. The examples offered below are intended to do nothing more than suggest the body of literature that is emerging and exemplifying various approaches to computer-assisted composition. Some examples of computer-generated compositions are Barry Vercoe's *Synthesism* (1969), Hugh Le Caine's *Mobile* (1970), Curtis Rhodes' *nscor* (1980), and Barry Truax's *The Wings of Nike* (1987) to be used with computer images. There are many more such works. This is just a point-of-departure listing.

Although live performers have been provided with works allowing for tape/live interaction since at least the early 1960s, in the late 1980s, and into the 1990s, there has been growing interest in live performers interfacing with the computer and both generating and controlling the sounds that it will produce. These efforts have taken various forms and have been responsible for producing a literature that retains one aspect of conventional music not apparent in much of the other electronic music we have been considering, that is, the infinite variability of the works from one performance to another and the inherent possibility for the performer to put her or his imprint on the work in very human terms. Several such works employing differing technologies include Zak Settel's *Hok Pwah* (for voice and percussion with the IRCAM sound board and Max software); Steve Solum's *Concerto for MIDI'd Grand Piano* (1993) for generic MIDI grand piano and various MIDI devices; Scott Miller's *Angel of Progress II* (1994) for MIDI grand piano, clarinet (with pickup mike embedded in its barrel), and various MIDI devices. In each of these works, the performer produces the music required by the score while controlling the electronic sounds which mimic, play counterpoint with, provide delayed response to, and otherwise provide an "orchestrated environment" under the triggering control of the live performer and preprogrammed trigger points in the music (arriving at a specific note may trigger a series of events from the computer).

The literature that has been produced is vast and almost as varied as the number of works extant. The electronic resources of *musique concrète*, analog synthesis, digital synthesis both MIDI and non-MIDI, combinations of each of these with another, and the interaction between live performers and all of these approaches has provided an enormous expanse of artistic possibilities that we have only begun to explore. The advent of this technology has created controversy and strong responses from the musician's unions, has virtually taken over the popular music world, and has begun to have an indelible effect on virtually all avenues of musical expression.

TYPES OF ELECTRONIC MUSIC

The term *electronic music* is a generic one used to refer to all music that is produced employing electronics in one form or another. Use of this term can deceivingly imply a simplicity and singularity in the music that falls under its references that is far removed from actuality. In its earliest stages when its use was very sparing and possibly more novelty than for polished works of art, (e.g., use of the theramin), electronically produced sounds were used in live performances in an almost mystical way. Both the procedures and the results were, to the active music listener, quite simple, although the technology was sophisticated for its time.

The beginnings of the vigorous period of electronic music that started in the late 1940s was exclusively based on a form of music that was almost totally based on the use of the tape recorder and microphones: *musique concrète*. The term is French, coming from where work in this area began, and refers to music produced from the recording of natural sounds and manipulated into compositions. The techniques associated with this type of music have remained in use to the present, although greatly refined and modified over the years by the advent of rapidly improving and more versatile equipment. The process essentially required a composer to record sounds that were of interest—any naturally produced (acoustic) sounds experienced in everyday life. The composer would then manipulate these sounds into compositions using any combination (or all) of the techniques described below.

Typically, works derived from natural sounds would bear no resemblance to their source sounds. These would be altered by speeding up or slowing down the playback and re-recording the sounds in their new form. Depending on the degree of speed control employed, this would change the pitch of the sound and could even provide the effect of a new timbre entirely. The sounds might be subjected to any of the following splicing manipulations: spliced [i.e., cut and reconnected to different pieces of tape changing their position in the series of events, and their sound shape (envelope) might also be effected, i.e., a spliced change of position relative to an entire sound (not containing its attack and final decay)]; and spliced on to the master tape in reverse-play position so that the segment would be playing backward. In addition, the use of an echo effect could be added by a variety of means such as controlled feedback or out-of-phase playback on multiple tape recorders (later, multiple tracks of the same tape recorder). Variations in volume could be controlled in re-recording the master tape while changing level settings. Recognizing that tape travels at a definable speed, it is possible for the composer to be quite precise in timing the segments to be used and constructing the small and large time references for the flow of sound.

Musique concrète went through many refinements from the controlled feedback of Ussachevsky and Luening, and it has been incorporated into a wide variety of works employing newer technologies and has involved the use of live performers in many works. As noted earlier, the techniques of *musique concrète* remain today as resources for the composer, but many of them have been taken from the manual process to electronically controlled processes (e.g., creating desired envelopes with an envelope generator, or digitally reversing the play of a given segment). In this respect, it is clear that the evolution in electronic music has, at least in part, been a cumulative experience with early techniques and experiments becoming integral parts of the composer's working vocabulary.

Analog synthesis is the second mode of producing electronic music emerging in the 1950s and still very much a part of the electronic music scene. It was the first form of electronic music that produced sounds never before heard because they could not be produced by acoustic means. The oscillator is the fundamental sound source for analog synthesis. It may take the form of a random signal generator emitting noise (usually white or pink, two of several different kinds of noise differing by the degree of emphasis their respective band spectrums contained) of a specific wave form design e.g., sine, sawtooth, triangle or pulse (i.e., square or rectangular) waves. Oscillators were supplemented in the conventional analog setup with such devices as filters, envelope generators, amplifiers, ring modulators, mixers, and sequencers. Each of these played an important role in the shaping and molding of the final sound product.

The important distinction that must be understood about analog synthesis is that it produced a literal electrical two-dimensional analog of acoustic sound wave forms that are naturally spherical from the sound source could be represented two dimensionally on an oscilloscope display and which possessed all of the characteristics of their acoustic equivalent. It must be remembered that any sound carried through the air, whatever its initial generating source may be, moves spherically from its source until it decays. The two-dimensional image seen on an oscilloscope, therefore, is only accurate up to a point and must be recognized as having the limitations inherent in any such graphic representation. But it does effectively help us understand the "shapes" of waves and provides a visual reference for our aural experience.

In analog synthesis, the composer has the possibility of creating essentially any sound he or she is capable of imagining and can explore sound possibilities that may not have been preimagined. With the exception of sine waves, all other sounds have complexes of wave structures that may follow acoustic principles of an harmonic series (e.g., a fundamental of 64 vibrations per second), then added to itself one, two, or three times to an infinite number producing the octave above the fundamental (128), the fifth above (192), second octave (256), a major third (320), and so on or, in electronically generated sound, may provide a new configuration of a nonharmonic spectrum. All acoustic instruments (e.g., the traditional instruments of the orchestra) have their own unique harmonic spectrum derived from the overtone (harmonic) series but imbued with differing degrees of intensity for each of its respective constituent wave members. In addition, each acoustic instrument has its own distinctive envelope (i.e., attack, sustain, and decay pattern) that, together with the harmonic/amplitude spectrum special to that instrument, provides the distinctive timbre (tone characteristics) associated with that particular instrument. Although the timbre of acoustic instruments is directly dependent on their construction, timbres employed in analog electronic music must be constructed for each sound. The possibilities are, for all practical purposes, unlimited (or limited only by human hearing and imagination). As a result, the design of timbres for a composition has now become an integral part of the compositional process itself, unlike conventional composition where one writes for preexisting instruments with set and predictable timbres.

The composition techniques for analog electronic music require a broad new spectrum of operations employing a variety of new electronic modules (noted above). A basic sound source is selected which may consist of a single complex wave (e.g., white noise) or may employ a mixture of many oscillator-generated or other sounds superimposed on each other to produce a still more complex wave. That original sound could then be filtered in wide or narrow bands through any part of its spectrum. It is quite common for the resulting sound to be modulated (i.e., the behavior of the wave pattern is altered to assume a new quality, e.g., an undulating movement) by another single or set of wave forms — very commonly, low-frequency oscillators are used for such modulations. The phasing of the waves may be shifted, and the resulting sound may be channeled through a sequencer producing a precisely controlled repeating series of pitched events (similar to tape looping in much *musique concrète*). Depending on the amount of equipment available, it may be possible to produce two, three, four, or more different sound configurations at the same time which may be mixed onto a single track or sent separately to individual tracks of a multitrack tape recorder. The mixing process that takes place normally as the sounds are being recorded may include various effects that change the ambiance effect of the sounds (e.g., providing varying degrees of reverberation, giving the sound "depth"). At this point in the process, all of the tape-manipulation techniques of *musique concrète* may be employed to construct the final composition. After the development of the multiple-track tape recorder, those tape-manipulation techniques were expanded and refined to allow for overdubbing, precise alignment of tracks, and the building of many layers of tracks limited only by considerations of sound quality loss that occurs in any analog multiple-recording process.

The development of modular analog synthesizers provided an enormous amount of flexibility, allowing composers to add and delete modules as their aesthetic preferences dictated, and provided for very expansive systems with many oscillators, filters, envelope generators, amplifiers, and other modulating and controlling devices. More important to analog synthesis development and its effectiveness as a reliable compositional tool was the introduction of voltage control. Characteristic of the first MOOG synthesizers and most analog synthesizers that followed, voltage control provided precise degrees of control over a variety of parameters (e.g., oscillators, envelope generators, sequencers, and amplifiers). By adjusting measurable voltages up or down, consistent changes from subtle to dramatic would be produced in the output of the particular module. This provided a high degree of predictable and reliable control of these electronic devices for the compositional process.

Digital electronic music derives its name from the fact that it employs the on/ off digital processes of the computer. In fact, all digital electronic music instruments are dedicated computers. Every possible musical function must have a numerical value attached to it in order for it to serve the production of music through a digital environment. For example, velocity has a range of 0–127 with 0 being the lowest and 127 being the highest velocity level. To understand the way computers use this information, one must understand the "grammar" employed by the computer. Messages are constructed by *bits*, *nybbles*, *bytes*, and *words*. A bit is the single *on* or *off* function represented by the 0 and 1, respectively. Nybbles consist of four bits (e.g., 0011). Bytes consist of two or more nybbles (e.g., 0010 0011) and may have an additional starting and ending bit (as in the MIDI code) to alert the computer as to what kind of byte to expect and what to do when it is over. A standard has been adopted to provide a definition for each character, the American Standard Code for Information Interchange (the ASCII Code). For convenient reference, the digital code is represented by the binary, decimal, or hexadecimal systems (most commonly the hexadecimal). For example, the letter A would be 0100 0001 in the binary system, 65 in the decimal system, and 41 in the hexadecimal system. An extended study of these systems is outside of the purview of this article but can easily be pursued elsewhere. It is important, however, to understand that the digital system employed for electronic music uses these numerical bases and that the MIDI (Musical Instrument Digital Interface) standard that emerged in 1983 as the universal reference for electronic music is a direct application of these conventional computer digital references. Prior to MIDI, each manufacturer used their own form of application of the digital processes for their instruments, making it impossible for the instruments of one manufacturer to work with those of another. Upon the adoption of the MIDI standard, it became possible for all MIDI-designed instruments to interface with each other, bringing an enormous amount of flexibility to the collective operational system while retaining a degree of manufacturer proprietary control (especially true in the systems used to produce timbral differences, for example, wave table synthesis, frequency-modulation synthesis, phase-distortion synthesis, and others).

MIDI information travels at a rate of 31,200 bits per second over standard Deutsch Industry Norm (DIN) cables (using only three of the five lines in the cable). Its signal deteriorates over distance and the earliest MIDI cables had to be kept under 50 feet in length to avoid distortion. The small voltages that carry the MIDI information, instead of the variable control voltage frequency/amplitude interpretation associated with analog signals, are read as on/off fluctuations the patterns of which produce the "messages" of the MIDI code. It is viewed as an "event-based" network conveying information about specific actions (e.g., "note-on" or "note-off," the note to be played, or the amount of velocity to be used). It does not convey information such as sampled waveforms. Most MIDI devices must have three totally different cords attached: the power cord, the audio in and out cords, and the MIDI cords — they are not interchangeable and serve totally different functions.

All MIDI devices must have IN and OUT ports and may have a THRU port. The difference between the OUT and the THRU ports is that the former transmits information that has been effected by the device, whereas the latter passes the information coming from the IN port out without modification. Information coming in to a device that is not intended for use by that device (as provided by the MIDI message) will be ignored and passed out the THRU port to the next device in the chain that may be alerted to read and interpret that information. The MIDI code is transmitted *serially* (i.e., one item of information after another) through the chain of devices. If too many devices are connected in chain fashion, there will be deterioration of results (consequently, the development of a THRU BOX, shortening the travel time and distance between the source of the message and the receiving devices.

It should be understood that digital electronic music consists of vast amounts of numerical data which have no sound inherent in it. The data require converters to translate the numbers into sound. The analog-to-digital (AD) converter processes analog sound, providing digital information for it to be stored in databases (e.g., CD recordings or digital tape recorders). The digital-to-analog (DA) converter does the opposite, converting the numerical data into sound. Depending on the nature of the system, one or both of these converters may be present [e.g., a CD player only requires the digital-to-analog converter, whereas a digital tape recorder requires both (ADA) to permit it to both digitally record and playback the material recorded now stored in digital form]. The information represented will typically include the sound's wave shape (timbral quality), its frequency (pitch), the characteristics of its envelope (attack, sustain, and decay pattern), and its volume—all of the information required to replicate the sound in the reconversion process.

To gain some sense of the amount of data required for high-quality digital recording, consider the CD standard which is 44,100 samples per second or dependent upon bit resolution (e.g., 8,12,16), the numerical data for every second of music could constitute 705,600 bits of information at 16-bit resolution. This comes to 423,396,000 bits of data for every minute of music and 25,403,760,000 for every hour. A number of digital tape recorders offers the choice between 44,100 and 48,000 sampling rates, the latter providing a 10% increase in the amount of data to be stored. Music samplers, which routinely require only small amount of sound for manipulation to produce the required timbre, normally have quite a small memory capacity (e.g., 2–3 megabytes) compared to the figures cited above, but, at the same time, they often offer several different sampling rates ranging from as low as 22,000 samples per second to the CD quality of 44,100 samples per second. The lower rates do allow for quite satisfactory sampling of low-pitched instruments (e.g., tuba or string bass) because their frequency range is low enough to provide a substantial harmonic spectrum that will adequately replicate their sound quality under such low sampling rates (a subject beyond the purview of this essay).

Each of the three types of electronic music noted above *musique concrète*, analog, and digital) exist unto themselves as quite distinct ways of producing music by electronic means. However, throughout the evolution of these modes of producing music, there has been a frequent crossing of lines. As the new resources and techniques emerged, examples of works using two or more of the basic types together in single compositions became common occurrences. This mixing of technological resources together with the application of electronically produced materials with live performers (from soloists to full symphony orchestra) has become a widely adopted working compositional premise (e.g., Charles Whittenberg's *Electronic Study No. 2 for String Bass and Tape* and Roberto Gerhardt's *Collage: Symphony No. 3* for tape and orchestra). From the earliest interactive works of Ussachevsky and Luening to works for MIDI'd piano (e.g., Stephen Solum's *Concerto for MIDI'd Grand Piano*), clarinet, and other acoustic instruments, and interactive works for live performer and computer (e.g., those by Cort Lippe and Zak Settel), electronic sound has been incorporated into the live performance environment and each has had a significant influence on and has enriched the other. Although *musique concrète*, analog, and digital electronic music are clearly definable types, there have been so many crossings between them and with live performers that we can fairly speak of a broad spectrum of electronic music types from very pure representatives of each of the basic types to complex mixes of all of the options available.

HARDWARE EMPLOYED IN ELECTRONIC MUSIC

Frequent references have been made during the course of the preceding discussion to various pieces of equipment employed in the production of one or another kind of electronic music. An effort will be made in this section to identify the primary equipment employed in the different kinds of electronic music and to concisely explicate their operation and function. It is this hardware (and yet to be discussed software) that reflects the technological evolution of and distinctions between the different types of electronic music that have been considered in the preceding section.

The *tape recorder* has been the single most important piece of equipment employed in electronic music from its inception. It has gone through its own significant evolution from one-track monaural machines using paper-backed tape to discrete-channel multitrack machines allowing for large numbers of tracks of music to be recorded, edited, and mixed together. The early machines were heavy and very quick to emit tape noise. For multiple tracks to be employed, multiple machines had to be used, leading to severe problems of synchronization of the materials on the respective machines (representing the several tracks the composer may have desired to mix). The evolution of the tape recorder produced two-track monaural, two-track stereo, four-track stereo, discrete four-track quadraphonic (i.e., each track could be controlled independently for playback and recording, which was not possible on the standard four-track stereo), and a variety of larger-format discrete-track multitrack machines (e.g., 8- and 16-track recorders). In addition to the vast improvement of the recording and playback quality of the machines themselves, as well as the tape products available, several formats were developed for noise reduction units (e.g., Dolby A, B, and C, and Dbx) which might be incorporated directly into the recorders or used as external devices through which the sound was directed both in the record and playback modes. These devices are quite specific in their design and require that recording and playback occur using the same format device for the benefit of noise reduction to be experienced (i.e., they are not interchangeable).

Tape recorders (one-track to four-track) use ¼-in. tape, whereas those embodying greater numbers of tracks will use larger tape (e.g., ½- or 1-in. tape). These machines also have a variety of built-in options that can be quite helpful to the composer in editing and processing the recorded materials. These include variable speeds (e.g., 7.5, and 15 inches per second), adjustments for the kind of tape being used to obtain the highest quality recording results; VU meters to help monitor the recording levels, counters to assist in identifying locations on the tape, and editing releases that permit listening to tiny fragments of the tape by hand manipulation without engaging the forward or reverse motors.

For all practical purposes, electronic music began with the advent of the tape recorder and it has remained heavily dependent on it ever since, throughout all other evolutionary changes. The position of the machine may be challenged in the years ahead by the relatively new introduction of the digital tape recorder, which will provide all of the opportunities and quality that are inherent in digital music in general and allow for more precise editing and other manipulation of the recorded materials. At this writing, however, the analog tape recorder remains the workhorse of the electronic music composer.

Several small items of equipment are necessary for the effective music compositional use of the tape recorder. Most significant among these are a variety of *microphones* (e.g., crystal, carbon, dynamic, condenser, and ribbon) with several recording-spectrum configurations (e.g., omni-directional, bi-directional, and cardoid) which have enjoyed increasing sophistication and reliability in their own evolution throughout much of this century. *Splicers* for cutting and joining tape have taken various configurations from simple precisely molded metal blocks to more complex mechanical devices. Necessary small but critical adjuncts to the splicer have been the *grease pencil* for marking the tape and a sharp *cutting edge* (typically, a razor blade). *Recording tape* has experienced considerable improvement and refinement over the period of the tape recorder's use, starting with paper-backed tape (which would become rather brittle, and recognizing some motor problems in earlier tape recorders, was prone to break fairly easily, requiring splicing unrelated to compositional choices), mylar-based tape, which was significantly more durable than the paper tape but could stretch under tension and distort the recording or playback, and polyester tape, which is very strong, with a long reliable life, and resistant to humidity. In addition, tape has been produced in a variety of thicknesses for varying lengths of recording time (e.g., .5 mil, 1.0 mil, and 1.5 mils) and a few different widths (e.g., ¼ in., ½ in., and 1 in.) to provide different numbers and configurations of recording track, and have been treated to produce several levels of recording sensitivity and noise resistance. Finally, two other items considered basic to a tape studio (and all others) are the patch bay and the mixing board. The former permits the connection of a number of pieces of equipment (and individual tracks of multitrack machines) for convenient routing of sound, and the latter provides for a number of inputs and outputs to allow for the mixing of sound sources and the selective introduction of sound processing effects (e.g., reverberation). Both types of units have appeared in various sizes, from just a few jacks for in and out patching on the patch bay, and a few inputs and one output to larger systems allowing for 20, 24, and more inputs with 2, 4, or more outputs on the mixing boards.

The *synthesizer* is the second major item of equipment that has been present in every electronic studio since the mid-1950s. Essentially, a synthesizer is a device that comprises several different components that work together to permit the user to generate sound and to electronically manipulate different facets of that sound to produce different timbral possibilities. The basic components of analog synthesizers are oscillators to generate the sound waves (e.g., sine, triangle, rectangle, sawtooth, and white noise), envelope generators to shape the attack, sustain, and release behavior of the sound, and filters (e.g., low- and high-pass filters) to permit focusing on a particular band of sound in the spectrum offered by the oscillators. Oscillators and envelope generators normally appear in banks (groupings) with several in a bank and often several banks of each on a synthesizer. Other devices commonly included in commercially produced synthesizers with some differences between analog and digital systems include modulation modules (e.g., ring modulators and modulation wheels), controller modules (e.g., keyboards and sequencers), portamento (glide) controls, and, specifically on digital systems, specialized tools (e.g., memory capacity for storage of program's sound data and data banks of sounds), low-frequency oscillators, split and layering capabilities, velocity controls, viewing windows, providing digital information about the particular mode in which one is working, and MIDI IN, OUT, and THRU jacks, permitting communication with other MIDI devices.

The first piece of equipment spoken of as a synthesizer and consisting of its most basic components was developed by E. Compleaux and A. Givelet in 1929. The first significant such device was the large system developed by Harry Olson and Robert Belar, the RCA MARK II synthesizer that was installed at the Columbia–Princeton Center for Electronic Music located at Columbia University in 1959. Composers were working with the electronic components that comprise a synthesizer in the early 1950s (e.g., Stockhausen and Varese), but these were not self-contained integrated systems that had a singular identity. In the early to mid-1960s, Robert Moog introduced the first commercially available modular voltage-controlled synthesizer, which was quickly followed by several others (e.g., the ARP and Buchla synthesizers). Digital synthesizers began to appear in the 1970s and quickly became very attractive to pop bands and, in various forms, appealed to everyone from children to hobbyists and amateur musicians. These synthesizers ranged from very modest and inexpensive units to extremely sophisticated and very expensive systems. The most recent development has been to place synthesizers on "sound cards" to be inserted into computers, providing for all sound production and manipulation capabilities in one compact piece of equipment. The major new development from the advent of the MIDI code for the manipulation of digital sound has been the emergence of a wide range of computer software (to be discussed later) to permit the user to do all of the things that were once done by manipulating buttons, switches, potentiometers, and sliders on separate pieces of equipment.

The tape recorder (usually at least two or three are present) and synthesizer, together with the array of supporting equipment mentioned above, constitute the heart of the analog studio. Studio sizes may range from a couple of tape recorders and a modest synthesizer to several multitrack tape recorders and possibly several large modular synthesizers. This "classical studio" is typical for the analog facility and is quite different from the new digital studios which typically will have the tape recorders, multiple digital synthesizers possibly using several different modes of synthesis (e.g., wavetable, FM, phase distortion, and linear-arithmetic synthesis), samplers, computers (at least one—with a variety of music software), and a variety of other digital equipment [e.g., drum machines, sound processors, different controllers (keyboard, guitar, or wind controllers), and sequencers (different from the analog sequencer in both intent and function)]. The equipment presented in the following paragraphs is designed for use in a digital studio, although some have found application in analog studios as well (e.g., sound processors).

Samplers constitute an extremely important companion to synthesizers and, to some, are preferred over them. They function quite differently in terms of the sounds employed but allow similar manipulations to take place on that sound. Samplers are specialized recording devices that are used to take comparatively small fragments of sound recordings which become the basic sound source for further manipulation (or is used to simulate acoustic instruments, an increasingly more popular function of the sampler that strongly influenced the extension of the MIDI code to include General MIDI, a set order of acoustically identified sounds that can be used for "conventional" orchestration and arrangement of digitally scored or recorded music). The sampler records a fragment of sound (the length and quality respectively limited by the memory capacity of the sampler and its level of operation, e.g., 8 bit or 16 bit). That sound sample can be analyzed quite precisely, allowing components to be deleted from it (or added to it, as in the case of an envelope), discrete looping to allow for indefinite sustain of the sound, and then other typical synthesizing manipulations (e.g., filtering and modulating) to be performed on the sound. The results of these procedures could produce either a digital refinement or enhancement of the acoustic sound originally recorded or an entirely new timbre.

Sequencers appear in both analog and digital worlds of electronic music, but they are two dramatically different devices. The analog sequencer is a controller that provides for a number of prescribed events to take place and be stopped or repeated indefinitely. These can be sped up to the point where they essentially constitute a new timbre, or slowed down to provide an extremely slow articulation of sound, possibly as a looped ground bass track for the music. They can add precisely defined rhythmic patterns to the series of events unfolding, limited by the number of events the sequencer is capable of producing.

Digital sequencers are essentially digital recorders with a number of editing capabilities built into them. They first appeared as hardware (pieces of equipment) but have largely become software products. Sequencers usually have very large numbers of independent tracks (sometimes over 400) and are limited by the amount of memory the hardware (discrete unit or computer) has available. Tracks of music can be "laid down" (similar to multitrack tape recorders which, however, do not have the editing capability) and edited with enormous flexibility. The tracks can be looped (individually), passages cut, moved, or added with great precision, sped up or slowed down, mixed with other tracks, and each of the parameters of a sound (e.g., volume, length, and timbre) edited in great detail (tiny fractions of time or loudness can be controlled).

In addition to the sound information that may be sent to a sequencer, the unit can also accept controlling information and system-exclusive proprietary information allowing for the transmission of instructions to each piece of equipment employed in playback. In playback, the tracks can be mixed and balanced in relationship to each other. Digital sequencers accept MIDI information from any suitable sending device and provide for playback through appropriately designed equipment (i.e., compatible with the information recorded that may require proprietary equipment configurations, e.g., for the timbral qualities desired). The track capacity and flexibility provided by such numbers of tracks make the sequencer an indispensable tool for producing polished final products within the MIDI environment.

MIDI controllers may be any specifically designed instrument that directly produces MIDI information or may be acoustic instruments fitted with attachments that convert the actions of the performer on the acoustic instrument (e.g., velocity of finger motion, wind flow, or string and instrument body response) to MIDI information which can then be transmitted or manipulated as any other MIDI sound information. A controller (e.g., a MIDI or MIDI'd keyboard, guitar, wind or string instrument) is used to perform the music either for a live performance environment or for recording purposes. It is essentially any device that can begin the production of a sound, can produce, directly or indirectly, MIDI information about that sound, and can influence the way that sound is heard by the expressive performance techniques of the player. As implicit in the foregoing comments, there are a large number of MIDI instruments as well as MIDI-fitted acoustic instruments that can serve as controllers.

Drum machines are another piece of equipment frequently found in digital music studios. They are essentially dedicated closed samplers in the sense that they contain a substantial collection of sampled drum sounds that can be selected and played by a performer on the pads provided on the unit itself. Specific sounds can be assigned to specific pads; the performance can be recorded in the units own memory and can then be edited into desired rhythmic and timbral patterns that can be looped and later set down on a sequencer's track as a part of a composition (or the performance can be recorded directly to the sequencer). Percussion is the only family of instruments represented as an individual piece of equipment in a studio for somewhat obvious reasons [i.e., they are a fundamental component of almost all pop music (the area of music most committed to and dependent on digital electronic music sound)].

There are a large number of *sound processors* on the market that provide a number of different options to composers. When MIDI sound information is sent into a processor, there are a wide range of manipulations and transformations that can be accomplished (e.g., adding varying amounts of delay, echo, resonance, or reverberation to the sound, making it behave in certain ways or appear to have been recorded in a vast cathedral or a small room). Processors are almost indispensable pieces of equipment when it comes to providing "depth" or "presence" to a sound and to juxtaposing different degrees of these qualities to different sounds that are interacting with each other in a composition. They can be used in live performance and for recorded studio work.

Finally, the *computer* is central to the operation of a MIDI studio and plays the central role in a different world of electronic music that is academically based and is not necessarily dependent on (or may not even employ) MIDI. Centers such as those at Stanford University, San Diego State University, MIT, and many others have been devoted principally to research and composition of digital electronic music based on self-contained languages and programs that had their own manner of handling all of the functions that we quickly recognize in the MIDI code (i.e., all of the functions that can be performed in producing or modifying sound). Many MIDI-based choices have emerged from these research institutions (e.g., FM synthesis and powerful software packages). In MIDI, the computer handles a variety of software types, most of the functions that were initially performed directly (and much more clumsily) on the pieces of equipment designed for the respective function. Timbre design, sequencing, sampling, and all of the editing options available are now routinely performed on the computer. In addition, it serves as a valuable library storage facility for individual sounds, banks of sound, sequences, and digitally produced musical scores. The latter has become the primary base for preparing final copies of all scores — for acoustic or electronic instruments. The speed, clarity, and ease of operation for what are sometimes extremely complex procedures has made the computer the primary hardware resource of any digital studio. As suggested earlier, in some studios it may be the only piece of equipment necessary (with the exception of the supporting printer and audio playback system).

MUSICAL INSTRUMENT DIGITAL INTERFACE

Many references have been made to MIDI (Musical Instrument Digital Interface) throughout much of the preceding discussion and those comments may have provided some sense as to the nature of this computer code. Recognizing the importance of the adoption of this standard, in 1983, to the entire industry and electronic music world, a closer look should prove valuable.

MIDI is a computer code devoted to defining musical functions in computer language that is designed to permit the transmission of data from one MIDI-fitted device to another. Its adoption permitted manufacturers to develop a large number and variety of MIDI-fitted instruments (both digital and acoustic) that, by means of this code, could "talk" to each other. It operates within the digital language of computers (i.e., binary code of ON/OFF). The small voltages that carry MIDI signals, instead of the variable-control voltage frequency/amplitude fluctuations associated with analog signals, are read as ON/OFF fluctuations the patterns of which produce the "messages" of the code. It is viewed as an *event*-based network conveying information about specific actions (e.g., note on, note off, the note selected, or velocity). It does not convey information such as the specific structure of *sampled waveforms*.

MIDI code is transmitted *serially* (i.e., one item of information after another) over MIDI cables using standard five-pin DIN plugs and jacks (although only three of the pins are used for MIDI purposes). The information travels at 31,250 bits per second. Information for 16 different channels can be transmitted on a single MIDI cable. Although the resultant effect is that of simultaneous musical events on each of the channels, each byte of information for all 16 channels moves along in a single stream of data. The time deviations resulting from the speed of the one-at-a-time flow of data are too small for the human ear to distinguish, making this serial procedure possible. As in all digital processes, the information results from groupings of bits (either 0 or 1)—the smallest element of a digital signal—into "nybbles," "bytes," and "words." A nybble consists of four bits, and two or more nybbles constitute a byte. Words consist of groupings of bytes. Instead of writing out the cumbersome binary form of the information represented, this information is typically represented by the use of the more efficient hexadecimal system, a system based on 16 parts represented by 0–15. Table 1 is an example of the hexadecimal system as compared to the binary and the decimal system.

Table 1 provides 2 "cycles" of the sixteen components of the hexadecimal system. The patterns for the binary and hexadecimal systems begin to become apparent even in this brief example. If we were to progress beyond this point, each hexadecimal cycle would begin with the next digit or letter of the first group of 16. For example, the next cycle would run from 20 to 2F, the cycle following that would be 30 to 3F, and so forth. The 11th cycle would be from A0 to AF, and the 16th would run from F0 to FF.

TABLE 1   Comparison of Binary,
Decimal, and Hexadecimal Systems

Binary	Decimal	Hexadecimal
0000 0000	0	0
0000 0001	1	1
0000 0010	2	2
0000 0011	3	3
0000 0100	4	4
0000 0101	5	5
0000 0110	6	6
0000 0111	7	7
0000 1000	8	8
0000 1001	9	9
0000 1010	10	A
0000 1011	11	B
0000 1100	12	C
0000 1101	13	D
0000 1110	14	E
0000 1111	15	F
0001 0000	16	10
0001 0001	17	11
0001 0010	18	12
0001 0011	19	13
0001 0100	20	14
0001 0101	21	15
0001 0110	22	16
0001 0111	23	17
0001 1000	24	18
0001 1001	25	19
0001 1010	26	1A
0001 1011	27	1B
0001 1100	28	1C
0001 1101	29	1D
0001 1110	30	1E
0001 1111	31	1F

The MIDI code is monitored by the International MIDI Association (IMA) which is responsible for working with the digital instrument manufacturers in working to improve the code over time. Since its 1983 adoption, there have been a number of important amplifications of the code (e.g., the announcement of the adoption of "General MIDI" in the Winter, 1990, *IMA Bulletin*), "General MIDI" provides a specific designation for 128 instruments that will be constant from one manufacturer to another (e.g., an acoustic grand piano will always be 0, whereas a violin will always be 40). The IMA is also responsible for publishing the code information for software developers and other interested users. It is from its publication that the following information has been summarized in capsule form (14).

One of the goals in establishing the code was to attempt to define in code every

TABLE 2   Channel Messages

Message	Hex code
Note off	8n
Note on	9n
Polyphonic aftertouch	An
Control change	Bn
Program change	Cn
Channel aftertouch (pressure)	Dn
Pitch bend	En

possible action that may be required for a musical performance or incorporated into the control of a musical sound. A numerical representation of each of these requirements is *system* messages. System messages are further subdivided to include *common* and *real-time* messages. Tables 2 and 3 list the messages that are found in each of these principal groupings.

All MIDI devices *must* have an *IN* and an *OUT* port, and many have a *THRU* port as well. The difference between the OUT and the THRU ports are that the former sends information from the settings of that specific device, whereas the THRU port passes on data that entered the IN port without being affected by that device's settings—the information literally just passes through unaffected by the unit through which it is passing. The information passing through may be providing commands intended for another MIDI instrument. In such cases (where several instruments are linked in a series, referred to as "Daisy Chaining," each instrument will be assigned to a different channel and will respond only to information arriving on that channel—the other instruments will ignore that information, responding only to the information on their assigned channel. By this means, a variety of different instruments can be employed in a composition in a variety of ways while each retains the integrity of its particular characteristics—especially in regard to sound quality, mode of synthesis (e.g., wave table or FM synthesis), or, for samplers, its use of sampled sound. The controlling device (computer, keyboard, or

TABLE 3   System Messages

Common messages	Hex code	Real-time messages	Hex code
System exclusive	F0	Timing clock	F8
MIDI time code (¼ frame)	F1	Undefined	F9
Song position pointer	F2	Start	FA
Song select	F3	Continue	FB
Undefined	F4	Stop	FC
Undefined	F5	Undefined	FD
Tune request	F6	Active sensing	FE
End system exclusive	F7	System reset	FF

other controller) serves as the "Master," whereas the responding devices are referred to as "Slaves." This same process can be accomplished more efficiently with the use of a "THRU box," which provides for one or two inputs and several outputs. This allows all messages to arrive at their respective instruments more quickly and with a shorter length of MIDI cabling. All information coming into the THRU box goes to all instruments but is simply ignored if it does not pertain to their assigned channel. There are a number of different configurations that can be used in putting instruments together and these are principally dependent on the number of instruments being used, the relationships desired for those instruments, and, ultimately, the musical goals of the user.

There is one other aspect of MIDI that must be considered and which will suggest alternatives to the channel use and configuration suggested above. The MIDI modes are provided to accommodate differing needs and circumstances (not all MIDI equipment is equal in terms of their respective capabilities and, as a result, require other options). The four MIDI modes consist of combinations of the commands OMNI and POLY in ON or OFF positions (POLY OFF is termed MONO ON). The four modes are Mode 1 (OMNI ON/POLY ON), Mode 2 (OMNI ON/POLY OFF), Mode 3 (POLY ON/OMNI OFF), and Mode 4 (MONO ON/OMNI OFF), providing different ways of transmitting data. In Mode 1 (called OMNI), all voice data travels over one basic channel (normally Channel 1). When two instruments are connected in this mode, either can be played and both will respond. In Mode 2, messages will be sent on an assigned channel, permitting the Master to be played and only the Slave to sound. In Mode 3 (called POLY), messages for each channel (or voice on multitimbral instruments) will be sent over individually assigned channels, permitting multiple instruments (or timbres in multitimbral instruments) to be played simultaneously and recorded and played back on individual channels. Mode 4 (called MONO) permits each voice (timbre) on a multitimbral instrument to have its own assigned channel, allowing it to operate independent of the other voices. The capacities of each synthesizer are important in determining which modes are possible or necessary for particular performance or recording needs.

Finally, to help clarify a MIDI setup, a basic MIDI layout is provided in Figure 2. The most basic configuration wherein MIDI is an integral part of the process of producing and manipulating sound would involve a MIDI controller (e.g., a keyboard) and a computer patched directly to each other with at least one of them audio patched to a sound system. In order to provide a view of MIDI in a slightly more sophisticated system, a "slave" is included in Figure 2. In this system, the controller synthesizer would be able to produce its sound, and the sound module (Slave) would be able to produce its own sound (activated by the Master). Each of these units has its own audio connection to the sound system through the Mixer, allowing each to be heard independently or mixed to varying degrees. The MIDI circuit is quite direct: from the Master to the Slave, from the Slave to the Computer, and from the Computer to the Master. Employing such a configuration allows all materials played both on the Master and Slave to be recorded on a Sequencer (as software in the Computer) and then played back from the Computer through the two sound units (assuming the Master Controller to be a sound source—there are controllers that do not produce sounds of their own). Also, the computer can provide a library of sounds that could be "dumped" into the respective modules to

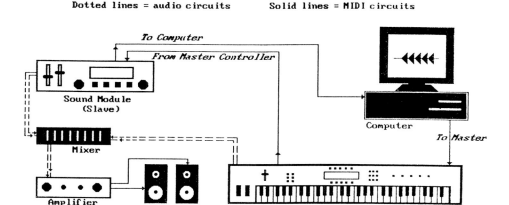

FIGURE 2   One basic MIDI configuration.

provide a new "bank" of sounds on which to draw. A system like this could be expanded to include additional Slaves in this "Daisy Chain" fashion or through the use of a THRU BOX discussed earlier.

MUSIC SOFTWARE

Software is simply a set of instructions to a computer (generic or dedicated) to perform the functions desired, and the environment within which the user works to make selections and perform the related tasks. There is "user-friendly" software that provides the easiest and most intuitive environment within which to work, and other software that imposes varying degrees of complexity and discomfort to tasks that might otherwise be accomplished more simply. Typically, the latter uses a variety of coded commands, whereas the former uses straightforward language and mouse or keyboard clicking on clearly identified commands or selections.

Music software is, of course, that which has been designed to perform music functions either within a MIDI context or employing direct computer instructions apart from the MIDI code. As there are several quite specific types of functions that users normally require, different types of software categories have emerged. These include software for producing a musical score, for sequencing, for editing old and constructing new sounds, and for the storage of individual and banks of sounds. There are many other types unrelated to electronic music that are used for educational purposes (e.g., those designed for ear training and music theory).

Scoring software (e.g., Personal Composer, Score, and Finale) is designed to produce the best possible professional quality scores and parts. Its functions normally include the following: note entry both through the use of a computer keyboard (or mouse) and through a MIDI keyboard, allowing the pitches played to appear on the screen; entry of all expression symbols (e.g., slurs, ties, staccatos, and dynamics); text entry (for lyrics, titles, and other text needs); and the wide variety of other graphics required to produce an effective score. In addition, such programs typically provide for MIDI playback of the score through a MIDI/audio system including tempo, dynamic, and other controls. The great convenience of easy transposition of parts of the score and the extraction of instrumental parts from the score are very powerful and especially attractive capabilities of these programs. Such programs typically allow for different zoom levels, that is, magnification levels, permitting precise entry and editing of information. Also, because they can produce and read MIDI files, these programs can export and import files from other music programs, permitting the user to select different programs to perform specific functions—those functions done best by each of the respective programs. Ultimately, the purposes of these programs is to produce handsome scores which makes their sophisticated printing capabilities vital components of this kind of software.

Sequencing software (e.g., Cakewalk, Master Tracks, and Vision) is designed to allow for direct recording of music from MIDI controllers to the computer and to provide extensive editing capabilities of that music. Recording can be done, tracks instantly duplicated, passages moved around within the composition, single (or multiple) tracks looped (repeated in playback as many times as may be defined), all or any combination of tracks listened to in replay, playback one note at a time, tempos changed, several different modes of editing (e.g., basic score, event list, and piano roll), as well as a wide range of other options. The editing capabilities include changing the note, the velocity of the note, the time of attack (definable to a very precise degree, e.g., 1/120 of a beat—regardless of tempo), the length of the note, and the timbre (within the limitations of the MIDI equipment being employed). The score options on such programs are typically quite basic and are present for the convenience of users rather than for purposes of producing final printed copies (in fact, some programs may not provide for printing of such scores). Consequently, these files can be exported to scoring programs for such purposes, normally after the sound editing has been completed in the sequencing program.

Editor/librarian software (e.g., MIDI Quest and Galaxy) is designed to permit the user to take the sounds (timbres) from a selected piece of MIDI equipment and modify them; that is, a timbre from a compatible instrument will be brought ("dumped") into the computer and all of its parameters (e.g., velocity, pitch, envelope, oscillator, and amplifier use) will be analyzed and displayed on the screen. The software then provides for the possibility of manipulating any of these components of the sound, changing it very subtly or so dramatically that the original sound is no longer recognizable (or any where in between). A long, quiet attack can be changed into an instantaneous and loud attack. A pure flutelike sound could be changed into a raucous "white noise" rich quality. A steady, even sound could be altered to fluctuate slowly or quickly. The possibilities, for all practical purposes, are limited only by one's imagination. The sound(s) brought from the MIDI device to this software (this can be done individually or in "banks") can then be regrouped (placing them into different combinations in sets called "banks"). Their position in the bank also can be redefined (the order of sounds in a bank sometimes can be important in live performance to allow for a quick and easy change of timbre), and these banks (or individual sounds) can be stored in the "Library" of sounds.

In addition to the principal types of MIDI software discussed above, there are a few other kinds that are in use to some degree. These include software that accompanies sound cards (e.g., Advanced Gravis Ultrasound) that allow the user to have the opportunity to check out the sounds available without using other programs; software that provide for sampling and editing sampled sounds; and some "compositional" software which ranges from providing matrices (for tone row or other serial manipulations) to programs that offer computer improvisational possibilities. As mentioned earlier, there are a wide variety of educational software programs, some using MIDI, for many different educational needs ranging from the most rudimentary introduction to music (e.g., notation and rhythm) to advanced study of music theory, analysis, and ear training.

Another very important area of music software is that designed without using MIDI (e.g., C-SOUND). Such programs in many instances have emerged initially from university research into the properties of sound and the musical applications of the sound spectrum with its seemingly infinite number of possible subtle nuances. In programs of this kind, not typically available commercially, a substantial number of options are included, but the user is expected to be able to do programming in computer languages (e.g., C or Pascal) to develop their own subprogram components that work seamlessly with the original program. Each musical parameter is designed and controlled by such programming from the tiniest to the most expansive elements. The completed work is directed to a digital-to-analog converter and then to an audio system for realization in audible sound. The computer, through the design of the program, serves as the generator of the sound, including such elements as its wave shape, pitch, envelope, dynamic characteristics, and timbral quality. Perhaps more important is the fact that the composer controls every possible facet of the composition directly and precisely, from the definition of sounds and their behavior through the articulation of every nuance of the composition through its total realization — the piece is composed entirely at the computer and, until put on tape or other audio storage device, is totally dependent on the computer. The composer exercises a level of control heretofore impossible in any musical/technological context.

REFERENCES

1. C. Sachs, *The History of Musical Instruments*, W. W. Norton Co., Inc., New York, 1940, p. 286.
2. M. Praetorius, *Syntagma Musicum*, Part II, David C. Crookes (transl.), Oxford University Press, New York, 1986, Plate XXIV.
3. D. Ernst, *The Evolution of Electronic Music*, Schirmer Books, New York, 1977, p. xviii.
4. D. Ernst, *The Evolution of Electronic Music*, Schirmer Books, New York, 1977, p. xxi.
5. D. Ernst, *The Evolution of Electronic Music*, Schirmer Books, New York, 1977, p. xix.
6. J. B. de Laborde, *The Electric Harpsichord: With a New Theory for the Mechanism and Phenomena*, 1759, E. Ann Grannis (transl.), Americole R. Biasini, Bellingham, WA, 1979.
7. V. Ussachevsky and O. Luening, *Electronic Tape Music: The First Compositions*, Highgate Press, New York, 1977, p. 32.
8. M. Berenbaum, *The World Must Know*, Little Brown and Co., Boston, MA, 1993, pp. 42–43.
9. M. Matthews, remarks made at the International Computer Music Association conference at the University of Illinois, 1988.

10. V. Ussachevsky and O. Luening, *Electronic Tape Music: The First Compositions*, Highgate Press, New York, 1977, p. 4.

11. *Hugh Le Caine: Pioneer in Electronic Music Instrument Design*, liner notes, produced by Gayle Young, JWD-02.

12. K. H. Worner, *Stochhausen: Life and Work*, University of California Press, Berkeley, 1976.

13. *Columbia Princeton Electronic Music Center*, liner notes, Columbia Record MS 6566.

14. International MIDI Association, *MIDI 1.0 Detailed Specifications*, Ver. 4.0, International MIDI Association, Los Angeles, CA, 1988.

BIBLIOGRAPHY

Anderton, C., *MIDI for Musicians*, Amsco Publications, New York, 1986.

Anderton, C., *The Electronic Musician's Dictionary*, distributed by MIX Publishers, Emeryville, CA, 1990.

Appleton, J. H. and R. Perera, *The Development and Practice of Electronic Music*, Prentice-Hall, Englewood Cliffs, NJ, 1975.

Bartlett, B. *Stereo Microphone Techniques*, Focal Press, Stoneham, MA, 1990.

Borwick, J., *Loudspeaker and Headphone Handbook*, Focal Press, Stoneham, MA, 1990.

Chowning, J. and D. Bristow, *FM Theory and Applications*, Hal Leonard Publ. Corp., New York, 1987.

Cross, L. M., *A Bibliography of Electronic Music*, University of Toronto Press, Toronto, 1967.

DeFuria, S., Scacciaferro, J., *The MIDI System Exclusive Book*, distributed by MIX Publishers, Emeryville, CA, 1987.

de La Bourde, J. B., *The Electronic Harpsichord: With a New Theory for the Mechanism and the Phenomena*, 1759, E. Anne Grannis (transl.), Americole R. Biasini, Pub., Bellingham, WA, 1979.

Deutsch, H. A., *Synthesis: Introduction to History, Theory and Practice of Electronic Music*, Alfred Publ. Co., New York, 1976.

Dodge, C. and T. J. Jerse, *Computer Music*, Schirmer Books, New York, 1985.

Douglas, A., *Electronic Musical Instruments Manual: A Guide to Theory*, DePitman Publ. Co., New York, 1962.

Douglas, A., *Electronic Music Production*, 2nd ed., MacDonald Press, London, 1982.

Ernst, D., *The Evolution of Electronic Music*, Schirmer Books, New York, 1977.

Graham, B., *Music and the Synthesiser*, Argus Books, Watford Hertshire, England, 1980.

Heifetz, R. J., *On the Wires of Our Nerves: The Art of Electronic Music*, Bucknell University Press, Cranbury, NJ, 1988.

Hiller, L. A. and L. M. Isaacson, *Experimental Music*, McGraw-Hill Book Co., New York, 1959.

Hofstetter, F., *Computer Literacy for Musicians*, Prentice-Hall, Englewood Cliffs, NJ, 1988.

Horn, D. T., *The Beginner's Book of Electronic Music*, Tab Books, Blue Ridge Summit, PA, 1982.

Howe, H. S., *Electronic Music Synthesis*, W. W. Norton Co., New York, 1975.

Jenkins, J. and J. Smith, *Electronic Music: A Practical Manual*, Indiana University Press, Bloomington, IN, 1975.

Judd, F. C., *Electronic Music and Musique Concrete*, Neville Spearman Co., London, 1961.

Keane, D., *Tape Music Composition*, Oxford University Press, New York, 1980.

Kettlekamp, L., *Electronic Musical Instruments: What They Do: How They Work*, William Morrow and Co., New York, 1984.

Mackay, A., *Electronic Music*, Phaidon Press, London, 1981.

Manning, P., *Electronic and Computer Music*, Clarendon Press, London, 1985.

Mathews, M., *The Technology of Computer Music*, M.I.T. Press, Cambridge, MA, 1969.
MIDI 1.0 Detailed Specifications, ver. 4.0, International MIDI Association, Los Angeles, 1988.
Molenda, M. (ed.), *Electronic Musician*, Peter Hirschfield, Publ., Emeryville, CA.
Montague, S., *Live Electronics*, Gordon & Breach Science Publ., London, 1991.
Montague, S., *New Electronic Instruments*, Gordon & Breach Science Publ., London, 1991.
Moore, F. R., *Elements of Computer Music*, Prentice-Hall, Englewood Cliffs, NJ, 1990.
Naumann, J. and J. Wagoner, *Analog Electronic Music*, Schirmer Books, New York, 1985.
Orton, R. (ed.), *Electronic Music for Schools*, Cambridge University Press, New York, 1981.
Petit, J., *Le Poéme Electronique, Le Corbusier*, Editions de Minuit, Paris, 1958.
Praetorius, M., *Syntagma Musicum, Part II*, David C. Crookes (transl.), Oxford University Press, New York, 1986.
Roads, C. (ed.), *Composers and the Computer*, William Kaufman, Los Altos, CA, 1985.
Roederer, J. G., *Introduction to the Physics and Psychophysics of Music*, Springer-Verlag, Berlin, 1973.
Rona, J., *MIDI – In's Out's and Thru's*, Hal Leonard Publ. Co., New York, 1986.
Rothstein, J., *MIDI: A Comprehensive Introduction*, distributed by MIX Publishers, Emeryville, CA, 1991.
Russcol, H., *The Liberation of Sound: An Introduction to Electronic Music*, Prentice-Hall, Englewood Cliffs, NJ, 1972.
Sachs, C., *The History of Musical Instruments*, W. W. Norton Co., New York, 1940.
Schrader, B., *Introduction to Electro-Acoustic Music*, Prentice-Hall, Englewood Cliffs, NJ, 1982.
Schwartz, E., *Electronic Music: A Listener's Guide*, Praeger, New York, 1975.
Shawn, J. (ed.), *Digital Audio Engineering: An Anthology*, William Kaufman, Los Altos, CA, 1985.
Shawn, J. (ed.), *Digital Audio Signal Processing: An Anthology*, William Kaufman, Los Altos, CA, 1985.
Strange, A., *Electronic Music System Technology and Controls*, 2nd ed., Wm. C. Brown Co., Dubuque, IA, 1983.
Tjepkema, S. L., *Bibliography of Computer Music*, University of Iowa Press, Iowa City, 1981.
Traylor, J. G., *Physics of Stereo/Quad Sound*, Iowa State University Press, Ames, 1977.
Trubitt, D. (ed.), *Making Music With Your Computer*, EM Books, Emeryville, CA, 1993.
Trythall, G., *Principles and Practices of Electronic Music*, Grosset and Dunlap Co., New York, 1973.
Ussachevsky, V. and O. Luening, *Electronic Tape Music: The First Compositions*, , Highgate Press, New York, 1977.
Wadhams, W., *Dictionary of Music Production and Engineering Terminology*, Schirmer Books, New York, 1988.
Watkinson, J., *The Art of Digital Audio*, Focal Press, Stoneham, MA, 1990.
Wells, T. H., *The Technique of Electronic Music*, Schirmer Books, New York, 1981.
Wilkinson, S. R., *Tuning In: Microtonality in Electronic Music*, distributed by MIX Publishers, Emeryville, CA, 1988.
Wittlich, G., J. W. Schaeffer, and L. R. Babb, *Microcomputers and Music*, Prentice-Hall, Englewood Cliffs, NJ, 1986.
Worner, K. H., *Stockhausen: Life and Works*, University of California Press, Berkeley, 1976.
Young, G., *The Sackbut Blues: Hugh LeCaine – Pioneer Electronic Musician*, University of Toronto Press, Toronto, 1989.
Zaza, A., *The Mechanics of Sound Recording*, Prentice-Hall, Englewood Cliffs, NJ, 1991.

LLOYD ULTAN

FUZZY LOGIC IN ARTIFICIAL INTELLIGENCE

INTRODUCTION

In 1948, Alan Turing wrote an article (1) marking the beginning of a new era, the era of the intelligent machine, which raised questions that still remain unanswered today. This era was heavily influenced by the appearance of the computer, a machine that allowed humans to automate their way of thinking.

However, human thinking is not exact. If you had to park your car *precisely* in one place, you would have extreme difficulties. To allow computers to really mimic the way humans think, the theories of fuzzy sets and fuzzy logic were created. They should be viewed as formal mathematical theories for the representation of uncertainty, which is essential for the management of real-world systems, as it mimics the crucial ability of the human mind to summarize data and focus on decision relevant information.

Marvin Minsky, one of the founding fathers of artificial intelligence, once defined the latter as

> . . . the science of making machines do things that would require intelligence if done by men.

Similarly, Lotfi A. Zadeh, who in 1965 wrote the founding paper on fuzzy set theory (2), once described the aim of this theory as being

> the construction of smarter machines.

Zadeh recently coined the term MIQ (machine intelligence quotient) to refer to this particular aspect of the growing number of intelligent consumer products and industrial systems (3).

Proponents of the so-called "strong" artificial intelligence believe that eventually these machines will be as intelligent as we human beings are now. Thinking positively about technology, everything that is conceivable to be solved by artificial means will eventually be realized if it is interesting enough. Of course, some intellectual processes have been shown to be emergent properties, such as "consciousness." The concept of emergent properties of complex systems was first observed by von Bertalanffy (4) in the 1920s in his study of complex biological systems. He noted that complex assemblies of entities organized in particular ways can reveal unique properties not possessed by the individual entities alone. Emergent properties cease to exist if the whole is broken into components or if the components are organized in a different way. Additionally, emergent properties cannot be understood by the study of isolated components. Similar to the notion of a critical mass in physics, an emergent property will suddenly pop up when a sufficient amount of mass has been accumulated. Contrary to reductionistic approaches, these approaches normally assume a holistic view of the world; that is, something complex can be more than simply the accumulation or "sum of its parts." Of course, as with the atomic bomb, which was in a certain sense the first artificial application of the physical effect described above, the ethical aspects have to be carefully considered. One has to be aware that any technology can be used for good or for evil. However, not the technology in itself is good or bad, but instead the humans that use it are so, as technology has so far been only a tool for human beings. In the case of intelligence, this might not be true anymore because advanced intelligence may entail new ethical needs, but these new forms of intelligence have not yet reached a level where ethical aspects become prevalent.

SOME ELEMENTS OF FUZZY LOGIC

In this section, we briefly outline how fuzzy logic extends classical Boolean logic (or, equivalently, how fuzzy set theory generalizes Cantorian set theory).

Given a (crisp) universe of discourse X, a *fuzzy subset A* of X (see, e.g., Refs. 2 and 5) is characterized by its *membership function*

$$\mu_A : X \to [0, 1],$$

where for $x \in X$ the number $\mu_A(x)$ is interpreted as the *degree of membership* of x in the fuzzy set A or, equivalently, as the *truth value* of the statement "x is an element of A."

The membership function of a fuzzy set is a natural generalization of the *characteristic function* of a (classical) subset A of X,

$$\mathbf{1}_A : X \to \{0, 1\},$$

assigning to each element x in X the value 1 whenever x belongs to A, and the value 0 otherwise.

In order to generalize the set-theoretical operations like *intersection* and *union* (or the corresponding Boolean logical operations *conjunction* and *disjunction*, respectively), we need triangular norms and conorms (6–8): A *triangular norm (t-norm)* is a binary operation on $[0, 1]$, that is, a function $T: [0, 1]^2 \to [0, 1]$, which is commutative, associative, monotone in both components, and satisfies the boundary condition

$$T(x, 1) = x.$$

If T is a *t*-norm, then the dual *triangular conorm (t-conorm)* $S: [0, 1]^2 \to [0, 1]$ is defined by

$$S(x, y) = 1 - T(1 - x, 1 - y).$$

There are many, in fact infinitely many, *t*-norms and *t*-conorms, only few of which are used in applications. The most important *t*-norms, together with their dual *t*-conorms, are the following:

Minimum T_M, Maximum S_M

$$T_M(x, y) = \min(x, y), \qquad S_M(x, y) = \max(x, y)$$

Product T_P, Probabilistic Sum S_P

$$T_\mathbf{P}(x, y) = x \cdot y, \qquad S_\mathbf{P}(x, y) = x + y - x \cdot y$$

Łukasiewicz *t*-norm $T_\mathbf{L}$, Bounded Sum $S_\mathbf{L}$

$$T_\mathbf{L}(x, y) = \max(x + y - 1, 0), \qquad S_\mathbf{L}(x, y) = \min(x + y, 1)$$

Weakest *t*-norm $T_\mathbf{W}$, Strongest *t*-conorm $S_\mathbf{W}$

$$T_\mathbf{W}(x, y) = \begin{cases} \min(x, y) & \text{if } \max(x, y) = 1 \\ 0 & \text{otherwise,} \end{cases}$$

$$S_\mathbf{W}(x, y) = \begin{cases} \max(x, y) & \text{if } \min(x, y) = 0 \\ 1 & \text{otherwise.} \end{cases}$$

Given a *t*-norm T, its dual *t*-conorm S, and fuzzy subsets A and B of the universe X, the membership functions of the intersection $A \cap B$, the union $A \cup B$, and the complement A^c are given by

$$\mu_{A \cap B}(x) = T(\mu_A(x), \mu_B(x)),$$
$$\mu_{A \cup B}(x) = S(\mu_A(x), \mu_B(x)),$$
$$\mu_{A^c}(x) = 1 - \mu_A(x).$$

The values $\mu_{A \cap B}(x)$, $\mu_{A \cup B}(x)$, and $\mu_{A^c}(x)$ describe the truth values of the statements "x is an element of A AND x is an element of B," "x is an element of A OR x is an element of B," and "x is NOT an element of A," respectively.

Given a *t*-norm T, its dual *t*-conorm S and propositions P and Q with truth values $\|P\|$ and $\|Q\|$, respectively, there are two main extensions of the Boolean implication $P \Rightarrow Q$:

S-implication

$$\|P \Rightarrow_s Q\| = S(1 - \|P\|, \|Q\|)$$

R-implication

$$\|P \Rightarrow_R Q\| = \sup\{\alpha \in [0, 1] \mid T(\alpha, \|P\|) \leq \|Q\|\}$$

In Boolean logic, that is, with truth values 0 and 1 only, *S*- and *R*-implication always are equivalent, which is no longer true in fuzzy logic: For the *t*-norm $T_\mathbf{M}$, the corresponding *S*-implication becomes the Kleene–Dienes implication and the *R*-implication of the Gödel implication (9) which are quite different. Note, however, that in the case of the Łukasiewicz *t*-norm $T_\mathbf{L}$, *S*- and *R*-implication coincide: They both yield the Łukasiewicz implication.

The fact that there is a wide range of possibilities for extending Boolean operations to fuzzy logic may look disturbing for beginners in the field. However, it reflects the richness of fuzzy logic, as it allows for a very sensitive fine-tuning when modeling real-world situations.

FUZZY LOGIC, ARTIFICIAL INTELLIGENCE, AND COMPUTATIONAL INTELLIGENCE

It is important to note that the term fuzzy logic is used in two distinct senses. In its narrower sense, fuzzy logic is only one branch of fuzzy set theory. Fuzzy set theory was invented by Zadeh to be better able to represent such everyday notions as the set of "tall persons." Of course, this set is defined vaguely, and persons will more or less be a member of it, that is, member to a certain degree. Fuzzy logic in this narrow sense deals in a natural way with the representation and inference from such vaguely formulated or uncertain knowledge, similar to classical logic, which deals with crisp knowledge where statements can only be either true or false (well, almost, at least if you do not count the findings of Kurt Gödel). In recent years, however, it has become increasingly common to employ the term fuzzy logic in a much broader sense, making the difference between the notions of fuzzy set theory and fuzzy logic vanish. To avoid confusion, we follow the trend of using fuzzy logic in its general sense.

James Bezdek, editor-in-chief of the *IEEE Transactions on Fuzzy Systems* defined fuzzy logic in a delightful essay (10) to be one part of "computational intelligence," altogether with such research areas as neural networks, evolutionary computation, and genetic algorithms. Bezdek contrasts the ABCs on intelligence: artificial, biological, and computational. In the strictest sense, computational intelligence "depends on numerical data supplied by manufacturers and [does] not rely on 'knowledge.'" Artificial intelligence, on the other hand, uses what Bezdek calls "knowledge tidbits." Heuristically constructed artificial intelligence such as an expert system is an example. Practicing knowledge engineers and neural smiths know the distinction is at times not precise. Expert extraction of feature data for training a layered perceptron certainly falls in the area of artificial intelligence. Using these features to train the layered perceptron is primarily computational. Fuzzy inference engines crafted by experts fall into the definition of artificial intelligence. Algorithmic tuning of the engine with raw data, however, is computational intelligence.

Even though the boundary between computational intelligence and artificial intelligence is not distinct, we can, making certain assumptions, monitor the volume of research activity in each. Indeed, the separate identities of computational intelligence and artificial intelligence are confirmed by inspection of the recent volume of publishing and patent activity (11).

However, the term "computational intelligence" itself is not undisputed, as it had already been widely used to mean artificial intelligence before it was redefined by Bezdek; see, for example, the journal *Computational Intelligence*, published since 1985, the conference "Computational Intelligence" taking place annually since 1988, and numerous other publications and organizations using the term in this traditional sense.

In both cases, artificial intelligence as well as fuzzy logic, one tries in some sense to imitate life in its problem-solving capability. The ways in which to achieve this goal are different in many respects, but there are also many common points where the two fields overlap: Robert Marks (11) counted 4811 entries on fuzzy logic in the INSPEC database from 1989 to 1993, containing citations from over 4000 selected journals, books, conference proceedings, and technical reports — "22% of them [were] cross categorized in the expert system category, and 12% with neural networks." Based on various "bean countings," Marks concludes that the overlapping areas cover, depending on the method of counting, from 14% to 33%.

It should be noted that there has been a lot of scientific antagonism between fuzzy logic and artificial intelligence, and, accordingly, skeptics on both sides exist and treat the other side with reservation, if not with open hostility. There are many reasons for this; for example, some critics of fuzzy logic credit the word "fuzzy" for being too controversial and misleading in itself, others maintain that anything that can be done with fuzzy logic and fuzzy set theory can be done equally well with classical logic and probability theory (12),* and still others insist on denying fuzzy logic the status of a logic itself (13). Of course, these claims were refuted (Refs. 14 and 15, or see discussions in the archives of the new-groups mentioned later in this article). Fuzzy logic in its narrow sense is simply a logic *of* fuzziness, not a logic which *itself* is fuzzy. Just as the laws of probability are not random, so the laws of fuzziness are not vague.

On the other hand, critics of artificial intelligence have observed that the sometimes overambitious predictions made in the past did not come true. Some even go as far as to deny that there has been even one successful expert system implemented that really was used. Others believe that the aim of creating artificial intelligence is useless and impossible on philosophical grounds. However, such views are likely to become muted with the passage of time and a better understanding of the basic ideas underlying the theories of both artificial intelligence and fuzzy logic. We observe nevertheless that, nurtured by the current success of fuzzy logic in the real world, dangerously unrealistic predictions and claims appear again. For instance, Bart Kosko, a respected scholar in the field and author of a best-selling textbook *Neural Networks and Fuzzy Systems* (16), predicts for the next few decades fuzzy-logic-based natural-language-understanding, machines that write interesting novels and screenplays in a selected style such as Hemingway's, or even sex robots with a humanlike repertoire of behavior (14). Some researchers suggest, however, that as attempts are made to make fuzzy systems larger, they will encounter similar difficulties as conventional reasoning methodologies. Fuzzy logic is certainly not a philosopher's stone for solving all problems that confront us today, but it has a considerable potential for practical applications. The management of uncertainty will be of growing importance. This uncertainty can have various reasons, ranging from uncertainty due to the lack of knowledge or evidence, due to an abundance of complexity and information, to uncertainty due to the fast and unpredictable development of scientific, political, social, and other structures nowadays.

APPLICATIONS OF FUZZY LOGIC

The applications of fuzzy technologies fall mainly into two categories. Fuzzy control applications, which are often rather simple but very efficient fuzzy-rule-based systems, such as autofocusing systems in cameras, washing machines, automobile transmissions, subway control, or even handwriting recognition. In these applications, fuzzy logic is used as a powerful knowledge representation technique that allows to hide unessential details and to handle uncertain data. However, their efficiency also depends heavily on the use of sensors and effectors; thus, their success should really be explained by the interaction of these various parts. The

---

*But Cheeseman, the author of Ref. 12, also rejects nonmonotonic reasoning, default logic, and Dempster Shafer's theory, arguing that probabilities are better suited to model the world, and that the other methods are at most harmless if not outright wrong.

second category consists of those much more complex systems that aim at supporting or even replacing a human expert. Such applications are exemplified by medical diagnosis systems, securities funds and portfolio selection systems, traffic control systems, fuzzy expert systems, and fuzzy scheduling systems. In this second category, there are still many problems that remain to be addressed, and there is an equally pressing need for a better understanding of how to deal with knowledge-based systems in which knowledge is both uncertain and imprecise.

Areas where fuzzy logic and artificial intelligence meet in current research include fuzzy expert systems (e.g., for medical diagnosis or intelligent tutoring systems), theoretical investigations (e.g., combinations of fuzzy logic with modal logics and other forms of defeasible reasoning, i.e., based on questionable knowledge; this also includes investigations into fuzzy logic programming languages such as fuzzy extensions of PROLOG), machine learning (e.g., combinations of fuzzy logic with neural networks, genetic algorithms, associative memories, symbolic learning methods such as case-based reasoning), robotics (involving motion control and planning capabilities, e.g., when flying a fully automated helicopter or driving a car on a freeway), pattern matching (e.g., face recognition), fuzzy deductive databases (e.g., to ease data retrieval in geographic information systems), or constraint satisfaction problem-solving methods (applied, e.g., in manufacturing process scheduling (17) or in bridge design).

FUZZY EXPERT SYSTEMS

Let us take a closer look at fuzzy expert systems as the archetypical spin-off coming from the combination of techniques from fuzzy logic and artificial intelligence. Classical expert systems are computer programs that emulate the reasoning of human experts or perform in an expert manner in a domain for which no human expert exists. This could be due to a dangerous working environment or simply because of a domain that is too large for one human being. These expert systems typically reason with uncertain and imprecise information, using various methods besides fuzzy logic to handle them. There are many sources of imprecision and uncertainty. The knowledge that the expert systems embody is often not exact, in the same way as a human's knowledge is imperfect. Given facts or user-supplied information are also often uncertain.

An expert system is typically made up of at least three parts: an inference engine, a knowledge base, and a working memory. The inference engine uses the domain knowledge together with acquired information about a problem to provide an expert solution. The knowledge base contains the expert domain knowledge for use in problem solving, very often in form of explicit facts and IF-THEN rules.

A fuzzy expert system, usually, is an expert system that uses a collection of fuzzy membership functions and rules to reason about data. The rules in a fuzzy expert system are typically of a form similar to the following:

IF heat is *low* AND pressure is *high* THEN valve is *closed*

where heat and pressure are (linguistic) input variables, that is, names for known data values, valve is a (linguistic) output variable, that is, a name for a data value to be computed, *low* is one of the possible linguistic values of the variable heat described by membership function of the corresponding fuzzy set, *high* is a linguistic value of the variable pressure and *closed* is a linguistic value of the variable valve. The antecedent (the rule's premise) describes to what degree the rule applies, whereas the conclusion (the rule's consequent) assigns a fuzzy set or, if defuzzification takes place, a crisp value to each of the output variables. Most tools for working with fuzzy expert systems allow for more than one conclusion per rule. The set of rules in a fuzzy expert system is known as the rule base or knowledge base.

The general inference process proceeds in three (or four) steps.

1. In the fuzzification step, the linguistic terms defined through their associated fuzzy membership functions are matched with the actual values of the input variables, to determine the degree of truth for each rule's premise.

2. In the inference step, the truth values for the premises are propagated to the conclusion part of each rule. This results for each rule in one fuzzy subset that is assigned to an output variable. Usually, only *minimum* or *product* are used as inference methods. In *minimum* inferencing, the output membership function is clipped off at the height corresponding to the rule premise's computed degree of truth. In *product* inferencing, the output membership function is scaled by the rule premise's computed degree of truth.

3. In the composition step, all fuzzy subsets assigned to given output variables are combined to form a single fuzzy subset for each output variable. Also in this case, two ways of composition dominate in most applications, namely, *max* and *bounded sum*. In *max* composition, the combined output fuzzy set is constructed by taking the pointwise maximum over all of the membership functions of the fuzzy sets assigned to the output variable by the inference rule. In *bounded sum* composition, the combined output fuzzy set is constructed by taking the pointwise sum (cut off at level 1 whenever it would be exceeded) of all the membership functions of the fuzzy sets assigned to the output variable by the inference rule.

4. The optional defuzzification step is used when it is useful and/or necessary to convert the output fuzzy set into a crisp value by choosing a crisp number which is representative for the fuzzy output set. This is almost always the case in technical control problems where the output must be crisp, less often in expert systems where output fuzzy sets are sometimes linguistically approximated. There are at least 30 different defuzzification methods. Two of the more common techniques are the *center of gravity* and *center of maxima* methods. In the *center of gravity* method, the crisp value of the output variable is computed by finding the variable value of the center of gravity of the membership function for the fuzzy value. In the *center of maxima* method, the midpoint of the region where the fuzzy set assumes its maximum truth value is chosen as the representative crisp value for the output variable.

It should be mentioned that *min* and *product* are two out of an infinite number of possible multiple-valued generalizations of the logical operation "and" (conjunction) in Boolean (two-valued) logic.

A TYPICAL EXAMPLE

To cite one of the most prominent and successful fuzzy expert systems, we have to refer to a very long ranging project initiated as early as 1976 by Klaus-Peter Adlassnig and resulting in a system in use today. CADIAG-2, which is currently evolving to become CADIAG-3, is a medical diagnosis system based on fuzzy expert system technology (Ref. 3 contains a recent paper about this very large project which has resulted in an enormous amount of publications; Ref. 5 also contains a description of CADIAG-2). A typical rule of this system looks as follows (the rule has been slightly simplified for this example):

IF	fever	is	*frequent*	AND
	high fever	is	*frequent*	AND
	knee dropsy	is	*rare*	AND
	carditis	is	*very-rare*	AND
	articular pain	is	*almost-always*	AND
	erythema	is	*frequent*	AND
	previous tonsillitis	is	*very-frequent*	AND
	staphylokokkus	is	*never*	AND
	increased AST	is	*almost-always*	
THEN	rheumatic fever	is	*plausible*	

Here one can see again the two key concepts which play a central role in the application of fuzzy logic in expert systems. The first is that of a linguistic variable such as "high fever," that is, a variable whose values are words or sentences in a natural or synthetic language such as *frequent* or *rare*. The other is that of a fuzzy IF-THEN rule in which the antecedent and consequent are propositions containing linguistic variables. The essential function served by linguistic variables is that of granulation of variables and their dependencies. In effect, the use of linguistic variables and fuzzy IF-THEN rules results—through granulation—in soft data compression which exploits the tolerance for imprecision and uncertainty. Of course, the effective membership functions represented by words such as *very-rare* have also to be determined and must be known at inference time to the inference engine.

For a detailed account of what expert systems, in general, and fuzzy expert systems, in particular, are and how they work, we refer to Refs. 5, 18, and 19.

CAN FUZZY LOGIC HELP TO REDUCE COMPUTATIONAL COMPLEXITY?

In the final "Future Perspectives" section of his book (5), Hans-Jürgen Zimmermann, who is also editor-in-chief of the influential journal *Fuzzy Sets and Systems*, points out an important potential benefit that fuzzy logic could bring to the field of artificial intelligence. In particular, for many problems encountered in subfields of artificial intelligence, such as logic programming, deductive databases, or constraint satisfaction, complexity analysis results range from intractable to undecidable; that is, these problems are computationally very hard to solve. It is very easy to encounter problems not solvable with current computing power. Zimmermann, therefore, raises the question of whether fuzzy logic can help to solve such large and complex problems. At the time of the writing of his book, the answer was still no.

We shortly restate here some common notions from complexity theory to analyze whether another answer can be found. Many of the complex problems most commonly encountered in the mentioned subfields of artificial intelligence have been proven to be so-called NP-hard problems, referring to their combinatorially explosive need for computing resources. Especially, the run-time behavior of algorithms that solve these hard problems is at least exponential in the size of the problem description. NP-hardness formally implies that these problems are "at least as hard" as so-called NP-complete problems. According to Garey and Johnson (20), NP-complete problems are known to be

> . . . "just as hard" as a large number of other problems that are widely recognized as being difficult and that have been confounding the experts for years.

> . . . the knowledge that [a problem] is NP complete does provide valuable information about what lines of approach have the potential of being most productive. Certainly the search for an efficient, exact algorithm should be accorded low priority.

The main result is that an exact and efficient solution for NP-hard problems has eluded many researchers until now. These problems have, therefore, been termed intractable. However, it is possible to relax one of two criteria, either exactness or efficiency, in which case the other criterion can be fulfilled in many cases. One suggestion could be to relax the problem somewhat in its unimportant characteristics, that is, to model a simplified version that does yield an acceptable solution efficiently. This is often sufficient for real-world optimization problems. Another suggestion is indicated by the second sentence in the above quotation, which is worth some more investigation. In particular, it is interesting to know that NP-complete problems can be solved in polynomial time by a nondeterministic computer. The scenario is often such that a solution has to be "guessed," for instance by consulting an "oracle," followed by calling a polynomial algorithm to check whether the guessed solution is correct. This would suggest than an algorithm that intelligently "guesses" a complete instantiation and then checks whether it is a solution could be used to construct an algorithm that finds a "reasonably good" solution for "almost all" problems.

The following paragraph provides a little more background about the introduced notions. It is an open problem of complexity theory whether NP is equal to P, P being the problems solvable in polynomial time, that is, the tractable problems. Indeed, many researchers even believe that this question is currently the most important open question in computer science as a whole. However, most researchers think that P and NP are different. This would mean that NP-complete problems would remain, at least in the worst case, intractable; that is, their execution time grows more than polynomially when the structural parameters grow linearly. In such a case, doubling the speed of the computer does not really help because only negligible larger problems will be solvable by that computer, which is usually by far not enough. The NP-complete problems are characterized by the fact that they are NP problems and that *all* other NP problems can be polynomially reduced to these NP-complete problems. This means that NP-complete problems are at least as difficult as any other NP problem. To prove that a problem A is NP-complete, it is sufficient to show that A belongs to NP and that one other problem B known to be NP-complete can be polynomially transformed into A. A general search problem H

belongs to the NP-hard problems if and only if there exists a *polynomial time algorithm* for some decision problem C known to be NP-complete, assuming that H could be used arbitrarily often for further computations at a computational cost of one unit-time interval by the polynomial time algorithm solving C (i.e., C must be polynomial time Turing-transformable into H).

Therefore, the answer to the question posed by Zimmermann has to remain negative on theoretical grounds. On the contrary, the computational complexity will often increase when a problem is fuzzified because, in general, the search space will be enlarged.

However, knowledge modeled using fuzzy logic can easily approximate a problem in its important characteristics. In particular, problems encountered in the real world, such as in manufacturing, exhibit a tendency to obey certain intangible rules, thus allowing the approximation to be done successfully. The same would not be possible for random data, representing the worst case that must also be correctly handled by exact (but much slower) algorithms. Additionally, some heuristics such as described in Ref. 17 match particularly well with fuzzy knowledge representation schemes and, thus, help to efficiently solve large and complex problems. In this connection, a "solution" to a problem is often understood pragmatically as the result of a search for the best solution that can be found using all the available resources such as *available* computers, *available* time, and *available* algorithms. So, to provide a more positive answer to the question raised by Zimmermann, we conclude that fuzzy logic *can* help to reduce complexity *if* the problem to be solved can be adequately approximated, which is true for many real-world problems.

SYNERGY EFFECTS

To emphasize again in what respect artificial intelligence and fuzzy logic can mutually benefit from each other, we want to point out that all complex systems and machines that were built so far required more than just one basic technology in order to be successful. In a large measure, techniques from artificial intelligence and from fuzzy logic are complementary rather than competitive. We believe that it is possible to fruitfully combine techniques from both fields in many areas. The resulting hybrid systems will be more and more important in the future. Following the line of reasoning given earlier concerning emergent properties, the synergy effect resulting in this combination is necessary to achieve the ultimate goal of creating machines that act more and more intelligently for the benefit of mankind.

FURTHER READINGS

For readers interested in gaining a better understanding of one of the two fields, fuzzy logic and artificial intelligence, we would like to refer to some good introductory texts such as Winston's book on artificial intelligence (21), or, more recently, McNeill and Freiberger's book on fuzzy logic (14). For those wanting to dig deeper or to answer more elaborate questions, we recommend to consult some of the following texts and media (the list could, of course, be much longer, but we limit ourselves to the most accessible items):

- The excellent *Encyclopedia of Artificial Intelligence* edited by Shapiro (19) covers almost all possible subjects related to this field, including numerous articles on fuzzy logic.
- The *Readings in Fuzzy Sets for Intelligent Systems* (22) to rapidly find the most influencing articles published in this field, as well as *Fuzzy Sets and Applications: Selected Papers by L. A. Zadeh* (23).
- The internet news-groups comp.ai and comp.ai.fuzzy, also accessible electronically via various mailing lists and blackboards, including their respective frequently-asked-questions (with answers) lists, which contain pointers to other electronic sources of information such as worldwide-web-servers, pointers to the most important conferences, major journals, scientific societies, research centers, major scientific projects, book-lists, as well as names of persons-to-know and companies related to the respective fields. These news-groups are also forums to discuss all topics related to the two fields and are equipped with searchable archives extending over several years (15,24).

For readers searching for references covering primarily the intersection of artificial intelligence and fuzzy logic, we have compiled a list of some important textbooks (18,25–28) and conference proceedings (3,29) in the Reference section.

REFERENCES

1. A. M. Turing, "Intelligent Machinery," in *Mechanical Intelligence, Collected Works of A. M. Turing*, D. C. Ince (ed.), North-Holland, Amsterdam, 1992. Original article appeared in *Machine Intell., 5*, 3–23 (1969) but was actually written as early as in 1948.
2. L. A. Zadeh, "Fuzzy Sets," *Inform. Control, 8*, 338–353 (1965). Republished in Ref. 23.
3. E. P. Klement and W. Slany (eds.). *Fuzzy Logic in Artificial Intelligence. Proceedings of the 8th Austrian Artificial Intelligence Conference, FLAI'93*, Springer-Verlag, Berlin, 1993. A conference report is available on the net: URL: ftp://mira.dbai.tuwien.ac.at/pub/slany/flai.txt.
4. L. von Bertalanffy, "The Organism Considered as a Physical System," in *General System Theory*, L. von Bertalanffy (ed.), Braziller, New York, 1968. Republished from 1940.
5. H.-J. Zimmermann, *Fuzzy Set Theory—and Its Applications*, 2nd rev. ed., Kluwer Academic Publishers, Boston, 1991.
6. E. P. Klement, "Operations on Fuzzy Sets and Fuzzy Numbers Related to Triangular Norms," in *Proceedings of the Eleventh International Symposium on Multiple-Valued Logic*. IEEE, New York, 1981, pp. 218–225.
7. B. Schweizer and A. Sklar, *Probabilistic Metric Spaces*, North-Holland, Amsterdam, 1983.
8. D. Butnariu and E. P. Klement, *Triangular Norm-Based Measures and Games with Fuzzy Coalitions*, Kluwer, Dordrecht, 1993.
9. R. Kruse, J. Gebhardt, and F. Klawonn. *Foundations of Fuzzy Systems*, John Wiley & Sons Ltd., Chichester, 1994.
10. James C. Bezdek, "On the Relationship Between Neural Networks, Pattern Recognition and Intelligence," *Int. J. Approximate Reasoning, 6*, 85–107 (1992).
11. R. J. Marks II, "Intelligence: Computational Versus Artificial," *IEEE Trans. Neural Nets, 4*, 737–739, (September 1993).
12. P. Cheeseman, "In Defense of Probability," in *Proceedings of the Ninth International*

Joint Conference on Artificial Intelligence, Morgan Kaufmann Publishers, San Mateo, CA, 1985, pp. 1002–1009.

13. C. Elkan, "The Paradoxical Success of Fuzzy Logic," in *Proceedings of the Eleventh National Conference on Artificial Intelligence, AAAI'93*, 1993, pp. 698–703. URL: ftp://cs.ucsd.edu/pub/elkan/paradoxicalsuccess.ps.Z; Responses: URL: ftp://ftp.cs.cmu.edu/user/ai/areas/fuzzy/doc/elkan/response.txt.

14. D. McNeill and P. Freiberger, *Fuzzy Logic*, Simon & Schuster, New York, 1993.

15. E. Horstkotte, C. Joslyn, and M. Kantrowitz, comp.ai.fuzzy faq: Fuzzy logic and fuzzy expert systems 1/1 [monthly posting]. URL: ftp://ftp.cs.cmu.edu/afs/cs.cmu.edu/project/ai-repository/ai/pubs/faqs/fuzzy/fuzzy.faq, January 1994.

16. B. Kosko, *Neural Networks and Fuzzy Systems*, Prentice-Hall, Englewood Cliffs, NJ, 1992.

17. W. Slany, "Scheduling as a Fuzzy Multiple Criteria Optimization Problem," CD-Technical Report 94/62, Christian Doppler Laboratory for Expert Systems, Technical University of Vienna, 1994. URL: ftp://mira.dbai.tuwien.ac.at/pub/slany/cd-tr9462.ps.Z.

18. A. Kandel (ed.), *Fuzzy Expert Systems.*, CRC Press, Boca Raton, FL, 1992.

19. S. C. Shapiro (ed.), *Encyclopedia of Artificial Intelligence*, 2nd rev. ed., John Wiley & Sons, New York, 1992.

20. M. R. Garey and D. S. Johnson, *Computers and Intractability: A Guide to the Theory of NP-Completeness*, Freeman and Co., San Francisco, 1979.

21. P. H. Winston, *Artificial Intelligence*, Addison-Wesley, Reading, MA, 1977.

22. D. Dubois, H. Prade, and R. R. Yager (eds.), *Readings in Fuzzy Sets for Intelligent Systems*, Morgan Kaufmann, San Mateo, CA, 1993.

23. R. R. Yager, S. Ovchinnikov, R. M. Tong, and H. T. Nguyen (eds.), *Fuzzy Sets and Applications: Selected Papers by L. A. Zadeh*, John Wiley & Sons, New York, 1987.

24. M. Kantrowitz. comp.ai faqs: 6 parts [monthly posting]. URL: ftp://ftp.cs.cmu.edu/afs/cs.cmu.edu/project/ai-repository/ai/pubs/faqs/ai/ai__[1-6].faq and other directories at the same site, January 1994.

25. D. Dubois and H. Prade, *Possibility Theory: An Approach to Computerized Processing of Uncertainty*, Plenum Press, New York, 1988.

26. R. Kruse, E. Schwecke, and J. Heinsohn, *Uncertainty and Vagueness in Knowledge Based Systems—Numerical Methods*, Springer-Verlag, New York, 1991.

27. C. V. Negoiță, *Expert Systems and Fuzzy Systems*, Benjamin/Cummings, San Francisco, 1985.

28. M. Zemankova-Leech and A. Kandel, *Fuzzy Relational Data Bases—A Key to Expert Systems*, Verlag TÜV Rheinland, Germany, 1984.

29. D. Heckerman and A. Mamdani (eds.), *Uncertainty in Artificial Intelligence* (*Proceedings of the 9th Conference*), Morgan Kaufmann, San Mateo, CA, 1993.

ERICH PETER KLEMENT

WOLFGANG SLANY

FUZZY MODULES AND THEIR BASES

INTRODUCTION

The nearly three decades that have transpired since the publication of Zadeh's seminal paper (1) have been a period of remarkable growth for the theory of fuzzy sets. Research has proceeded in many different directions, and much progress has been made in both theoretical and applied areas. The goal of theoretical research has been to lay down the theoretical underpinnings of the field, thereby providing a foundation for application-minded researchers on which to build. Much of the theoretical research has been directed toward the development of a theory of fuzzy sets that generalizes and extends the theory of various kinds of structures studied in classical mathematics. In particular, fuzzy generalizations of various kinds of algebraic structures (such as semigroups, groups, rings, and modules), as well as generalizations of structures studied in analysis and topology, such as measurable spaces, metric spaces, and normed spaces, have been studied.

Applications of the theory of fuzzy sets are found in many areas. In engineering, the theory finds application in the control of different kinds of systems (2,3). In computer science, the theory finds important applications in the areas of neural networks, expert systems, and robotics (4,5). Many of the computer science applications are in problem domains that have traditionally been associated with artificial intelligence; it is in such domains, where it is often necessary to represent and use information which may be vague or imprecise, that the theory has proved particularly invaluable.

With the growing recognition of the usefulness of fuzzy logic in representing information not easily represented through classical logic has come a realization of the need for programming languages which have built in support for working with fuzzy logic. A number of such fuzzy programming languages have been proposed (6). Some of these fuzzy programming languages have built in support of automated reasoning and deduction and may be regarded as fuzzy extensions of logic programming systems (7) on one hand, and as fuzzy extensions of classical automated theorem provers on the other hand (8). Unlike the situation with classical programming languages, however, little or no work has been done to formally characterize the semantics of these new languages. Because the formal semantic descriptions of classical programming languages makes heavy use of various kinds of universal algebras (9,10), it is reasonable to expect that fuzzy universal algebras will play a correspondingly large role in describing the semantics of fuzzy languages.

This article presents an overview of what is known about fuzzy algebras. The article concentrates mainly on groups and modules; the study of other kinds of algebras employs similar techniques. Many examples of both fuzzy groups and fuzzy modules are provided, and the article points out a number of places where the theory of fuzzy modules and fuzzy groups differs from the theory of their crisp counterparts. A current area of active research is the generation of fuzzy modules or groups from their fuzzy subsets; in connection with this, we point out some open problems, and also point out some areas of contact with the theory of algorithms. Finally, the conclusion contains a brief discussion of free fuzzy groups, free fuzzy modules, and free universal algebras; this is an area that is likely to be of major importance for fuzzy programming languages and logics, considering the role that free algebras have played in the semantics of classical programming languages and logics.

FUZZY SETS

The notion of a fuzzy set is best understood by regarding it as a generalization of the notion of an ordinary set. (We will sometimes refer to an ordinary set as a *crisp* set to distinguish it from its fuzzy counterpart.) When talking about sets, one typically has in mind some universal set X, and all sets under discussion are implicitly understood to be subsets of this universe. Now if s is a set in the universe X, we can associate with s a function $\chi_s : X \to \{0, 1\}$, called the *characteristic function* of s, that assigns a *grade of membership* to each element $x \in X$: if an element x of the universe is a member of s, the x is assigned a membership grade of 1, but if x is not in s, then x is assigned a membership grade of 0. It is convenient to identify the set s with its characteristic function χ_s, and we will use the notation $s : X \to \{0, 1\}$ to denote both the set s and its characteristic function χ_s.

Most of the "sets" encountered in everyday life are not easily described by crisp sets, and degrees of membership other than just 0 and 1 are often required to give an adequate characterization of such sets. Thus, a college professor, in describing the set of "good" students in a calculus course, may assign grades such A, B, C, D, and F, and the Internal Revenue Service, in describing the set of "rich" people in the nation, institutes various tax brackets. Both of the above two sets, the set of good students and the set of rich people, are fuzzy sets. Thus, fuzzy sets are like crisp sets, except that the set $\{0, 1\}$ of membership grades is replaced with some more general set H with some suitable order structure. By using different sets H for the membership grades, we get different classes, or *categories*, of fuzzy sets. For many applications, it suffices to take H to be the closed unit interval I with its usual ordering based on size. We give formal definitions below, starting with one that is particularized to the case $H = I$. A more general definition of a fuzzy set will then follow.

Definition 1   Let X be a nonempty set (the universe), and let $I = [0, 1]$ be the closed unit interval. A *fuzzy set s in X* is a function $s : X \to I$.

The various operations possible on crisp sets, such as taking intersections and unions of families of sets, extend in a natural manner to families of fuzzy sets. Let $s : X \to I$ and $t : X \to I$ be fuzzy sets in X. Then the *union s $\cup$ t*, and the *intersection s $\cap$ t* are the fuzzy sets in X defined by

$$(s \cup t)(x) = \max\{s(x), t(x)\} \quad \text{and}$$
$$(s \cap t)(x) = \min\{s(x), t(x)\} \quad\quad\quad\quad\quad\quad [1]$$

for all $x \in X$. We can similarly define the *union* and *intersection* of arbitrary families of fuzzy sets: let $\{s_\alpha\}_{\alpha \in A}$ be a family of fuzzy sets in X. The union and intersection of the family are defined by

$$\left(\bigcup_{\alpha \in A} s_\alpha \right)(x) = \sup_{\alpha \in A} s_\alpha(x) \quad \text{and} \quad \left(\bigcap_{\alpha \in A} s_\alpha \right)(x) = \inf_{\alpha \in A} s_\alpha(x) \qquad [2]$$

for all $x \in X$. If s and t are fuzzy sets in X, we say that s is a *subset* of t if

$$s(x) \leq t(x) \quad \text{for all } x \in X, \qquad [3]$$

and write $s \subseteq t$ or even $s \leq t$ to indicate this.

Let us now consider the structure that is necessary on a set of membership grades H, in order for the resulting category of fuzzy sets to have useful properties. We would like such an H to be a generalization of I in some way that will allow us to use Eqs. (1)–(3) to define unions, intersections, and the subset relation between two fuzzy sets.

First, it is reasonable to expect that the subset relation defined by Eq. (3) will be a partial order, so H must, itself, be a partial order. In addition, we stipulate that H should be a lattice, so that the $\min\{\delta_1, \delta_2\}$ and $\max\{\delta_1, \delta_2\}$ operations used in the definition of intersection and union in Eq. (2) will make sense. Thus, $\min\{\delta_1, \delta_2\}$ and $\max\{\delta_1, \delta_2\}$ denote the greatest lower bound and the least upper bound of δ_1 and δ_2, respectively. Finally, we stipulate that H be a complete lattice; this will ensure that an arbitrary subset A of H will have a greatest lower bound (denoted by inf A), as well as a least upper bound (denoted by sup A). With this proviso, the definition of intersection and union for arbitrary families of fuzzy sets given in Eq. (2) makes sense.

Ideally, we would like to use as general a complete lattice as possible for our set of membership grades to ensure that results obtained will be widely applicable. In practice, however, the assumption of additional structure on H is necessary to allow us to obtain interesting results. An appropriate level of generality, which encompasses almost all cases encountered in practice, but still allows us to prove interesting results, is to assume that H is a complete Heyting Algebra (11).

Definition 2   A *complete Heyting algebra H* is a complete lattice in which the two equivalent identities

    1. $\sup_{a \in A} \min\{a, b\} = \min\{\sup A, b\}$
    2. $\inf_{a \in A} \max\{a, b\} = \max\{\inf A, b\}$

for every $A \subseteq H$ and $b \in H$.

The closed unit interval I used in Definition 1 as well as the power set algebra $\mathcal{P}(S)$ of all subsets of any set S are both complete Heyting algebras.

All examples of fuzzy sets in this article will assume that the lattice H of membership grades is either I or the power set algebra of some set. In the latter case, the partial order relation $a \leq b$ of H is simply the subset relation $a \subseteq b$, the lattice operation $\min\{a, b\}$ denotes the intersection $a \cap b$, the operation $\max\{a, b\}$ denotes union, whereas inf and sup denote intersection and union of arbitrary sets, respectively.

The greatest and least elements of the complete lattice H will be denoted by 1_H

and 0_H, respectively; when there is no possibility of ambiguity, we will simply write 1 or 0.

Definition 3   Let H be a complete Heyting algebra, and let X be a nonempty set. An *H-fuzzy set s* in X is a function $s : X \to H$.

We will simply say *fuzzy set* whenever the membership lattice H can be understood from the context. We will refer to X as the *carrier* of s and will often write (X, s) in place of the more cumbersome $s : X \to H$.

Let (X, s) be a fuzzy set. If $f : X \to Y$ is a mapping, we define the *image f(s)* of s under f to be the fuzzy set in Y defined by

$$f(s)(y) = \sup\{s(x) | f(x) = y\} \quad \text{for all } y \in Y. \tag{4}$$

Finally, let (X, s) and (Y, t) be two H-fuzzy sets. A *mapping* or *function f*: $(X, s) \to (Y, t)$ from s to t is a function $f : X \to Y$ between the underlying carriers which satisfies the condition

$$f(s) \le t.$$

FUZZY SETS WITH ALGEBRAIC STRUCTURE

In what follows, we assume some familiarity with groups, rings, fields, and other elementary concepts from abstract algebra. We will refer to objects such as groups, rings, and fields by the generic term "algebra," and to their fuzzy counterparts as "fuzzy algebras." Basically, a fuzzy algebra (X, s) is a fuzzy set whose carrier X is an algebra, such that s satisfies a fuzzy closure condition for each operation of the algebra X. This simply means that if $f : X \times X \times \cdots \times X \to X$ is an operation of X of arity n, say, then

$$s(f(x_1, \ldots, x_n)) \ge \min\{s(x_1), \ldots, s(x_n)\}$$

for all $x_1, \ldots, x_n$ in X. We will now give specific definitions and examples of some fuzzy algebraic structures that have been widely studied, namely, fuzzy groups and fuzzy modules. We begin with fuzzy groups, as they are the simpler of the two.

Definition 4   Let G be a group with identity e, and let H be a complete Heyting algebra. A mapping $s : G \to H$ is called a *fuzzy group* in G if s has the fuzzy closure property under the group operations:

(a) $s(x^{-1}) \ge s(x)$ for each $x \in G$
(b) $s(xy) \ge \min\{s(x), s(y)\}$ for all x and y in G
(c) $s(e) = 1$.

An ordinary group is clearly a H-fuzzy group with $H = \{0, 1\}$. We give examples of noncrisp fuzzy groups below.

Example 1   Let X be a nonempty set and denote by S_X the set of all permutations of X. It is clear that S_X is a group under the operation of function composition. Let $\varphi : S_X \to \mathcal{P}(X)$ be defined by

$$\varphi(f) = \{x \in X | f(x) = x\} \quad \text{for each permutation } f : X \to X.$$

Then φ is a fuzzy group in S_X. This fuzzy group may be regarded as the fuzzy group of permutations of X that fix X: The larger the subset of X fixed by a permutation f, the greater the membership degree f in the fuzzy group.

Example 2 Let Z denote the additive group of integers, and define $\psi : Z \rightarrow [0, 1]$ as follows. For each $m \in Z$, let

$$\psi(m) = \sup\{1 - 2^{-k} \,|\, k \geq 0 \text{ and } 2^k \text{ divides } m\}. \qquad [5]$$

It is clear that $\psi(0) = 1$, because 2^k divides 0 for infinitely large k. It is further clear that (Z, ψ) satisfies fuzzy closure under the operation of taking additive inverses. To give an idea of some of the proof techniques used in the field, we will sketch a proof of fact that ψ satisfies fuzzy closure under addition. Let m_1 and m_2 be integers. Suppose that k_1 and k_2 are non-negative integers such that 2^{k_1} and 2^{k_2} divide m_1 and m_2, respectively. It is then clear that $2^{min\{k_1,k_2\}}$ divides $m_1 + m_2$, which by Eq. (5), implies

$$\psi(m_1 + m_2) \geq 1 - 2^{-min\{k_1,k_2\}}$$
$$= \min\{1 - 2^{-k_1}, 1 - 2^{-k_2}\}.$$

The definition of a least upper bound in a lattice, along with the first condition in the definition of a complete Heyting algebra, may now be used to prove fuzzy closure under addition. Thus, (Z, ψ) is a fuzzy group.

The above example may be regarded as a fuzzy group that in some sense, measures each integer m for divisibility by 2: The higher the power of 2 that divides m, the greater the degree of membership assigned to m. There is another fuzzy group in Z, closely related to the preceding, that also measures the integers for divisibility by 2.

Example 3 Let Z be the additive group of integers and let N denote the set of non-negative integers. Define $\psi : Z \rightarrow \mathcal{P}(N)$ by

$$\psi(m) = \{k \in N \,|\, 2^k \text{ divides } m\}.$$

Then (Z, ψ) is a fuzzy group.

There is a sense in which each of the above fuzzy groups may be regarded as a natural construction on its carrier, in that it measures each member x of the carrier by the degree to which x has a certain property. Fuzzy groups may, therefore, provide a useful new way of studying various group-theoretic properties.

Definition 5 Let R be a ring with identity 1_R. A *fuzzy R-module* is a fuzzy set $\mu : M \rightarrow H$ where M is an R-module and μ satisfies the following conditions:

    (a)   For all x, y in M, $\mu(x + y) \geq \min\{\mu(x), \mu(y)\}$
    (b)   For all x in M and $r \in R$, $\mu(rx) \geq \mu(x)$
    (c) $\mu(0_M) = 1_H$

Here, 0_M denotes the additive identity of the module M.

Just as every abelian group is actually a Z-module, every fuzzy group with abelian carrier is also a fuzzy Z-module. Thus, the last two examples furnish us with examples of Z-modules. Here are some more examples of fuzzy modules.

Example 4   Let R be a ring, and let M be an R-module. Define $\mu : M \to \mathcal{P}(R)$ by

$$\mu(x) = \{r \in R \mid rx = 0\}.$$

Then μ is the fuzzy module in M that measures each member of M by its order ideal [12].

Definition 6   Let K be a field. A fuzzy K-module is called a *fuzzy K-vector space*.

We will say "fuzzy module" instead of "fuzzy R-module" whenever the ring R can be inferred from the context, and similarly, we will shorten the term "fuzzy K-vector space" to "fuzzy vector space" whenever possible.

Example 5   Let $n \geq 1$, let $X = R^n$ be the real vector space of dimension n, and let $H = \mathcal{P}(\{1, \ldots, n\})$ be the power set of the set of the first n positive integers. Define $\vartheta : R^n \to H$ by

$$\vartheta(x_1, \ldots, x_n) = \{k \mid 1 \leq k \leq n \text{ and } x_k = 0\}.$$

Then ϑ is a fuzzy vector space. This fuzzy vector space may be regarded as measuring each vector x in X by the set of vectors in the usual basis to which x is orthogonal.

Example 6   Let K be a field, and let $K[x]$ denote the vector space of all polynomials over K. Define $\vartheta : K[x] \to \mathcal{P}(K)$ by

$$\vartheta(p) = \{x \mid p(x) = 0\}.$$

Then ϑ is a fuzzy vector space which measures each polynomial by the set of its roots.

FUZZY MODULES AND THEIR BASES

Fuzzy algebras, like their crisp counterparts may be very large objects, and in fact, as demonstrated by the above examples, may even be infinite. Because large objects are difficult to manipulate (for example, when it is desired to store such an object in the memory of a digital computer), we must cast about for some indirect, and preferably finitary, method of representing these algebraic objects. Our search for such a succinct method of representation leads us directly to the notion of a generating fuzzy set. We will discuss generating sets for fuzzy modules and refer the interested reader to the literature for discussions on generating sets of fuzzy sets with other kinds of algebraic structure. The notion of a generating fuzzy set requires an expanded definition of the notion of a fuzzy subset. Specifically, we would like to talk about a subset relation holding between two fuzzy sets which do not necessarily have the same carrier.

Definition 7   Let (X, s) and (Y, t) be fuzzy sets. We say (X, s) is a *subset* of (Y, t) if X is a subset of Y and $s(x) \leq t(x)$ for all x in X.

It is often convenient to be able to regard a fuzzy subset (X, s) of the fuzzy set (Y, t) as a *fuzzy set in Y*. We do this by defining $s(y) = 0$ for all $y \in Y \setminus X$. We will refer to such an extension of s as the *inclusion* of s in Y and denote the extended fuzzy set by $\mathrm{inc}(s)$. Thus,

$$\text{inc}(s)(y) = \begin{cases} s(y) & \text{if } y \in X \\ 0 & \text{if } y \in Y \setminus X. \end{cases} \quad [6]$$

Definition 8 Let M be a module, and let (S, s) be a fuzzy subset of M, that is, $S \subseteq M$. The *span* of the fuzzy set s is the intersection of all fuzzy modules in M which include inc(s).

It is easily proved that the intersection of fuzzy modules containing a fuzzy set s is itself a fuzzy module containing s. Thus, the span of a fuzzy set is the smallest module containing with that fuzzy set. We say that s is a *generating set* for a fuzzy module (M, μ) if μ is the span of s.

The utility of a generating fuzzy set s for a fuzzy module μ lies in the fact that s may have a finite carrier even when the carrier of μ is infinite. Even in the case where the carrier of μ is finite, a generating fuzzy set for μ may still be more manageable if its carrier is much smaller than that of μ. Because the carrier M of a fuzzy module (M, μ) is an integral part of μ, we must expect that a fuzzy generating set of μ will have a carrier that is a generating set for M. The carrier of a minimal generating set for a fuzzy module, however, may be much larger than a minimal generating set for the carrier of the fuzzy module. For example, the fuzzy Z-module (Z, ψ) of Example 2 cannot be generated by any fuzzy set (S, s) with a finite carrier, even though the module Z is cyclic and can be generated by a set of cardinality 1. Roughly speaking, this is due to the fact that the function $\psi : Z \to I$ uses infinitely many degrees of membership (that is, ψ has infinite range), whereas the span of fuzzy set (S, s) with S finite can have at most finitely many values in its range (cf. Theorem 1 below).

Because we are striving for economy in the representation, it makes sense to seek a generating fuzzy subset with a linearly independent carrier. Ideally, for any $x \in M$, we should be able to recover the value of $\mu(x)$ from the generating fuzzy set s by an easy computation. We are, thus, led to the following definitions.

Definition 9 Let B be a subset of an R-module M, and let x be an element of M. an *irredundant representation* of x by elements of B is an expression

$$x = \sum_{i=1}^{k} r_i \beta_i \qquad (r_i \in R, \beta_i \in B) \quad [7]$$

in which all β_i are distinct and each $r_i \beta_i \neq 0$.

Definition 10 Let (M, μ) be a fuzzy module, and let $B \subseteq M$. A fuzzy set (B, s) is a *basis* for μ if

1.   The crisp set B is a basis for M.
2.   For all $x \in M$, if $x = \Sigma_{i=1}^{k} r_i \beta_i$ is an irredundant representation of x by elements of B, then $\mu(x) = \min_{1 \le i \le k} s(\beta_i)$

The first condition in Definition 10 ensures that the carrier M of a fuzzy module (M, μ) can be recovered from the carrier B of the fuzzy basis.

The second condition similarly allows the recovery of the degree of membership $\mu(x)$ for any x in M. The second condition in the above definition also plays an important role in the definition of fuzzy linear independence.

Definition 11 Let (M, μ) be a fuzzy module, and let $B \subseteq M$. A fuzzy set (B, s) is a *linearly independent subset* of μ if

1. The crisp set B is a linearly independent subset of M.
2. For all $x \in M$, if $x = \Sigma_{i=1}^{k} r_i \beta_i$ is an irredundant representation of x by elements of B, then $\mu(x) = \min_{1 \leq i \leq k} s(\beta_i)$.

The above definitions generalize the classical definitions of linear independence and bases in the context of crisp modules. We observe also that if (B, s) is a linearly independent subset of a fuzzy module (M, μ), the s is simply the restriction of μ to B, so that in the context of (M, μ), the specification of B suffices to completely define (B, s). It easy to see, though, that a crisp linearly independent subset of M may fail to be the carrier of *any* linearly independent fuzzy subset of (M, μ). This raises the possibility that a fuzzy module (or vector space) (M, μ) may fail to have a basis even when its carrier M does.

Example 7 (13)   Let $\mu : R^2 \to [0, 1]$ be the characteristic function of the real linear subspace $\{(x_1, x_2) | x_1 = x_2\}$, and let $B = \{\beta_1, \beta_2\}$ be the standard basis of R^2. Then B cannot be the carrier of any basis (B, s) for μ: For example,

$$(1, 1) = \beta_1 + \beta_2$$

is an irredundant representation of $(1, 1)$ that violates condition 2 of Definition 10:

$$\mu(1, 1) = 1 \neq 0 = \min\{s(\beta_1), s(\beta_2)\}.$$

We do see, however, that the fuzzy set (B', s') defined by $B' = \{(1, 1), (1, 0)\}$ is a basis for μ.

Example 8   The fuzzy vector space (R^n, ϑ) of Example 5 has a basis the restriction of ϑ to $B \subseteq R^n$, where B is the standard basis of R^n.

In the crisp case, it is well known that every vector space must have a basis. In the fuzzy case, however, fuzzy vector spaces may fail to have a basis, even when they have finite-dimensional carriers. In general, proving the existence or nonexistence of a basis for a particular family of fuzzy vector spaces requires some ingenuity. Depending on the particular vector space, such a proof may require use of techniques from fields as varied as algebra, functional analysis, and combinatorics. Below, we will give an example of fuzzy vector space that fails to have a basis. Our proof of nonexistence of a basis will rely on a combinatorial argument based on the following result.

Theorem 1   *Let X be a K-vector space with dimension n, and let (X, ϑ) be a fuzzy K-vector space in X. If ϑ has a basis, then the cardinality $|\vartheta(X)|$ of the range of ϑ is at most 2^n.*

Proof.   Let B be a basis of X. The above result follows from the observation that the mapping

$$B' \to \begin{cases} \min_{1 \leq i \leq k} \mu(\beta_i) & \text{if } B' \subseteq B \text{ and } B' = \{\beta_1, \ldots, \beta_k\}. \\ 1_H & \text{if } B' = \emptyset. \end{cases}$$

from the power set of B to the range of ϑ is onto.

Example 9 (13)   Let X be a K-vector space with finite dimension $n \geq 2$, set $q = 2^n - 1$, and let H be the power set of the set $\{1, \ldots, q\}$. Let $\{\beta_1, \ldots, \beta_n\}$ be a basis for X, and for each $j = 1, \ldots, q$, let S_j be the one-dimensional subspace of

X generated by $\Sigma_{i=1}^{n} r_i \beta_i$, where each scalar $r_i \in \{0, 1\}$ and the sequence $r_1 r_2 \cdots r_n$ encodes j as a binary number. Then

$$S_i \cap S_j = \{0\} \quad \text{for all } i \neq j.$$

Now the $q + 2$ sets

$$\{0\}, \quad X \setminus \cup_{k=1}^{q} S_k, \quad S_k \setminus \{0\} \quad (1 \leq k \leq q)$$

partition X, and we can define a fuzzy set $\vartheta : X \to H$ by

$$\vartheta(x) = \begin{cases} \{1, \ldots, q\} & \text{if } x = 0 \\ \{k\} & \text{if } 1 \leq k \leq q \text{ and } x \in S_k \setminus \{0\} \\ \emptyset & \text{if } x \in X \setminus \cup_{k=1}^{q} S_k. \end{cases}$$

It is easily verified that ϑ is a fuzzy vector space. Because ϑ uses $q + 2 = 2^n + 1$ different values in H as degrees of membership, it is impossible for ϑ to have a basis.

We observe that if we insist that the membership lattice H be the complete Heyting algebra on two elements, namely, $\{0, 1\}$, we return to the crisp case, where every fuzzy vector space then possesses a basis. We look for some general kind of conditions, which, when placed on H, ensure the existence of a basis for all H-fuzzy vector spaces. In the light of the preceding discussion, it seems natural to require that ordering on H be linear. At the present time, it is not known whether this condition is sufficient to imply the existence of a basis for a fuzzy vector space. There is an additional condition, however, which, in conjunction with linearity of the partial order of H, does suffice to imply existence of a basis.

Definition 12 An H-fuzzy set (X, s) satisfies the *sup property* if for each nonempty subset T of X, there exists t^* in T such that $s(t^*) = \sup\{s(t) | t \in T\}$.

The following result is in essence proved in Ref. 13 and also in Ref. 14. Related results may be found in Ref. 15.

Theorem 2 *Let H be linearly ordered, and let (X, ϑ) be an H-fuzzy vector space that enjoys the sup property. Then (X, ϑ) has a basis.*

Given a fuzzy vector space (X, ϑ), finding a basis for ϑ, or even just determining whether ϑ does have a basis, can be quite difficult. In addition, we may seek answers to other questions concerning ϑ: For instance, we may wish to know for a given degree of membership $\delta \in H$, whether there exist any x in X satisfying $s(x) = \delta$. If the carrier X is finite, we may attempt to answer these questions by programming a computer to carry out a search of X. It is then natural to raise questions about the computational complexity of such search processes, and ask whether specific questions concerning ϑ can be answered in polynomial time (16). A convenient measure of the size of the problem might be either the size of X, or the dimension of X. Consider, for example, the following vector space.

Example 10 Let $n \geq 1$, and let $K = Z_2 = \{0, 1\}$, the Galois field of two elements. Then $X = K^n$ is a K-vector space, as is the set $L(n, K)$ of all K-linear maps $f : K^n \to K^n$. Define $\vartheta^n : L(n, K) \to \mathcal{P}(X)$ by

$$\vartheta_n(f) = \{x \in X \mid f(x) = 0 \text{ or } f(x) = x\}.$$

Then ϑ is a fuzzy vector space for each n.

From Example 10, we get for each n a fuzzy vector space ϑ_n. Because no general result characterizing those n for which ϑ_n has a basis is known, we can attempt to answer the question of whether a particular ϑ_n has a basis by using a computer search. To do this, we can represent each K-linear map $f \in L(n, K)$ by its matrix representation M_f with respect to the standard basis of K^n. Such a representation and the fact that the scalar field K is Z_2 make this particular example especially amenable to computation, because a linear combination reduces to simple matrix addition. Unfortunately, $L(n, K)$ has 2^{n^2} elements, so an algorithm that relies on exhaustive search can never do better than $\Omega(2^{n^2})$ time. Further research into the structure of ϑ_n is needed to determine whether subexponential basis-finding algorithms exist.

FREE OBJECTS

In this section, we generalize the ideas of the last section to other kinds of fuzzy algebraic structures. We are particularly interested in free fuzzy algebras: These may be regarded as generalizing the notion of a fuzzy module with a basis. The notion of a free fuzzy algebra is related to the notion of a crisp free algebra in the same sense that linear independence and bases for fuzzy modules are related to linear independence and bases for crisp modules. We will limit our discussion of free fuzzy algebras to defining free fuzzy modules and free fuzzy groups. After the discussion of the main ideas in the context of groups and modules, the reader who is familiar with other kinds of algebras (17) will have no trouble defining free objects for other classes of fuzzy algebras.

Definition 13   Let (X, s) and (Y, t) be two H-fuzzy R-modules. A *homomorphism* from s to t is a function $f: (X, s) \rightarrow (Y, t)$ between the underlying fuzzy sets which is also a homomorphism $f: X \rightarrow Y$ of the underlying crisp modules.

Now suppose that (M, μ) is a fuzzy R-module with a basis (B, b). Let (N, η) be another fuzzy R-module, and let $f: (B, b) \rightarrow (N, n)$ be a mapping of fuzzy sets. The mapping $f: B \rightarrow N$, considered as a mapping of crisp sets, can be extended to a unique homomorphism $f: M \rightarrow N$ of crisp modules, by defining

$$\bar{f}(x) = \begin{cases} \sum_{i=1}^{n} r_i f(\beta_i) & \text{if } 0 \neq x = \sum_{i=1}^{n} r_i \beta_i \\ 0 & \text{if } x = 0, \end{cases} \tag{8}$$

where $x = \sum_{i=1}^{n} r_i \beta_i$ is an irredundant representation of x by elements of B. This homomorphism $\bar{f}$ of crisp modules turns out to be a homomorphism $\bar{f}: \mu \rightarrow \eta$ of fuzzy modules.

Definition 14   A fuzzy R-module (M, μ) is *free* over a fuzzy subset (B, b) if every mapping $f: (B, b) \rightarrow (N, \eta)$ into a fuzzy R-module (N, η) can be extended to a unique homomorphism $\bar{f}: (M, \mu) \rightarrow (N, \eta)$ of fuzzy modules.

We call a fuzzy module *free* if it is free over some fuzzy set. It is clear that every fuzzy module with a basis is free. The converse is also true: It can be shown that every free fuzzy module has a basis (13). We thus have the following characterization of free modules.

Theorem 3 *A fuzzy module is free if and only if it possesses a basis.*

Consider now the case of fuzzy groups. To define the notion of a free fuzzy group, we proceed as in the case of fuzzy modules. The only difference is that we use group homomorphisms in place of module homomorphisms.

Definition 15 Let (X, s) and (Y, t) be two H-fuzzy groups. a *homomorphism* from s to t is a function $f: (X, s) \rightarrow (Y, t)$ between the underlying fuzzy sets which is also a homomorphism $f: X \rightarrow Y$ of the underlying crisp groups.

Definition 16 A fuzzy group (G, s) is *free* over a fuzzy subset (B, b) if every mapping $f: (B, b) \rightarrow (G', s')$ into a fuzzy group (G', s') can be extended to a unique homomorphism $\bar{f}: (G, s) \rightarrow (G', s')$ of fuzzy modules.

Fuzzy free groups and fuzzy free modules are discussed at length in Refs. 13, 18, and 19.

FURTHER READING

For an introduction to fuzzy sets and their many applications, one can do no better to consult Ref. 4. A good understanding of mordern algebra, at the level of the first four chapters of Ref. 20, is necessary for the understanding of current research in the field. A knowledge of universal algebra at the level of the first few chapters of Ref. 17 is also useful. Some knowledge of category theory is required in the discussion of fuzzy free algebras and programming language semantics; for this, Refs. 11, 21, and 22 can be consulted. In the area of fuzzy algebra, Refs. 23 and 24 are some early treatises which are still among the best to read for an introduction. For material on the semantics of programming languages, the reader should consult Ref. 25 and the references therein.

REFERENCES

1. L. A. Zadeh, "Fuzzy Sets," *Inform. Control, 8*, 338–353 (1965).
2. S. Aoki, S. Kawachi, and M. Sugeno, "Application of Fuzzy Control Logic for Dead-Time Processes in a Glass Melting Furnace," *Fuzzy Sets Syst., 38*, 251–265 (1990).
3. A. O. Esogbue, M. Theologidu, and K. Guo, "On the Application of Fuzzy Set Theory to the Optimal Flood Control Problem Arising in Water Resources Systems," *Fuzzy Sets Syst., 48*, 155–172 (1992).
4. H.-J. Zimmermann, *Fuzzy Set Theory and its Applications.* Kluwer Academic Publishers, Boston, 1991.
5. B. Kosko, *Neural Networks and Fuzzy Systems*, Prentice-Hall, Englewood Cliffs, NJ, 1992.
6. J. F. Baldwin, "Support Logic Programming," *Int. J. Intell. Syst., 1*, 73–104 (1986).
7. J. W. Lloyd, *Foundations of Logic Programming*, Springer-Verlag, Berlin, 1984.
8. C. L. Chang and R. C. T. Lee, *Symbolic Logic and Mechanical Theorem Proving*, Academic Press, New York, 1973.

9. G. Goguen, J. W. Thatcher, E. G. Wagner, and J. B. Wright, "Initial Algebra Semantics and Continuous Algebras," *J. Assoc. Comput. Mach., 24*, 68–95 (1977).
10. M. Hennessy, *Algebraic Theory of Processes*, The MIT Press, Cambridge, MA, 1988.
11. M. Barr and C. Wells, *Category Theory for Computer Science*, Prentice-Hall, Englewood Cliffs, NJ, 1990.
12. J. J. Rotman, *An Introduction to the Theory of Groups*, WCB Publishers, Dubuque, IA, 1984.
13. G. C. Muganda, "Free Fuzzy Modules and Their Bases," *Inform. Sci., 72*, 62–82 (1993).
14. P. Lubzonok, "Fuzzy Vector Spaces," *Fuzzy Sets Syst., 38*, 329–343 (1991).
15. D. S. Malik and J. N. Mordeson, "Fuzzy Vector Spaces," *Inform. Sci., 55*, 271–281 (1991).
16. A. Aho, J. Hopcroft, and J. Ullman, *The Design and Analysis of Computer Algorithms*, Addison-Wesley, Reading, MA, 1974.
17. S. Burris and H. P. Sankappanavar, *A Course in Universal Algebra*, Springer-Verlag, New York, 1981.
18. G. C. Muganda, and M. Garzon. "On the Structure of Fuzzy Groups," in *Advances in Fuzzy Theory and Technology, Volume 1*, P. P. Wang, (ed.) BookWrights, Durham, NC, 1993.
19. M. Garzon and G. C. Muganda, "Fuzzy Groups and Fuzzy Group Presentations," *Fuzzy Sets Syst., 48*, 249–255 (1992).
20. T. W. Hungerford, *Algebra*, Springer-Verlag, New York, 1974.
21. B. C. Pierce, *Basic Category Theory for Computer Scientists*, MIT Press, Cambridge, MA, 1991.
22. T. S. Bylth, *Categories*, Longman, London, 1986.
23. A. K. Katsaras and D. B. Liu, "Fuzzy Vector Spaces and Fuzzy Topological Vector Spaces," *J. Math. Analy. Appl., 58*, 135–146 (1977).
24. R. Lowen, "Convex Fuzzy Sets," *Fuzzy Sets Syst., 19*, 291–310 (1980).
25. D. A. Schmidt, *Denotational Semantics*, Allyn and Bacon, Newton, MA, 1986.

GODFREY C. MUGANDA

HUMAN ERROR BEHAVIOR IN CONCEPTUAL AND LOGICAL DATABASE DESIGN

INTRODUCTION

The widespread availability of information technology and the increasing competence of users has resulted in user-developed applications (1). These applications are developed without the direct help of the information systems (IS) department (2). Most users feel reasonably comfortable with popular software like word processors and spreadsheets. Although such information workers can perform simple tasks using database software, there is no evidence that these users can design nontrivial databases. Further, database languages are still too difficult for most users. Instead, they turn to personal information managers (PIMs), a new kind of software customized for specific tasks (3). However, PIMs are suitable only for standard, routine tasks. Thus, new applications involving database systems are still designed primarily by systems analysts in the IS department.

Although systems analysts usually have the requisite technical skills, they are far less knowledgeable than the users about the application. Systems developed by analysts are likely to be inferior because they may not mirror the users' method of working. Further, IS-developed systems are expensive, may require a long waiting period, and their development takes a considerable amount of time. Although for very critical or very complex systems the development of systems must be handled by the IS department, there is still a vast number of systems that can potentially be developed by users.

Database systems designed and developed by users are likely to be low cost, timely, and acceptable quality, provided the users have the requisite skills to design a good system. Because such users are unlikely to have an inordinate amount of time or motivation for gaining database design skills, effective and efficient training of these users is a pertinent issue. The primary emphasis in training would be to minimize the occurrence of errors. This makes human error behavior in conceptual and logical database design an important research area.

This article addresses research on human errors in the conceptual and logical design of databases. It explains the important elements of database design. It then illustrates why such design is so complex for an end user, who is likely to be a nonexpert. It includes a survey of past research, frameworks relevant to the domain, and what has been achieved in this line of research. It discusses the heuristics used by nonexperts and the typical resulting biases. It provides a brief description of the status of expert systems that have been developed to address this domain. It summarizes the major problems and provides recommendations for tasks in the domain. Finally, it proposes an agenda for future research in this area.

ELEMENTS OF CONCEPTUAL AND LOGICAL DATABASE DESIGN

Conceptual database design involves representing the data requirements as entities, attributes of entities, and relationships among entities. Data models like the entity relationship model (4) provide representation primitives for such basic concepts. Semantic and object-oriented models provide additional semantics like generalization (5,6); however, the basic concepts are adequate for most applications. Conceptual database design is predominantly independent of implementation. When this step is completed, the design needs to be translated to logical database to allow implementation. For example, the relational model (7) specifies the structure of database at the logical level.

An entity is an object that has descriptive data. Specifically, it can be a person, a thing, or an event. For example, EMPLOYEE is an entity if it has descriptive data like employee number, employee name, age, position, and so on. Such descriptive data constitute the attributes. In this case, EMP_NUMBER, EMP_NAME, AGE, and POSITION will be attributes of the entity EMPLOYEE. An example of an entity is called an instance. For example, the employee with number 1843 and name "Jim Lehrer" is an instance of the entity EMPLOYEE. The primary key of an entity is an attribute or set of attributes that serves to distinguish instances of the entity. For example, EMP_NUMBER is the primary key of EMPLOYEE. The remaining attributes are called nonkey attributes or descriptors.

A relationship is an association between entities. For example, the entity EMPLOYEE may associate with another entity DEPARTMENT. This relationship can be called ASSIGNED and indicates which employee belongs to which department. There are many characteristics of a relationship that need to be shown. Three important characteristics are degree, connectivity, and optionality.

The degree of a relationship is the number of entities that participate in the relationship. Binary relationships involve two entities and are the most common. For example, ASSIGN is a binary relationship (Fig. 1a). Sometimes, an association involves three entities; such a relationship is called a ternary relationship. For example, if one needs to show the skills used by an employee in a given project, the relationship is ternary assuming EMPLOYEE, SKILL, and PROJECT are entities (Fig. 1b). Connectivity indicates the mapping of instances of an entity with respect to those of other entities involved in a relationship. The value of connectivity of an entity in a relationship is either "one" or "many." In this article, the connectivity "many" is shown by a shaded triangle and the connectivity "one" by an unshaded triangle. This notation is similar to that used in Refs. 8 and 9.

Connectivity of an entity is determined by considering one instance of each of the other entities in the relationship and determining the number of associated instances of the entity under consideration. For example, consider the relationship ASSIGNED. To determine the connectivity of the entity EMPLOYEE, ask "how many instances of this entity are associated with one instance of DEPARTMENT?" The answer in the general case is "many." Next, determine the connectivity of the entity DEPARTMENT by asking the question, "how many instances of this are associated with one instance of EMPLOYEE?" Assuming that an employee can belong to no more than one department, the connectivity of department is "one." Thus, ASSIGN is a one–many relationship (Fig. 1a). In a ternary relationship, determining the connectivity is more difficult. Consider a relationship EMP_

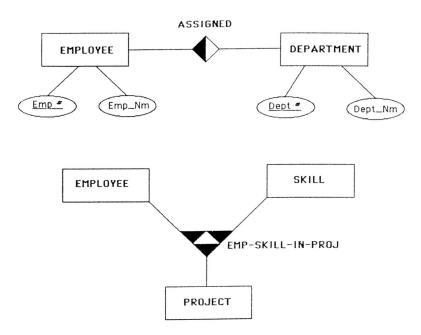

FIGURE 1   (a) Example illustrating ER constructs. (b) Ternary relationship.

SKILL__IN__PROJ between EMPLOYEE, SKILL, and PROJECT. To determine the connectivity of say PROJECT, ask "how many instances of this entity are associated with one entity each of EMPLOYEE and SKILL?" Suppose that an employee can use the same skill in many projects; the connectivity then is "many." Similarly, the connectivity of EMPLOYEE and of SKILL can be determined (Fig. 1b).

Another important characteristic of a relationship is optionality. Suppose an employee does not have to belong to a department, but a department must have at least one employee. Thus, the entity EMPLOYEE is mandatory and DEPARTMENT is optional. Optionality can be expressed along with connectivity by asking the minimum instead of the maximum number of instances associated. If the minimum number is 0, the existence of entity is optional; if it is at least 1, it is mandatory. Employee connectivity can be expressed as [1, n] and the department [0, 1]. Thus, optionality does not involve an altogether new concept and its usability is not discussed separately in this article.

COMPLEXITY IN CONCEPTUAL AND LOGICAL DATABASE DESIGN

Naturally, concepts like entity, relationship, and attribute are based on the metaphor of real world. The designer is likely to develop a mental model of database design based on similar notions in the real world. In training designers, the idea of a database relationship is presented in terms of real-world relationships. For example, a designer is apt to consider the "database" relationship between the two entities

EMPLOYEE and DEPARTMENT in the same terms as the real-world relationship between them. However, the analogy does not hold well when many entities are considered.

In database design, all possible relationships among entities are not shown. Relational design is governed by normalization rules. Entity relationship (ER) model-based methodologies usually have relational design as the target. If the translation from the ER representation to relational representation is to be automatic (e.g., performed using a CASE tool), one needs to capture all semantics in the ER representation. The resulting design from an ER-based approach that leads to a normalized solution does not directly capture all relationships; most relationships end up as derived. This conflicts with the real-world analogy because a large number of relationships are possible with a limited number of entities.

For example, consider the application: An order involves a sale by salespersons to a customer. Assume that ORDER, SALESPERSON, and CUSTOMER are the entities. In the real world, one can visualize four relationships: between ORDER and SALESPERSON, between ORDER and CUSTOMER, between SALESPERSON and CUSTOMER, and among ORDER, CUSTOMER, and SALESPERSON. Thus, a designer may choose to model the application as a ternary one–many–many relationship with CUSTOMER on the "one" side (Fig. 2a) arguing that an order involves many salespersons and one customer. This relationship would be deemed

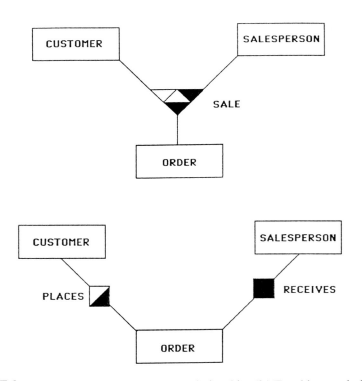

FIGURE 2   (a) Ternary one–many–many relationship. (b) Two binary relationships.

incorrect. It can be decomposed into two binary one–many relationships: one between ORDER and SALESPERSON, and the other between ORDER and CUSTOMER (Fig. 2b). As an order by itself corresponds to one customer, the relationship between ORDER and CUSTOMER should not involve the entity SALESPERSON.

Also, the ternary one–many–many relationship conveys wrong semantics. The connectivity of an entity in an n-ary relationship is specified by considering one instance of each of the other $(n - 1)$ entities and determining if the mapping of the instances of the entity is "one" or "many." By stating that the connectivity of CUSTOMER is "one" in the relationship, it is implied that given an order and a salesperson, there is only one customer. However, this does not preclude one order from having multiple customers—if we consider another salesperson, there is only a constraint on having one customer, but it does not necessarily have to be the same customer. Thus, the ternary relationship shown in Figure 2a does not capture the constraints that an order has only one customer. Table 1 illustrates the problem using two records. Note that for the sake of clarity, customer and salesperson names instead of their numbers are used. Note that given one order and one salesperson, there is only one customer, yet there can be more than one customer per order. This is contrary to the semantics of the application which limits one customer per order.

Another way of proving that the ternary relationship is incorrect for the given application is by considering the dependencies implied by this solution. Assume that the primary keys of the three entities are ORDER#, CUSTOMER#, and SPERSON#. The implied dependency is (see Ref. 9 for a detailed explanation):

Order#,Sperson# → Customer#

Thus, the constraint Order# → Customer# (an order pertains to one customer) is lost. A similar problem is encountered when relations are not in second normal form. The correct ER representation is shown in Figure 2b and the correct relational representation (that includes some nonkey attributes) is

ORDER(*Order#*, Order-dt, Customer#)
SALESPERSON(*Salesperson#*, Salesperson-nm)
SALES(*Order#, Salesperson#*)

Note that although salespersons sell to customers, this fact is not directly captured. This fact can be derived by linking ORDER and SALES. Note that if a relationship is shown between CUSTOMER and SALESPERSON, and any one of the remaining two binary relationships is shown, the third relationship cannot be derived. A novice designer may not easily comprehend the distinction.

Thus, clearly there can be an inconsistency between the relationships as visual-

TABLE 1 Order Example

Order	Salesperson	Customer
22834	Coles	Rice
22834	Stockton	Malone

ized in the real world and as represented in a database. Certain relationships are modeled and others are precluded because the solution needs to be normalized and minimal.

The previous example involved only three entities. When this number increases, the number of possible relationships between entities increases in a combinatorial fashion. The problem of choosing a few relationships among the numerous possible becomes difficult. Note that the problem gets exacerbated because the various possible configurations of connectivities between the same entities increases the possible relationships by another factor.

Consider an application that has two entities. Four binary relationships are possible: one–one, one–many, many–one, and many–many. Now consider an application with three entities. There are C_2^3 or three ways of defining binary relationships. Because each binary relationship can have 2^2 or 4 connectivities, 12 ways are possible. One ternary relationship is possible; as there are 2^3 or 8 possible connectivities, in all, there are 20 potential ways. When the number of entities is 4, the total number jumps to 24 binary, 32 ternary, and 16 four-ary. Thus, there are 72 possible configurations among 4 entities. However, the correct solution may include only three of these relationships; some are not possible and others are derived. Note that as the number of entities increases, the number of relationships increases in a nonpolynomial fashion. The crux of the database design task, therefore, is to choose the correct configuration among a large number of possible relationships.

What criteria allow a designer to choose the right set of relationships? Most relationships can be derived from others, so the problem in modeling relationships is selecting a minimum set that captures the semantics effectively and can be used to derive the others. For a right choice of relationships, at least the following criteria should be met: (i) semantics in the application should not be lost, (ii) relationships should not be captured redundantly, and (iii) each relationship should be of minimum degree. If the semantics of an application are specified clearly, and these criteria are met, there is usually only one among the numerous possible configurations that accurately depicts the semantics. Thus, it is not surprising that nonexperts find the conceptual database design a complex task. Past research has confirmed that novices commit a number of errors in modeling data requirements.

RETROSPECTION: FINDINGS FROM RECENT STUDIES

Usability studies dealing with database design have typically compared designer performance between two or more data models. Due to the popularity of relational systems, these studies have invariably considered the relational data model as one of the treatments. The other popular data model used in these studies is the entity-relationship (ER) model. The focus of these studies is quantitative measures like degree of correctness, and although one may argue that such a measure is inversely related to the number of errors, the studies have not explicitly focused on the nature of errors made.

Brosey and Shneiderman (10) compared relational and hierarchical models using instance diagrams. They found that the hierarchical model was slightly better. However, the task was also inherently hierarchical, so the study may have been confounded. Durding et al. (11) presented subjects with a group of words and asked them to organize the words as a hierarchy, list, table, or network. They found that subjects made the choice based on the inherent structure of the group of words. The results suggested that designers would commit more errors if there was a mismatch between the structure of data in an application and the structure of the modeling formalism. Juhn and Naumann (12) focused on the user validation task and presented subjects with a database using different data representations like relational and ER. They found that graphical models (like ER) lead to fewer errors than table models (like relational). Hoffer (13) found that novices have individualized images of a database, and a process flow structure is the most frequently used image. They have difficulty in specifying data relationships.

Recent studies have confirmed that the use of an ER model minimizes data modeling errors. Batra et al. (14) presented subjects with a text description of the application to compare designer performance using the entity relationship and the relational models. They found that subjects using the extended ER model could easily model binary relationships. However, subjects using the relational model committed many errors in modeling binary relationships. Further, both groups of subjects had considerable difficulty in modeling ternary relationships. Jarvenpaa and Machesky (15) compared the logical data structure (LDS) with the relational model. LDS, which is similar to the ER model, led to better performance. The use of relational model led to more errors. Bock and Ryan (16) found that the extended ER model outperformed Kroenke's object-oriented representation in some aspects of data modeling. In this experiment, practically no errors were reported for modeling entity, identifier, category, and unary one–one, binary one–many, and binary many–many relationships using the ER model.

One study, however, has shown favorable results for the relational model. Shoval and Even-Chaime (17) compared normalization, which uses the relational model, with the information analysis approach, which is based on the binary relationship model (18). The study used systems analysts (as opposed to novice designers) and found that the relational group committed fewer errors than the information analysis group.

Although it seems that these studies were done piecemeal and there was no line of research, one consistent finding emerged: Errors in modeling binary relationships could be minimized by the use of the ER model. Further, novice designers did not seem to face any difficulty in modeling entities, identifiers, and nonkey attributes. As most real-world relationships are binary, one would tend to conclude that the human–computer interaction studies have solved a major piece of the puzzle. However, if one analyzes the tasks employed by these studies, it seems that the problem descriptions tended to hint at the solutions. Further, even though these studies could provide information about which models minimized human errors, none attempted to explain *why* the subjects committed other errors and what could be done to improve performance. Recently, human–computer interaction studies on database design have changed the focus from comparing different data representations to understanding what causes design errors. This is essential if effective expert tools and tutoring systems are to be developed to improve novice designer performance.

Batra (19) developed a framework to illustrate human error behavior in modeling conceptual databases. The framework was adapted from ideas, frameworks, and models suggested in the literature on human–computer interaction and human reliability. The primary source was Hutchins, Hollan, and Norman's (20) concept of "gulf" or directness distance between a user's goals and the human–computer interface. They specified two components of this distance — semantic and articulatory. Semantic distance separates what the user wants to say from the meaning of an expression in the interface language. Articulatory distance separates the meaning of an expression from its physical form. If the gulf between the user's goals and the interface is large, the user would require considerable effort to accomplish his goals.

The framework suggested by Batra (19) specified four aspects of "gulf" in the context of conceptual database design — syntax, mapping, rules, and consistency. Syntax referred to articulatory distance, and the remaining three to semantic distance. Based on the model, six types of errors were suggested — syntactic, abstraction, simplification, overload, convergence, and divergence. These were then matched to errors found in four empirical studies on database representation. Four types of errors — abstractions, simplification, convergence, and overload — were typically found in these studies. Brief descriptions of these errors are provided below.

> **Abstraction:**   This is an error caused by inappropriate *mapping* from reality to representation. Change of level of abstraction involves a shift in concepts and structure (21). If the representation is distorted during the abstraction process, the designer is likely to commit errors. Such errors are called abstraction errors. A *unary* relationship as modeled by the entity relationship (ER) model provides an apt example of the possibility of this error. If a binary fact in the real-world level maps to a unary fact at the representation level, the disparity can cause confusion and errors. The supervisor relationship is binary in the real world (e.g., "Rebecca is supervisor of David"); in the ER model, however, the supervisor relationship is unary (as both Rebecca and David pertain to the same entity, i.e., employee).
>
> **Simplification:**   If a situation or a piece of the application is complex, requiring too many rules for representation, a designer may divide it into simpler pieces. However, the situation may not be divisible, that is, any attempt to break it up would lead to distorted semantics, and hence the representation would be erroneous. For example, a designer may simplify a ternary relationship by decomposing it into binary relationships. However, the resulting semantics may be different.
>
> **Overload:**   An overload error is similar to a simplification error, because both involve a complex situation and are caused by inappropriate use of *rules*. In this case, however, the designer does recognize the situation as a whole and does not use a simplifying approach. They are, therefore, less severe than simplification errors. In the case of overload error, there are many elements of a situation, and the process of analysis and/or integration places a heavy burden on a person's memory. Further, the application description may not provide information about all such elements — some may have to be inferred or obtained by eliciting more from the user; but failure to consider all elements may lead to incomplete or erroneous representations. For example, a designer may recognize a ternary relationship but fail to accurately specify the connectivity.
>
> **Convergence:**   This is one of the errors caused by the lack of *consistency* between the real world and the representation. If similar (i.e., convergent) situations in the real world lead to dissimilar representations, the resulting

REFERENCES

1. S. Rivard and S. L. Huff, "Factors of Success for End-User Computing," *Commun. ACM, 31*, 552–561 (1988).
2. T. Cronon and D. Douglas, "End User Training and Computing Effectiveness in Public Agencies: An Empirical Study," *J. MIS, 6*(4), 21–40 (1990).
3. K. C. Laudon and J. P. Laudon, *Business Information Systems: A Problem Solving Approach*, Dryden Press, Fort Worth, TX, 1993.
4. P. P. Chen, "The Entity–Relationship Model—Toward a Unified View of Data," *ACM Trans. Database Syst., 1*(1), 9–36 (1976).
5. J. M. Smith and D. C. P. Smith, "Database Abstractions: Aggregation and Generalization," *ACM Trans. Database Syst., 2*(2), 105–133 (1977).
6. J. Banerjee, H. T. Chou, J. F. Garza, W. Kim, D. Woelk, N. Ballou, and H. J. Kim, "Data Model Issues for Object-Oriented Applications," *ACM Trans. Office Inform. Syst., 5*(1), 3–27 (1987).
7. E. F. Codd, "A Relational Model of Data for Large Shared Banks," *Commun. ACM, 13*, 377–387 (1970).
8. D. Reiner, G. Brown, M. Friedell, J. Lehman, R. Mckee, P. Rheingans, and A. Rosenthal, "A Database Designer's Workbench," in *Proceedings Entity–Relationship Approach*, S. Spaccapietra, ed., Elsevier Publishers, Amsterdam, 1987.
9. T. J. Teorey, D. Yang, and J. F. Fry, "A Logical Design Methodology for Relational Databases Using the Extended Entity-Relationship Model," *Comput. Surveys, 18*(2), 197–222 (1986).
10. M. Brosey and B. Shneiderman, "Two Experimental Comparisons of Relational and Hierarchical Database Models," *Int. J. Man–Machine Studies, 10*, 625–637 (1978).
11. B. M. Durding, C. A. Becker, J. D. Gould, "Data Organization," *Human Factors, 19*, 1–14 (1977).
12. S. Juhn and J. D. Naumann, "The Effectiveness of Data Representation Characteristics on User Validation," in *Proceedings of the Sixth International Conference on Information Systems*, 1985, pp. 212–226.
13. J. A. Hoffer, "An Empirical Investigation into Individual Differences in Database Models," in *Proceedings of the Third International Conference on Information Systems*, 1982, pp. 153–168.
14. D. Batra, J. A. Hoffer, and R. P. Bostrom, "Comparing Representations Developed Using Relational and EER Models," *Commun. ACM, 33*, 126–139 (1990).
15. S. L. Jarvenpaa and J. J. Machesky, "Data Analysis and Learning: An Experimental Study of Data Modeling Tools," *Int. J. Man–Machine Studies, 31*, 367–391 (1989).
16. D. B. Bock and T. Ryan, "Accuracy in Modeling with Extended Entity Relationship and Object Oriented Data Models," *J. Database Manag., 4*(4), 30–39 (1993).
17. P. Shoval and M. Even-Chaime, "Database Schema Design: An Experimental Comparison Between Normalization and Information Analysis," *Database, 18*(3), 30–39 (1987).
18. J. Verheijen and J. Van Bekkum, "NIAM: An Information Analysis Method," in *Information Systems Design Methodologies*, T. W. Olle, H. G. Sol, and A. A. Verryn-Stuart, eds., North-Holland, Amsterdam, 1982.
19. D. Batra, "A Framework for Studying Human Error Behavior in Conceptual Database Modeling," *Inform. Manag., 25*, 121–131 (1993).
20. E. L. Hutchins, J. D. Hollan, and D. A. Norman, "Direct Manipulation Interfaces," *Human–Computer Interact., 1*, 311–338 (1985).
21. J. Rasmussen, "Cognitive Control and Human Error Mechanisms," in *New Technology and Human Error*, J. Rasmussen, K. Duncan, and J. Leplat, eds., John Wiley & Sons, London, 1987.

22. J. D. Ahrens and C. S. Sankar, "Tailoring Database Training for End Users," *MIS Quart.*, *17*, 419–439 (December 1993).
23. J. H. Gerlach and F. Y. Kuo, "Understanding Human–Computer Interaction for Information Systems Design," *MIS Quart.*, *15*, 527–549 (1991).
24. J. M. Carroll and A. P. Aaronson, "Learning by Doing with Simulated Intelligent Help," *Commun. ACM, 31*, 1064–1079 (1988).
25. S. H. Zanakis and J. R. Evans, "Heuristic 'Optimization': Why, When and How to Use It." *Interfaces, 11*, 84–91 (1981).
26. A. Tversky and D. Kahneman, "Judgement Under Uncertainty: Heuristics and Biases," *Science 185*, 1124–1131 (1974).
27. R. M. Dawes, "The Mind, the Model and the Task," in *Cognitive Theory*, F. Restle et al., eds., Vol. I, Lawrence Earlbaum Associates, Hillsdale, NJ, 1975, pp. 97–125.
28. R. N. Taylor, "Psychological Determinants of Bounded Rationality: Implications for Decision-Making Strategies," *Decision Sci., 16*, 409–429 (1975).
29. H. A. Simon, *Administrative Behavior*, Macmillan, New York, 1957.
30. D. Kahneman, P. Slovic, and A. Tversky, *Judgment Under Uncertainty: Heuristics and Biases*, Cambridge University Press, Cambridge, 1982.
31. C. P. Slovic and S. Lichtenstein, "Comparison of Bayesian and Regression Approaches to the Information Processing in Judgement," *Organiz. Behav. Human Perform., 6*, 649–744 (1971).
32. A. Tversky and D. Kahneman, "Evidential Impact of Base Rates," in *Judgement Under Uncertainty: Heuristics and Biases*, D. Kahneman, ed., Cambridge University Press, New York, 1982, pp. 153–160.
33. M. Moskowitz, R. E. Schaefer, and K. Borcherding, "Irrationality of Management Judgments: Implications for Information Systems," *Omega, 4*, 125–140 (1976).
34. R. M. Hogarth and S. Makridakis, "The Value of Decision Making in a Complex Environment: An Experimental Approach," *Manag. Sci., 27*, 93–107 (1981).
35. A. P. Sage, "Behavioral and Organizational Considerations of Information Systems and Processes for Planning and Decision Support," *IEEE Trans. Syst. Man Cybernet. SMC-11*, 640–678 (1981).
36. S. Makridakis and S. C. Wheelwright (eds.), *Forecasting*, North-Holland, New York, 1979.
37. R. E. Nisbett and L. Ross, *Human Inference: Strategies and Shortcomings of Social Judgement*, Prentice-Hall, Englewood Cliffs, NJ, 1980.
38. B. Fischhoff, "Hindsight and Foresight: The Effect of Outcome Knowledge on Judgement Under Uncertainty," *J. Exp. Psychol.: Human Percep. Perform., 1*, 288–299 (1975).
39. E. J. Langer, "The Illusion of Control," *J. Personality Soc. Psychol., 32*, 311–328 (1975).
40. A. Tversky and D. Kahneman, "Belief in the Law of Small Numbers," in *Judgement Under Uncertainty: Heuristics and Biases*, D. Kahnerman, ed., Cambridge University Press, New York, 1982, pp. 23–31.
41. R. M. Hogarth and S. Makridakis, "Forecasting and Planning: An Evaluation," *Manag. Sci., 27*, 115–138 (1981).
42. H. J. Einhorn, "Learning from Experience and Suboptimal Rules in Decision Making," in *Cognitive Processes in Choice and Decision Behavior*, T. S. Wallsten, ed., Lawrence Earlbaum Associates, Hillsdale, NJ, 1980, pp. 1–20.
43. D. Kahneman and A. Tversky, "On Psychology of Prediction," *Psycholog. Rev., 80*, 237–351 (1973).
44. F. H. Barron and R. John, "Reference Effects: A Sheep in Wolf's Clothing," *Organiz. Behav. Human Perform., 25*, 365–374 (1980).

45. D. Batra and S. Antony, "Novice Errors in Database Design," *Eur. J. Inform. Syst.*, 3(1), 59–69 (1994).
46. J. T. Reason, "Generic Error-Modeling System (GEMS): A Cognitive Framework for Locating Common Human Error Form," in *New Technology and Human Error*, J. Rasmussen, K. Duncan, and J. Leplat, eds., John Wiley & Sons, London, 1987, pp. 63–83.
47. A. Rizzo, S. Bagnara, and M. Visciola, "Human Error Detection Process," *Int. J. Man-Machine Studies, 27*, 555–570 (1987).
48. V. C. Storey, and R. C. Goldstein, "Knowledge-Based Approaches to Database Design," *MIS Quart., 17*, 25–46 (March 1993).
49. D. Reiner, *Database Design Tools in Conceptual Database Design: An Entity–Relationship Approach*, C. Batini, S. Ceri, and S. B. Navathe, eds., Benjamin/Cummings, Redwood City, CA, 1992.
50. A. Kawaguchi, N. Taoka, R. Mizoguchi, T. Yamaguchi, and O. Kakusho, "An Intelligent Interview System for Conceptual Design of Database," *ECAI 1986: The Seventh European Conference on Artificial Intelligence*, 1986, pp. 1–7.
51. V. C. Storey, *View Creation*, ICIT Press, Washington, DC, 1988.
52. V. C. Storey and R. C. Goldstein, "A Methodology for Creating User Views in Database Design," *ACM Trans. Database Syst., 13*(3), 305–338 (1988).
53. B. Demo and M. Tilli, "Expert System Functionalities for Database Design Tools," in *Applications of Artificial Intelligence in Engineering Problems: Proceedings of the First International Conference*, D. Sriram and R. Adey, eds., Springer-Verlag, Berlin, 1986, pp. 1073–1082.
54. B. Tauzovich, "An Expert System for Conceptual Data Modeling," in *Proceedings of the Eight International Conference on the Entity–Relationship Approach*, 1989, pp. 329–344.
55. J. Choobineh, B. R. Konsynski, M. V. Mannino, and J. F. Nunamaker, "An Expert System Based on Forms," *IEEE Trans. Software Eng., 14*(2), 242–253 (1988).
56. I. T. Hawryszkiewycz, "A Computer-Aid for ER Modeling," in *Proceedings of the Fourth International Conference on the Entity–Relationship Approach*, Chicago, IL, 1985, pp. 64–69.
57. C. Wagner, "View Integration in Database Design," Ph.D. dissertation, University of British Columbia, Vancouver, Canada (1989).
58. M. Bouzeghoub, G. Gardarin, and E. Metais, "Database Design Tools: An Expert System Approach," in *Proceedings of the Eleventh International Conference on Very Large Databases*, A. Pirotte and Y. Vassiliou, eds., Morgan-Kaufmann, San Mateo, CA, 1985, pp. 82–95.
59. H. Briand, H. Habrias, J. F. Hue, and Y. Simon, "Expert System for Translating an E-R in Diagram into Databases," *Proceedings of the Fourth Entity–Relationship Conference*, North-Holland, Amsterdam, 1985, pp. 199–206.
60. A. Dogac, B. Yuruten, and S. Spaccapietra, "A Generalized Expert System for Database Design," *IEEE Trans. Software Eng., 15*(4), 479–491 (1989).
61. A. L. Furtado, M. A. Casanova, and L. Tucherman, "The Chris Consultant," in *Entity–Relationship Approach*, S. T. March (ed.), Elsevier Science Publishers, Amsterdam, 1988, pp. 515–532.
62. R. Yasdi and W. Ziarko, "Conceptual Schema Design: A Machine Learning Approach," in *Methodologies for Intelligent Systems*, Z. W. Ras and M. Zemankova, eds., Elsevier Science Publishers, Amsterdam, 1987, pp. 379–391.
63. C. Proix and C. Rolland, "A Knowledge Base for Information System Design," in *Data and Knowledge (DS-2)*, R. A. Meersman and A. C. Sernadas, eds., Elsevier Science Publishers, Amsterdam, 1988, pp. 293–306.

64. D. Batra and S. H. Zanakis, "A Conceptual Database Design Methodology Based on Rules and Heuristics," *Eur. J. Inform. Syst.*, *3*(3), 228–239 (1994).
65. D. Batra and M. K. Sein, "Improving Conceptual Database Design Through Feedback," *Int. J. Human-Computer Studies*, *40*, 653–676 (1994).

DINESH BATRA

HUMAN RESOURCE MANAGEMENT

INTRODUCTION

Human resource management (HRM) is the utilization of human resources (HR) at work to achieve organizational and individual goals (1–3). It helps an organization achieve its future objectives by providing competent, well-motivated employees. HRM is also the management of various activities designed to enhance the effectiveness of an organization's workforce in achieving organizational goals in terms of recognizing human resources (HR) as a crucial element in the strategic success of organizations (4,5). HRM is a new approach to the management of employees. It differs from traditional approaches to personnel management. The importance of HRM recognizes that the people (employees) element is a special kind of resource that is complex and difficult to handle and people's investment is often more effective than other resources.

Personnel, HRM, and industrial relations are used to describe a unit, department, or group of people. HRM is more concerned than traditional personnel management with the management of managers (6). It has been well recognized that HRM is sometimes used in an expansive fashion to embrace any one of a variety of approaches to the management of labor. A meaningful version of HRM would seem to comprise four key aspects (i.e., benefits and assumptions of managers and employees, strategic aspects, significance of managers, key levers) to distinguish HRM from traditional personnel and industrial relations (7). Here, three models are useful for an in-depth understanding of HRM characteristics. The human relations model postulates a straight-line relationship from participation to satisfaction to increased productivity. This model had to be replaced by the HR model based on findings that participation improved the quality of decision making and this, in turn, improved subordinate satisfaction and morale (8). The Harvard analytic framework for HRM (9) offers an improvement conceptualization of the links among HR policy choices about employee influence, HR flow, reward systems, and other organizational variables (e.g., stakeholder interests, workforce characteristics, business strategy, labor market, laws, unions, and management philosophy).

Human Resource Management consists of numerous activities or functional areas, including HR planning, job analysis, recruitment, selection and placement, financial compensation, HR development, labor–management relations, safety and health, and HR resource research (10). Many quantitative or qualitative techniques have been developed to support the HRM activities, classified as management sciences/operations research, multiattribute utility theory, multiple-criteria decision making, ad hoc approaches (e.g., use of versatile materials, behavior analysis), and human resource information systems (HRIS). More importantly, HRIS can include the three systems of expert systems (ES), decision support systems (DSS), executive information systems (EIS) (11) in addition to transaction processing systems (TPS) and management information systems (MIS) conventionally accepted as an HRIS. An HRIS is regarded as a computer-aided HRM system.

HRM ENVIRONMENT

Many interrelated factors affect achieving HRM goals and objectives. The following eight elements contribute the component of a diagnostic model to develop an HRM system: focus, domain, external pressure, internal pressure, organizational type, methodology, people, and data and knowledge sources. This focus denotes what an HRM system gives organizations as goals. The domain denotes appropriate functional activities or means what to do under the focus. Remaining components are related to how to do.

Those factors that affect a firm's HR from outside its boundaries comprise the external pressures. They usually include union procedures and requirements, legal regulations, composition of labor force, geographic location of the organization, society, customers, and economic condition. For legal regulations, when an organization makes hiring, promotion, performance evaluation, and layoff decisions, it must weigh the impact of government laws and regulations. Three aspects of economic conditions affect HRM programs: productivity, the nature of competitiveness, and the nature of the labor market. In the area of competitiveness, for example, an HR manager is important for answering the competitiveness-related questions: "Does the firm have the HR needed to increase the size of the manufacturing facility to handle global demands?" For another example, a surplus in the labor market can reduce the union's pressures for compensation and benefit increases.

Internal pressures are considered as the internal environment of HRM. Factors that affect a firm's HR from inside its boundaries comprise the internal environment. The primary internal factors include the firm's goal or mission, policies, corporate culture, nature of the task, work group, and management style of upper managers. In addition, the information about employees stored in personnel or payroll databases should be regarded as a major factor affecting a firm's HR. Internal pressures have an impact in determining the interaction between HR departments and others within the organization. On the other hand, the different HRM strategy should be considered as the organization's goals change. For example, a company involved in little risk-taking will likely need a different workforce as compared to a company involved in risk taking. A work group consists of two or more people who consider themselves a group and are interdependent of one another. If the work group opposes HRM programs, it can ruin them. The style of leadership involves skills, experiences, personalities, and motives of individuals. Organizational culture refers to a system of shared meaning held by members that distinguishes the organization from other organizations. Culture provides a benchmark of the standards of performance among employees. HRM is described as the effective matching of the nature of the task (e.g., degree of environmental unpleasantness, physical location) with the nature of the employee performing the task. The internal and external pressures maybe a bottleneck in the development of HRM systems.

Organizational characteristics can be divided into profit (e.g., manufacturing firms) and nonprofit organizations (e.g., government), and the different types affect the development of a unified HRM system; these can be classified as size, complexity, and stability.

Some conventional techniques and glossaries (2,10) that support HRM activities are discussed in Table 1.

People elements are users and developers. As with senior HR executives, their interest in personnel data is typically key promotions, executive searches, or succession plans. HR functioning professions are trained in and assigned to a specific area of HR. HR managers typically have some knowledge of all areas of HR but have less specific expertise than the functional professions. The HR manager is primarily responsible for coordinating the management of HR to help the organization achieve its goals. They look to reduce the time they spend worrying about administrative activities (e.g., payroll processing), or look for data to guide or to justify strategic decisions.

The HR manager faces a multitude of problems, ranging from a constantly changing workforce to coping with government regulations (12). Conducting a job analysis for managerial jobs offers a significant challenge to the HR manager. The management position description questionnaire (13) implies the following manager's jobs: informing, receiving information, influencing, promoting, selling, directing, côordinating, integrating, negotiating, supervising, rating, planning, decision making, monitoring, controlling and administering.

Line managers are concerned with personnel-level data about the employees they manage or summary-level data (e.g., performance review). Finally, employees are clients as well as servers to perform an HRM system. They not only give the organizations labor but also receive benefits and direction from the system.

Knowledge sources and HR-related data or information can be acquired from MIS (management information systems), TPS (transaction processing systems) human experts, and organizational manuals. TPS are able to include a hardware-oriented system such as automatically checking employee assiduity. The attributes of personnel data bases become the information to control an employee (Table 2).

Additional environmental factors for the diagnostic evaluation of HRM and development of an HRM system include communication between people, compensation association, customer's demand, economy of nation, employee preference, finance status, marketing status, operation status, labor budget, social responsibility, and organizational hierarchy (Table 3). It is useful to build an information base to evaluate the factors using preferences of HR managers.

Measures are required to evaluate an HRM system's effectiveness. Criteria such as grievance rates, turnover, and accident rates evaluate whether outcomes of an HRM system developed in an organization under the HRM environment satisfy the employees' need and organizational goals somewhat. These criteria are used as an index for the verification of the system, as well as searching for urgent activities compared to others. Performance measures involve such things as the unit labor cost per unit of output and the cost per employee of HRM programs.

HRM ACTIVITIES

Human Resources planning eliminates any gaps that may exist between supply and future personnel needs. It has to be integrated internally (e.g., all HR functions)

TABLE 1 Glossary on Techniques for Achieving HRM Activities

HR planning

Zero-base forecasting: A method for estimating future employment needs regarding the organization's current level of employment as zero.

Bottom-up approach: A forecasting method beginning with the lower organizational units and progressing upward to ultimately provide an aggregate forecast of employment needs.

Delphi technique: A set of procedures to obtain the most reliable consensus of opinion of a group of experts.

Management inventory: Detailed data regarding each manager to be used in identifying individuals processing the potential to move into higher-level positions.

Skill inventory: Information maintained on nonmanagerial employees as to their ability and preparedness.

Recruiting

Job posting: A procedure for communicating to company employees that fact that job opening exists.

Advertising: A way of communicating the firm's employment needs to the public through media such as radio, newspaper, or industry publications.

Employee referrals: A method for assisting recruitment process by employee's friends and associates.

Internship: A special form of recruitment that involves placing students in temporary jobs with no obligation either by company to permanently hire the student or by the student to accept a permanent position with the firm.

Special events recruiting: When the supply of employees available is not large or when the organization is new or not well known, some organizations have successfully used special events, e.g., open houses.

Reference checks: A means of providing additional insight into the information furnished by applicant and a way to verify the accuracy of the information provided.

Selection

Physical examination: A method to screen out individuals who have a contagious disease and to determine whether an applicant is physically capable of performing the work.

Graphic rating scale: Ratings can be in a series of boxes on a continuous scale (0-9, or so).

Behaviorally anchored rating scale: A rating scale that uses critical incidents as anchor statements placed along a scale. Typically 6-10 performance dimensions, each with 5-6 critical incident anchors are rated per employee.

Forced choice: A method choosing from a set of descriptive statements (e.g., rank from 1 to 4) about an employee because the graphic rating scales allowed supervisors to rate high.

Critical incident technique: A method to maintain a log of behavioral incidents that represent either effective or ineffective performance for each employee being rated.

Compensations

Pay survey: Survey of compensation paid to employees by all employers in a geographic area, an industry, or an occupational group using personal interview, mailed questionnaires, and telephone inquiries.

Classification or grading system: A job evaluation method that groups jobs together into a grade or classification.

Point system: A job evaluation method that requires evaluators to quantify the value of the elements of a job. Points are assigned to the degree of various factors required to do the job.

Training

Case method: Description of a real decision-making situation in the organization or a situation that occurred in another organization.

Role playing: The acting out of a role by participants. Participants play act a role that others in the training session observe.

Behavior modeling: A training method that utilizes video tapes prepared specifically to illustrate how managers function in various situations for the purpose of developing interpersonal skills.

Transactional analysis: An organizational development method that considers the three ego states of the Parent, the Adult, and the Child in helping people understand interpersonal relations and thus assists in improving an organization's effectiveness.

In-basket training: A simulatin in which the participant is asked to establish priorities for handling a number of business papers, such as memoranda, reports, and telephone messages, that would typically cross a manager's desk.

Labor–management relations

Collective bargaining: A process by which the representatives of the organization meet and attempt to work out a contract with the employees' representative.

---

and externally (e.g., organization's overall plans), forecasting manpower requirements inside and outside. The major components of the HR planning process are as follows:

1. Strategic planning
2. Evaluation of current HR situation using skills inventory
3. HR forecast of present workforce, demand, and supply
4. Implementation plans such as recruitment, layoff, career planning, training, and transfer
5. Audit and adjustment.

Job analysis fits each job into the total fabric of the organization. Simply stated, job analysis is a procedure for obtaining pertinent job information. It plays a role in HR planning, recruitment and selection, pay, and design of training programs. Observations, questionnaires, interviews, and checklists are used for gathering job information. The immediate products of this analysis are job descriptions and job specifications. Job design focuses on content and structure regarding productivity and employee motivation.

Recruitment distinguishes between qualifications of potential applicants and desirable ones. This is used to develop a pool of applicants using more of the sources because the greater the number of applicants, the more selective the organization can be in hiring. Selection meets the organization's standards of performance and increases the proportion of successful employees selected. Selection decisions include reject, hold, hire, promote, transfer, terminate, and layoff.

Compensation includes financial returns and tangible services and benefits employees receive as part of an employment relationship. Compensation meets all the criteria equitable for employer and employee and incentive providing it is acceptable to the employee. Compensation objectives are controlling labor costs, fair

TABLE 2   List of Attributes on Personnel Inventory

Address	Joining union
Age	Joining party
Birthplace	Leave of absence type
Deduction type	Marital status
Department	Blood type
Division	Medical examination
Domestic training date	Military history
Domestic training field	Spouse
Driver's license	Number of dependents
Educational progress	Overtime history
Educational degree	Performance rating
Educational major	Performance increase
Hearing ability	Position
Height	Prior career
Weight	Professional license
Employment type	Punishment type
Employment date	Punishment date
Foreign training service	Retired reason
Foreign training study	Reward type
Foreign training date	Salary class
Foreign language skill	Sex
Grievance type	Sick history
Handicap status	Sideline business
Incentive amount	Skill proficiency level
Injury type	Skill type
Injury date	Job title
Transfer reason	Transfer date
Job description	Vacation leave used
Job preference	

treatment for all employees, and conforming to various laws and regulations. For a compensation decision, pay level is the average of the array of rates paid by an organization. Pay structures are the pay relationships among different jobs within a single organization. Among different pay systems, knowledge-based pay systems compensate employees for the work-related skills they possess, rather than for the specific job they do.

Human resources development includes career planning and performance appraisal. Large-scale HR development programs are often referred to as organization development, intended to help employees perform more productively (14). Career planning is a process of setting HR goals (individual careers and organizational needs) and establishing the means to achieve them (15). Performance evaluation evaluates employee performance to meet standards. It affords employees the opportunity to capitalize on their strengths and overcome identified deficiencies (16,17). Training matches the organization's objectives with the firm's human talent, structure, climate, and efficiency. Labor–management relations negotiate with the union on the contract.

Safety involves protecting employees from injuries caused by work-related

TABLE 3   Environmental Factors for Diagnostic Evaluation

Communication between people	Marketing status
Compensation association	Nature of task (unpleasantness, difficulty)
Competition of labor force	Operation status
Corporate culture	Organization's continuing purpose
Court decisions	Organizational image
Customer's demand	Organizational characteristics (size, complexity)
Direction in decision making	
Economy of the nation	Organizational hierarchy, structure
Employee attitude and preference	Patterns of human interaction
Executive order	Pools of individuals external to firms
Finance status	Production status
Force of union	Sales status
Geographical location	Shareholders' decision
Government regulations	Social responsibility
HR certification institute programs	Society for training and development
Labor budget	Speed of decision making
Law	Technological changes
Life stages for career planning	Top management support
Management style of upper managers	Work group
Organizational type	

accidents, and health refers to the employees' freedom from illness and their physical and mental well-being (18). Employees who work in a safe environment and enjoy good health are more likely to yield long-term benefits to organizations. Organizational responses to health and safety challenges include safety design and preventive approaches; inspection, reporting, and accident research; safety training and motivation programs; auditing safety program; and health programs for employees (19).

Finally, HR research is the systematic study of a firm's HR beginning to realize the full significance of the HRM areas on an organization's ability to achieve its goals (20). This includes describing how quantitative methods may be used, how the HR function may be evaluated, and how technological advances can affect HRM.

Performing HRM activities needs the significant information in a diagnostic HRM environment. It depends on the current status and concern of organizations. Some input items and examples as shown in Table 4 will help understand these activities.

INFORMATION TECHNOLOGIES SUPPORT FOR HRM

Technological advances in computer hardware and software occur virtually everyday. This can improve HRM and raise employee productivity. Even during tough economic times, technological changes must be tracked to maintain a competitive edge (21). Failure to keep up with developments in this rapidly changing area can threaten a firm's competitive position and possibly even its survival. According to

TABLE 4   Information Sources for the HRM Activities

HRM activities	Items	Examples
HR planning	Employment requirement	Number and type of employees by skill level and occupation
	Existing employment inventory	Supply of employees
	Strategic planning	More sales workers than clerical workers
Job analysis	Organization and process chart	Supervisor of jobs, job relationships
	Characteristics of the job	Education, skill, experience
	Required behaviors	Job responsibility and duty
	Employee characteristics	Individual preference, need strength for the job
Recruiting	Employer's requirements	Personal characteristics of recruiters, image of the employer
	Candidate's performance	Qualified workers
	Recruiting goals	Recruit from outside the organization
	Status of labor market	A lot of job openings or very few
	Status of possible inside recruits	Internal recruiting
Selection	Application blank	Career, education
	Personality and performance	Programming test for computer test operators
	Physical examination	Serious diseases
	Selection criteria	How to weigh the criteria
Compensation	Individual difference	Pay for each individual relative to pay of others
	Profit amount of organization	Financial availability
	Contributions to meeting	Employee satisfaction, understanding how pay organizational goal is determined
Performance evaluation	Accuracy of work	Quality and quantity of work
	Job knowledge	Statement of the performance dimensions
	Personal qualities	Appearance, leadership, integrity
Performance standards	Criteria for evaluation	
	Evaluation policies	When, how often, who evaluates
Training	Organization's needs	Use of performance evaluation
	Employee's needs	Self-assessment of individual skills
	State of the economy	Consumer price index, inflation
Labor– management relations	Goals of the bargaining parties	Wage cut, work-rule changes
	Public sentiment	Mood of society
	Issues being discussed	Welfare, retirement pension
	Labor law and regulation	Minimum pay
	Precedents in bargaining	Past contracts

Porter and Miller (22), the concept of the value chain divides a firm's activities into the technologically and economically distinct activities it performs to do business. The value is measured by the amount that buyers are willing to pay for a product or service. A firm's value activities fall into nine generic categories classifying primary activities and support activities with the margin, or net revenue. To gain competitive advantage over its rivals, a firm must either perform those activities at a lower cost or perform them in a way that leads to differentiation and changing competitive scope.

In the value-chain analysis, HRM is a kind of support activity. However, HRM can be considered as a target of the business model rather than as a support activity because the assumption that technological changes affect HRM and HRM is supported by it. In the HR's value chain, support activities are changed to information technologies (IT). Here, the primary activities become HRM activities. Linkages between a support IT and a primary activity become a potential task under the primary HRM activity. The HR's value-chain analysis starts by systematically examining how activities interact and how they can provide sources of competitive advantage within a particular industry. For example, if a company decides a broader geographic scope is needed to acquire better recruiting sources, the competitive scope is changed by IT to act as a consultant to a human.

Major IT components include application and communication software, teleconferencing, voice mail, telecommuting, ES, graphical user interfaces, and multimedia. Through telecommuting, employees work at home and transmit data over telephone lines tied to a computer. Through multimedia, employees are immediately drawn to the presentation with stereo sound or full motion video, which makes multimedia useful in sales presentations and in training and development (Fig. 1).

DECISION SUPPORT FRAMEWORK OF HRM

A decision support framework is a tool for the analysis of HRM activities and is used as a source of the HRIS design. It is useful to employ the same dimensions as the MIS framework (23) by searching for a task among HRM activities based on decision types and management levels supported. The taxonomy for the managerial activities consists of three categories. Strategic planning is concerned with long-term planning, broad policies, and goals for HR executives. Managerial control deals with tactical issues for middle management. At the first-line level, managers handle operational issues that are largely of a day-to-day nature. The task orientation of operational control requires information of a well-defined and narrow scope. The three decision types are structured, unstructured, and semistructured. To the extent that a given problem is semistructured or unstructured, there is an absence of a routine procedure, ambiguity in the problem definition, and the lack of a decision-making procedure.

The framework as shown in Figure 2 devoted to providing the following:

- HRM systems are understood based on a global view of MIS, which should take into account the MIS structure.
- HRM efforts are more productive if they are directed to developing specialized systems to meet the needs of specific management levels.

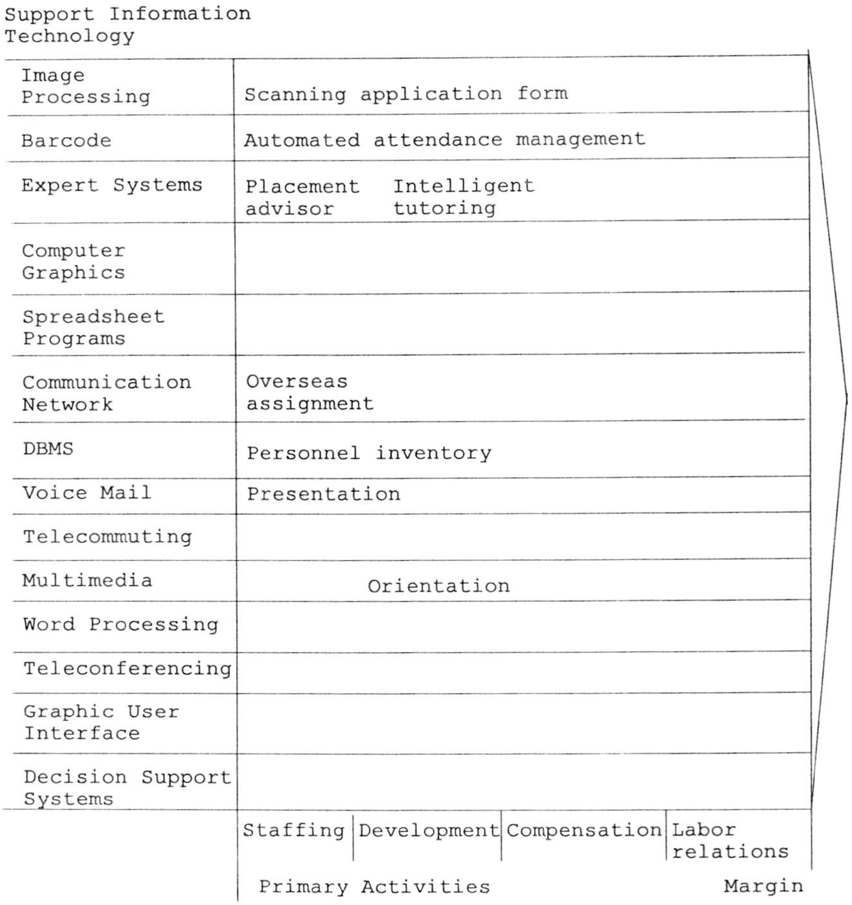

Support Information
Technology

Image Processing	Scanning application form			
Barcode	Automated attendance management			
Expert Systems	Placement advisor	Intelligent tutoring		
Computer Graphics				
Spreadsheet Programs				
Communication Network	Overseas assignment			
DBMS	Personnel inventory			
Voice Mail	Presentation			
Telecommuting				
Multimedia		Orientation		
Word Processing				
Teleconferencing				
Graphic User Interface				
Decision Support Systems				
	Staffing	Development	Compensation	Labor relations
	Primary Activities			Margin

FIGURE 1   The HR's value chain.

- It is possible to plan and make sensible resource allocation decisions which result in effective use of HRM.

COMPLEXITY ANALYSIS OF HR FIRMS

Situations for an HRM environment are different in each firm regarding hardware and software techniques. A two-dimensional model that analyzes the complexity of organizations can be used when the firm is developing an HRM system. In the model, the two dimensions include not only the complexity of knowledge such as many people, depth of expertise, many sources of information, and uncertainty in information, but also the complexity of technology such as diversity of platforms needed, diversity of IT, and degree of system integration. In Figure 3, the arrow on the gird of the two-dimensional model represents a system development sequence

Type of Control / Type of Decision	Operational Control	Managerial Control	Strategic Planning
Structured	Application control, Interview preparation, Attendance control, Employee data preparation and entry	Workforce analysis, Availability analysis, Forecasting labor shortages, Labor cost management	HR action plans, Return on investment measures, Tracking expenditures
Semistructured	Staffing schedule	Skill inventory design, Career planning, Job assignment, Pay budgets, Recruitment evaluation	Employment planning, HR project initiation, Determining incentive strategy
Unstructured	Selecting training techniques, Evaluating training outcomes	Pay structure design, Job design, Performance policy, Choosing applicant qualifications, Choosing recruitment sources, Health planning	Resource allocation, Contract negotiations, Employee welfare

FIGURE 2 Decision support framework for HRM.

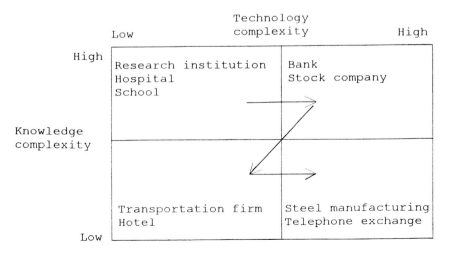

FIGURE 3 Two-dimensional model.

recommended for a firm's HRM system. The industry with the lower complexity of knowledge and technology has a greater guarantee of success.

Of course, there needs to be a different classification of industries according to organizational status even though the industry is included in the same category. In service firms with many employees that must work in diverse areas, highly developed technologies need to be used because the difficulty in gathering information about employees may be through a telecommunications network. But, the complexity of knowledge is relatively low because of strict evaluation criteria that exactly follow their performance jobs. On the other hand, research centers are usually classified as nonprofit organizations and have a high level of knowledge complexity, whereas the complexity of its technology is low. Because the employee's evaluation often depends on the manager's judgment, it is burdensome to quantitatively evaluate an individual job performance. But the technology for systematization is relatively easy.

HUMAN RESOURCE MANAGEMENT INFORMATION SYSTEMS

An HRIS was defined as a computer-based system for simply collecting, storing, maintaining, retrieving, and validating certain data needed by an organization about its employees (24). It is also designed to assist the planning, administration, decision making, and control activities of HRM (1). An HRIS should be considered as an integrated approach to acquiring, storing, analyzing, and controlling the flow of information throughout an organization (25). An HRIS can be seen as a computer-based information system (26) grouped into the following six categories: TPS, MIS, DSS, Group DDS (GDSS), ES, case-based reasoning systems (CBRS), and EIS. This implies that HRIS should be developed to solve HR problems appropriately reflecting the problem characteristics of HRM activities. For example, according to a number of HRIS user-group trends, an HRIS should be developed and managed considering the need of more users with diverse expertise as well as the increase of complexity of the HR field (11).

A TPS focuses on processing data resulting from the occurrence of employee transactions, such as the employees' data entry, payments, and report generation. MIS use personnel and payroll databases that store large quantities of detailed data concerning transaction processing. They summarize information from TPS to produce routine reports and allow on-line access to current information at the operational and tactical levels. The MIS approach to personnel focuses on the use of data about the corporation and builds a database that consists of skills inventory, payroll master including various taxes withheld, personnel history, and training data elements.

A DSS interactively helps HR managers utilize data and models such as forecasting models for HR planning to solve complex, unstructured, and semistructured problems. Typically, "what–if" analysis is an important feature of DSS that enables decision-makers to find what happens to certain conclusions if changes are being made in the assumptions (27). For a case example, the main components of DSS deal with staff attendance, placement, generating feasibility, optimization, analysis, and evaluation (28). A DSS for HRM that would provide for clerical processing and allow the integration and ease of interaction to support decision making was called "industrial relations information system" (IRIS) (29). It is regularly in daily use in the highly diverse industrial enterprise as a transaction-driven data system. A

DSS for large numbers of personnel assignments comprises the decision modules of utility and ordinary and special assignments (30). The army's personnel planning DSS combines a variety of modeling techniques such as goal programming, network models, and linear programming (31).

A GDSS (group decision support system) facilitates solution by groups of people that have a joint responsibility for making decisions in order to improve group performance and organizational effectiveness (32,33). A GDSS can support the group interviewing process for employee selection and the contract negotiation between union and management.

Expert systems allow HR managers to make better decisions with their heuristic knowledge. ES have been successfully applied to the HR problem domains of performance evaluation, qualification test, and career counseling (34–36). The intelligent tutoring systems (37,38) are regarded as types of training ES. There is the representative ready-made ES: Negotiation Edge for personnel, labor relations; and Hiring Edge for personnel management [from Human Edge in Palo Alto, CA (29)].

Case-based reasoning systems (CBRS) show a possibility of success in HR problem domains. Originally CBRS (39) have been applied to solve decision-making problems including HR problems from old cases or past experiences by overcoming the limitation of rule-based reasoning systems. The PERSUADER system is a mediator in simulated labor negotiations using case-based reasoning capability (40). More importantly, a generalized CBRS for personnel performance evaluation compensates both case-based reasoning's and rule-based reasoning's shortcomings in a knowledge-poor domain (41).

Finally, originally an EIS (executive information system) serves the information needs of top executives. It provides rapid access to current, timely information (42,43). The information is collected from internal and external sources. Internal information is usually generated from MIS-related reports within organizations. External information is generated from on-line databases, newspapers, personal contacts, and government reports. It provides an extremely user-friendly interface, supported by color graphics, exception reports, summarized reports, drill-down capabilities, and tracking on critical data.

Human Resource Management Expert Systems

A human resource management expert system (HRMES) is defined as an ES for HRM, or ES in HR problem domains to support several HRM activities (44). HRMES emerge to overcome the limitation of traditional database-oriented HRIS. Figure 4 presents the conceptual structure of HRMES. The important notions include that, for example, the two users (employer and employee) with different requests are involved on the system (Table 5) and that the employees receive multiple orders under the time horizon. The behavior means all information to employees including payroll, performance, job attitude, and career. Two users can acquire useful information from the database management systems for making decisions from the ES that they communicate with each other. The know-how and strategy acquired from HR managers are probably major sources of knowledge in small-scale ES.

Knowledge Representations of HR Domains Using Rules

Production rules are procedural or operational knowledge that specify what to do under specific conditions. In HR planning (Fig. 5), rules consist of the selection of

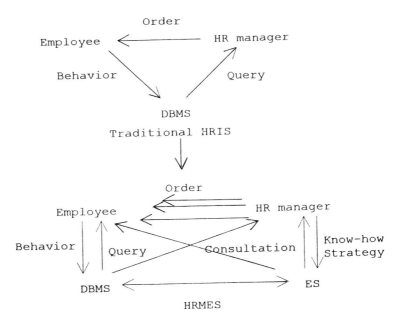

FIGURE 4   Traditional HRIS versus HRMES.

planning methods, checking preliminary conditions for the demand analysis and internal inventory analysis, and actions according to a current employee status. Job analysis (Fig. 6) includes the rules of selection of the appropriate analysis method, precondition for the process, and composition of the document required as a result, such as the job description. In recruiting (Fig. 7), rule sets include checking of the preliminary condition for the recruiting process, selection of recruiting methods and sources, selection of candidates, and the overall policies taken by organizations. Selection focuses on such decisions as hire, hold, reject, and transfer through employee test (Fig. 8). Compensation (Fig. 9) covers the two rules of pay level and pay strategy. In labor–management relations (Fig. 10), rules cover how to determine a decision in the negotiation process.

EXECUTIVE INFORMATION SYSTEMS FOR HRM

HR Executives and EIS Applications

The characteristics of EIS indicate the needs of the system in HRM areas. Suppose an HRIS was designed to provide information that is timely, accurate, concise, and relevant (10); this is made to conform to the ability of the EIS. Monday and Noe (10) argued that weekly and monthly employment status reports may be sent to the general manager, whereas quarterly reports may be forwarded to top management. Through exception reports which are completed when the number of product de-

TABLE 5 Outline of Dialog with Two User Groups

Type of question	Reply	User
Training techniques	On-the-job training	ER[a]
Training result	High cost	ER
Pay class	Class-I	ER
Number of job items	100	ER
Promotion decision	Not O.K.	ER
Job knowledge	Outstanding	ER
Quality of work	Good	ER
Personality test	Pass	ER
Employee appraisal	Training	ER
Retirement policy	Age 60–65	ER
Retirement decision	Preretirement	ER
Safety hazards	30%	ER
Recruiting source	College	ER
Pay raise	5%	ER
Estimated turnover	10%	ER
Collective bargaining	Lockout	ER
Financial compensation	Incentive providing	ER
Pay level	Competitive	ER
Career planning	Sales department	EE
Collective bargaining	Boycott	EE
Negotiation issue	Working condition	EE
Occupational health hazards	70%	EE
Pay raise	10%	EE

[a]ER: employer; EE: employee.

fects exceeds a predetermined maximum, the HR manager is made aware of this type of information in order to identify additional training needs.

The concern of senior HR executives is at a high level of aggregation, mainly summary reports comparing divisions/functions or highlighting opportunities through the use of variance reports (11). Their primary interest with individual data is also regarding key promotions, executive searches, or succession plans. The EIS of the future may include summary-level HR data (e.g., turnover rates, attitude survey data, performance data, labor costs). HR executives have to become increasingly oriented toward growth and efficiency of the organization instead of merely administrating traditional personnel activities (45). This denotes greater emphasis on planning the structure of the future organization and its personnel requirements, identifying and selecting the right people to meet these expected needs, developing and using the organization's present-day HR, and assessing and rewarding performance. They also need to review the efficient use of existing personnel at their present and future levels of organization, and concern themselves with the enhancement of the individual's skills and talents currently and in the future in order to improve productivity and overall contribution of the workforce.

In practice, the EIS applications at Marine Midland Bank include tracking of

```
RULE: selection of HR planning techniques
IF    consensus-of-a-group = reliable AND
      questionnaires = available AND
      estimation-of-employment-needs = best
THEN  Delphi
RULE: analysis of present and future requirements of job
IF    estimation-of-org-condition = accomplishment AND
      linking-business-activity-to-HR-requirement =
      accomplishment AND forecasting-HR-requirement =
      accomplishment
THEN  demand-analysis = ok
RULE: examining the current internal inventory of employees
IF    forecasting-technique = available AND
      analysis-of-activity-change = ok AND
      forecasting-inside-outside-movement = accomplishment
      AND skill-inventory-analysis = accomplishment
THEN  internal-analysis = ok
RULE: comparison of demand and supply
IF    external-analysis = ok AND
      internal-analysis = ok AND demand-analysis = ok AND
      external-supply + internal-supply > demand
THEN  condition = surplus
RULE: action decisions with a shortage of employees
IF    employee-shortage = small AND
      highly-skilled-employees = yes
THEN  action = overtime
IF    employee-shortage = small AND
      highly-skilled-employees = no
THEN  action = training or promotion
RULE: action decisions in surplus conditions
IF    employee-condition = shortage AND
      early-retirement = disagreement OR
      union = aggressive
THEN  action = work sharing
IF    labor costs = high AND
      downsizing-motivated-by-business goal = true
THEN  action = quit
```

FIGURE 5   Rules for HR planning.

staff counts, personnel expenses, recruitment, turnover rates, staffing trends, salary analysis, and other related statistics (46). The Fisher Price EIS menu concept is being expended into a more macro-level menu concept with the inclusion of an HR module (HR information is currently being entered) (47). Here the HR module includes information about all management employees, their skills and potential development, salaries, benefits, and recruiting strategies. In a useful EIS approach to specific areas (45), for example, wage and salary administration in an EIS environment focus on graphically presenting various types of wages and salary analyses to get at personnel exceptions; exception reporting gives an executive alertness when monthly personnel expenses rise or fall by 10%. Another example is in personnel selection placement, where the HRM software system is able to provide top-level executives with an answer to the question: If a 5% increase were given to all salaried

```
RULE: selection of the job analysis method
IF    number-of-employees > 500 AND incomplete-information-
      received = ok AND target = salary-and-hourly-worker
THEN  method = questionnaires
RULE: qualified interviewer
IF    interest-in-worker = sincere AND terminology-used =
      worker's language AND job-study-skill-or-knowledge = ok
      AND verification-of-the-job-information-prepared = ok
THEN  interview = ok
RULE: checking the completeness of the job description
IF    job-title = ok AND job-summary = ok AND job-duty = ok
      AND working-condition = ok AND definition-of-equipment =
      ok
THEN  job description = ok
RULE: an example of job specification
IF    degree-of-intelligence-required = high AND education >
      high school AND experience-level > average
THEN  job = software handling
```

FIGURE 6   Rules for job analysis.

personnel and a 4% increase to nonsalaried personnel, what will salaries look like in the coming year?

Human Resource Management Executive Information Systems

A human resource management executive information system (HRMEIS) contains the following two notions: an independent system from the global EIS (GEIS) developed for the chief executive officer and covering all business functions, or a set of HR modules supporting GEIS. In the first notion, HRMEIS are an EIS to support only HR executives, specially designed for dealing primarily with HR-related data. The second notion assures the bottom-up approach attempt at first building an individual EIS and then integrating these EIS into a single GEIS.

Modular design on each business function is a usual approach in the development of GEIS. HR executives focus on managing more HR divisions than the business divisions. Sometimes it is useful to save development costs if we build a specially designed EIS with data and capabilities focusing more on a specific business area, such as marketing and finance, than the entire business areas. On the assumption that GEIS can be divided into an individual EIS with domain-dependent and domain-independent capabilities, the ingredients of HRMEIS are derived from the analysis of the structure of GEIS as follows:

$$\text{User}_{GEIS} = \text{HR executive} + \text{Non-HR executive};$$ [1]

$$\text{Data}_{EIS} = \text{Internal} + \text{External};$$ [2]

$$\text{Data}_{Internal} = \text{Resource} + \text{Organizational structure} + \text{Operations} + \text{Product}$$
and service + · · ·

```
RULE: checking the availability of recruiting plan
IF    required-applicant-qualification = agree AND
      recruitment-sources = ok AND inducement-plan = ok AND
      quality-of-recruiter = agree
THEN  recruiting-plan = ok
RULE: decisions about how to generate source of the applicants
IF    external-recruiting = ok AND necessity-of-special-worker
      AND cost-for-program = available
THEN  recruiting-method = internship
IF    motivation-of-employee-movement = high AND HR-planning =
      agree AND computer-system = not-available
THEN  method = job-posting
IF    org-size = large AND org-complexity = low AND org-
      stability = high
THEN  radio-commercial
RULE: finding recruiting sources for each job
IF    cost-of-recruiting = low AND recruiting-policy =
      outside-referral AND past-image = good AND number-of-
      schools = large AND qualified-worker = true
THEN  sources = school
RULE: evaluation of candidates
IF    past-work-experience = true AND college-major = agree
      AND salary-requirement = agree OR military-experience =
      agree OR awards = true
THEN  qualified-worker = true
RULE: policy on internal or external recruiting
IF    labor-market = shortage AND government-regulation = high
      AND inducement-plan = bad AND organization-location =
      bad OR organization-image =bad
THEN  policy = positive
IF    short-term-change-in-need = high AND uncertainty-of-
      environment = high AND growth-of-service-industry = high
THEN  policy = temporary
```

FIGURE 7   Rules for recruitment.

```
RULE: employee test
IF    intelligence = ok AND personality = good AND achievement
      = ok AND aptitute = ok AND physical-examination = ok
THEN  employee-test = ok
IF    neurotic-tendency = high AND self-sufficiency = low AND
      introversion = low AND self-confidence = high AND
      sociability = average
THEN  personality-test = good
RULE: selection decision
IF    age < 30 AND sex = male AND education > college AND
      employee-test = ok
THEN  decision = hire
IF    age > 30 OR sex = female AND employee-test = ok
THEN  decision = hold
```

FIGURE 8   Rules for selection.

```
RULE: pay-level decisions on influencing factors
IF    minimum-wage-rate = high AND maximum-hour = low AND
      union-attitude =strong AND economic-condition-of-others
      = competition AND labor-market = tight AND org-status =
      ok
THEN  higher-wage
IF    labor-budget = available AND size-of-org = large AND
      managerial-pay-strategy = high
THEN  org-status = ok
IF    match-to-long-range-policy = yes AND managerial-attitude
      = positive
THEN  managerial-pay-strategy = high
RULE: pay policies to compensation objectives
IF    ability-to-attract = positive AND ability-to-retain-
      quality-employees =positive AND reducing-pay-
      dissatisfaction = positive
THEN  above-market
IF    ability-to-attract = negative AND ability-to-retain-
      quality-employees =negative AND increasing-productivity
      = unknown
THEN  below-market
RULE: job evaluation methods
IF    ranking-of-job = ok OR grading-system = ok OR
      point-system = ok OR factor-comparison = ok
THEN  job-evaluation = ok
RULE: clerical worker grading-system
IF    work = simple AND supervisory-responsibility = no AND
      public-contact = no
THEN  class-I
IF    work = complex AND supervisory-responsibility = yes
      AND public-contact = yes
THEN  class-V
RULE: point-system
IF    skill-required > 60 AND education-required > 70 AND
      job-complexity > 90 AND physical-requirement > 80
THEN  first-degree-job
RULE: classifying occupation groups
IF    vice-presidents = yes OR managers = yes OR project-
      leaders = yes
THEN  skill-group = managerial-group
```

FIGURE 9   Rules for compensations.

$$= (\text{Capital} + \text{Facilities} + \text{Human resource} + \cdots) + (\text{Department} + \text{Division} + \cdots) + (\text{Cost} + \text{Schedule} + \text{Productivity} + \cdots)$$

$$= \text{HR executives related} + \text{Non-HR executive related} + \text{CEO related;} \quad [3]$$

$$\text{Data}_{\text{External}} = \text{Customers} + \text{Economy} + \text{Competitors} + \cdots$$

$$= \text{HR executives related} + \text{Non-HR executives related} + \text{CEO related;} \quad [4]$$

$$\text{Capability}_{\text{GEIS}} = \text{Special functions} + \text{General functions}$$

$$= \text{Unscheduled meeting support} + \text{Telephone call} + \text{Travel schedule support} + \cdots) + (\text{Drill-down} + \text{Graphic support} + \cdots). \quad [5]$$

```
RULE: preparing labor and management relations
IF    labor-contract = ok AND grievance = accept AND
      mediator = ok AND arbitration = ok
THEN  bargaining = ok
RULE: reaching a formal contractual agreement
IF    hours-of-work = agree AND rates-of-pay = agree AND
      overtime = agree AND arbitration = agree
THEN  labor-contract = ok
RULE: reflection on a complaint about organization policy
IF    gather-grievance = yes AND work-with-union-representative
      = yes AND weighing-grievance = yes
THEN  grievance = accept
RULE: evaluation of mediator who helps labor and management
      reach agreement
IF    impartiality = low AND sincerity = high AND
      communication-skill =high AND expertise = high AND
      self-control = high
THEN mediator = ok
RULE: decisions on unsolvable dispute for binding settlement
IF    grievance = not-accept AND (arbitrator = full-time   OR
      arbitrator = labor-economics ) AND time-delay = no AND
      expense = low
THEN arbitration = ok
RULE: decisions on types of strikes
IF    economy = booming OR cost-of-strikes = high OR
      unemployment = high
THEN strikes = short
RULE: decisions on lockout
IF    strikes = long OR slow-down = high OR
      damage-to-property = high OR labor-disorder = high
THEN lockout = agree
```

FIGURE 10   Rules for labor–management relations.

From these relationships,

$$\text{HRMEIS} = (\text{User}_{\text{GEIS}} - \text{Non-HR executive} - \text{CEO}) + (\text{Data}_{\text{GEIS}} - \text{Data}_{\text{Non-HR executives related + CEO related}}) + (\text{Capability}_{\text{GEIS}} - \text{Insignificant capabilities}_{\text{GEIS}}). \quad [6]$$

From Eq. (6), an HRMEIS is distinguished from a GEIS based on the three views of data, user, and capability. In practice, detailed data and capabilities cannot be derived through a requirement analysis (48). Based on the assumption of a ready-made GEIS, the minus sign guarantees the typical authorization privilege for HR executives.

Comparisons of HRIS, HRMES, and HRMEIS

HRMEIS and HRMES seem to be different and unrelated computerized systems similar to differences between ES and EIS (29). As can be viewed in Table 6, there are significant dimensions to identifying the characteristics of these systems. Here HRIS denotes the conventional systems depending on TPS and MIS.

TABLE 6   Comparisons of HRIS, HRMES, and HRMEIS

Dimension	HRIS	HRMES	HRMEIS
Purpose	Internal monitoring, payroll, record-keeping, maintaining, retrieving	Decision-making	Internal and external tracking
User	HRIS group	HRIS group, mainly HR managers	HR executives
Output	Periodic reports	Consultation queries	Ad hoc reports, queries
Operation	Information processing	Inference, expertise transfer	Tracking, drill-down
Database	Personnel, payroll database	Information base, knowledge base	External database
Decision capabilities	Structured routine problems	Unstructured, use of rules	None
Type of information	Summary reports	On-line advice and explanations	Exception reporting, status access
Organizational level served	Middle, low management	Entire management and specialists	Senior executives
Degree of HR data oriented	High	Middle	Low
Time orientation	Past	Past	Past, present

SUMMARY

Although we have discussed the definition of HRM and its major activities, it is difficult to confine HRM research areas. HRM environment consisting of complex interdependent factors provides a research framework for understanding HRM. Among HRM techniques that perform these activities, we recommend information technologies including high-level information systems such as expert systems and executive information systems. The value chain as well as the decision support framework describes how information technologies are important and the possibility of applying these information systems to HR domains. The set of rules for HRM activities helps HRM system builders understand better the HRM procedures and design knowledge bases. Other novel techniques prominently announced in computer sciences such as artificial intelligence and software engineering can also be applied as a vehicle for HRM.

ACKNOWLEDGMENT

I wish to thank Professor Eui-Ho Suh for his sincere comments and encouragement.

REFERENCES

1. G. DeSanctis, "Human Resource Information Systems: A Current Assessment," *MIS Quart., 10*(1), 15–17 (1986).
2. J. M. Ivancevich, *Human Resource Management: Foundations of Personnel*, Irwin, Homewood, IL, 1992.
3. G. T. Milkovich and J. W. Boudreau, *Human Resource Management*, Irwin, Homewood, IL, 1991.
4. K. M. Bartol and D. C. Martin, *Management*, McGraw-Hill, New York, 1991.
5. H. G. Heneman, D. P. Schwab, J. A. Fossum, and L. D. Dyer, *Personnel/Human Resource Management*, Irwin, Homewood, IL, 1989.
6. K. Legge, "Human Resource Management: A Critical Analysis," in *New Perspectives on Human Resource Management*, J. Storey (ed.), Routledge, London, 1989.
7. J. Storey, "The Take-Up of Human Resource Management by Main-Stream Companies: Key Lessons from Research," *Int. J. Human Resource Manag., 4*(3), 529–533 (1993).
8. R. E. Miles, "Human Relations or Human Resources?," *Harvard Bus. Rev., 43*(4), 148–163 (1965).
9. M. Beer, B. Spector, P. R. Lawrence, M. D. Quinn, and R. E. Walton, *Managing Human Assets*, Free Press, New York, 1984.
10. R. W. Mondy and R. M. Noe, *Human Resource Management*, Allyn and Bacon, Boston, 1993.
11. S. I. Tannenbaum, "Human Resource Information Systems: User Group Implications," *J. Syst. Manag., 41*(1), 27–32 (1990).
12. B. W. Shimko, "All Managers are HR Managers," *HRMagazine, 35*, 67–70 (January 1990).
13. W. W. Tornow and P. R. Pinto, "The Development of a Managerial Job Taxonomy: A System for Describing, Classifying, and Evaluating Executive Positions," *J. Appl. Psychol., 61*, 410–418 (August 1976).
14. G. F. Kimmerling, "The Future of HRD," *Training Dev. J., 43*, 46–55 (June 1989).
15. L. D. Foxman and W. L. Polsky, "Aid in Employee Career Development," *Personnel J., 69* 22–24 (January 1990).
16. G. English, "Tuning Up for Performance Management," *Training Dev. J., 45*, 56–60 (April 1991).
17. R. J. Sahl, "Design Effective Performance Appraisals," *Personnel J., 69* 53–60 (October 1990).
18. D. W. Chappell, "How to Involve Employees in Safety Management," *Safety & Health, 142* 52–55 (October 1990).
19. J. M. Ivancevich and M. T. Matteson, "Optimizing Human Resources: A Case for Preventive Health and Stress Management," *Organiz. Dynam., 8*, 4–25 (Autumn 1980).
20. A. Redwood, "Human Resources Management in the 1990s," *Bus. Horizons, 33*, 74–80 (January–February 1990).
21. A. Laplante, "The Needing Edge," *Computerworld, 25*(11), 65 (1991).
22. M. Porter and V. E. Miller, "How Information Gives You Competitive Advantage," *Harvard Bus. Rev., 63*(4), 149–160 (1985).
23. G. A. Gorry and M. S. Scott-Morton, "A Framework for Management Information Systems," *Sloan Manag. Rev., 13*(1), 57–72 (1971).
24. A. J. Walker, *HRIS Development: A Project Team Guide to Building an Effective Personnel Information System*, Van Nostrand, New York, 1982.
25. M. J. Kavanagh, H. G. Gueutel, and S. I. Tannenbaum, *Human Resource Information and Decision Support Systems*, PWS-Kent, Boston, 1989.
26. D. W. Kroeber and H. J. Watson, *Computer-Based Information Systems: A Management Approach*, Macmillan, New York, 1988.

27. R. H. Sprague, "A Framework for the Development of Decision Support Systems," *MIS Quart., 4*(4), 1–26 (1980).
28. R. Buhner and P. Kleinschmidt, "Reflections on the Architecture of a Decision Support System for Personnel Assignment Scheduling in Production Cell Technology," *Decision Support Systems, 4,* 473–480 (1988).
29. E. Turban, *Decision Support and Expert Systems: Management Support Systems,* Macmillan, New York, 1990.
30. P. Constantopoulos, "Decision Support for Massive Personnel Assignment," *Decision Support Systems, 5,* 355–363 (1989).
31. H. S. Weigel and S. P. Wilcox, "The Army's Personnel Decision Support System," *Decision Support Systems, 9,* 281–306 (1993).
32. G. DeSanctis and R. B. Gallupe, "A Foundation for the Study of Group Decision Support Systems," *Manag. Sci., 33*(5), 509–609 (1987).
33. G. P. Huber, 'Issues in the Design of Group Decision Support Systems," *MIS Quart., 8*(3), 195–204 (1984).
34. M. R. Edwards, "Using Expert Systems to Improve International Productivity," *Int. J. Manag., 9*(2), 166–174 (1992).
35. M. M. Extejt and M. P. Lynn, "Expert Systems as Human Resource Management Decision Tools," *J. Syst. Manag., 39*(11), 10–15 (1988).
36. F. Lehner, "Expert Systems for Organizational and Managerial Tasks," *Inform. Manag., 23,* 31–41 (1992).
37. J. R. Anderson and E. Skwarecki, "The Automated Tutoring of Introductory Computer Programming, *Commun. ACM, 29*(9), 842–849 (1986).
38. B. Woolf and A. Patricia, "Multiple Knowledge Sources in Intelligent Teaching Systems," *IEEE Expert, 2*(2), 41–54 (1987).
39. J. L. Kolodner, "Improving Human Decision Making Through Case-Based Decision Aiding," *AI Mag., 12,* 52–68 (1991).
40. K. P. Sycara, "Negotiation Planning: An AI Approach," *Eur. J. Oper. Res., 46*(2), 216–234 (1990).
41. T. H. Chi, M. Chen, and Y. Kiang, "A Generalized Case Based Reasoning System for Personnel Performance Evaluation," in *Proceedings of the 24th Annual Hawaii International Conference on System Science,* 1991, pp. 82–89.
42. J. F. Rockart and D. W. DeLong, *Executive Support Systems,* Irwin, Homewood, IL, 1988.
43. J. F. Rockart and M. E. Treacy, "The CEO Goes On-Line," *Harvard Bus. Rev., 60*(1), 84–88 (1982).
44. D. H. Byun and E. H. Suh, "Human Resource Management Expert Systems," *Expert Systems, 11*(2), 109–119 (1994).
45. R. J. Thierauf, *Executive Information Systems: A Guide for Senior Management and MIS Professionals,* Quorum Books, New York, 1991.
46. L. Volonino and S. Robinson, "The Experience of Marine Midland Bank in Sustaining an EIS," in *DSS-90 Transactions,* The Institute of Management Sciences, Province, RI, 1990, pp. 164–172.
47. L. Volonino and H. J. Watson, "The Strategic Business Functions (SBF) Approach to EIS Planning and Design," in *Proceedings of the 23rd Annual Hawaii International Conference on System Science,* 1990, pp. 170–177.
48. H. J. Watson and M. N. Frolick, "Determining Information Requirements for an EIS," *MIS Quart., 17*(4), 255–269 (1993).

DAE-HO BYUN

MANAGING INFORMATION TECHNOLOGY:
A RESOURCE ENHANCEMENT PERSPECTIVE

INTRODUCTION

> The creation of a new device can create *new ways of being* that previously did not exist and a *framework for actions* that would not have previously made sense.
>
> Terry Winograd and Fernando Flores
> from *Understanding Computers and Cognition* (1)

Organizations are facing challenges on two different fronts: *changes in their external environment* due to the opening of global markets and competition, customer demands for better quality product and faster service, and uncertain legal, social and governmental pressures, and so forth, and *rapid advances in the tools and techniques* used to support the streamlining of various organizational operations. One such tool/technique that is of interest here is the *computer-based information technology* (henceforth referred to as IT). It is creating new opportunities for business to meet its external demands while forcing changes in the way organizations manage their internal operations, if they are to exploit these opportunities. Earlier use of IT has primarily been to process basic business transactions and report salient information to decision-makers. In other words, computers (a capital resource) replaced labor (human resource) in performing these tasks. Organizations have managed this type of *resource substitution* in a way similar to all other resource substitutions of labor by capital during the postindustrial era (2). However, the role of IT has changed dramatically in the last decade, from resource substitution to one of supporting the individual (i.e., enhancement), especially since the introduction of powerful, cost-effective personal computers, and workstations. This change in the role of IT, from resource substitution to *resource enhancement*, has necessitated associated changes in the management of IT.

The objective of this article is to examine the issues in the management of IT under a resource enhancement perspective, specifically when it affects labor productivity. The next section provides some definitions, and the third section discusses the differences in management thinking needed to address the new role of IT (i.e., new ways of being). The fourth section provides some issues organizations have to address (i.e., framework for actions) to manage IT effectively.

DEFINITIONS

Technology is defined as the application of science and other advances to business and commerce (adapted from *Webster's Dictionary*).

Information technology is the application of science and other advances to providing *information* needed in support of business and commerce. Some of these are *product technologies* (e.g., CD-ROM to store and provide access to large amounts of information, fiber-optic cable to facilitate quick transfer of a large volume of information, etc.); others are *process technologies* (e.g., spreadsheet modeling to support interactive decision making, object-oriented approaches to improve the software development process, etc.). Often the process technologies are also referred to as methodologies.

Managing is defined as the act, manner, or practice of planning, organizing, allocating resource, coordinating, and controlling (adapted from *American Heritage Dictionary*).

Managing information technology is , hence, the "the act, manner or practice of planning, organizing, allocating resource, coordinating and controlling" information technologies in support of business and commerce. In a rapidly changing business environment, organizations need to manage IT not only to address current needs but also to remain competitive over time.

Specifically, managing IT calls for the following:

- **Planning** for strategic information technology deployment so organizations can remain competitive (now and in the future)
- **Organizing** its infrastructure (technical and organizational) to effectively adopt and diffuse these technologies
- **Allocating resource** (human, capital, etc.) in order to successfully implement IT deployment plans
- **Coordinating** activities using appropriate personnel and project management techniques
- **Controlling** operations to ensure that any deviations from IT deployment plans are monitored and changed as needed

CHANGES IN MANAGEMENT PHILOSOPHY: NEW WAYS OF BEING

During the seventies and early eighties, IT was primarily used to replace labor-intensive data/information processing tasks with computers in order to realize processing efficiencies and cost savings. The continuing shift of American industry from manufacturing to the service sector has changed the work-force activities from those that are labor intensive to those that are knowledge intensive (2). This has changed the use of IT from one of replacing data/information processing tasks of the work force with computers to one of improving the work-force productivity. This is often done by enhancing their knowledge base, facilitating the use of interactive algorithmic and heuristic modeling for decision support, improving access to and communication of corporate information, and so forth. This shift in the role of IT—*enhancing human resource as opposed to replacing it*—calls for a different management thinking. The following discussion highlights some of these differences in each of the management activities and are summarized in Table 1.

Planning

Planning has been used to *identify candidate projects and selecting those with highest return* for deployment.

Typically, the *identification of candidate projects* is based on the premise that

TABLE 1   Summary of Differences in Thinking

	Resource substitution	Resource enhancement
Planning		
Identification	Task automation	Improve productivity
Selection	Monetary return	Value on multiple dimensions
Organization		
Technical	Mainframe based for processing efficiency and system integrity	PC/workstations that are user environment friendly and decision process sensitive
Organization	Hierarchical organization	Matrix or network-type organizations
Resource allocation	Teams of individuals with special skills	Teams with changing skills and composition
Coordination	Life-cycle approaches	Spiral/concurrent approaches
Control	Monitor preestablished requirements and yearly budgetary and performance goals	Assess impact on business decisions and business

substituting the computer for labor-intensive information processing tasks (i.e., task automation) can reduce cost, error rates, processing time, and so on. Under the resource enhancement focus, the project identification is based on the role IT can play in *improving individual productivity* (better decision quality, improved service, etc.).

The selection of appropriate task automation projects for deployment is usually based on the impact such projects have on *monetary return* using techniques such as payback period, net present value, and internal rate of return. However, projects that are intended to enhance individual productivity may have to be evaluated based on their overall *value on multiple*, qualitative and quantitative, *dimensions* (such as strategic importance, risk, reduced decision uncertainty, and improved consistency in decision making).

The selection of new projects is often constrained by the amount of resources committed to the maintenance or enhancement of existing projects. It is assumed that most new projects need a major investment at the start and a smaller incremental investment subsequently. However, most of the projects proposed for productivity improvement, by definition, are never complete because the business processes they support are operating in a rapidly changing environment. Hence, each candidate project proposed merely represents a version of support needed at a given point in time, and continued revisions to this version are called for as the environment changes. This makes both the investment made and value derived *incremental* in nature.

In summary, the planning process under enhancement perspective calls for the identification and selection of the first version of new systems and revised versions of existing systems for deployment, in order to meet the changing needs of an organization.

Organizing

Organizing IT calls for a *technical and organizational infrastructure* to implement the plans.

Typically, the technical infrastructure has been *mainframe based* to ensure *processing efficiency* (as computers processed large volumes of business transactions) and to maintain *system integrity* (as computer systems maintained huge amounts of corporate data and processed highly visible and sensitive corporate transactions such as customer orders and chart of accounts). The role of IT under an enhancement perspective often calls for a PC/workstation-based technical infrastructure that is *user environment friendly* (i.e., available where and when needed) to process mostly low volume transactions while remaining *decision process sensitive* (i.e., support relatively autonomous individual access reliable and secure information).

The organizational infrastructure has often been *hierarchical* in nature to manage various subtasks of the information system development function such as analysis, design, programming, maintenance, and operations. This structure is used to extract requirements and build systems using specialists such as analysts, designers, programmers, operators, and database specialists, each performing a specific development subtask. Under resource enhancement, the role of IT is intended to support continuously evolving business requirements, and this calls for a shorter and iterative system development life cycle. In addition, the role of users and developers may overlap in many of the system development subtasks due to the continual changes that are occurring in both the business and technology. Hence, a *matrix type* of organizational structure that distributes development responsibilities to both users and developers may be appropriate. Recently, significant focus has been placed on "networktype organizations" to address many of the complexities businesses are facing as they move to the 21st century (3).

Resource Allocation

Resource allocation focuses on *personnel allocation* among projects.

By disaggregating the system development function into subtasks (analysis, design, etc.), one can assign individuals with specialized skills to each of these subtasks (i.e., personnel are allocated to these subtasks based on their "skills"). The project *team*, hence, is a composition of individuals with specific skills, each playing a significant role in the project at a given point in time. When IT is supporting task enhancement, requiring overlapping skills and shorter development life cycle, the personnel allocation to a project is much more difficult and has to consider factors such as user's availability and competence, concurrent use of individuals with specialized skills, and availability of people with multiple skills. In other words, resource enhancement projects call for a *fluid project team*, whose skill and personnel composition changes frequently during the project life cycle. Recent research seems to suggest the need for a similar approach for strategic decision making as well: the formulation of "strategic teams" with interdisciplinary skills (4).

Coordination

Coordination of IT development focuses on the use of *project management techniques* to ensure that systems meet their requirements.

The life-cycle approaches, specifically those that are sequential in nature, are used to typically manage projects in a sequential manner: from initial conception in the planning phase to final user acceptance during the implementation phase, through the establishment of milestones. The deliverable at the end of each of these milestones is based on the premise that the completion of one subtask (or phase) should precede the initiation of the other. With the unstructured and evolving nature of many enhancement projects, coordination has to rely on techniques such as *spiral* (5) and *concurrent* (6) system development, where greater amount of parallelism is proposed within phases, as well as within versions of the same system.

Control

Control objectives are established to ensure that *individual projects have met user needs* and IT function, as a whole, met its *budgetary and performance goals.*

The success of an IT project is often measured in terms of how it met preestablished requirements such as user satisfaction, system performance against stated requirements, and time and budget guidelines. Under the new role, IT assessment is an ongoing activity and may be made based on how it impacts business decisions (individual productivity, decision effectiveness, etc.) as well as its impact on the task and organization.

Typically, IT management [often a Management Information Systems (MIS) department in a firm] is concerned with meeting its *budgetary and performance goals* through periodic reporting of variances between budgeted and actual outcomes. The performance goals are system based, (such as reliability and accessibility) and budgetary goals are monetary based. Given the changing dynamics of a business, the success of an IT function has to be based on its ability *both* to identify new IT opportunities for productivity improvements and competitive advantage, and to manage their effective assimilation into the organization. Simply put, the assessment of an IT function has to be based on its impact on business over time rather than simply meeting yearly budgetary/performance goals.

MANAGING IT CHALLENGES: A FRAMEWORK FOR ACTION

Planning

It is necessary to identify candidate projects that improve productivity and select those that add value on multiple qualitative and quantitative dimensions. The candidate projects basically are systems of different versions: first version of new systems and later versions of existing systems.

Identify Productivity Improvement Projects

In order to identify candidate projects that improve productivity, one needs to proactively monitor the dynamics of both the business and IT environments. For example, a Federal Credit Union has introduced an expert system (ES) to process loans of certain type consistently and broaden its loan portfolio to improve service, only after the firm went through a SWOT (strengths, weaknesses, opportunities, and threats) analysis and determined that one of its weaknesses is its inability to provide a broader customer service. A manufacturing organization has decided to explore the use of an ES to configure complex products to reduce errors and provide better customer service, after it has observed success in similar types of applications by firms such as Digital Equipment Corporation and Honeywell.

Often, users' lack of awareness of changing information technologies and their impact on the decision making process as well as the developers' inability to understand the dynamics of changing business climate *both* contribute to the difficulty in identifying such candidate projects. This problem is further aggravated by the simultaneous occurrence of both these phenomena: rapid changes in the technical advances and the business climate. The challenge here remains one of monitoring trends in IT and business climate and detecting opportunities for enhancing individual productivity and service quality.

Porter defines a value chain (7) for an organization that includes a firm's *primary activities* (inbound logistics, operations, outbound logistics, marketing and sales, and service) and *support activities* (technology development, human resource management, procurement, and corporate infrastructure). These can be used to identify *productivity improvement opportunities* within various primary and secondary activities. Parasuraman et al. (8) have provided a conceptual model that describes various determinants of service quality, and these can help an organization assess service improvement opportunities.

Assess Value on Multiple Dimension

When IT projects are used for resource enhancement, their value is assessed on multiple dimensions: some qualitative, such as development risk, productivity gains, competitive advantage or necessity, and organizational compatibility, and others quantitative, such as rate of return and payback period. For example, an insurance company invested heavily in ES technology, when this technology was in its infancy, to ensure that its underwriting activity provided competitive service to a potential client. Similarly, a credit union used ES technology for loan evaluation not for the time it saved but for the consistency it provided in the decisions. Both these examples illustrate the use of qualitative dimensions to assess the technology potential. When projects are evaluated on multiple dimensions and one needs to arrive at a combined rank for each of these projects, techniques such as Analytical Hierarchy Process (9), decision tree models (10), and multidimensional prioritization (11) can often be used.

The major challenge in the evaluation process, when technologies and businesses are changing rapidly and measures used to evaluate projects are highly qualitative, is to keep one's commitment to a project contingent on a continuous assessment of costs and value, and discontinue projects that do not seem to add value. For example, one company made a strong commitment to ES technology after initial exploration and today considers it a standard technology for the configuration of all its products, whereas a bank decided to abandon a loan evaluation ES, even after it was shown to be locally beneficial, because its "net" impact on the organization was considered negative. Many organizations are now moving toward approving only smaller versions of larger projects so they can reassess their value periodically. In fact, one of the reasons for significant interest in business process redesign (12) now is because most of the earlier projects never went through a periodic scrutiny for the value they provide.

measures, before deciding on a redesign of the process and/or a reconfiguration of the technology that is used to support it (23).

Assess the Long-Term Impact of the IT Function

Measuring the success of an IT function as a whole, in terms of how it impacts individual productivity, is much harder because this requires a long-term evaluation. Also, given the rapidity with which technologies are changing, the IT function has to continually update its human resource skills, seek new IT-based opportunities to support individual decision making in a changing environment, diffuse new technologies effectively into individual decision processes, abandon technologies and operations that are known to be not effective, and so forth. For example, the IT function in an insurance company, which introduced ES for underwriting, has not made major commitments to diffusing this technology to other functions because it saw no major productivity gains. The IT function in a firm that manufactures electrical supplies has decided to update their staff skills so they can better identify IT opportunities to meet business needs. A manufacturing firm has decided to outsource its data center operations so it can focus on application development and service support. A film processing company has outsourced its entire IT function to those that know how to manage it. An insurance company and a manufacturing firm are both outsourcing their maintenance functions so that they can focus on introducing new technologies to address changing business problems.

The above examples are all indicative of a change in the role of the IT function: from designing systems that meet "stated user needs" to proactively seeking ways to use IT for productivity and service quality gains. This calls upon the IT organization to periodically assess its own management competencies in a changing business and technology environment and to focus on a few activities it can do well.

TABLE 2   Summary of Actions/Challenges

	Resource enhancement	Challenges
Planning	Improve productivity	Identify opportunities
	Value determination	Continuously assess a project's value
Organization	User environment and decision friendly	Open architecture
		Seamless integration
		Object approaches
	Matrix structure	Hybrid structure
Resource allocation	Matching skills with activities	Fluid project teams
		Cross-disciplinary skills
Coordinate	Spiral/concurrent approaches	Match methodology with technology
		Match project scope with methodology steps
Control	Decision impact	Assess when and what to measure
	Impact over time	Assess the IT function's impact on business

The challenge to the IT function is, thus, twofold: determine its effectiveness in managing technologies in support of individual and organizational productivity and outsource or subcontract those activities it cannot manage well, and adapt continuously its activities and management philosophies to meeting the changing business and technology climate.

These observations are summarized in Table 2.

CONCLUSIONS

The initial focus of information technology industry has been to replace routine, error-prone, and monotonous data processing and reporting activities of labor with computers. With such a resource substitution, knowledge workers (i.e., those that process information and make/support decisions) are given more time to plan and guide "competitive" organizational efforts in a changing marketplace. With both technology and business changing rapidly, the use of IT in support of such knowledge workers (i.e., resource enhancement) will continue to dominate in the future. To address these challenges, IT management has to focus on the following activities:

- **Planning:** identifies opportunities that enhance productivity and selects those projects (versions of various systems) which meet organizational criteria (both quantitative and qualitative)
- **Organizing:** establishes a technical infrastructure that brings processing power to individuals that need it, and a bureaucratic infrastructure that allows both users and developers share responsibility for IT application development
- **Allocating resource:** matches projects with "skilled" individuals during the entire project life cycle
- **Coordination:** manages projects using techniques that allow for the continual evolution of systems of various versions
- **Control:** monitors the success of IT projects and function to ensure that they support the organizational goals/objectives

REFERENCES

1. T. Winograd and F. Flores, *Understanding Computers and Cognition: A New Foundation for Design*, Earlbaum Associates, Norwood, NJ, 1986.
2. P. J. Drucker, "The Coming of the New Organization," *Harvard Bus. Rev.,* 66(1), 45–53 (1988).
3. R. Nolan, A. J. Pollock, and J. P. Ware, "Creating the 21st Century Organization," *Stage by Stage,* 8(4) (1988).
4. R. Charan, "How Networks Reshape Organizations – For Results," *Harvard Bus. Rev.,* 69, 104–115 (1991).
5. B. W. Boehm, "A Spiral Model of Development and Enhancement," *Software Eng. Notes,* 11(4) (1986).
6. P. Dewan and J. Riedl, "Toward Computer-Supported Concurrent Software Engineering," *IEEE Computer*, 1993, 17–27 (January 1993).
7. M. E. Porter and V. E. Miller, "How Information Gives you Competitive Advantage," *Harvard Bus. Rev.,* 63 (1985).

8. A. Parasuraman, V. A. Zeithami, and L. L. Berry, "A Conceptual Model of Service Quality and its Implications for Future Research," *J. Marketing, 42* (Fall 1985).

9. T. L. Saaty, *The Analytical Hierarchy Process*, McGraw-Hill, New York, 1980.

10. E. K. Clemons and B. W. Weber, "Strategic Information Technology Investments: Guidelines for Decision Making," *J. MIS, 7*(2), 9–28 (1990).

11. R. Agarwal, L. Roberge, and M. Tanniru, "MIS Planing: A Methodology for Systems Prioritization," *Inform. Manag.* (in press).

12. M. Hammer and J. Champy, *Reengineering the Corporation: A Manifesto for Business Revolution*, Harper Business, New York, 1993.

13. A. Rin, "CASE and Application Development Technologies," in *Information Technology in Action: Trends and Perspectives*, R. Wang (ed.), Yourdon Press/Prentice-Hall, Englewood Cliffs, NJ, 1993, pp. 83–117.

14. A. Beitz, P. King, and K. Raymond, "Comparing two Distributed Environments: DCE and ANSAware in *DCE–The OSF Distributed Computing Environment*, Springer-Verlag, New York, 1993.

15. E. V. Berard, *Essays on Object-Oriented Software Engineering*, Prentice-Hall, Englewood Cliffs, NJ, 1993.

16. J. I. Cash, Jr., E. G. Eccles, N. Nohria, and R. L. Nolan, *Building the Information-Age Organization: Structure, Control, and Information Technologies*, Irwin, Inc., Homewood, IL, 1994, pp. 29–33.

17. J. C. Weatherbe and N. P. Vitalari, *Systems Analysis and Design: Best Practices*, West Publishing Co., Boulder, CO, 1994, pp. 143–147.

18. A. L. Kristof, K. G. Brown, H. P. Sims, Jr., and K. A. Smith, "The Virtual Team: An Example from AES Corporation," *Advances in Interdisciplinary Studies of Work Teams*, JAI Press (in press).

19. R. Agarwal, S. Brown, and M. Tanniru, "Assessing the Impact of ES: The Experiences of a Small Firm," *Expert Syst. Appl., 7*(2), 249–257 (1994).

20. J. J. Sviokla, "An Examination of the Impact of ES on the Firm: The Case of XCON," *MIS Quart.*, 127–139 (June 1990).

21. W. H. DeLone and E. McLean, "Information Systems Success: The Quest for the Dependent Variable," *Inform. Syst. Res., 3*(1), 60–95 (1992).

22. R. Agarwal and M. Tanniru, "Assessing the Organizational Impacts of Information Technology," *Int. J. Technol. Manag., 7*(6/7/8), 623–643 (1992).

23. T. H. Davenport and J. E. Short, "The New Industrial Engineering: Information Technology and Business Process Redesign," *Sloan Manag. Rev.*, 11–27 (Summer 1990).

BIBLIOGRAPHY

Cash, J. I., Jr., E. G. Eccles, N. Nohria, and R. L. Nolan *Building the Information-Age Organization: Structure, Control, and Information Technologies*, Irwin, Inc., Homewood, IL, 1994.

Frenzel, C. W., *Management of Information Technology*, Boyd & Fraser, 1992.

Martin, E. W., D. W. DeHayes, J. A. Hoffer, and W. C. Perkins, *Managing Information Technology: What Managers Need to Know*, MacMillan Publishing, New York, 1994.

Wang, R. *Information Technology in Action: Trends and Perspectives*, Yourdon Press/Prentice-Hall, Englewood Cliffs, NJ, 1993.

Weatherbe, J. C. and N. P. Vitalari, *Systems Analysis and Design: Best Practices*, West Publishing Co., Boulder, CO, 1994, pp. 143–147.

MOHAN R. TANNIRU

THE MODULARITY OF FACE RECOGNITION

INTRODUCTION

> no single object presented to our senses . . . engrosses so large a share of our thoughts, emotions, and associations as that small portion of flesh and blood a hand may cover, which constitutes the human face. (1)

Faces hold the key to huge amounts of information. Unfamiliar faces signal emotional state, age, sex, race, health, attractiveness, and perhaps even social status and character. Familiar faces unlock biographical information about their owners and our experiences with them, crucial information for predicting their behavior, especially toward us (are they friend or foe?), and for modulating our own behavior toward them (for overviews, see Refs. 2–4). Without access to such information, even the simplest forms of social organization would be impossible.

Our ability to recognize many hundreds or even thousands of faces despite their similarity, sometimes even managing to tell "identical" twins apart, is impressive. Few other recognition tasks require us to discriminate among such homogeneous objects, all with the same basic parts in the same basic configuration. To recognize faces, the visual system must solve this difficult computation problem. It must find a way to detect and represent the subtle differences in this shared configuration that individuate faces.

Evolution has provided neonates with innate mechanisms that focus their attention on faces (for a review, see Ref. 5) and allow them to discriminate their mother's face from that of a stranger within days of birth (6,7).* Despite this head start, face recognition skills continue to develop throughout childhood (for a review, see Ref. 11), taking about 10 years before the adult level of expertise is reached (for a review, see Ref. 12). This expertise is finely tuned by massive amounts of experience and is easily disrupted if faces appear in an unfamiliar orientation (e.g., upside-down) (for reviews, see Refs. 13 and 14) or come from an unfamiliar racial group (15).

Is There a Face Recognition Module?

The idea that faces might be special has fascinated many scientists (e.g., Refs. 16–19). Perhaps in addition to our innate interest in faces, evolution has also given us a special-purpose face recognition system or *module* to solve the computational problem presented by the homogeneity of faces.† A module is a special-purpose, autono-

---

*Neonates can also discriminate facial expressions (8) and imitate facial gestures (9,10).

†There may also be modules for other aspects of face processing, such as recognition of expressions and analysis of lip movements associated with speech (3,20).

mous, computational system with its own dedicated neural architecture (21). Fodor argues that perceptual analysis is conducted by a collection of modules specialized for face recognition, color perception, shape coding, analysis of 3-D (three-dimensional) spatial relations, grammatical analysis, voice recognition, the analysis of melody, and so on. The modules deliver information about the current state of the world to our central, cognitive system, which interprets this information in the light of prior knowledge, goals, expectations, and other relevant factors.

In the next three sections, I will address three key questions for deciding whether we have a face recognition module. First, is face recognition computationally specialized, with different processing operations used than for other objects? Second, is face recognition neurally specialized and if so where is its neural substrate? Third, is face recognition autonomous, with its operations insulated from higher-level knowledge (expectations, beliefs, goals, etc.) and information within other modules? If the answer to all three questions is "yes," then face recognition is modular.

ARE FACES COMPUTATIONALLY SPECIAL?

Are all objects recognized in the same way? At one extreme, there may be different systems for recognizing many different kinds of objects. For example, based largely on dissociations of impairment following brain damage, Konorski (18) proposed different systems for the following classes: (1) small, manipulable objects, (2) larger, partially manipulable objects, (3) nonmanipulable objects, (4) human faces, (5) emotional facial expressions, (6) animated objects (e.g., animals), (7) signs, (8) handwriting, and (9) limb positions. The opposite and more popular view is that all objects are recognized by a single general-purpose recognition system (e.g., Refs. 22–28). The basic idea of most of these models is that objects are analyzed into their component parts and the spatial relations among those parts (22,24,26, 27). On the first view, face recognition would be modular, whereas on the second view, it would not.

The truth, however, may lie somewhere between these two extremes. Consider the claim that all objects are recognized by a part-based recognition system. Such a system is ideally suited to recognition of objects at the basic level (cat, table, car, tree, etc.) (29), where objects (especially manufactured objects) differ primarily in the parts that they have (30). It is also suitable for distinguishing objects that differ in the overall arrangement of parts, such as a cup (handle on the side) versus a bucket (handle on the top). However, this kind of analysis will not work for face recognition, because faces all have the same basic parts in the same basic arrangement. A part-based analysis could tell us that we are looking at a face, but not whose face it is. Therefore, a different system seems to be needed for face recognition, one that can encode the variations in the shared facial configuration that individuate faces (e.g., Refs. 13, 14, 31–34). Researchers are trying to determine just what computations are used to recognize faces and whether these are unique to faces.

One line of work has identified the importance of coding *relational features*, such as the spacing of internal features, ratios of distances between parts of the face, and global shape. Yin (35,36) discovered that inversion disrupts the recognition of faces much more than within-category discriminations of other mono-oriented objects (for recent reviews of inversion effects on face recognition, see Refs. 13, 14, and 37). Inversion disrupts the processing of relational features more than isolated features* (visibility of teeth, presence/absence of facial hair, glasses, wrinkles, etc.) (eg., Refs. 14 and 39) and so the disproportionate inversion decrement for face recognition indicates a greater reliance on relational features for faces than other objects (13,14). Developmental studies also show that learning to use such features is part of becoming a face expert (see Ref. 12 for a review). However, although relational features play a special role in face recognition, reliance on such features is not unique to faces because a disproportionate inversion effect is found for other homogeneous classes (e.g., dogs) with which subjects have expertise (13). Therefore, a computational module specialized for coding relational features within shared configurations would not uniquely process faces.

Closely related to this focus on relational features is the idea that faces are represented more *holistically* than other objects, that is, their parts are not explicitly represented and recognition is based on template matching (31,33,40). If so, the parts of a face should be especially difficult to recognize when taken out of the face context and presented in isolation, compared with the parts of other objects, which are explicitly represented. Tanaka and Farah (33) showed that this was indeed the case, with parts presented in the whole object recognized better than parts in isolation for faces but not for scrambled faces, inverted faces, or houses. However, although consistent with their holistic hypothesis, this result is also consistent with the relational feature hypothesis, because relationships between the target part and other parts of the face are disrupted when the part is presented in isolation.

Farah (32,40) conjectures that we have two computational systems, one for part decomposition and the other for more holistic representations of complex parts (although as indicated above, present evidence seems equally consistent with the latter coding relational features rather than holistic representations). However, these systems do not map directly onto object types. Rather, she suggests that words are represented by the part-based system, faces by the holistic system, and common objects by both systems. This hypothesis is consistent with several neuropsychological observations (40). First, impaired recognition of common objects (visual agnosia) always occurs along with impaired recognition of either words (alexia) or faces (prosopagnosia). Second, visual agnosia never occurs with intact recognition of both words and faces, and, third, impaired recognition of both words and faces never occurs with intact recognition of objects.† Therefore, there may be two recognition systems, but, again, neither is a dedicated face recognition system.

Another line of work suggests that faces are coded as *deviations from a norm* or average face, an efficient method for representing variations in the shared facial configuration that individuate faces. Caricatures, which exaggerate the distinctive

---

*Of course, all the features are still present in the inverted images, in an objective sense, but something about the unfamiliar orientation seems to make relational features particularly difficult to encode. Perhaps the mismatch between the intrinsic and retinal/gravitational tops of inverted but normally mono-oriented objects (38), is especially disruptive to coding relational features, which already require reference to more than one part of the face.

†The hypothesis also predicts that some degree of visual agnosia should consistently co-occur with alexia and with prosopagnosia, but this does not seem to be the case (see below).

information in a face relative to a norm, are at least as recognizable as undistorted faces and both are more recognizable than anticaricatures, which reduce distinctive information (34,41–44). The effectiveness of caricatures suggests that we use norm-based coding for faces because only features coded with reference to the norm (e.g., vector deviations from the norm) are transformed systematically. Features coded in any other frame of reference are distorted haphazardly. However, caricatures can also enhance the recognition and discrimination of many stimuli other than faces (see Ref. 43 for a review). Therefore, like relational feature coding and holistic coding, norm-based coding may not be unique to faces.

The preceding discussion strongly suggests that face recognition is handled differently from basic level object recognition. It relies on relational feature coding, holistic coding, and/or norm-based coding, in contrast to the part-based analysis used for basic level object recognition. However, none of these computational strategies is unique to face recognition. Rather the difference between face recognition and other discriminations within spatially homogeneous classes seems to be a matter of degree rather than of kind. Relational feature coding is used whenever a person must distinguish homogeneous objects with which they have expertise (13) and the same may be true of norm-based coding (45). It is less clear when holistic coding is used, although Corballis (31) has speculated it may be important for natural objects, with part-based coding used for manufactured objects.

To summarize, there is no evidence for a *dedicated* computational system used exclusively with faces (see also Refs. 46–49). However, there does seem to be a specialized computational system designed to represent variations in a shared configuration that deals *primarily*, but not exclusively, with faces. Given the adaptive importance of face recognition, this system may be a face recognition module in the teleological sense, having evolved to solve the problem of recognizing faces but which has been co-opted for other discriminations that present a similar computational problem.

ARE FACES NEURALLY SPECIAL?

Somewhat paradoxically, considering the failure to find clear evidence for a computational module dedicated to faces, brain damage can disrupt face recognition in a remarkably selective way (subsection entitled Prosopagnosia). This paradox could be resolved if the (damaged) neural substrate turned out to correspond to the computational system described above rather than to a system that deals exclusively with faces, and I will examine this possibility below. I will also review evidence for cells that respond selectively to faces. The existence of such cells does not ensure modularity because different classes of cells *could* represent different objects without any computational specificity (see Ref. 50). Nor is it clear what, if any, role these cells play in recognition. Nevertheless, the existence of such cells is consistent with a face recognition module (subsection entitled Face Cells in Monkeys). Finally, I will review evidence about where the neural substrates of face recognition are located (subsection entitled Where Is the Neural Substrate?)

Prosopagnosia

The first clinical reports of face recognition disorders appeared in the 19th century (51,52). However, these patients also had problems recognizing other objects and it was not until 1947 that Bodamer described a small group of patients whose face recognition problems occurred in the context of relatively preserved object recognition (53). He coined the term, *prosopagnosia*, for, "the selective disruption of the perception of faces, one's own face as well as those of others, which are seen but not recognised as faces belonging to a particular owner . . . A well-characterised, strictly defined disorder, . . . affecting only a certain part of the gnostic activity, i.e. that of the recognition of faces" (quoted in Ref. 54, p. 83).

*Is Prosopagnosia Genuinely Face-Specific?**

Considerable effort has been directed at determining whether prosopagnosia is genuinely face-specific and, hence, whether there is a neurally distinct substrate for face recognition. Of course, restriction of the deficit to faces could arise simply because faces are harder to recognize (e.g., they may be more similar) than other kinds of object. This differential difficulty hypothesis must be ruled out before one could conclude that faces were neurally special. This could be done by showing that the two abilities can be impaired independently, that is, by showing a *double dissociation* between impaired recognition of faces and other objects. Even then, the face deficit might stem from a more general problem in making discriminations within basic level categories† (e.g., discriminating different cars, houses, dogs, etc) or it might be a problem in distinguishing the members of homogeneous classes using relational features or norm-based coding, consistent with the computational considerations discussed above.

Face recognition can certainly be impaired independently of basic level object recognition. Many prosopagnosics can recognize common objects without difficulty (for a review, see Refs. 55 and 61) and there are other patients who are much more impaired at recognizing common objects than faces (62–65). Therefore, prosopagnosia is not simply a weak form of visual agnosia.

But can face recognition be impaired independently of other within-category discriminations? Prosopagnosics typically have associated difficulties recognizing other classes of objects, such as animals, buildings, cars, chairs, foods, flowers, houses, monuments, and/or personal effects (66–73). These associated deficits have led Damasio and his colleagues to claim that prosopagnosia is really a problem in

---

*The ability to recognize faces is independent of the ability to recognize facial expressions (for reviews see Refs. 55 and 56). Some prosopagnosics have preserved recognition of facial expressions (e.g., Refs. 57 and 58) and some patients who cannot recognize facial expressions are not prosopagnosic (59). The conclusion that separate systems analyze facial identity and facial expressions is supported by research with normals showing that performance sorting faces on one of these dimensions is unaffected by their values on the other dimension (60). In this section, I consider whether the recognition deficit in prosopagnosia is specific to faces or not.

†A general problem in making within-category discriminations might be especially apparent with faces, even if it was not restricted to faces. For example, faces are unusually homogeneous, other objects are often identified at the basic level (e.g., dog versus car versus table) rather than at the within-category or individual level (29), and difficulties might be more readily noticed with faces, given the obvious and embarrassing social consequences of failing to recognize friends, relatives, and associates.

making within-category or other discriminations between similar items (70,74). However, such a conclusion is probably not correct. Apart from the general consideration that associations or co-occurrences of deficits provide weak evidence about underlying capacities,* there are other reasons to doubt this claim. Problems discriminating within categories are found much less consistently than one would expect if prosopagnosics had this general problem (75), and, more importantly, there is at least one case where prosopagnosia is not accompanied by such difficulties. De Renzi (76) describes an Italian prosopagnosic who could identify his own wallet, razor, glasses, necktie, and handwriting when each was shown together with 6–10 similar items. He could also sort foreign from Italian coins and identify a Siamese cat from various kinds of cat. A critic might worry that these discriminations were easier than face recognition, but other results show a selectivity for faces that cannot be attributed to differential difficulty. The prosopagnosic L. H. did as well as normal subjects at distinguishing new pairs of glasses from previously seen pairs (77), a task that normal subjects found more difficult than an analogous face recognition test, and another prosopagnosic who took up sheep farming became proficient at recognizing sheep faces, which normal subjects found extremely difficult (78). Therefore, prosopagnosia cannot simply be a manifestation of a general problem in making within-category discriminations.

The most straightforward interpretation of these data is that prosopagnosia is a face-specific deficit brought about by damage to a neural system for face recognition. However, it seems odd (but not impossible)† that there should be a dedicated neural system when there is no special-purpose computational system for faces. If, as suggested above, we have a computational system specialized for distinguishing homogeneous objects (at least those with which we have expertise) rather than faces per se, then it would make more sense if prosopagnosia was really the result of damage to this broader system. Note that this homogeneity hypothesis does not predict an across-the-board problem with within-category discriminations. If the stimuli can be discriminated on the basis of cues such as color, texture, pattern, size, presence/absence of parts, or other isolated features, performance would be intact (e.g., De Renzi's patient).‡ In fact, much of the inconsistency in deficits associated with prosopagnosia may be due to differences in the homogeneity of the stimuli used and differences in the patients' expertise with that class.

The homogeneity hypothesis predicts that prosopagnosics should have difficulty discriminating homogeneous objects with which they are experts. The fact that for many people faces are the only homogeneous class for which they are genuine experts may account for the face-specificity of the deficit in many prosopagnosics.

---

*Associated deficits do not allow strong inferences about underlying capacities because they can arise when distinct capacities are carried out by neighboring regions of cortex as well as when a common capacity underlies both skills. For example, color agnosia (deficits in recognizing colors) typically co-occurs with deficits in face recognition, simply because of the proximity of face and color processing areas.

†There could be a localized neural substrate simply because faces were learned at some critical point during cortical development (for further discussion see Ref. 50).

‡Such cues are less available for the glasses used by Farah and so L. H.'s normal performance with them seems problematic. However, although L. H.'s performance on glasses was normal, normal performance was only a little above chance and he actually recognized glasses as badly as he recognized faces!

However, if a prosopagnosic has expertise with another homogeneous class, then performance on that class should be impaired. There is some support for this prediction from cases where ornithologists and farmers have become prosopagnosic and lost the ability to recognize species of birds (66) and their individual animals (79,80). Another prosopagnosic lost the ability to recognize racehorses (72). Prosopagnosics also have trouble with classes such as animal faces (using isolated feature cues to recognize them, such as the beard for a goat and whiskers for a cat) (e.g., Ref. 73) and animals (see Ref. 55 for a review), which although less homogeneous than faces are still relatively homogeneous and with which we have some expertise.

However, not all the data fit so well. McNeil and Warrington's prosopagnosic who was excellent at recognizing sheep is a problem. However, he became a sheep expert after becoming prosopagnosic and may have learned to recognize sheep using cues other than relational features (although from the published examples, it is not obvious that all the sheep had markings that could serve as isolated feature cues). This possibility could be tested by examining whether he showed the large inversion decrement in sheep recognition associated with reliance on relational features. If he did, then the relational feature/expertise hypothesis would be disconfirmed. Assal et al.'s farmer is also problematic because he recovered from prosopagnosia but still could not recognize his cows. However, cows may well have been harder than faces for this patient (who remained mildly prosopagnosic), so that differential difficulty may explain the selective improvement. Another potentially problematic case is that of a farmer who became prosopagnosic but, according to anecdotal evidence, could still recognize his cows and dogs (57). However, the animals varied in color and markings, and variations in the shared configuration may not have been used for recognition.

In summary, prosopagnosia can be remarkably selective for faces and may well be the result of damage to a dedicated neural system for faces. However, there is some support for the hypothesis that prosopagnosia is due to damage to a broader system for distinguishing homogeneous objects. Future tests paying careful attention to the homogeneity of stimuli and the expertise of the patient will be needed to settle this issue.

Face Cells in Monkeys

In 1969 cells were discovered in monkey inferotemporal (IT) cortex (see Fig. 1) that responded selectively to a particular type of object, a hand (81). Shortly afterward, other IT cells were found that responded to faces (82,83) and many more face-specific cells have since been found in IT and other visual areas (see the subsection entitled Where Is the Neural Substrate?). At least some of these cells are sensitive to the correct facial configuration, responding poorly if features are rearranged (84–86), missing (84), or presented in isolation (85). Some cells are sensitive to the relative position of features within a face, especially the distance between the eyes and from the eyes to the mouth (87), consistent with the importance of relational features for human face recognition (see section entitled Are Faces Computationally Special?). In apparent contrast to the human system, these cells respond as well to inverted as to upright faces (84), but monkeys recognize inverted faces just as well as upright faces (88). Other cells respond to features such as the mouth, hair, and (especially) eyes (85,89).

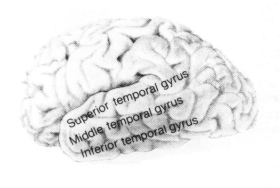

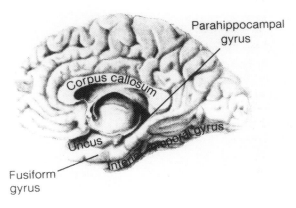

FIGURE 1   Lateral (top) and medial (bottom) views of the temporal lobe. (Adapted from Ref. 122.)

Are these "face" cells truly selective for faces? This question is impossible to answer definitively because one can never test all objects or object features (if we knew what they were). However, some heroic attempts have failed to find alternative stimuli to which these "face" cells will respond. Stimuli tested include textures, brushes, gratings, bars and edges of various colors, as well as models of objects like spiders, snakes, and food, that ought to interest monkeys (for a review, see Ref. 90). In contrast, these cells respond to real faces, plastic models of faces, and photographs of faces (although line drawings produce weak responses) and they respond to faces irrespective of their size, angle of view, position in the visual field, or spatial frequency content. Some reviewers conclude that these cells are face-selective (90) although others would like to see more testing of nonface objects (55). With the exception of hands, no cells have been found that are selective for other objects (e.g., fruit, tree branches, monkey genitalia, etc.), so that faces (and for monkeys, hands) may be unique in having cells devoted to them.

Different cells code different aspects of faces, such as identity, expression, and direction of attention (for review see Refs. 20 and 90). Some respond selectively to the direction of gaze or head orientation (e.g., Refs. 91–94; see Ref. 95 for a review), others respond to identity, and still others to expression. Hasselmo et al. (91) measured the responses of face cells to nine pictures of three different monkey faces, each with three different expressions (calm, slight threat, or full threat). A third of the cells responded selectively to identity and a fifth responded to expression, with only 7% responding to both. Interestingly, none of the cells that responded to either expression or identity responded exclusively to a single expression or identity, respectively. All were broadly tuned, consistent with the idea that identities and expressions are coded by ensembles of cells rather than "grandmother cells" that respond to a unique stimulus (see the following subsection).

Where Is the Neural Substrate?

Information about the location of the neural substrate(s) of face recognition is reviewed below. Tovée and Cohen-Tovée have recently reviewed the neural bases of other aspects of face processing such as emotional expression, direction of attention, facial speech analysis, and access of multimodal information associated with faces (20).

Prosopagnosia

Following Lissauer's (96) distinction between apperceptive and associative agnosia, perceptual and mnestic forms of prosopagnosia have been distinguished and are associated with different areas of damage (74).* *Apperceptive* prosopagnosia is due primarily to faulty perception of faces. These patients have trouble matching pictures of unfamiliar faces and seeing the face as a whole. In *associative* prosopagnosia, the percept is relatively intact but is stripped of meaning.† Knowledge about the person is intact and can be accessed from other cues such as their voice, clothing, or gait. These patients almost certainly do not have normal face percepts, but the classic view is that the perceptual deficits are insufficient to account for the recognition difficulties. However, the discussion of face-specificity above suggests that associative prosopagnosia may really be a high-level perceptual disorder in a computational system for representing configural variation [cf. Farah's claim that associative agnosia generally is a high-level perceptual disorder (55)]. Some authors have also distinguished face-specific deficits at earlier and later stages of processing respectively, that is, *visual* and *amnesic* deficits. With the visual deficit, faces but not other objects appear distorted (e.g., flattened or like fish heads) despite normal visual acuity (56). In contrast, with an amnesic disorder, identity information cannot be accessed from *any* cues (74).

Apperceptive prosopagnosia is associated with damage to visual association cortex in the occipital and parietal lobes of the *right hemisphere* (Fig. 2). It appears that both the inferior and superior components (mesially and laterally) of areas 18 and 19, plus fields 37 and 39 (Fig. 3), must be damaged for this type of prosopag-

---

*The discussion of face-specificity in the subsection Prosopagnosia focused on associative prosopagnosia because there is very little evidence on the face-specificity of apperceptive prosopagnosia (for a review, see Ref. 56).

†Despite the failure of overt recognition, some patients show "covert" recognition, learning correct name–face pairings faster than incorrect ones (57) or showing increased skin conductance when the correct name for a face is read out (97).

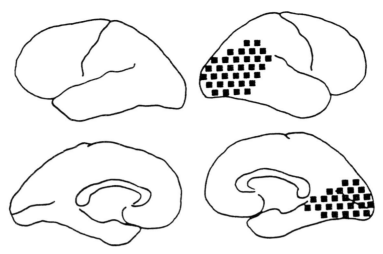

FIGURE 2   Areas of damage found in apperceptive prosopagnosia. (From Ref. 74, with permission.)

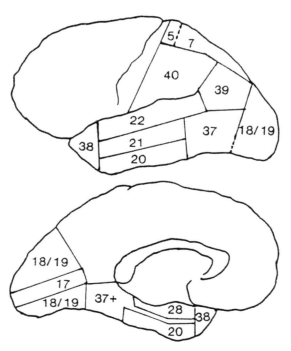

FIGURE 3   Human cytoarchitectonic areas whose damage is associated with prosopagnosia. (From Ref. 74, with permission.)

nosia to occur. The association of right hemisphere damage with apperceptive prosopagnosia is consistent with evidence that the right hemisphere has a special role in the perception and recognition of faces. For example, unilateral right-sided lesions can produce partial defects of face recognition (for reviews, see Refs. 20 and 98) and split-brain subjects with surgically disconnected cerebral hemispheres recognize faces better when they are presented to the right hemisphere than the left hemisphere* (e.g., Ref. 99). Similarly, normal subjects typically show a right-hemisphere advantage when faces are presented to their left and right visual fields, and hence (initially) to the opposite hemispheres (for reviews, see Refs. 20, 98 and 100). Finally, recent PET (positron emission tomography) studies of brain activity have shown asymmetric involvement of the posterior right hemisphere during a face identification task (see below for details) (61,101). This cerebral asymmetry for face recognition parallels the left-hemisphere focus on language functions, and the expansion of language areas near the temporal cortex in the left hemisphere may have forced face processing functions to the right hemisphere (102).

Despite this cerebral asymmetry, the most common kind of brain damage associated with prosopagnosia is bilateral damage (74). *Associative* prosopagnosia is caused by *bilateral* damage to the inferior occipital and temporal visual association cortices, areas 18, 19 and part of area of 37 (see Figs. 3 and 4) and *amnesic associative* prosopagnosia is caused by more anterior *bilateral* damage to the temporal lobes, including hippocampal structures as well as the surrounding cortex (see Figs. 3 and 5). The association of bilateral damage with these types of prosopagnosia might simply be a by-product of vascular organization, because the infero-

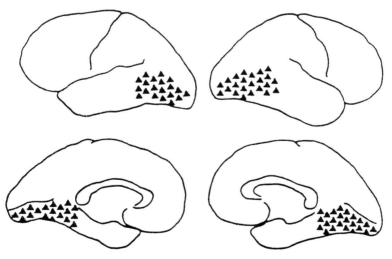

FIGURE 4   Areas of damage found in associative prosopagnosia. (From Ref. 74, with permission.)

---

*However, if a naming response is required, subjects choose the face presented to the left hemisphere, apparently responding to isolated, nameable features such as glasses or mustaches.

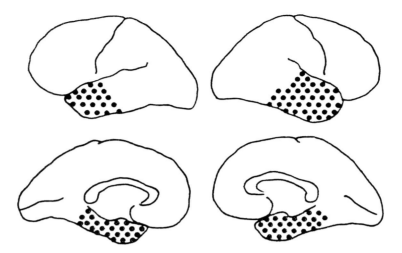

FIGURE 5   Areas of damage found in amnesic prosopagnosia. (From Ref. 74, with permission.)

medial part of the occipitotemporal cortex is supplied by branches of the posterior cerebral arteries which originate from a common trunk, the basilar artery (20), and even unilateral strokes in the posterior cerebral artery tend to be followed by ischemic attacks contralaterally (103). However, given other evidence that the left hemisphere can recognize faces (see Ref. 98 for a review, also Ref. 99), it may reflect a genuine contribution of the left hemisphere to face recognition.

Much of the debate about whether bilateral damage is needed for prosopagnosia (for reviews see Refs. 103 and 104) has failed to recognize the heterogeneity of prosopagnosic disorders. However, neither prosopagnosia nor face recognition are unitary, and determining the neural substrates of face recognition will require a careful analysis of the actual deficits shown by prosopagnosics and their associated areas of damage. Damasio et al.'s analysis suggests that unilateral damage is sufficient to produce disorders in the perceptual analysis of faces, whereas bilateral damage is needed to produce high-level disorders in accessing the semantic and biographical information associated with faces.

The anatomical data provided by prosopagnosic patients give an indication of brain areas that contribute to face recognition. However, they may not give the full picture. The problem is that structural integrity does not guarantee normal functioning. For example, Marciani et al. (71) describe a prosopagnosic whose MRI (magnetic resonance imaging) scan showed unilateral damage confined to the occipitotemporal regions of the *right* hemisphere. However, they also found that EEG (electroencephalography) activity was disturbed *bilaterally* and that when tested 2 months later, the patient's face recognition performance had improved and the left-sided EEG activity had returned to normal. These findings strongly suggest that the abnormal functioning of the structurally intact left hemisphere contributed to the patient's face recognition problems. Another problem is that focal damage in one area can affect the performance of distant intact areas that receive inputs from the damaged area (for further discussion, see Refs. 61 and 101). Fortunately, evidence is available from PET studies of brain functioning to round out the picture.

Positron Emission Tomography

Positron emission tomography (PET) studies identify areas of activity in the brain while normal subjects perform various tasks. Sergent and her colleagues (61,101) identified face-specific areas by "subtracting" areas activated in a face gender classification task and an object recognition task (classify as living/nonliving) from those activated during a face recognition task (classify as politician/actor). Face-specific areas were (i) the medial fusiform gyrus (areas 19–37) of the right hemisphere, (ii) the parahippocampal gyrus (area 36) of the right hemisphere, and (iii) the anterior temporal lobes of both hemispheres. These results are broadly consistent with the evidence from prosopagnosia, in that the first two areas are associated with apperceptive prosopagnosia and the third with amnesic prosopagnosia (Ref. 74 — see above).

In another PET study, blood flow was measured during a face-matching task, in which subjects had to indicate which of two photographs was of the same person (but taken from a different angle of view and under different lighting conditions) as a target photograph (105). This task, which taps high-level perceptual matching processes, activated inferotemporal cortex (area 37) but not more anterior temporal cortex, consistent with the idea that the former is associated with perceptual analysis and the latter with the semantic analysis of faces. In contrast to Sergent's results, the activation was clearly bilateral.

Electrical Recordings from Human Cortex

Electrical recordings made from the surface of occipitotemporal cortex in 24 epileptic patients during passive observation of faces and other objects also implicate neurons in the middle portion of the fusiform gyrus in area 37 (and part of the inferior temporal gyrus posterior to this region) in face processing, although in this study both hemispheres were involved (106). Many sites responded (large negative potentials 200 msec after stimulus onset) to faces but not to scrambled faces, cars, scrambled cars, or butterflies. However, only a small portion of these were active in any given individual, suggesting that small face-specific regions are dispersed among other functionally specialized small regions, which might account for the frequent co-occurrence of prosopagnosia and agnosia for other objects. Allison and his colleagues also suggest that face neurons in the fusiform and inferior temporal gyri were responsible for the perceptual analysis of faces because the subjects were viewing unfamiliar faces. This interpretation is consistent with Sergent et al.'s results but seems difficult to reconcile with their own observation that cortical stimulation of these sites often disrupted the naming of familiar faces, while leaving their appearance intact.

Single-Cell Recordings in Monkey Cortex

Additional information about the neural substrate of face recognition comes from single-cell recordings in monkey cortex (for reviews, see Refs. 20, 90, 107 and 108). As already noted, there are face-specific cells in IT, the final stage in the analysis of form and color in the occipitotemporal pathway (see Ref. 107). In contrast with cells early in the visual system (e.g., V1), which have small receptive fields (RFs) and code objects retinotopically (lesions in V1 cause defects in retinal space that move as the eyes move), cells in IT have large RFs and respond to objects or properties of objects largely independently of their retinal position. The selectivity of many IT neurons for shape is maintained over changes in stimulus size, contrast, and wavelength (107), as well as changes in orientation and illumination (109). Thus, these cells are coding real objects or object properties pretty much independent of viewpoint and they may pool inputs from face-specific cells in the superior temporal sulcus (STS) which tend to be view-specific and respond at shorter latencies than the IT cells (95). However, other evidence does not support this hierarchical picture. Rather, STS and IT cells seem to code different information about faces. STS cells code emotional expression (95,110), direction of (an observed monkey's) attention (91), and possibly other social cues based on familiarity or social status (110), whereas IT cells code facial identity (20,90,108,111).

A more detailed picture can be obtained if these areas are further subdivided. Face-specific cells are found in the inferior temporal gyrus and STS. The lower banks of STS and the inferior temporal gyrus form part of IT. The upper bank of STS, which contains many polysensory neurons, is called the superior temporal polysensory area (STP). IT and STP can be further subdivided using cytoarchitecture and anatomical connections into six subdivisions: TE_m and TE_a located within IT, TA_a, TPO, and PG_a located within STP, and IP_a on the boundary between IT and STP (see Fig. 6). Although face cells are found in all six subdivisions, they are most heavily concentrated in areas TE_m (IT) and TPO (STP) (112). The different patterns of connectivity of these two areas suggest that cells in these two areas are involved in the recognition of identity and expression of faces, respectively (20,90). This proposal is consistent with the fact that bilateral removal of STS does not render monkeys prosopagnosic (110) and with human evidence that identity and expression recognition can be independently impaired (60,113).

Consistency of Human and Animal Data

There are some striking anomalies between the human and animal data. For example, Sergent et al.'s PET studies with humans showed no activation in the areas

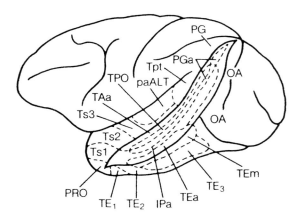

FIGURE 6   Multimodal areas in the superior temporal sulcus (lateral view). (Adapted from Ref. 122.)

where face-specific cells are found in monkeys—STS and lateral IT; Nor does damage to these regions of the human brain result in prosopagnosia (74). The STS anomaly can be resolved by the fact that monkey cells in this area probably do not code identity. As we saw earlier, cells in this area seem to code expression and direction of attention, and lesions there do not produce prosopagnosia in monkeys. However, we are still left with a mismatch between the location of face-selective cells in the lateral inferotemporal cortex of monkeys and the location of damage in human prosopagnosics (107). One possibility is that the simian and human substrates of face processing are not the same (61).

How Does All This Operate?

A speculative account of the neural organization of human face recognition suggested by the evidence reviewed earlier is that perceptual representations of faces are computed in the visual association cortices (possibly with greater involvement of the right hemisphere), that memory representations of faces are stored bilaterally in the anterior temporal lobes, and that the inferior occipitotemporal region of both hemispheres is important for accessing these stored representations and matching them with perceptual representations. It is unlikely that either perceptual or memorial representations of faces are coded by "grandmother cells" [cf. pontifical cells (114)], each dedicated to a unique face, that sit at the top of a processing hierarchy that progresses from simple features to complex objects. Instead, given that face-selective neurons respond to more than one face (e.g., Ref. 111), identity is probably coded by spatially and temporally distributed activity of ensembles or groups of cells. Interestingly, however, recent results suggest that quite small populations of cells may be used to code each individual face (111). More detailed arguments and a discussion of the advantages of ensemble coding can be found in Refs. 107 and 108).

Two questions remain unresolved. One is whether view-independent and view-specific representations of faces operate in parallel or form part of a hierarchy in which the outputs of view-specific cells are pooled by cell ensembles that respond to individual faces irrespective of viewpoint (as conjectured in Ref. 108). The other is whether component features and whole-face configurations are coded in parallel or whether configurations are coded by groups of cells that pool the outputs of feature-selective cells (as suggested in Ref. 115).

IS FACE RECOGNITION INFORMATIONALLY ENCAPSULATED?

For Fodor (21), the most interesting feature of a module is that its specialized computations are carried out without assistance or interference from the central semantic system or other modules; that is, it is informationally encapsulated. Rhodes and Tremewan (116) recently examined the encapsulation of face processing by asking whether a familiarity decision about a face could be influenced or *primed* by the prior presentation of a name (processed by a different module). Name priming had clear effects on the ability to discriminate between known and unknown faces, suggesting that face processing is not informationally encapsulated and, hence, that face recognition is not modular. However, Fodor's encapsulation requirement is controversial. Many theorists would not accept encapsulation as a criterion for modularity, believing that top-down influences are ubiquitous in perception (117–121).

CONCLUSIONS

In conclusion, it appears that face recognition is modular, but in a restricted sense. The first restriction is that the module does not *exclusively* process faces. Rather it may be used whenever we need to distinguish homogeneous objects with which we have expertise. The second restriction is that it may not be informationally encapsulated. However, as already noted, many would disagree that strict encapsulation is a realistic requirement for a module. Therefore, although face recognition may not be modular in a strict sense, it may be one of the most modular perceptual systems around!

REFERENCES

1. E. Eastlake, *Quarterly Review*, 90, 62 (1851).
2. V. Bruce, *Recognising Faces*, Erlbaum, London, 1988.
3. V. Bruce and A. W. Young, *Br. J. Psychol.*, *77*, 305–327 (1986).
4. A. W. Young and V. Bruce, *Eur. J. Cogn. Psychol.*, *3*, 5–49 (1991).
5. M. H. Johnson and J. Morton, *Biology and Cognitive Development: The Case of Face Recognition*, Blackwell, Oxford, 1991.
6. I. W. R. Bushnell, F. Sai, and J. T. Mullin, *Br. J. Dev. Psychol.*, *7*, 3–15 (1989).
7. G. E. Walton and T. G. R. Bower, "Newborn Preference for Familiar Faces," *Society for Research in Child Development*, Seattle (1991).
8. T. M. Field, R. Woodson, R. Greenberg, and D. Cohen, *Science, 281*, 179–181 (1982).
9. A. N. Meltzoff and M. K. Moore, *Science, 198*, 75–78 (1977).
10. A. N. Meltzoff and M. K. Moore, *Child Dev., 54*, 702–709 (1983).
11. H. D. Ellis, "The Development of Face Processing Skills," in *Processing the Facial Image*, V. Bruce, A. Cowey, A. W. Ellis, and D. I. Perrett, eds., Clarendon Press, Oxford, 1992, pp. 105–111.
12. S. Carey, "Becoming a Face Expert," in *Processing the Facial Image*, V. Bruce, A. Cowey, A. W. Ellis, and D. I. Perrett, eds., Clarendon Press, Oxford, 1992, pp. 95–103.
13. R. Diamond and S. Carey, *J. Exp. Psychol. General, 115*, 107–117 (1986).
14. G. Rhodes, S. Brake, and A. Atkinson, *Cognition, 47*, 25–57 (1993).
15. R. K. Bothwell, J. C. Brigham, and R. S. Malpass, *Pers Social Psychol. Bull., 15*, 19–25 (1989).
16. F. Galton, *Inquiries into the Human Faculty and Development*, Macmillan, New York, 1883.
17. N. Geschwind, *Sci. Am., 241*, 180–199 (1979).
18. J. Konorski, *Integrative Activity of the Brain*, University of Chicago Press, Chicago, 1967.
19. H-L. Teuber, "Alteration of Perception and Memory in Man: Reflections on Methods," in *Analysis of Behavioural Change*, L. Weiskrantz, ed., Harper & Row, New York, 1968.
20. M. J. Tovée and E. M. Cohen-Tovée, *Cogn. Neuropsychol., 10*, 505–528 (1993).
21. J. A. Fodor, *The Modularity of Mind*. MIT Press, Cambridge, MA, 1983.

22. I. Biederman, *Psychol. Rev., 94*, 115–147 (1987).
23. C. B. Cave and S. M. Kosslyn, *Perception, 22*, 229–248 (1993).
24. D. D. Hoffman and W. A. Richards, "Parts of Recognition," in *Visual Cognition*, S. Pinker, ed., MIT Press, Cambridge, MA, 1984, pp. 65–96.
25. D. G. Lowe, *Int. J. Computer Vision, 1*, 57–72 (1987).
26. D. Marr, *Vision*, Freeman, San Francisco, 1982.
27. D. Marr and H. K. Nishihara, *Proc. Roy. Soc. London, B, 200*, 269–294 (1978).
28. S. Ullman, *Cognition, 32*, 192–254 (1989).
29. E. Rosch, C. B. Mervis, W. D. Gray, D. M. Johnson, and P. Boyes-Braem, *Cogn. Psychol., 8*, 382–439 (1976).
30. B. T. Tversky and K. Hemenway, *J. Exp. Psychol., General, 113*, 169–193 (1984).
31. M. C. Corballis, *The Lopsided Ape: The Evolution of the Generative Mind*, Oxford University Press, New York, 1991.
32. M. J. Farah, *Curr. Direct. Psychol. Sci., 1*, 164–169 (1992).
33. J. W. Tanaka and M. J. Farah, *Quart. J. Exp. Psychol., 46A*, 225–245 (1993).
34. G. Rhodes, S. Brennan, and S. Carey, *Cogn. Psychol., 19*, 473–497 (1987).
35. R. K. Yin, *J. Exp. Psychol., 81*, 141–145 (1969).
36. R. K. Yin, *Neuropsychologia, 8*, 395–402 (1970).
37. T. Valentine, *Br. J. Psychol., 79*, 471–491 (1988).
38. I. Rock, *Sci Am, 230*, 78–85 (1974).
39. J. C. Bartlett and J. Searcy, *Cogn. Psychol., 25*, 281–316 (1993).
40. M. J. Farah, *Cogn. Neuropsychol., 8*, 1–19 (1991).
41. P. J. Benson and D. I. Perrett, *Eur. J. Cogn. Psychol., 3*, 105–135 (1991).
42. R. Mauro and M. Kubovy, *Memory and Cogn., 20*, 433–440 (1992).
43. G. Rhodes, Superportraits: Caricatures and Recognition. Erlbaum, London, 1995. Forthcoming.
44. G. Rhodes and T. Tremewan, *Visual Cogn., 1*, 275–311 (1994).
45. G. Rhodes and I. G. McLean, *Perception, 19*, 773–794 (1990).
46. J. B. Davidoff, "The Specificity of Face Perception: Evidence from Psychological Investigations," in *The Neuropsychology of Facial Perception and Facial Expression*, R. Bruyer, ed., Erlbaum, Hillsdale, NJ, 1986, pp. 147–166.
47. H. D. Ellis and A. W. Young, "Are Faces Special?" in *Handbook of Research on Face Processing*, A. W. Young and H. D. Ellis, eds., North-Holland, Amsterdam, 1989, pp. 1–26.
48. D. C. Hay and A. W. Young, "The Human Face," in *Normality and Pathology in Cognitive Functions*, A. W. Ellis, ed., Academic Press, New York, 1982, pp. 173–202.
49. S. C. Levine, "The Question of Faces: Special Is in the Brain of the Beholder," in *Handbook of Research on Face Processing*, A. W. Young and H. D. Ellis, eds., North-Holland, Amsterdam, 1989, pp. 37–48.
50. J. Morton and M. Johnson, "Four Ways for Faces to Be Special," in *Handbook of Research on Face Processing*, A. W. Young and H. D. Ellis, eds., North-Holland, Amsterdam, 1989, pp. 49–56.
51. J. M. Charcot, *Prog. Med., 11*, 568–571 (1883).
52. H. Willbrand, *Di seelenblindheit als Herderscheinung und ihre Beziehung zur homonymen Hemianopsie, zur Alexie und Agraphie*, Bergmann, Wiesbaden, 1887.
53. J. Bodamer, *Archiv für Psychiatrie und Nervenkrankleiten, 179*, 6–53 (1947).
54. H. D. Ellis and M. Florence, *Cogn. Neuropsychol., 7*, 81–105 (1990).
55. M. J. Farah, *Visual Agnosia: Disorders of Object Recognition and What They Tell Us About Normal Vision*, MIT Press, Cambridge, MA, 1990.
56. R. A. McCarthy and E. K. Warrington, *Cognitive Neuropsychology: A Clinical Introduction*, Academic Press, San Diego, CA, 1990.
57. R. Bruyer, C. Laterre, X. Seron, P. Feyereisen, E. Strypstein, E. Pierrard, and D. Rectem, *Brain Cogn., 2*, 257–284 (1983).

58. E. C. Shuttleworth, V. Syring, and N. Allen, *Brain and Cogn., 1,*, 302–332 (1982).
59. J. Kurucz and G. Feldmar, *J. Am. Geriatr. Soc., 27*, 225–230 (1979).
60. N. L. Etcoff, *Neuropsychologia, 22*, 281–295 (1984).
61. J. Sergent and J-L. Signoret, *Philos. Trans. Roy. Soc. London, B, 335*, 2–30 (1992).
62. T. E. Feinberg, L. J. Gonzalez-Rothi, and K. M. Heilman, *Neurology, 36*, 864–867 (1986).
63. J. M. Ferro and M. E. Santos, *Cortex, 20*, 121–134 (1984).
64. H. Hécaen, M. C. Goldblum, M. C. Masure, and A. M. Ramier, *Neuropsychologia, 12*, 447–464 (1974).
65. R. A. McCarthy and E. K. Warrington, *J. Neurol. Neurosurg. Psychiatry, 49*, 1233–1240 (1986).
66. B. Bornstein, "Prosopagnosia," in *Problems of Dynamic Neurology*, L. Halpern, ed., Hassadah Medical Organisation, Jerusalem, 1963.
67. M. Cole and J. Perez-Cruet, *Neuropsychologia, 2,* 237–246 (1964).
68. E. De Renzi and H. Spinnler, *J. Nervous Mental Dis., 142*, 513–525 (1966).
69. J. Lhermitte, F. Chain, R. Escourolle, B. Ducarne, and B. Pillon, *Rev. Neurol., 126*, 329–346 (1972).
70. A. R. Damasio, H. Damasio, and G. W. Van Hoesen, *Neurology, 32*, 331–341 (1982).
71. M. G. Marciani, G. A. Carlesimo, M. C. E. Maschio, M. Sabbadini, N. Stefani, and C. Caltagirone, *Int. J. Neurosci., 60*, 27–32 (1991).
72. F. Newcombe, "The Processing of Visual Information in Prosopagnosia and Acquired Dyslexia: Functional Versus Physiological Interpretation," in *Research in Psychology and Medicine*, Vol. 1, D. J. Oborne, M. M. Gruneberg, and J. R. Eiser, eds., Academic Press, London, 1979, pp. 315–322.
73. C. A. Pallis, *J. Neurol. Neurosurg. Psychiatry, 18*, 218–224 (1955).
74. A. R. Damasio, D. Tranel, and H. Damasio, *Ann. Rev. Neurosci., 13*, 89–109 (1990), by Annual Reviews Inc.
75. H. Ellis, "Past and Recent Studies of Prosopagnosia," in *Developments in Clinical and Experimental Neuropsychology*, J. R. Crawford and D. M. Parker, eds., Plenum Press, New York, 1989, pp. 151–166.
76. E. De Renzi, "Current Issues in Prosopagnosia," in *Aspects of Face Processing*, H. D. Ellis, M. A. Jeeves, K. F. Newcombe, and A. Young, eds., Martinus Nijhoff, Dordrecht, 1986, pp. 243–252.
77. M. J. Farah, *The Neuropsychology of High Level Vision: Collected Tutorial Essays*, M. J. Farah and G. Ratcliff, eds., Erlbaum, Hillsdale, NJ, 1994, pp. 133–146.
78. J. E. McNeil and E. K. Warrington, *Quart. J. Exp. Psychol. 46A*, 1–10 (1993).
79. G. Assal, C. Favre, and J. P. Anderes, *Rev. Neurol., 140*, 580–584 (1984).
80. B. Bornstein, H. Stroka, and H. Munitz, *Cortex, 5*, 164–169 (1969).
81. C. G. Gross, D. B. Bender, and C. E. Rocha-Miranda, *Science, 166*, 1303–1306 (1969).
82. C. Bruce, R. Desimone, and C. G. Gross, *J. Neurophysiol., 46*, 369–384 (1981).
83. C. G. Gross, C. E. Rocha-Miranda, and D. B. Bender, *J. Neurophysiol., 35*, 99–111 (1972).
84. R. Desimone, T. D. Albright, C. G. Gross, and C. Bruce, *J. Neurosci., 4*, 2051–2062 (1984).
85. D. I. Perrett, E. T. Rolls, and W. Caan, *Exp. Brain Res., 47*, 329–342 (1982).
86. D. I. Perrett, A. J. Mistlin, A. J. Chitty, P. A. J. Smith, D. D. Potter, R. Broennimann, and M. H. Harries, *Bhvrl Brain Res., 29*, 245–258 (1988).
87. S. Yamane, S. Kaji, and K. Kawano, *Exp. Brain Res., 73*, 209–214 (1988).
88. C. Bruce, *Neuropsychologia, 20*, 515–521 (1982).
89. G. C. Baylis, E. T. Rolls, and C. M. Leonard, *Brain Res., 342*, 91–102 (1985).
90. R. Desimone, *J. Cogn. Neurosci., 3*, 1–8 (1991).
91. M. E. Hasselmo, E. T. Rolls, and G. C. Baylis, *Bhvrl Brain Res., 32*, 203–218 (1989).

92. M. H. Harries and D. I. Perrett, *J. Cogn. Neurosci., 3*, 9–24 (1991).
93. D. I. Perrett, P. A. J. Smith, D. D. Potter, A. J. Mistlin, A. S. Head, A. D. Milner, and M. A. Jeeves, *Proc. Roy. Soc. London, B, 223*, 293–317 (1985).
94. D. I. Perrett, M. O. Oram, M. H. Harries, R. Bevan, J. K. Hietanen, P. J. Benson, and S. Thomas, *Exp. Brain Res., 86*, 159–173 (1991).
95. D. I. Perrett, J. K. Hietanen, M. W. Oram, and P. J. Benson, *Philos. Trans. Roy. Soc. London, B, 335*, 23–30 (1992).
96. H. Lissauer, *Arch. Psychiatr. Nervenfrankh., 21*, 222–270 (1890).
97. R. M. Bauer, *Neuropsychologia, 22*, 457–469 (1984).
98. G. Rhodes, *Br. J. Psychol., 76*, 249–271 (1985).
99. J. Levy, C. Trevarthen, and R. Sperry, *Brain, 95*, 61–78 (1972).
100. J. L. Bradshaw, *Hemispheric Specialization and Psychological Function*, John Wiley & Sons, Chichester, 1989.
101. J. Sergent, S. Ohta, and B. MacDonald, *Brain, 115*, 15–36 (1992).
102. M. C. Corballis, *Am. Psychologist, 35*, 284–295 (1980).
103. O.-J. Grusser and T. Landis, *Visual Agnosias*, Macmillan, London, 1991.
104. T. Landis, M. Regard. A. Bliestle, and P. Kleihues, *Brain, 111*, 1287–1297 (1988).
105. J. V. Haxby, C. L. Grady, B. Horwitz, L. G. Ungerleider, M. Mishkin, R. E. Carson, P. Herscovitch, M. B. Schapiro, and S. Rapoport, *Proc. Natl. Acad. Sci. USA, 88*, 1621–1625 (1991).
106. T. Allison, H. Ginter, G. McCarthy, A. C. Nobre, A. Puce, M. Luby, and D. D. Spencer, *J. Neurophys., 71*, 821–825 (1994).
107. C. G. Gross, *Philos. Trans. Roy. Soc. London, B, 335*, 3–10 (1992).
108. E. T. Rolls, *Philos. Trans. Roy. Soc. London, B, 335*, 11–21 (1992).
109. L. Weiskrantz, "Visual Prototypes, Memory and the Inferotemporal Cortex," in *Vision, Memory and the Temporal Lobe*, E. Iwai and M. Mishkin, eds., Elsevier, New York, 1990.
110. C. A. Heywood and A. Cowey, *Philos. Trans. Roy. Soc. London, B, 335*, 31–38 (1992).
111. M. P. Young and S. Yamane, *Science, 256*, 1327–1331 (1992).
112. G. C. Baylis, E. T. Rolls, and C. M. Leonard, *J. Neurosci., 7*, 330–342 (1987).
113. N. L. Etcoff, "The Neuropsychology of Emotional Expression," in *Advances in Clinical Neuropsychology*, Vol. 3, G. Goldstein and R. E. Tarter, eds., Plenum Press, New York, 1985.
114. C. S. Sherrington, *Man on His Nature*, Penguin Books, Middlesex, U.K., 1955.
115. D. I. Perrett, A. J. Mistlin, and A. J. Chitty, *Trends Neurosci., 10*, 358–364 (1987).
116. G. Rhodes and T. Tremewan, *Cogn. Psychol., 25*, 147–187 (1993).
117. J. S. Bruner, *Psychol. Rev., 64*, 123–152 (1957).
118. K. S. Goodman, "Reading: A Psycholinguistic Guessing Game," in *Theoretical Models and Processes of Reading*, H. Sinder and R. B. Ruddell, eds., International Reading Association, Newark, DE, 1970.
119. R. L. Gregory, *The Intelligent Eye*. McGraw-Hill, New York, 1970.
120. A. M. Liberman, *J. Acoust. Soc. Am., 29*, 117–123 (157).
121. U. Neisser, *Cognition and Reality*, W. H. Freeman, San Francisco, 1976.
122. B. Kolb and I. Q. Whishaw, *Fundamentals of Human Neuropsychology*, W. H. Freeman, New York, 1990.

BIBLIOGRAPHY

Bruce, V., *Recognizing Faces*. Erlbaum, London, 1988.
Bruce, V., A. Cowey, A. W. Ellis and D. I. Perrett (eds.), *Processing the Facial Image*, Clarendon Press, Oxford, 1992.

Damasio, A. R., D. Tranel, and H. Damasio, *Annu. Rev. Neurosc., 13*; 89–109 (1990).

Diamond, R., and S. Carey, *J. Exp. Psychol. General, 115*; 107–117 (1986).

Farah, M. J., *Visual Agnosia: Disorders of Object Recognition and What They Tell Us About Normal Vision*, MIT Press, Cambridge, MA, 1990.

Farah, M. J., *Curr. Direct. Psychol. Sci., 1*; 164–169 (1992).

Fodor, J. A. *The Modularity of Mind,* MIT Press, Cambridge, MA, 1983.

Johnson, M. H. and J. Morton, *Biology and Cognitive Development: The Case of Face Recognition*, Blackwell, Oxford, 1991.

Rhodes, G., S. Brake, and A. Atkinson, *Cognition, 47*; 25–57 (1993).

Rhodes, G. and T. Tremewan, *Cogn. Psychol., 25*; 147–187 (1993).

Tovée, M. J. and E. M. Tovée, *Cogn. Neuropsycho., 10*; 505–528 (1993).

Young, A. W. and H. D. Ellis (eds.), *Handbook of Research on Face Processing*, North-Holland, Amsterdam, 1989.

GILLIAN RHODES

Expression (4) is called a *clause*, $p(\overline{X})$ is the head of that clause, whereas $q_1((\overline{X}))$, ..., $q_m(\overline{X})$ is the body of the clause. Such clause possesses a *logical interpretation*. It is a formula

$$\forall_{\overline{X}}(q_1((\overline{X})) \wedge \cdots \wedge q_m(\overline{X}) \supset p(\overline{X}))$$

ground (P), where P is a program, is the family of all ground substitutions of clauses from P.

With a program P we associate an operator T_P, mapping subsets of Herbrand base into subsets of Herbrand base, by the following:

$$T_P(I) = \{p : \exists_{C \in \text{ground } P} I \models \text{body}(C) \wedge p = \text{head}(C)\}$$

(Ref. 46). Operator T_P is monotone and compact. Hence, by the Knaster–Tarski Lemma, T_P possesses the least fixpoint. This fixpoint coincides with the least Herbrand model M_P of P. Moreover, if P_1 and P_2 are two programs and $P_1 \subseteq P_2$, then $M_{P_1} \subseteq M_{P_2}$.

When we introduce negation into the body of clauses of the program, we get *general logic programs*. They consist of clauses of the form

$$p(\overline{X}) \leftarrow q_1((\overline{X})), \ldots, q_m(\overline{X}), \neg r_1(\overline{X}), \ldots, \neg r_n(\overline{X}). \qquad [5]$$

The notion of the logical interpretation and the operator T_P generalize directly to general logic program in a natural fashion.

Although a general logic program always possesses a model (Herbrand base is a model of every program), the existence of the least Herbrand model is no longer guaranteed. There are, however, always minimal models of the general logic program. There may be several minimal models of a general programs. The question of how to assign the meaning of a general program is one of the most important issues in foundations of logic programming. We will look at several proposals for assigning such meaning.

Minimal Models

As noted above, minimal models of a program always exist. However, a minimal model may be fairly artificial and may not be connected with the process of computation. To see that, look at the program P_1 consisting of a single clause $p \leftarrow \neg q$. Intuitively, the "correct" model of P is $\{p\}$ (q cannot be computed, so p can), but P possesses two minimal models (the other is $\{q\}$). Moreover, adding new clauses to a program changes semantics drastically. A minimal model of a larger program does not need to be minimal as a model of a smaller program. For complexity results on minimal models, see Ref. 47.

Supported Models

One can assign to a general program its *completion* (48). Completion of the program is a first-order theory obtained from P by the following procedure. For each predicate p, a formula

$$\forall \overline{X} p((\overline{X})) \equiv (B_1 \vee \cdots \vee B_k)$$

is the *completion* of p. Here, formulas B_j, $1 \leq j \leq k$, are obtained by elimination of terms in the heads of clauses with head p. Completion of a program is the theory consisting of completions of predicates of the programs incremented by axioms about equality (so called the Clark Equational Theory) A supported structure for P is a model of completion of P. Such a structure is a model of P and so it is called a supported model of P. Apt and van Emden (49) proved that Herbrand models of completion of P are characterized as fixpoints of the operator T_p.

Perfect Model

Some programs allow for identification of a particular minimal model which has particularly nice properties. Call a program P *stratified* (50) if there is a function *rank* on the set of predicates of the program P such that whenever we have a clause of the form (5), then for all i, rank(q_i) $\leq$ rank(p) and for all j, rank(r_j) $<$ rank(p). The intuition is that the negative information necessary to compute the extension of the predicate p in the desired model of P must be computed *before* the stage in which p is computed. Checking if P is stratified can be done in time linear in $|P|$. The desired model is computed in stages. First, compute extensions of predicates of rank 0. This information is then used to compute extensions of predicates of rank 1 and so on. The resulting model is called the prefect model of P. Not every program is stratified, and so a perfect model is not always defined. If it exists, then it is unique and does not depend on a particular stratification used in its construction. Moreover, the perfect model of P is a model of completion of P as well. If P is a propositional program that is stratified, then its perfect model can be computed in time linear in $|P|$. In the predicate case, Apt and Blair (51) show that a program with n strata can compute a Σ_n^0 complete set. Conversely, the perfect model of a stratified program with n strata is Σ_n^0.

A "local" version of stratification is due to Przymusiński (52). Here we require that the rank is defined not on the set of all predicates of the language of the program but rather on the Herbrand base. The stratification conditions are similar but pertain to clauses in ground(P). Again, one can assign to a locally stratified program the perfect model. There is no difference between stratification and local stratification in the case of finite propositional programs. In the predicate case testing, if P is locally stratified, is Π_1^1 complete, (53). A perfect model of a locally stratified, recursive program is hyperarithmetical, and all hyperarithmetical sets are extensions of predicates in a perfect model of a suitably chosen locally stratified program.

Stable Models

Gelfond and Lifschitz (54) defined the notion of a stable model of a program. Let M be a subset of the Herbrand base of P. Reduce the program ground(P) as follows. Given a clause C

$$p \leftarrow q_1, \ldots q_m, \neg r_1, \ldots, \neg r_n$$

in ground(P), eliminate C altogether if for some j, $r_j \in M$. Otherwise, let C^M be

$$p \leftarrow q_1, \ldots q_m.$$

P^M consists of C^M for those C's that are not eliminated. Because P^M is a Horn program, it possesses a least model N_M. We call M a stable structure for P if $N_M =$

M. A stable structure for *P* (if exists) is a model of *P*. Moreover, it is a model of completion of *P* and a minimal model of *P*. If *P* is stratified or locally stratified, then *P* possesses a unique stable model. It is its perfect model. It turns out that stable models of general logic programs are closely connected with default logic (55,56). There exist programs without stable models. The existence problem for stable models of propositional general logic programs is NP-complete (57). For finite-predicate general logic programs, the existence of a stable model is a Σ_1^1-complete problem (58).

MODAL NONMONOTONIC LOGICS

The modal flavor of nonmonotonic reasoning has been noted at the very beginning of developments. In facts, Reiter's notation suggests that he considered the formulas in justification as modalized formulas, at least conceptually. McDermott and Doyle (26) suggested a construction in the language of modal logic which handles non-monotonicity well. The McDermott and Doyle construction is based on the analysis of the notion of introspection. Let $\mathcal{L}_L$ be a modal language with modal unary functor *L*. Given a theory *T*, we say that *T* is closed under *positive instrospection* if

$\varphi \in T$ implies $L\varphi \in T$.

Thus, closure under positive introspection is nothing more than closure under the necessitation rule of modal logic. Similarly, we say that *T* is closed under *negative introspection* if

$\varphi \notin T$ implies $\neg L\varphi \in T$

Negative introspection has a distinctly nonmonotonic flavor — if φ is not in *T*, then $\neg L\varphi$ is in *T*. Theories closed under propositional provability (in the language of modal logic) and both forms of introspection are called *stable* (59). They are precisely theories of Kripke models with universal accessibility relation.

McDermott and Doyle (26,27) considered the following operator:

$$\text{MDD}(T) = \text{Cn}_S(I \cup \{\neg L\varphi : \varphi \notin T\}).$$

There are two parameters in this operator: first, *I* — the set of initial beliefs (or initial knowledge) of a reasoning agent; second, a modal logic S. The fixpoints of that operator, that is, solutions of the equation

$$T = \text{Cn}_S(I \cup \{\neg L\varphi : \varphi \notin T\}),$$

are called S-expansions of *I*. The consequence operator Cn_S used here is stronger than in usual modal logics — necessitation is applicable to all formulas and not only to axioms of S. The strength of the McDermott and Doyle construction lies in the additional parameter S. Varying S can lead to very different solutions. McDermott noted that as long as S contains necessitation, every expansion is a stable theory. Moreover, an S-expansion is closed under an S5-consequence. McDermott (27) noted that for S = S5, S-expansions of *I* coincide with theories of S5-models of *I* with universal relations. This implies that the formulas true in all S5-expansions of *I* are precisely S5-consequences of *I*. This was considered counterintuitive at a time.

Moore (60) considered a different operator, explicitly taking into account both positive and negative introspection with respect to T,

$$M_0(T) = \text{Cn}(I \cup \{L\varphi : \varphi \in T\} \cup \{\neg L\varphi : \varphi \notin T\}),$$

and argued that this operator is more natural than the McDermott and Doyle operator. Fixpoints of the Moore operator, that is, solutions to the equation

$$T = \text{Cn}(I \cup \{L\varphi : \varphi \in T\} \cup \{\neg L\varphi : \varphi \notin T\}),$$

are called autoepistemic (or stable) expansions of I. It turned out, however, that as long as consistent theories are concerned, Moore construction is a special case of McDermott and Doyle construction, namely, $\mathbb{S} = KD45$ (61). Another special case is the so-called *reflexive autoepistemic logic* of Schwarz (62), where reflexive autoepistemic expansions are solutions of the equation

$$T = \text{Cn}(I \cup \{L\varphi \equiv \varphi : \varphi \in T\} \cup \{\neg L\varphi : \varphi \notin T\}).$$

This is again a special case of McDermott and Doyle construction, corresponding to modal logic $S4.4$ (see Ref. 16 for more information on modal logics). All the operators mentioned above are nonmonotonic. Logic based on fixpoints of the Moore operator is called autoepistemic logic. It is currently believed that this logic properly models beliefs of a fully introspective, reasoning agent.

The notion of $\mathbb{S}$-expansion behaves monotonically in $\mathbb{S}$; that is, given $I \subseteq \mathcal{L}_L$, $\mathbb{S}_1$, and $\mathbb{S}_2$, if $\mathbb{S}_1 \subseteq \mathbb{S}_2$, then every $\mathbb{S}_1$-expansion of I is also an $\mathbb{S}_2$-expansion of I.

It turns out that different modal logics may generate uniformly in I the same expansions. This happens, for instance, for modal logics 5 (subnormal modal logic without the scheme K), $K5$, $K45$, and $KD45$. Many other areas (called ranges) where expansions coincide are known presently. One such area is between $S4$ and $S4F$ for all *finite* theories I (63).

The degree of freedom (the choice of $\mathbb{S}$) present in modal nonmonotonic logics makes them a very powerful mechanism for representation of other forms of nonmonotonic reasoning. There are many representations of nonmonotonic reasonings in modal nonmonotonic logics with various degree of faithfulness. These include Konolige interpretation of default logic in autoepistemic logic (64), Truszczyński interpretation of default logic in nonmonotonic $S4F$ (65), and many others. Stable semantics of logic programs can be faithfully represented in both autoepistemic logic (66) and in reflexive autoepistemic logic (67). Similarly, supported semantics for logic programs can be faithfully represented in autoepistemic logic (68).

Lifschitz (69) introduced a general mechanism for uniform treatment of modal nonmonotonic logics in a single bimodal logic $MBNF$.

Computational mechanisms associated with modal nonmonotonic logics vary greatly in complexity. Because of existence of ranges, there is no simple correlation between the complexity of the underlying modal monotonic logic and the corresponding nonmonotonic modal logic. In the case of logic $S4$ modal nonmonotonic logic, is computationally simpler than modal monotonic $S4$, (70). The case of autoepistemic logic has been especially thoroughly investigated by Gottlob (39) and Niemelä (71). Similarly to default logic, the problems associated with autoepistemic expansions are on the second level of polynomial hierarchy. Specifically, the existence problem is Σ_2^P-complete, membership in some expansion is Σ_2^P-complete, and membership in all expansions is a Π_2^P-complete problem. Generally, the complexity problems for nonmonotonic logics are not completely solved yet.

CIRCUMSCRIPTION

Circumscription is a second-order technique for minimizing extensions of predicates. In its simplest and most natural form, the circumscription scheme says that a theory implicitly defines a predicate it circumscribes (72). Specifically, by circumscribing a predicate P in a theory T, we assume that all the information about the predicate is given by T. Thus, only those models where P is minimal need to be considered. Formally, let $\varphi = \varphi(P)$ be the conjuction of axioms of a finite theory T in the first-order language containing the predicate P. The result of circumscribing P is the second-order statement

$$\varphi(P) \wedge \neg \exists_Q (Q \subseteq P \wedge \varphi(Q)),$$

where Q is a new predicate (not in the language under consideration). We then say that $T_{\text{circ}} \models \psi$ if $\text{Circ}(T, P) \models \psi$. Clearly, circumscription is syntactically a second-order formula (it quantifies a predicate). In fact, for a theory T consisting of the axioms $\forall_{x,y} R(x, y) \supset P(x, y)$ and $\forall_{x,y,z} R(x, y) \wedge P(y, z) \supset P(x, z)$, the result of circumscribing P by T defines the transitive closure of R, which is not first-order definable, in general. There are cases when circumscription reduces to a first-order sentence. For instance, theory T consisting of a single axiom $\forall_x Q(x) \wedge R(x) \supset P(x)$ after circumscribing P gives $\forall_x (Q(x) \wedge R(x)) \equiv P(x)$. Lifschitz, in a series of articles (73–76) analyzed the most important properties of circumscription.

When the theory T is a propositional theory, circumscribing theory T reduces to minimizing models of T (in general, we can minimize some or all proposition variables in T). Minimization of all propositional variables at once is known as extended generalized Closed World Assumption (GCWA) and has been studied by Yahia and Henschen (77); see also Ref. 78. Clearly, the entailment problem for propositional circumscription is decidable. An algorithm has been proposed by Przymusinski (79). In the predicate case, the circumscription is very complex. Schlipf (80) shows that all Δ_2^1 ordinals are definable with circumscription, so this mode of reasoning goes beyond anything currently accepted as computable. The complexity of propositional circumscription has been studied by Eiter and Gottlob (81) who found that the problems associated with circumscription are, generally, located on the second level of polynomial hierarchy. Circumscription is a very powerful technique and it is known (82) that at a least fragment of default logic can be embedded into circumscription.

Suchenek (83) gave an analysis of various orderings of models and corresponding circumscriptions.

MANY-VALUED INTERPRETATIONS

Many-valued logics has been studied in the context of nonmonotonic reasoning, primarily as a technique to obtain semantics for some logic programs. A four-valued interpretation is a pair $\langle A, B \rangle$, where A and B are two sets of atoms (or elements of

Herbrand base of a program). When $A \cap B = \emptyset$, we talk about a three-valued interpretation. Three- and four-valued logics provide semantics for logic programs. Fitting (84) noted that the operator T_p applied to three-valued interpretations is monotone and so has the least fixpoint. He proposed that fixpoint as a semantics for logic programs. A stronger semantics, the so-called well-founded semantics, has been introduced by Van Gelder, Ross, and Schlipf (85). It turns out that using a three-valued version of stable semantics, one can identify well-founded semantics with the least stable three-valued model of the program (86). Using the theory of bilattices, Ginsberg (87) and Fitting (88) characterized three-valued stable models.

Well-founded semantics generalizes perfect semantics for stratified logic programs, and in the case where it produces a two-valued interpretation, the resulting interpretation determines a unique stable model of the program. Van Gelder (89) gave a polynomial computational procedure for computing well-founded semantics of propositional programs. Schlipf (90) proved that in the predicate case well-founded semantics can define a complete Π_1^1-set.

TRUTH MAINTENANCE AND NONMONOTONIC RULE SYSTEMS

Doyle (91) considered truth maintenance systems (TMS). These are systems of rules consisting of objects of the form $\langle A, B \rangle \rightarrow c$, where A and B are finite sets of atoms and c is an atom. The meaning of such rule is "when all the atoms in A are IN and all the atoms in B are OUT, then infer c." Doyle did not give a precise semantics for such systems. De Kleer (92,93) gave a semantics, very close to supported semantics, of logic programs for systems with rules having $B = \emptyset$. Elkan (94) found a semantics for TMS, essentially the stable semantics of logic programs.

Marek, Nerode, and Remmel (95,96) considered rules of the form

$$\frac{a_1, \ldots, a_m : b_1, \ldots, b_n}{c} \qquad\qquad [6]$$

with $a_1, \ldots, a_m, b_1, \ldots, b_n$, and c from an arbitrary set U (not necessarily of atoms) and considered *nonmonotonic rule systems*, that is, pairs $\langle U, N \rangle$, where U is a set and N consists of rules of form (6). It turns out that by manipulating the parameter U, one can provide a proper description of all the first-order forms of nonmonotonic reasoning mentioned above, namely, default logic stable and supported semantics of logic programs, McDermott and Doyle systems, and truth maintenance systems. Moreover, stripping the systems of specific and unimportant features allows for proving various properties of such systems in a uniform and efficient way.

IMPLEMENTATIONS

As mentioned earlier, there are various algorithms for computations of structures associated with nonmonotonic reasoning. These algorithms have been or presently are being implemented by various groups of researchers. Historically, first implementation of (a fragment of) default logic has been reported by Poole (97). Dixon and de Kleer (98) reported massively parallel implementation of TMS. Ginsberg

(99) reported implementation of circumscription. Warren et al. (100) reported an implementation of well-founded semantics. Bell et al. (101) implemented circumscription and stable semantics for propositional theories using an interpretation of these nonmonotonic systems in linear programming. Niemelä (102) reported a fast implementation of full autoepistemic logic. Marek and Truszczyński (103) reported implementation of a default reasoning system.

CONCLUSIONS AND PERSPECTIVES

Nonmonotonic reasoning is an active area of research in artificial intelligence. This research is actively pursued in many places around the world. Many areas not discussed in our short review are currently under development. These include abduction (104), nonmonotonic probabilistic reasoning (105), extended logic programming (106), belief revision (107), and several other areas. Object-oriented programming, especially its use of classes, inheritance, and overriding, use techniques of inheritance hierarchies with exceptions (108) and will, doubtlessly, drive developments in nonmonotonic reasoning. We can expect many discoveries; a definitive description of nonmonotonic reasoning has not been done yet.

REFERENCES

1. Aristotle, *Selections*, Oxford University Press, Oxford, 1942.
2. A. De Morgan, *Formal Logic, or, the Calculus of Inference, Necessary and Probable*, Taylor and Walton, London, 1847.
3. G. Boole, *An Investigation of Laws of Thought, on Which Are Founded Mathematical Theories of Logic and Probability*, Macmillan, London, 1854.
4. C. S. Peirce, *Collected Papers of Charles Sanders Peirce*, The Belknap Press of Harvard University Press, Cambridge, MA, 1933, Vol. 3.
5. G. Frege, *Die Grundlagen der Arithmetic*, M. & H. Marcus, Breslau, 1884.
6. E. Schröder, *Vorlesungen über die Algebra der Logik*. B. G. Teubner, Leipzig, 1890–1905, 3 volumes.
7. A. N. Whitehead and B. Russel, *Principia Mathematica*, Cambridge University Press, Cambridge, 1913.
8. D. Hilbert and W. Ackermann, *Principles of Mathematical Logic*, Chelsea, New York, 1950.
9. K. Gödel, "Die Vollständigkeit der Axiome des logische Funktionenkalküls," Monatsch. *Math. Phys., 37*, 349–360 (1930).
10. A. Tarski, *Logic, Semantics, Metamathematics*, Oxford University Press, Oxford, 1956.
11. A. Church, "A note on Entscheidungsproblem," *J. Symbol. Logic, 1*, 40–41 (1938).
12. K. Gödel, "Über formal unentscheidbare Sätze der Principia Mathematica und verwandter Systeme I," *Monatsch. Math. Phys., 38*, 173–198 (1930).
13. J. Herbrand, *Logical Writings*, Reidel, Hingham, MA, 1971.
14. S. C. Kleene, *Introduction to Metamathematics*, D. Van Nostrand, New York, 1952.
15. A. M. Turing, "On Computable Numbers with an Application to the Entscheidungsproblem," *Proc. London Math. Soc., 2*, 230–265 (1936).
16. B. F. Chellas, *Modal Logic, an Introduction*, Cambridge University Press, Cambridge, 1980.

17. J. van Benthem, *Modal Logic and Classical Logic*, Bibliopolis, Naples, 1983.
18. A. Colmerauer, H. Kanoui, P. Roussel, and R. Pasero, "Un systeme de communication homme-machine en francais," Technical Report, Groupe de Recherche en Intelligence Artificielle, Université Aix-Marseille, 1973.
19. T. Coquand and G. Huet, *Constructions: A Higher-Order Proof System for Mechanizing Mathematics*, Lecture Notes in Computer Science 242, Springer-Verlag, Berlin, 1985.
20. J.-Y. Girard, *Proof and Types*, Cambridge University Press, Cambridge, 1989.
21. R. L. Constable, S. F. Allen, H. M. Bromley, W. R. Cleaveland, J. F. Cremer, R. W. Harper, D. J. Howe, T. B. Knoblock, N. P. Mendler, P. Panangaden, J. T. Sasaki, and S. F. Smith, *Implementing Mathematics with the Nuprl Development System*, Prentice-Hall, Englewood Cliffs, NJ, 1986.
22. P. Martin-Löf, *Intuitionistic Type Theories*, Bibliopolis, Naples, 1984.
23. J. McCarthy, *Formalization of Common Sense, Papers by John McCarthy*, V. Lifschitz, (ed.), Ablex, Norwood, NJ, 1990.
24. R. Reiter, "On Closed World Data Bases," in *Logic and Data Bases*, H. Gallaire and J. Minker (eds.), Plenum Press, New York, 1978, pp. 55–76.
25. R. Reiter, "A Logic for Default Reasoning," *Artificial Intell., 13*, 81–132 (1980).
26. D. McDermott and J. Doyle, "Nonmonotonic Logic I," *Artificial Intell., 13*, 41–72 (1980).
27. D. McDermott, "Nonmonotonic Logic II: Nonmonotonic Modal Theories," *J. ACM, 29*, 33–57 (1982).
28. H. Rasiowa and R. Sikorski, *Mathematics of Metamathematics*, Polish Scientific Publishers, Warsaw, 1970.
29. J. A. Robinson, "Machine-Oriented Logic Based on Resolution Principle," *J. ACM, 12*, 23–41 (1965).
30. R. M. Smullyan, *First-Order Logic*, Springer-Verlag, Berlin, 1968.
31. A. Nerode and R. Shore, *Logic and Logic Programming*, Springer-Verlag, Berlin, 1993.
32. P. Besnard, *An Introduction to Default Logic*, Springer-Verlag, Berlin, 1989.
33. D. W. Etherington, *Reasoning with Incomplete Information*, Pitman, London, 1988.
34. G. Brewka, "Cumulative Default Logic: In Defense of Nonmonotonic Inference Rules," *Artificial Intell., 50*, 183–205 (1991).
35. W. Marek and M. Truszczyński, *Nonmonotonic Logics; Context-Dependent Reasoning*, Springer-Verlag, Berlin, 1993.
36. W. Łukaszewicz, *Non-Monotonic Reasoning: Formalization of Commonsense Reasoning*, Ellis Horwood, London, 1990.
37. K. Apt, "Logic Programming," in *Handbook of Theoretical Computer Science*, J. van Leeuven (ed.), MIT Press, Cambridge, MA, 1990, pp. 493–574.
38. F. Yang, H. Blair, and A. Brown, "Programming in Default Logic," Technical Report, University of Syracuse (1992).
39. G. Gottlob, "Complexity Results for Nonmonotonic Logics," *J. Logic Computat., 2*, 397–425 (1992).
40. V. Lifschitz, "On Open Defaults," in *Proceedings of the Symposium on Computational Logic*, J. Lloyd (ed.), Springer-Verlag, Berlin, 1990, pp. 80–95.
41. R. Guerreiro and M. Casanova, "An Alternative Semantics for Default Logic," *The Third International Workshop on Nonmonotonic Reasoning*, 1990.
42. W. Łukaszewicz, "Considerations on Default Logic," in *Proceedings of the International Workshop on Nonmonotonic Reasoning*, R. Reiter (ed.), 1984, pp. 165–193.
43. C. Baral and V. S. Subrahmanian, "Dualities Between Alternative Semantics for Logic Programming and Nonmonotonic Reasoning," in *Logic Programming and Nonmonotonic Reasoning*, A. Nerode, W. Marek, and V. S. Subrahmanian (eds.), MIT Press, Cambridge, MA, 1991, pp. 69–86.

44. W. Marek and M. Truszczyński, "Relating Autoepistemic and Default Logics," in *Proceedings of the 1st International Conference on Principles of Knowledge Representation and Reasoning, KR '89*, Morgan Kaufmann, San Mateo, CA, 1989, pp. 276–288.

45. G. Brewka, *Nonmonotonic Reasoning: Logical Foundations of Commonsense*, Cambridge University Press, Cambridge, 1991.

46. M. H. van Emden and R. A. Kowalski, "The Semantics of Predicate Logic as a Programming Language," *J. ACM, 23*(4), 733–742 (1976).

47. T. Eiter and G. Gottlob, "On the Complexity of Propositional Knowledge Base Revision, Updates and Counterfactuals," in *ACM Symposium on Principles of Database Systems*, 1992.

48. K. L. Clark, "Negation as Failure," in *Logic and Data Bases*, H. Gallaire and J. Minker (eds.), Plenum Press, New York, 1978, pp. 293–322.

49. K. R. Apt and M. H. van Emden, "Contributions to the Theory of Logic Programming." *J. ACM, 29*, 841–862 (1982).

50. K. Apt, H. A. Blair, and A. Walker, "Towards a Theory of Declarative Knowledge," in *Foundations of Deductive Databases and Logic Programming*, J. Minker (ed.), Morgan Kaufmann, Los Altos, CA, 1988, pp. 89–142.

51. K. Apt and H. A. Blair, "Arithmetical Classification of Perfect Models of Stratified Programs," *Fund. Inform., 12*, 1–17 (1990).

52. T. Przymusiński, "On the Declarative Semantics of Deductive Databases and Logic Programs," in *Foundations of Deductive Databases and Logic Programming*, Morgan Kaufmann, Los Altos, CA, 1988, pp. 193–216.

53. P. Cholak and H. A. Blair, "The Complexity of Local Stratification," *Fund. Inform., 21*, 333–344 (1994).

54. M. Gelfond and V. Lifschitz, "The Stable Semantics for Logic Programs," in *Proceedings of the 5th International Symposium on Logic Programming*, R. Kowalski and K. Bowen (eds.), MIT Press, Cambridge, MA, 1988, pp. 1070–1080.

55. N. Bidoit and C. Froidevaux, "Negation by Default and Unstratifiable Logic Programs," *Theoret. Computer Sci., 78*, 85–112 (1991).

56. W. Marek and M. Truszczyński, "Stable Semantics for Logic Programs and Default Theories," in *Proceedings of the North American Conference on Logic Programming*, E. Lusk and R. Overbeek (eds.), MIT Press, Cambridge, MA, 1989, pp. 243–256.

57. W. Marek and M. Truszczyński, "Autoepistemic Logic," *J. ACM, 38*, 588–619 (1991).

58. W. Marek, A. Nerode, and J. B. Remmel, "The Stable Models of Predicate Logic Programs," in *Proceedings of the International Joint Conference and Symposium on Logic Programming*, MIT Press, Cambridge, MA, 1992.

59. R. C. Stalnaker, "A Note on Nonmonotonic Modal Logic," unpublished manuscript, 1980.

60. R. C. Moore, "Semantical Considerations on Non-monotonic Logic," *Artificial Intell., 25*, 75–94 (1985).

61. G. F. Shvarts, "Stable Expansions of Autoepistemic Theories," in *Proceedings of the All-Union Conference on Artificial Intelligence*, 1988, pp. 483–487. [In Russian.]

62. G. F. Schwarz, "Autoepistemic Logic of Knowledge," in *Logic Programming and Non-monotonic Reasoning*, A. Nerode, W. Marek, and V. S. Subrahmanian (eds.), MIT Press, Cambridge, MA, 1991, pp. 260–274.

63. W. Marek, G. F. Shvarts, and M. Truszczyński, "Modal Nonmonotonic Logics: Ranges, Characterization, Computation," *J. ACM, 40*, 963–990 (1993).

64. K. Konolige, "On the Relation Between Default and Autoepistemic Logic," *Artificial Intell., 35*, 343–382 (1988).

65. M. Truszczyński, "Modal Interpretations of Default Logic," in *Proceedings of IJCAI-91*, Morgan Kaufmann, San Mateo, CA, 1991, pp. 393–398.

66. M. Gelfond, "On Stratified Autoepistemic Theories," in *Proceedings of AAAI-87*, Morgan Kaufmann, Los Altos, CA, 1987, pp. 207–211.

67. W. Marek and M. Truszczyński, "Reflexive Autoepistemic Logic and Logic Programming," in *Logic Programming and Non-monotonic Reasoning*, A. Nerode and L. Pereira (eds.), MIT Press, Cambridge, MA, 1993.

68. W. Marek and V. S. Subrahmanian, "The Relationship Between Stable, Supported, Default and Autoepistemic Semantics for General Logic Programs," *Theoret. Computer Sci., 103*, 365–386 (1992).

69. V. Lifschitz, "Minimal Belief and Negation as Failure," *Artificial Intell.* (1995).

70. G. F. Schwarz and M. Truszczyński, "Nonmonotonic Reasoning Is Sometimes Easier," Technical Report 213-92, Department of Computer Science, University of Kentucky (1992).

71. I. Niemelä, "On the Decidability and Complexity of Autoepistemic Reasoning," *Fund. Inform., 17*, 117–155 (1992).

72. J. McCarthy, "Circumscription — A Form of Non-monotonic Reasoning," *Artificial Intell., 13*, 27–39 (1980).

73. V. Lifschitz, "Computing Circumscription," in *Proceedings of IJCAI-85*, Morgan Kaufmann, Los Altos, CA, 1985, pp. 121–127.

74. V. Lifschitz, "Pointwise Circumscription," in *Readings in Nonmonotonic Reasoning*, M. Ginsberg (ed.), Morgan Kaufmann, Los Altos, CA, 1987, pp. 179–193.

75. V. Lifschitz, "Circumscriptive Theories: A Logic-Based Framework for Knowledge Representation," *J. Phil. Logic, 17*, 391–441 (1988).

76. V. Lifschitz, "Between Circumscription and Autoepistemic Logic," in *Proceedings of the 1st International Conference on Principles of Knowledge Representation and Reasoning*, Morgan Kaufmann, San Mateo, CA, 1989, pp. 235–244.

77. A. Yahia and L. J. Henschen, "Deduction in Non-Horn Databases," *J. Autom. Reason.*, 141–160 (1985).

78. J. Minker, *On Indefinite Databases and the Closed World Assumption*, Springer Lecture Notes in Computer Science 138, Springer-Verlag, Berlin, 1982, pp. 292–309.

79. T. C. Przymusinski, "An Algorithm to Compute Circumscription," *Artificial Intell., 38*, 49–73 (1989).

80. J. Schlipf, "Decidability and Definability with Circumscription," *Ann. Pure Appl. Logic, 35*, 173–191 (1987).

81. T. Eiter and G. Gottlob, "Complexity of Reasoning with Parsimonius and Moderately Grounded Expansions," *Fund. Inform.* (1992).

82. T. Imielinski, "Results on Translating Defaults to Circumscription," *Artificial Intell., 32*, 131–146 (1987).

83. M. Suchenek, "Preservation Properties in Deductive Data Bases," *Methods Logic Computer Sci.* (1994).

84. M. C. Fitting, "Kripke–Kleene Semantics for Logic Programs," *J. Logic Program., 2*, 295–312 (1985).

85. A. Van Gelder, K. A. Ross, and J. S. Schlipf, "Unfounded Sets and Well-Founded Semantics for General Logic Programs," in *ACM Symposium on Principles of Database Systems*, 1988, pp. 221–230.

86. T. Przymusiński, "Three-valued Nonmonotonic Formalisms and Logic Programming," in *Proceedings of the 1st International Conference on Principles of Knowledge Representation and Reasoning, KR '89*, Morgan Kaufmann, San Mateo, CA, 1989, pp. 341–348.

87. M. L. Ginsberg (ed.), *Readings in Nonmonotonic Reasoning*, Morgan Kaufmann, San Mateo, CA, 1987.

88. M. C. Fitting, "Well-Founded Semantics, Generalized," in *Proceedings of the International Symposium on Logic Programming*, MIT Press, Cambridge, MA, 1991, pp. 71–84.

89. A. Van Gelder, "The Alternating Fixpoints of Logic Programs with Negation," in *ACM Symposium on Principles of Database Systems*, 1989, pp. 1–10.

90. J. Schlipf, "The Expressive Powers of the Logic Programming Semantics," *J. Comp. Sys. Sci.* (1995). [A preliminary version appeared in *Ninth ACM Symposium on Principles of Database Systems*, 1990.]

91. J. Doyle, "A Truth Maintenance System," *Artificial Intell., 12*, 231–272 (1979).

92. J. de Kleer, "An Assumption-Based TMS," *Artificial Intell., 28*, 127–162 (1986).

93. J. de Kleer, "Extending the ATMS," *Artificial Intell., 28*, 163–196 (1986).

94. C. Elkan, "A Rational Reconstruction of Nonmonotonic Truth Maintenance Systems," *Artificial Intell., 43*, 219–234 (1990).

95. W. Marek, A. Nerode, and J. B. Remmel, "Nonmonotonic Rule Systems I," *Ann. Math. Artificial Intell., 1*, 241–273 (1990).

96. W. Marek, A. Nerode, and J. B. Remmel, "Nonmonotonic Rule Systems II," *Ann. Math. Artificial Intell., 5*, 229–263 (1992).

97. D. Poole, "A Logical Framework for Default Reasoning," *Artificial Intell., 36*, 27–47 (1988).

98. M. Dixon and J. de Kleer, "Massively Parallel Assumption-Based Truth Maintenance," in *Non-monotonic Reasoning*, M. Reinfrank, J. de Kleer, M. L. Ginsberg, and E. Sandewall (eds.), Springer-Verlag, Berlin, 1989, pp. 131–142.

99. M. L. Ginsberg, "A Circumscriptive Theorem Prover," in *Non-monotonic Reasoning*, M. Reinfrank, J. de Kleer, M. L. Ginsberg, and E. Sandewall (eds.), Springer-Verlag, Berlin, 1989, pp. 100–114.

100. D. S. Warren, W. Chen, and T. Swift, "Efficient Computation of Queries Under the Well-Founded Semantics," Technical Report 93-CSE-33, Southern Methodist University (1993).

101. C. Bell, A. Nerode, R. Ng, W. Pugh, and V. S. Subrahmanian, "Implementing Stable Semantics by Linear Programming," in *Logic Programming and Non-monotonic Reasoning*, A. Nerode and L. Pereira (eds.), MIT Press, Cambridge, MA, 1993.

102. I. Niemelä, "Autoepistemic Logic as a Unified Basis for Nonmonotonic Reasoning," Technical Report 24, Helsinki University of Technology (1993).

103. W. Marek and M. Truszczyński, "Deres – Default Reasoning System," unpublished manuscript, 1995.

104. A. C. Kakas, R. A. Kowalski, and F. Toni, "Abductive Logic Programming," *J. Logic and Comp., 6*, 719–770 (1993).

105. J. Pearl, *"Probabilistic reasoning in Intelligent Systems: Networks of Plausible Inference*, Morgan Kaufmann, San Mateo, CA, 1988.

106. M. Gelfond and V. Lifschitz, "Logic Programs with Classical Negation," in *Proceedings of the 7th International Conference on Logic Programming*, D. Warren and P. Szeredi (eds.), MIT Press, Cambridge, MA, 1990, pp. 579–597.

107. C. E. Alchourrón, P. Gärdenfors, and D. Makinson, "On the Logic of Theory Change: Partial Meet Contraction and Revision Functions," *J. Symbol. Logic, 50*, 510–530 (1985).

108. D. Touretzky, *The Mathematics of Inheritance Systems*. Pitman, London, 1986.

VICTOR W. MAREK

ANIL NERODE

OPEN SYSTEMS SECURITY STANDARDS

WHY SECURITY STANDARDS?

The still growing spread of computer systems combined with the introduction of telecommunication systems providing computer-based services literally allows for worldwide access to computer resources. Distributed computing is based on the use of computers linked together in local area or wide area networks. Security measures are introduced not only to protect users of such distributed systems from each other but also to protect the systems from user or outsider attacks.

By connecting several computer systems (nodes) to work together as a distributed system or connecting them in a network, the level of complexity and the number of possible threats are increased considerably. Not only has the security of one single node to be assured but all the components in the system (software and hardware) must work securely and must support host security. As not all nodes can be trusted or are working on the same level of trust, data transfers between differently trusted nodes must be strictly controlled. An excellent overview of network attacks and associated security mechanisms is given in Ref. 1.

Typically, the connected systems are heterogeneous in nature and installed in varying environments (e.g., the computers attached to the Internet are operated by commercial, government, or educational institutions). Openness implies properly defined interfaces, services and protocols, together with the availability of these specifications. Standardization in this context is essential because the elements of an open system (e.g., hardware components, operating systems, databases, communication links) must be able to offer security in concert with other elements. In addition, standardization can help to provide a basic level of security to all attached users. Toward secure open systems, standardization work needs to address the following aspects:

- Operational aspects: How can the security features of different manufacturers' systems or systems in different installations be compared:
- Functional aspects: What security functions need to be provided for implementing a required level of security?
- Interoperability aspects: How can different systems securely interoperate in a heterogeneous computer network?
- Portability aspects: How can software be ported to different systems without compromising the inherent security properties?

Outline

The following section introduces standardization bodies and their work areas as well as other groups that promote the standardization process, for example, by setting de facto standards. For a comprehensive overview of international standardization bodies and their work items, see Ref. 2. The section Generic Cryptographic Techniques gives an overview of the standardization of cryptographic mechanisms and techniques. The section Security Evaluation Criteria shows the development of computer system security evaluation criteria. Basic security mechanisms in operating systems are discussed in the section Security Mechanisms in Operating Systems. The following four sections deal with security standards for distributed open systems, starting with Internet layer enhancements followed by a discussion of OSI security architectures, frameworks and models, lower layer security protocols, and the application layer security services. The final section provides an outlook into further work on security standardization.

STANDARDIZATION BODIES

This section introduces the principal standardization groups driving the development of de facto or formal standards in open systems security. The range of activities covers the development of base standards, functional profiles, security evaluation criteria, and user and management guidelines. The standardization bodies typically are devoted to specific types of standardization efforts and to specific areas in the field (e.g., security architectures, IT security techniques, distributed applications security, or network security).

National standardization bodies participate in the development of international or regional (e.g., European) standards through technical committees established by the respective organization to deal with particular fields of technical activity. Other organizations, governmental and nongovernmental, also take part in the work.

International Standardization Groups

At the international level, security in open systems is primarily addressed by the International Organization for Standardization (ISO), the International Electrotechnical Commission (IEC), and the International Telecommunications Union (ITU).

In the field of information technology, ISO and IEC have established a joint technical committee, ISO/IEC JTC1. The activities of ISO/IEC JTC1 are harmonized with the Recommendations of ITU. Within JTC1, a Committee Draft (CD) adopted by a subcommittee is circulated to national bodies for approval before its acceptance as Draft International Standard (DIS). A DIS adopted by the joint technical committee is circulated to national bodies for approval before its acceptance as an International Standard. A DIS is approved in accordance with procedures requiring at least 75% approval by the national bodies voting. The following subcommittees (SCs) of ISO/IEC JTC1 are involved in the development of security standards:

SC6 (OSI Lower Layers): OSI protocol extensions at layers 3 and 4; lower layer security model

SC18 (Text and Office Systems): ODA security; secure message handling

SC21 (OSI Architecture, Management and Upper Layers): OSI security archi-

tecture; open system security frameworks; upper layer security model; FTAM and TP security; ODP security; management and directories
  SC22 (Languages): POSIX security
  SC27 (IT Security Techniques): Identification of generic requirements for IT security services; security guidelines; cryptographic and noncryptographic techniques and mechanisms; security evaluation criteria

The International Telecommunications Union — Telecommunications Sector (ITU-TS) was previously known as CCITT (Comité Consultatif International Télégraphique et Téléphonique). It has a steering group (SGVII) concerned in particular with the security of messaging, directory, and electronic data interchange (EDI) systems.

Regional and National Standardization Groups

At the European level, the standardization bodies which correspond to ISO, IEC, and ITU are the Comité Européen de Normalisation (CEN), the Comité Européen de Normalisation Electrotechnique (CENELEC), and the European Telecommunications Standards Institute (ETSI). ETSI committees active in the development of security standards are the following:

  STAG (Security Techniques Advisory Group): Security coordination and strategy.
  SAGE (Security Algorithms Group of Experts): Cryptographic algorithms; security protocols. SAGE is a closed group; its output is confidential.
  TC/TE (Terminal Equipment): X.400 MHS security; telephony terminal security; security aspects of directory systems; security aspects of intelligent card systems; teleconferencing security.
  TC/GSM (Global System for Mobile Communications): Mobile telephone system security (GSM, UMTS).
  TC/NA (Network Aspects): Universal personal telecommunications (UPT) security.
  TC/RES (Radio Equipment and Systems): Digital radio systems security (e.g., DECT — Digital European Cordless Telephone).

The leading standardization body for local area networks (LANs) is the North American Institute of Electrical and Electronic Engineers (IEEE). Besides LAN security, IEEE working groups are concerned with POSIX security.

National standards with major impact on international standardization are developed at the U.S. National Institute of Standards and Technology (NIST), for example, security guidelines, generic security mechanisms, and the federal criteria. Like its predecessor, National Bureau of Standards (NBS), NIST publishes Federal Information Processing Standards (FIPS).

Other Groups

The following groups are not standardization bodies themselves but promote the standardization process in different ways complementary to formal standards developments. Among those are the OSI Implementors Workshop (OIW) and the Standards Promotion and Application Group (SPAG), a consortium of European suppliers developing functional standards.

The European Workshop for Open Systems (EWOS) was established by European IT supplier and user organizations with the support of CEN, CENELEC, and ETSI. The main objective of EWOS is to provide an open forum to develop worldwide harmonized profiles and conformance tests for open systems. The following EWOS expert groups (EGs) are concerned with security aspects: EG SEC (Security), EG MHS (Message Handling Systems), EG DIR (Directory Systems), EG ODA (Office Document Architecture), and EG LL (OSI Lower Layer Profiles).

The European Computer Manufacturers Association (ECMA) also has several committees concerned with open systems security:

TC29: ODA security
TC32: OSI lower layer security; ISDN security; open systems security framework; security protocols, data elements and services; security management
TC36: Security evaluation criteria

Various national security evaluation criteria have been developed by governmental groups, for example:

DoD (U.S. Department of Defense): Trusted computer system evaluation criteria (Orange Book); trusted network interpretation (Red Book); trusted database interpretation
GISA (German Information Security Agency): German IT security criteria (Green Book); IT security evaluation manual

In a combined evaluation project between the U.S. Defense Intelligence Agency (DIA), the NCSC, and a group of computer manufacturers, the secure interworking of compartmented mode workstations and secure server systems is analyzed. The system requirements are laid out in a DIA document (3).

The DoD-initiated project SDNS (Secure Data Network Systems) has developed a network security architecture, security protocols for OSI layers 3 and 4, and de facto standards for secure messaging and key management.

The Internet Engineering Task Force (IETF) primarily sets the standards for the Internet network. However, recent security-related standards developed by IETF for the Internet are being more widely adopted (e.g., privacy enhanced mail, GSS-API, authentication techniques).

Finally, there are several vendor and/or customer associations concerned with open systems security, for example, the Open Software Foundation (OSF), the OSI Network Management Forum (OSI NMF), and X/OPEN.

GENERIC CRYPTOGRAPHIC TECHNIQUES

Cryptographic techniques are widely accepted as a basic means for enforcing security policies because security measures utilizing cryptographic mechanisms can provide efficient and flexible logical protection of information. In the following subsections, the principal classes of cryptographic security mechanisms and their status with respect to standardization are presented. Standardization of generic cryptographic techniques is primarily addressed by ISO/IEC JTC1/SC27.

Encipherment

An encipherment algorithm is an invertible function parametrized by a key that maps plaintext into ciphertext and, thus, provides concealment of information. A distinction is made between secret key ciphers (e.g., the Data Encryption Standard) and public key ciphers (e.g., the Rivest–Shamir–Adleman algorithm, RSA). Given an encipherment algorithm, there are techniques to construct other security mechanisms, such as keyed hash-functions or authentication protocols. The standardization of cryptographic algorithms that are intended to provide confidentiality is excluded from the scope of ISO/IEC JTC1/SC27. Nevertheless, there are several standards in the context of encipherment algorithms:

FIPS Publication 46 (1977): Data Encryption Standard. The Data Encryption Standard (DES), originally published by the NBS, is still the most widely used symmetric encipherment technique.

ISO/IEC 8372 (1987): Modes of operation for a 64-bit block cipher algorithm. The four different modes of operation specified for the DES by the NBS in FIPS Publication 81 (1980) have been taken over by ISO for the slightly more general case of 64-bit block ciphers. The standard modes are Electronic Code Book (ECB), Cipher Block Chaining (CBC), Output Feedback (OFB), and Cipher Feedback (CFB).

ISO/IEC 10116 (1991): Modes of operation for an *n*-bit block cipher algorithm. ISO/IEC 10116 specifies the four standard modes of ISO/IEC 8372 for the most general case of an *n*-bit block cipher. For $n = 64$, this standard is compatible with ISO/IEC 8372.

ISO/IEC 9979 (1991): Procedures for the registration of cryptographic algorithms. The ISO register of cryptographic algorithms is maintained by the National Computing Centre (Manchester, U.K.) which also provides information about the preparation of register entries and the current status of the register. Submission of new entries may only be made by an ISO member body, an ISO technical committee, or a liaison organization. Note that registration of an encipherment algorithm is a formal process which does not involve any evaluation of the algorithm to be registered.

Data Integrity and Digital Signatures

Data integrity is the property that data have not been altered or destroyed in an unauthorized manner. There are several types of crytographic mechanisms useful in this context. A Digital Signature is to serve as the electronic equivalent of a written signature. It allows the user to "sign" a message so that anyone can verify the signature (i.e., to prove to a third party that a message has been created by a specific entity). For digital signatures that provide message recovery, the additional specification of a special transformation introducing redundancy is necessary, whereas digital signatures with appendix require a cryptographic hash-function to produce a "footprint" of the data to be signed. A hash-function derives from any input an output of fixed length in such a way that it is infeasible to find two different messages that result in the same hash value (collision resistancy).

ISO/IEC 9797 (1994): Data integrity mechanism using a cryptographic check function employing a block cipher algorithm. ISO/IEC 9797 specifies a method to verify the integrity of stored or transmitted data using a message authentication code (MAC), also known as modification detection code (MDC), or keyed hash-function. The MAC calculation makes use of the CBC mode of a block cipher. This standard is a generalization of the data integrity mechanisms standardized in ISO 8731-1 and ANSI X9.9 that both are based on the DES.

ISO/IEC 9796 (1991): Digital signature scheme giving message recovery. ISO/IEC 9796 defines a method to calculate and verify digital signatures. The mechanism is based on the RSA algorithm and allows for recovery of the original data from the signature. The specified redundancy function doubles the length of the data before being signed.

FIPS Publication 186 (1994): Digital Signature Standard. The digital signature mechanism standardized by NIST is a variation of the ElGamal signature scheme based on the discrete logarithm problem. A hash-function to be used with the DSS has been standardized through FIPS Publication 180 (see below).

ISO/IEC 14888: Digital signatures with appendix. A multipart standard dedicated to digital signatures of hashed messages is under development within ISO/IEC JTC1/SC27. The following three parts are envisaged, all of them currently being at committee draft level:

- **ISO/IEC CD 14888-1: Digital signature with appendix — Part 1: General**.
- **ISO/IEC CD 14888-2: Digital signatures with appendix — Part 2: Identity-based mechanisms**. In its current status, this part contains two schemes known as Fiat-Schamir and Guillou–Quisquater signature schemes.
- **ISO/IEC CD 14888-3: Digital signatures with appendix — Part 3: Certificate-based mechanisms**. In its current status, this part specifies two ElGamal type signature schemes, the DSS (see above), and an elliptic curve based signature scheme.

ISO/IEC 10118 Hash-functions specifies different classes of cryptographic hash-functions:

- **ISO/IEC 10118-1 (1994): Hash-functions — Part 1: General**. Part 1 of ISO/IEC 10118 states definitions, notations, and general assumptions.
- **ISO/IEC 10118-2 (1994): Hash-functions — Part 2: Hash-functions using an *n*-bit block cipher algorithm**. Part 2 of ISO/IEC 10118 standardizes two constructions for hash-functions that are based on an *n*-bit block cipher algorithm.
- **ISO/IEC WD 10118-3: Hash-functions — Part 3: Dedicated hash-functions**. The current draft of part 3 of ISO/IEC 10118 contains two dedicated hash-functions, namely, the Secure Hash Standard (SHS) standardized by NIST (see below) and RIPEMD, a hash-function proposed by a European project consortium.
- **ISO/IEC WD 10118-4: Hash-functions — Part 4: Hash-functions using modular arithmetic**. The current draft of part 4 of ISO/IEC 10118 specifies a hash-function based on the "square mod *n*" operation.

FIPS Publication 180 (1993): Secure Hash Standard. This standard defines a dedicated hash-function to be used with FIPS Publication 186, the Digital Signature Standard (see above).

Authentication

Authentication mechanisms are concerned with assuring the identity of communicating entities to one another. Authentication is an essential security requirement for many applications, especially in the area of distributed systems and networks.

ISO/IEC 9798: Entity authentication specifies generic mechanisms which prove, based on cryptographic techniques, that an entity is the one it claims to be. The mechanisms are concerned both with the authentication of one entity only (unilateral authentication) and with mutual authentication. They use time-variant parameters such as time stamps, sequence numbers, or random numbers to prevent valid authentication information from being accepted at a later date. ISO/IEC 9798 currently consists of five parts:

- **ISO/IEC 9798-1 (1991): Entity authentication – Part 1: General model**. Part 1 of ISO/IEC 9798 states definitions, notations, and general assumptions. The general model optionally involves a third party of the distribution of keys or certificates.

- **ISO/IEC 9798-2 (1994): Entity authentication – Part 2: Mechanisms using symmetric encipherment algorithms**. Part 2 of ISO/IEC 9798 specifies six entity authentication mechanisms using symmetric encipherment algorithms. Two of the mechanisms require a trusted third party for the establishment of a shared secret key prior to authentication, whereas the remaining mechanisms deal with the situation where no trusted third party has to be involved.

- **ISO/IEC 9798-3 (1993): Entity authentication – Part 3: Entity authentication using public key algorithm**. Part 3 of ISO/IEC 9798 standardizes five entity authentication mechanisms using asymmetric techniques. Two of the mechanisms require a trusted third party for the establishment of a certificate prior to authentication.

- **ISO/IEC 9798-4 (1995): Entity authentication – Part 4: Mechanisms using a cryptographic check function**. Part 4 of ISO/IEC 9798 specifies four entity authentication mechanisms using a cryptographic check function (see, e.g., ISO/IEC 9797). The document only addresses the situation where no trusted third party has to be involved.

- **ISO/IEC WD 9798-5: Entity authentication – Part 5: Mechanisms using zero knowledge techniques**. Part 5 of ISO/IEC 9798 will specify entity authentication mechanisms using zero knowledge techniques. This envisaged standard currently is at working draft level.

Nonrepudiation

Nonrepudiation mechanisms protect against attempts to falsely deny having sent or received a message.

ISO/IEC 13888 Nonrepudiation will specify a set of generic nonrepudiation mechanisms. Part 3 of the envisaged standard currently is at working draft level.

- **ISO/IEC CD 13888-1: Nonrepudiation – Part 1: General model**. Part 1 of ISO/IEC 13888 will state definitions, notations, and the generic concept of nonrepudiation.

- **ISO/IEC CD 13888-2: Nonrepudiation – Part 2: Using symmetric enci-**

pherment algorithms. Part 2 of ISO/IEC 13888 specifies nonrepudiation techniques based on secret-key encipherment algorithms.
- **ISO/IEC WD 13888-3: Nonrepudiation—Part 3: Using asymmetric techniques**. Part 3 of ISO/IEC 13888 is to specify nonrepudiation techniques based on public-key algorithms.

Key Management Mechanisms

Key management is to provide procedures for handling cryptographic keying material to be used in symmetric or asymmetric cryptographic algorithms.

ISO/IEC CD 11770: Key management addresses the general concepts of key management and specifies a selection of generic mechanisms for key transport and for key establishment. All three parts of the envisaged standard currently are at committee draft level.
- **ISO/IEC CD 11770-1: Key management—Part 1: Key management framework**. The document identifies the objectives of key management, describes general models on which key management mechanisms are based, defines key management services, identifies the characteristics of key management mechanisms, and specifies requirements for the management of keying material during its life cycle.
- **ISO/IEC CD 11770-2: Key management—Part 2: Mechanisms using symmetric techniques**. Part 2 of ISO/IEC 11770 defines specific key establishment mechanisms using symmetric cryptographic techniques. Most of the mechanisms are derived from authentication mechanisms of ISO/IEC 9798-2 by specifying the use of text fields available in those authentication mechanisms. The described mechanisms are generic; that is, their implementation is not defined.
- **ISO/IEC CD 11770-3: Key management—Part 3: Mechanisms using asymmetric techniques**. Part 3 of ISO/IEC 11770 defines generic key establishment mechanisms using asymmetric cryptographic techniques. Some of the mechanisms are derived from authentication mechanisms of ISO/IEC 9798-3 by specifying the use of text fields available there.

FIPS Publication 185 (1994): Escrowed Encryption Standard. FIPS Publication 185 specifies a voluntary technology available for protecting telephone communications (e.g., voice, fax, modem) while meeting the needs of law enforcement (also known as the Clipper chip initiative). Within a key-escrowed system private device keys are held in a repository. Two key components kept by different escrow agents are needed to reconstruct a secret key in the case of a legal authorization for a wiretap.

SECURITY EVALUATION CRITERIA

For an IT system, in order to meet its security requirements, it will implement a number of security measures. Appropriate confidence in these functions is needed (i.e., confidence in the correctness and in the effectiveness of those security measures). The assessment of IT systems with respect to such confidence requires objective and well-defined security evaluation criteria.

History of Evaluation Criteria

Much work has been done on the development of IT security evaluation methods. Figure 1 gives an overview of the history of security evaluation criteria. This development was mainly driven by the National Computer Security Center (NCSC) to match the security policy of the U.S. Department of Defense (DoD). The first version of the Trusted Computer System Evaluation Criteria (TCSEC, also known as Orange Book) was published in 1983, with a follow-up in 1985 (DoD 5200.28-Std). The criteria are part of a set of publications including the well-known Trusted Network Interpretation [published in 1989 (4)] and the Trusted Database Interpretation [published in 1991 (5)].

In the late 1980s, several European countries developed security criteria of their own and established corresponding administrative bodies. The GISA (German Information Security Agency) was formally established in 1991. The German IT-Security Criteria (Greenbook) have been published in 1989, with the IT Evaluation Manual as a follow-up in 1990 (6). Also, since 1989, the four European countries Germany, France, Great Britain, and the Netherlands have been working on the so-called Harmonized Criteria (ITSEC), which have been published in version 1.2 in June 1991 (7). These criteria have become a (de facto) European standard after a 2-year trial period. They also have been proposed to ISO/IEC JTC1/SC27 to become an international standard. Based on ITSEC, the *IT Security Evaluation Manual V1.0* has been published for use in September 1993 after 1 year of public review.

In early 1992, the U.S. National Institute of Standards and Technology (NIST) published the so-called Minimum Security Functionality Requirements for Multi-User Operating Systems [MSFR (8)]. The MSFR set of criteria was a first step toward the Federal Criteria [FC (9)], which have been published for review as version 1.0 in December 1992. In the meantime, work has begun on the so-called Common Criteria (CC), which aim at specifying a common set of criteria to be used on an international basis for the security evaluation of computer systems. A first draft has undergone a review by government security experts, but applicable results are not yet visible.

1983	USA	Trusted Computer Security Evaluation Criteria
1985	USA	Trusted Computer Security Evaluation Criteria
1989	Germany	IT Security Criteria
1990	USA	Trusted Network Interpretation
	Germany	IT Evaluation Manual
1991	USA	Trusted Database Interpretation
	Europe	IT Security Evaluation Criteria (ITSEC V1.2)
1992	USA	Minimum Security Functionality Requirements
	Europe	IT Security Evaluation Manual
1993	USA	Federal Criteria
	Europe	IT Security Evaluation Manual (V1.0)

FIGURE 1   Historical view of IT criteria development.

The NCSC Orange Book (TCSEC)

The Orange Book defines seven sets of evaluation criteria (called classes), grouped into four divisions:

- D: being the lowest (catchall)
- C: C1 and C2, requiring audit and basic discretionary access control (DAC)
- B: B1, B2, B3, requiring mandatory access control (MAC), a security-oriented system structure, security model, user roles
- A: requires formal verification of the security model

The security model is an integral part of the Orange Book (Bell–LaPadula Model). It basically consists of a set of DAC rules and of MAC rules. The MAC rules very closely model the military confidentiality requirements. In particular, classifications and departments are defined to form a lattice model for information flow control (no read up, no write down). For each system under evaluation, an interpretation of the security model has to be defined.

The ITSEC Approach

The ITSEC takes a different approach, because it differentiates between the security functionality of a system and the different assurance levels for the effectiveness and the correctness of the claimed security attributes of the system. Seven assurance levels are defined, with E0 being the lowest (insufficient quality) and E6 being the highest (formally verified, see Fig. 2 for a complete list). The security functionality can be defined individually for each system, but, as an example, 10 functionality classes are predefined. The first five of these closely follow the Orange Book classes C1 to B3. Additional classes are defined for the following:

- Systems with integrity requirements (F-IN)
- Systems with availability requirements (F-AV)
- Systems with data integrity requirements during exchange (F-DI)
- Systems with data confidentiality requirements during exchange (F-DC)
- Networks with integrity and confidentiality requirements of information to be exchanged (F-DX)

Quality Classes		Function Classes	
E6	formally verified	F-DX	integritiy and confidentiality during
E5	formally analysed		information exchange
E4	semiformally analysed	F-DC	data confidentiality during info. exchg.
E3	methodically tested	F-DI	data integrity during information exchg.
	and analysed	F-AV	availability requirements
E2	methodically tested	F-IN	integrity requirements
E1	function tested	F-B3, F-B2, F-B1	
E0	insufficient assurance		corresponds to Orange Book B classes
		F-C2, F-C1	
			corresponds to Orange Book C classes

FIGURE 2   ITSEC quality and function classes.

It must be noted, however, that the mapping between Orange Book classes and ITSEC functional classes is not one-to-one, for example, DAC in F-C2 is more stringent than DAC in C2 (see, e.g., Ref. 10).

The Federal Criteria

The process of separating generic security qualities and functions, their analysis from specific products, and their evaluation has been taken one step further in the Federal Criteria, published as draft version V1.0 by NIST/NSA in 1993 (9). The overall security development is broken up in basically three steps. The first step is the definition and analysis of security profiles. The Federal Criteria are restricted to the definition and analysis of security profiles. Security profiles can be seen as generic security functions and security qualities of a wide range of products or systems. The profiles are based on security requirements of application scenarios, which must be fulfilled by products or systems to be used in such scenarios. Product evaluation as the second step uses existing security profiles as a reference for the required security functions and their qualities. Finally, in step three, systems consisting of several, not necessarily evaluated components need to be accredited for specific purposes.

Besides the information necessary to register a protection profile and to uniquely characterize the threats to be covered, the protection profile defines the following:

- The security functions of the profile (functional requirements)
- The requirements on the development process (development assurance requirements)
- The type and intensity of the evaluation process (evaluation assurance requirements)

Based on the generic process of defining protection profiles, sets of rules derived from other security criteria and from their use in security evaluations are defined for functional and assurance requirements.

In volume two of the two-volume Federal Criteria, two classes of protection profiles are completed for registration:

- Commercial Security Requirements (CS)
- Label Based Protection (LP)

Three CS subsets (CS1–CS3) are specified, which are planned to replace the earlier published MSFR criteria. The requirements are mainly oriented toward their broad use in private, civil, and defense communities. Products conforming to one of the CS subsets should be available off-the-shelf. Adherence to those requirements should be stipulated for a wide acceptance for security functions in the day-to-day operation of general-purpose, multiuser operating systems. For Label Based Protection, four subsets are specified which are aimed at replacing the Orange Book classes B1 to A. These profiles are aimed at classified government information as well as any information with the need for a label-based separation.

SECURITY MECHANISMS IN OPERATING SYSTEMS

Based on the definition of security functionality in ITSEC, an overview of currently implemented security mechanisms shall be given. These mechanisms are derived from open system implementations (such as UNIX®*; see Refs. 11–13). At first, associated standardization efforts are summarized.

Standardization of Security Mechanisms

In 1988, the POSIX working group 1003.6 was founded to cover aspects of security interfaces to UNIX systems (see also Ref. 14). The following aspects have been addressed:

- Discretionary access control and access control lists (ACLs)
- Auditing with audit data formats and auditable events
- Least privilege with privilege sets and management interfaces
- Mandatory access control with label definitions and interfaces

None of the standard proposals has been accepted during the several ballot runs. New projects are being discussed in P1003.6, targeted at identification and authentication, at data interchange, and at terminal I/O.

X/Open is an independent standardization body for open systems, formed by vendor and customer organizations. The Security Working Group (SWG) within X/Open has been created to define interfaces related to IT security and to provide advice for users. The interface specifications are largely consistent with the POSIX 1003.6 proposals. The *X/Open Security Guide* has been published in 1990 (16). The security guide is aligned with the *X/Open Portability Guides 3/4* (XPG3/XPG4). The guide is aimed at open system users and administrators to help them use the available security mechanisms and tools correctly. Also, security awareness of open system users shall be increased. An update of the security guide will be aligned with XPG4 and will have additional chapters on networks and communication, databases, transaction processing, window systems, and risk management.

In September 1992, the X/Open Secure Open Systems Procurement Guide (SOSPG) has been published (17). SOSPG shall help users of open systems in selecting the most adequate security measures for their applications. For that purpose, five scenarios (office systems, database applications, batch applications, software development environment, and control systems) have been set up to provide guidance on potential threats in those scenarios and corresponding security functions to counter those threats. In agreement with the ongoing POSIX and ITSEC work, six functionality classes have been set up (see also Fig. 3). To reflect the high priority of security requirements in general, X/Open has developed a security framework which sets requirements on future X/Open specifications to take security properties and requirements into account.

Mechanisms Typically Provided in Secure Systems

Authentication: To satisfy accountability requirements, all actions within the system must be traceable to a single identifiable user. To assure that the proper user is held accountable, the system authenticates each user at log-in

---

*UNIX® is a registered Trademark in the United States and other countries, licensed exclusively through X/Open Company Limited.

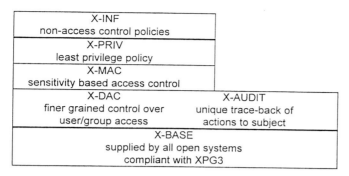

FIGURE 3 Proposed X/Open security functionality classes.

time. A unique log-in identifier (LUID) is set at log-in time. The LUID is inherited by child processes and may never be changed once set. For B-class security, it is required that a trusted path be provided between the user at a terminal and the system. This can be implemented by a secure attention key at the keyboard. Pressing this key assures the unique association between the user's input and the system log-in program. This mechanism suppresses spoofing programs trying to detect the user's password.

Discretionary Access Control (DAC): Access control lists (ACLs) are often used for a fine-grained control of object accesses (e.g., opening a file by user process). ACLs allow the owner of a file to define a list of users and groups for the file and read/write/execute permissions for each user and group on the list. Access can also be explicitly denied to users or groups.

Mandatory Access Control (MAC): A system maintained control over access to all system resources (including files, directories, and devices) can be implemented via sensitivity labels. Sensitivity labels combine a hierarchical classification level (e.g., unclassified, confidential, secret, top secret) and a nonhierarchical category (e.g., finance, sales, engineering). All object accesses are controlled by a MAC mechanism, which enforces the defined MAC security policy (e.g., Bell–LaPadula, see above). The MAC security policy requires that information can only flow from lower sensitivity levels to higher sensitivity levels.

Trusted Facility Management (TFM): Administrative roles are defined such that the person performing a given role has the least amount of privilege needed to do the job. A wide range of privileges is available to adapt to specific needs of a system installation. The roles operator, administrator, and security administrator are most often predefined, but additional roles can be configured. TFM is supported by a least-privilege mechanism, which assures that each process has only the least amount of privileges assigned at each point in time.

Administration Tools: The security of a system is also dependent on the security of the administrative tools (in particular, for security administration).

Audit: An audit mechanism has to be provided to track predefined system activity. Evaluation criteria typically define the minimally required audit records (e.g., log-in, log-out, changes to the security database). Additional system activity to be tracked can be configured by the security administrator. Each audit record contains at least LUID, time, activity, and security status (like MAC level). Tools are provided to store and analyze the accumulated audit data in a secure and efficient manner.

System Structure: For higher-level security requirements (B class), the system kernel has to be restructured for modularization and clearly defined interfaces (like minimal set of global variables). A covert channel analysis is performed to identify hidden channels, which could be exploited by malicious users.

Documentation: Due to evaluation requirements, the system documentation needs to be updated and enhanced. Specific manuals are required to cover all aspects of the security of a system. Typical examples are the security administrator's manuals and the security features manuals.

Compartmented Mode Workstations

A special case of generic computer systems are compartmented mode workstations (CMWs). These are stand-alone machines (the distributed case will be discussed below), supporting the management of trusted information. The correct labeling of information for mandatory access control requires special treatment in such an environment.

As discussed above, sensitivity levels such as {unclassified, confidential, secret, top secret} are used to label information in trusted environments. During the creation of objects, the subject's sensitivity level is inherited by the object. The same is the case during transfer of information between objects (under the constraints of mandatory access control). In many cases, the object label does not correctly reflect the security level of the object's contents. For example, if information of a secret file and a confidential file are copied to a new file, the new file's sensitivity level will become secret (see Fig. 4a). To reduce the induced overclassification, the concept of information levels has been introduced. Information levels are associated with data items in a finer granularity (often implemented via linked lists). In this case, copying of two files with different information levels would result in a third file with information levels dependent on the origin of its contents. Should the file be displayed in a window, the information level will change according to the displayed contents of the file. Figure 4b shows the handling of information levels during file copying. Note that the sensitivity levels are treated the same as in Figure 4a. The concept of information levels is mostly used in deciding on the classification of information during export out of a system or during declassification (via restricted commands). For more details, see Refs. 18–20.

SECURITY ON THE INTERNET

This section focuses on the DoD internetworking protocol suite, widely known as TCP/IP. The Internet Protocol (IP) provides a virtual packet-switched network. The Transmission Control Protocol (TCP) transforms the raw datagram-oriented service of IP into a full-duplex, reliable character stream. "Internet" will refer to

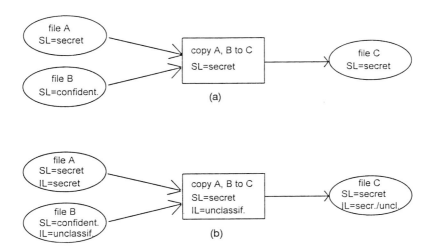

FIGURE 4   Sensitivity levels (a) and information levels (b) during file copy.

internets that use the TCP/IP protocols (21). Several efforts are currently under-taken to improve security on internets:

- Security options for the IP headers are defined by which security informa-tion can be exchanged between hosts.
- Session management functions are defined on top of TCP to support the correct set-up of secure communication paths.
- Application interfaces to the provided network services are defined.

Figure 5 provides an overview of the involved entities. On the IP level, exten-sions are required for trusted routing (routing dependent on packet labels), for packet labeling, and for import/export checks (dependent on packet labels). Above TCP, functionality is added for trusted session management. This includes identifi-cation and authentication, auditing of network events, and the transfer/transforma-tion of security attributes. In addition to a standard network interface like XTI

Security Functions
TLI
Session Management
Identification/Authentication
Auditing, Transfer of Security Attributes
TCP
Trusted Routing
IP   Packet Labeling
Import/Export Checks

FIGURE 5   Enhancements to TCP/IP Protocol.

(X/Open Transport Level Interface), additional interfaces are provided to take advantage of the network security functions.

The Internet community publishes its specifications in documents called "Request for Comments" (RFCs).

Internet Protocol Layer Enhancements

The proposed use of the option field of Internet headers is for communicating security information. The transferred information is used for assigning correct security labels to the associated data. It is also used to enforce the system defined mandatory access control policy to the host machine. Several format proposals for representing security information in this option field currently exist.

1. RIPSO: In RFC 1108 (Ref. 22, published in November 1991), the DoD specifies two security option types for transferring security information in DoD networks (Internet based). RFC 1108 replaces RFC 1038 (23), which defines the "revised IP security option" (= RIPSO).
   - "Basic security option" (option type = 130): this option carries classification levels and protection authority flags. The information is used for transmitting classification levels according to computer security models and for controlling the routing of datagrams in an Internet.
   - "Extended security option" (option type = 133): This option carries additional labeling information to meet the need of registered authorities. It is transmitted only in conjunction with the basic security option.
2. CIPSO: The "Commercial IP Security Option" (CIPSO) has been devised by the Trusted Systems Interoperability Group (TSIG is composed of a group of vendors and users developing/working with secure operating and network systems; the cooperation is aimed at improved interoperability of different systems with respect to security) to take requirements from an open system environment for transferring security information in internets into account (see Ref. 24 for more details). The format of the CIPSO option is shown in Figure 6. The CIPSO option number is 134. A length indicator shows the overall length of the option. To take interoperability between heterogeneous systems into account, a domain of interpre-

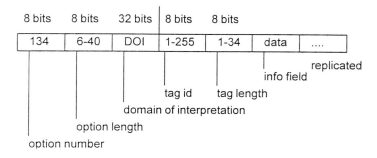

FIGURE 6   CIPSO security option definition.

tation (DOI) field is defined. This field defines the interpretation of the security information within the option. The DOI between communicating systems has to be negotiated. Then a number of security information fields are added. They contain level and category information. Categories can be represented via enumeration or bit maps. They are distinguished by tagging the category information (tag type 2 resp 1).

3. MaxSix Tokens: In project Max (25, 26), tokens are defined as a more general format of transferring security information via IP headers. Tokens are based on the CIPSO format, but additional tag types are defined for token information (types 3 and 4). Tokens can represent any of sensitivity labels, information labels, nationality caveats, log-in ids, process ids, privilege sets, and so on.

Session Management Functions

Trusted session (the session concept deviates from the ISO session definition) management is based on the secure transfer of security information (see above). It is responsible for the setup of sessions and the enforcement of system defined security policies. Besides, auditing of security-relevant actions is performed within session management.

1. DNSIX specification: DODIIS Network Security of Information Exchange (DNSIX) satisfies the technical security requirements for internetworking in DODIIS (DODIIS: Department of Defense Intelligence Information System). See Refs. 27–30 for details. The session management module gathers security relevant information as well as exceptional conditions and sends them to the network audit trail. The audit format is defined by DNSIX. DNSIX requires that mandatory access controls be performed at the network level.

2. TSIG work: Due to its general nature, TSIG work has to take session-level functions of different vendors or user groups (e.g., DNSIX) into account. The so-called Grand Unification Theory tries to cover compatibility with DNSIX specifications as well as proposes Kerberos-based authentication (see below). It is required to support multiple session management (SM) schemes. The transmission of authentication information between Telnet client and server compliant with the Kerberos V4 encryption method is specified in RFC 1411. The transmission of generic authentication information between Telnet client and server is specified in RFC 1416.

3. MaxSix session manager framework: The MaxSix framework allows for multiple SM implementations (e.g., the requirements for authentication and encryption strongly depend on the underlying physical layer). Security attribute mapping and translation are supported to cover different implementation schemes. The supported attributes can be negotiated between connected systems.

Application Interfaces

It is a basic requirement that applications should not be forced to change due to an underlying secure TCP/IP. However, the available security functions must be visible for administration and installation. Although implementations exist, they differ in the number of services they provide for trusted communication. Formal specifications must still be developed.

In Ref. 31, a proposal for a generic security service application program interface (GSS-API) has been made, which covers the following functional areas:

- Establishing a security context between two communicating peers to achieve peer entity authentication
- Providing per message data origin authentication and data integrity protection in conjunction with confidentiality services as a caller option

The interface has been specified with four goals in mind:

1. Mechanism independence: The interface is independent of underlying cryptographic mechanisms and can be based on secret-key techniques (e.g., Kerberos) or public-key techniques (e.g. X.509).
2. Protocol environment independence: To be useful in a broad range of protocol environments, the GSS-API services may be invoked via a suitable interface with a selected protocol.
3. Protocol association independence: The interface may be called either within different protocol associations or directly from application programs
4. Suitability to a range of implementation placements: The services may be called either from within a trusted computing base (as defined by the Orange Book) or outside, not making specific assumptions about the security environment of the calling client.

The interface specifications have been presented to the Internet standardization community (RFC 1508 and RFC 1509) and to ECMA (see below) to be used in the OSI security framework as defined in ECMA TR/46. Further development and harmonization is driven by X/Open, where GSS-API has been adopted as a work item in the Security Working Group. Preliminary specifications have been published recently (32, 33). This also reflects the high priority in the X/Open working process, which is given to authentication, authorization and access control services in distributed environments.

OSI SECURITY ARCHITECTURE, FRAMEWORKS, AND MODELS

There are many options for the integration of security services into a communications architecture. A network **Security Architecture** constitutes an overall security blueprint for a network. It describes security services and their interrelationships, and it shows how the security services map onto the network architecture. The purpose of **Security Frameworks** is to describe specific functional areas of security (e.g., authentication, access control, confidentiality) and to provide generic solutions to those security problems. The frameworks define the general means for protecting systems or objects and also are concerned with the interactions between systems. The intention of **Security Models** is to detail how and where the security elements of the frameworks and other security mechanisms and techniques can be combined to provide various types and levels of security.

OSI Security Architecture

ISO 7498-2 (1989) Open Systems Interconnection — Basic Reference Model — Part 2: Security Architecture. This basic standard defines the general security related architectural elements which can be applied appropriately in the circumstances for which protection of communications is required. In order to extend the field of application of the Basic Reference Model for Open Systems Interconnection (ISO 7498), ISO 7498-2 identifies a set of security services and possibilities of integrating them into the seven layers of the OSI architecture. Those services will typically be invoked at appropriate layers to satisfy a defined security policy and/or user requirements. Practical realizations of systems may implement particular combinations of the basic security services for direct invocation. The OSI security architecture supports five primary security services: authentication, access control, data confidentiality, data integrity, and nonrepudiation.

Figure 7 shows 14 specific security services identified in ISO 7498-2 and their possible allocation to each layer. It also illustrates that strict adherence to the OSI security architecture would limit LAN-specific security services (i.e., security services for layers 1 and 2) to data confidentiality. The following principles were used in order to determine the allocation of security services to layers and the consequent placement of security mechanisms.

*   The number of alternative ways to achieve a service should be minimized.
*   It is considered acceptable to build secure systems by providing security services in more than one layer.
*   Additional functionality required for security should not unnecessarily duplicate existing OSI functions.

Service	Layer						
	1	2	3	4	5	6	7*
Peer Entity Authentication	-	-	y	y	-	-	y
Data Origin Authentication	-	-	y	y	-	-	y
Access Control Service	-	-	y	y	-	-	y
Connection Confidentiality	y	y	y	y	-	y	y
Connectionless Confidentiality	-	y	y	y	-	y	y
Selective Field Confidentiality	-	-	-	-	-	y	y
Traffic Flow Confidentiality	y	-	y	-	-	-	y
Connection Integrity with Recovery	-	-	-	y	-	-	y
Connection Integrity w/out Recovery	-	-	y	y	-	-	y
Selective Field Connection Integrity	-	-	-	-	-	-	y
Connectionless Integrity	-	-	y	y	-	-	y
Selective Field Connectionless Integrity	-	-	-	-	-	-	y
Non-Repudiation, Origin	-	-	-	-	-	-	y
Non-Repudiation, Delivery	-	-	-	-	-	-	y

Legend:
y=   service should be part of the layer standards as a provider option
-=   not provided
*   application layer itself may provide security services

FIGURE 7   ISO/OSI layer association of security services.

- Violation of layer independence should be avoided.
- The amount of trusted functionality should be minimized.
- Whenever an entity is dependent on a security mechanism provided by an entity in a lower layer, any intermediate layers should be constructed in such a way that security violation is impractical.
- Wherever possible, the additional security functions of a layer should be defined in such a way that implementation as a self-contained module is not precluded.
- The definitions apply to open systems consisting of end systems containing all seven layers as well as to relay systems.

According to ISO 7498-2, the types of mechanisms that may be used to provide the security services identified are encipherment, digital signature, access control, data integrity, authentication exchange, traffic padding, routing control, and notarization. The standard specifies which mechanisms, alone or in combination, are considered to be appropriate for the provision of each type of service.

In addition, ISO 7498-2 sets up categories for OSI security management:

- System security management is concerned with the management of security aspects of the overall OSI environment (e.g., maintenance of consistency, audit management).
- Security service management is concerned with the management of particular security services (e.g., negotiation of available mechanisms).
- Security mechanism management is concerned with the management of particular security mechanisms (e.g., key establishment, certificate management).

Work on the management of security in open systems is performed in a combined effort between ISO/IEC JTC1/SC21 and ITU. Security management is seen as an integral part of system management.

ISO/IEC 10164: OSI systems management covers functions for managing security services and mechanisms (e.g., security alarm reporting, security audit trails, objects and attributes for access control). Details of network security management issues, in particular with respect to key management, can be found in Ref. 34.

OSI Security Frameworks

ISO/IEC 10181 Security Frameworks in Open Systems. This set of frameworks again is a result of a combined effort between ISO/IEC JTC1/SC21 and ITU. It consists of the following parts:

- **ISO/IEC CD 10181-1 (1994): Security Frameworks in Open Systems— Part 1: Security Frameworks Overview.** This part of the multipart standard describes the organization of the individual frameworks, their interrelationship, and basic security concepts.
- **ISO/IEC DIS 10181-2 (1993): Security Frameworks in Open Systems— Part 2: Authentication Framework.** This framework defines the basic concepts of authentication, classifies authentication mechanisms, and identifies functional and management requirements to support these classes.

- **ISO/IEC DIS 10181-3 (1994): Security Frameworks in Open Systems—Part 3: Access Control Framework**. This part of the multipart standard describes the basic concepts of access control, classifies access control mechanisms, and identifies functional and management requirements to support these classes.
- **ISO/IEC DIS 10181-4 (1994): Security Frameworks in Open Systems—Part 4: Nonrepudiation Framework**. This document describes the basic concepts of nonrepudiation and identifies functional and management requirements to support it.
- **ISO/IEC CD 10181-5 (1993): Security Frameworks in Open Systems—Part 5: Confidentiality Framework**. This framework addresses the basic concepts of confidentiality, the relationship to other security functions, and the management requirements for confidentiality.
- **ISO/IEC CD 10181-6 (1993): Security Frameworks in Open Systems—Part 6: Integrity Framework**. This framework addresses the basic concepts of integrity, the relationship to other security functions, and the management requirements for integrity.
- **ISO/IEC CD 10181-7 (1993): Security Frameworks in Open Systems—Part 7: Security Audit Framework**. This framework addresses the aspects of security audit, the relationship to other security functions, and interaction with other management functionality.

OSI Security Models

ISO/IEC TR 13594 (1994): Lower Layers Security Model. This technical report describes an architectural model that provides a basis for the development of services and protocols for security in the lower OSI layers (i.e., layers 2 to 4).

ISO/IEC 10745 (1993): Upper Layers Security Model. This document defines an architectural model that provides a basis for the development of application-independent services and protocols for security in the upper OSI layers (i.e., layers 5 to 7). Furthermore, it addresses their utilization to fulfill the security requirements of a wide area of applications.

ISO/IEC 11586 Generic Upper Layers Security. This Recommendation/International Standard is a multipart document, which provides a set of facilities to aid the construction of OSI Upper Layers protocols which support the provision of security services. The parts are as follows, parts 5 and 6 of the envisaged standard currently begin at working draft level:

- **ISO/IEC DIS 11586-1: Generic Upper Layers Security—Part 1: Overview, Models and Notation**. This document defines a set of generic facilities to assist in the provision of security services in OSI applications. These include notational tools, service definitions, protocol, and conformance specifications for application service elements and a security transfer syntax.
- **ISO/IEC DIS 11586-2: Generic Upper Layers Security—Part 2: Security Exchange Service Element Service Definition**. This part defines the service provided by the Security Exchange Service Element (SESE). The

SESE is an application service element which facilitates the communication of security information.

- **ISO/IEC DIS 11586-3: Generic Upper Layers Security – Part 3: Security Exchange Service Element Protocol Specification**. This part specifies the protocol provided by the SESE.
- **ISO/IEC DIS 11586-4: Generic Upper Layers Security – Part 4: Protecting Transfer Syntax Specification**. This document defines the protecting transfer syntax, associated with the Presentation Layer support for security services in the Application Layer.
- **ISO/IEC WD 11586-5: Generic Upper Layers Security – Part 5: Security Exchange Service Element PICS Proforma**.
- **ISO/IEC WD 11586-6: Generic Upper Layers Security – Part 6: Protecting Transfer Syntax PICS Proforma**.

ECMA Security Framework

ECMA TR/46 Security in Open Systems – A Security Framework. The ECMA security framework defines two important structural concepts: security domains and security facilities. Security domains are managerial concepts used to limit the scope of a particular security policy. A domain will cover a number of users (subjects) and computing resources (objects). Subdomains are introduced for ease of structuring large domains. Subdomains can interpret some aspects of their security policy to satisfy local needs. Besides the subdomain relationship, security domains may also be in a peer relationship to each other. Two domains are in peer relationship if neither domain is a subdomain of the other. The domain concept with the defined relationships can be used to identify common security features (services, facilities) and interfaces.

Security facilities are a modeling technique for developing and describing a framework for security in open systems. The facilities and their interactions are logical entities within the framework. The framework is designed to provide a model from which a comprehensive and complete set of security services and protocols may be developed. An implementation of an open secure system will make use of these services and protocols to support a specific security policy. The following security facilities have been defined:

- The subject sponsor serves as an intermediary between the security subject and the other security facilities.
- The authentication facility accepts and checks subject authentication information, communicating its conclusions to other security facilities as necessary under the security policy.
- The association management facility provides authorization for two entities to communicate, assurance of the identity of the communicating entities, and control over the kind and type of security of the underlying communication service.
- The security state facility maintains a view of the current security state of the system in terms of authenticated subjects and objects, their associations, and their security attributes.

- The security attribute management facility provides for the creation, distribution, revocation, archiving, and destruction of security attributes of subjects and objects within a given security domain.
- The authorization facility authorizes or denies requested accesses of subjects to objects depending on security state information.
- The interdomain facility maps one domain's interpretation of security attributes into another domain's interpretation.
- The security audit facility receives event information from other security facilities for recording and/or analysis.
- The security recovery facility reacts on an administrator defined policy or on administrator input to security events.
- The cryptographic support facility provides cryptographic services as required by other security facilities.

These defined security facilities can be used in two ways according to the OSI Reference Model: as supportive security applications or as application service elements.

LOWER LAYERS SECURITY PROTOCOLS

A **Security Protocol** is to provide cryptographic security services that are independent of specific cryptographic algorithms. It should not interfere with the operation of unprotected systems; it should provide optional communication between protected and unprotected systems and support transparent operation for protected systems. The specific capabilities of a security protocol depend on its location in the OSI reference model.

Several protocol extensions have been proposed for adding security services to OSI lower layers protocols. Most prominent are IEEE SILS (Standard for Interoperable LAN Security), the SDNS protocols SP3 (Security Protocol 3) and SP4 (Security Protocol 4), and the OSI Network Layer and Transport Layer Security Protocols (NLSP, TLSP). They all are designed to provide the primary security services confidentiality, integrity, and authentication and access control for OSI layers 2, 3 and 4, respectively.

IEEE 802.10 Standard for Interoperable LAN/MAN Security

A standard protocol for LAN security using cryptographic techniques has been developed by the IEEE working group 802.10 under the project title "Standard for Interoperable LAN/MAN Security" (SILS) (35). SILS is proposing a transparent Security Data Exchange sublayer (SDE) between the MAC (Media Access Control) and LLC (Logical Link Control) sublayers of the data link layer. Additional protocols for key and network management are under development. The SDE sublayer provides the following:

- Data confidentiality (by enciphering the LLC PDU)
- Connectionless integrity (by calculating an integrity check value and appending it to the LLC PDU)
- Data origin authentication (by placing the sender ID in the protected portion of the security header or by key management)
- Access control (by key management)

The SDE sublayer is optional; that is, not every node in a LAN or MAN has to employ the protocol. It depends on external key management for key establishment and for selecting algorithms for the confidentiality and for the data integrity service. The key management application makes use of the services provided by the SILS key management protocol. Key management is defined as a layer 7 functionality that provides cryptographic keys to be used by the SDE sublayer to provide security services.

Each of the individual protocols must identify objects that need to be managed by System Management. The layer management definitions in the key management and data exchange parts of SILS provide the encoding of those objects and their effects on the protocol state machines. If it becomes necessary for the system or the security management to communicate with another end system, the System Management Application Process uses either CMIP (Common Management Information Protocol) or IEEE 802.1 functionality. The Security Management Information Base (SMIB) provides the necessary objects for security management. The object structure is standardized in accordance with ISO/IEC 10165-2.

SDNS Security Protocols SP3 and SP4

In 1986, the DoD initiated a multiorganizational project titled Secure Data Network System (SDNS). SDNS has developed a security architecture within the OSI computer network model which includes security protocols for OSI layers 3 and 4. The SDNS transport protocol, SP4 (SDNS SDN.401), is defined as an addendum to the ISO transport protocol. The SDNS network protocol, SP3 (SDNS SDN.301), is defined as a sublayer of the ISO network protocol which resides directly below the transport layer. The key management and system management protocols utilize the OSI management approach and are application layer protocols between management application entities.

The SDNS security protocols have been developed for consistency with the OSI security architecture and with the ISO protocols. However, due to the similarity of the layer interfaces, SP3 and SP4 implementations can be adapted to work with the DoD protocols TCP and IP as well. With modifications, SP4 and SP3 have been adopted by ISO for inclusion into the OSI protocol suite (see below).

The basic security services provided by SP3 and SP4 are confidentiality and connectionless integrity. The protocols are designed to be independent of specific encipherment algorithms and the method of key distribution. Because SP3 and SP4 use pairwise keys, data origin authentication is offered in addition. Access control is provided by key management and by security label checking.

In addition, SDNS has specified a Key Management Protocol (SDNS SDN.90x) that can be used with the security protocols. The SDNS protocol for message security (SDNS SDN.70x) is an extension of CCITT recommendation X.400. Messages are encrypted end to end. The message security protocol includes an optional electronic signature which can be utilized for the additional service of nonrepudiation.

ISO Lower Layers Security Protocols

ISO has defined security protocols for the transport and the network layer that support all security services identified in ISO 7498-2 as relevant to those layers. The protocols support these services through the use of cryptographic mechanisms, security labeling, and attributes, such as keys and authenticated identities, preestablished by security management.

ISO/IEC 10736: Transport Layer Security Protocol (TLSP). This standard specifies an addendum to the connection-oriented (ISO 8073) and the connectionless ISO transport protocols (ISO 8602). The security protocol supports the basic security services confidentiality, integrity, data origin authentication, and access control. It depends on external key management for key establishment and for selecting the cryptographic algorithms to be used. TLSP, being placed within the transport layer, can only be implemented in an end system.

ISO/IEC 11577: Network Layer Security Protocol. This standard specifies a security sublayer for both the connection-oriented (ISO 8348) and the connectionless (ISO 8473) network protocols. The security protocol supports the basic security services confidentiality, integrity, data origin authentication, and access control. It depends on external key management for key establishment and for selecting the cryptographic algorithms to be used. The security protocol can be implemented in end systems (to achieve end-to-end security) or in intermediate systems (e.g., routers) for the protection of subnets.

APPLICATION LAYER AUTHENTICATION SERVICES

The most prominent example for an authentication and access control service for open systems is Kerberos (Ref. 36 gives a high-level technical view of Kerberos). Kerberos has been developed and used at MIT's project Athena (37). An updated version of Kerberos has been included in OSF's Distributed Computing Environment (DCE), and the Internet RFC 1510 has been published. With its wide availability and acceptance, the DCE version of Kerberos can be viewed as a de facto standard. In March 1994, the DCE security specifications have been distributed for review within X/Open. Several enhancements to Kerberos have already been proposed and will be briefly described in the sequel. A similar concept has been developed by ECMA using asymmetric cryptographic techniques (ECMA-138).

Kerberos Authentication

Figure 8 shows the basic structure of the Kerberos authentication scheme. At first (1), during log-in the user (actually the log-in program) requests in plain format from Kerberos a ticket for the ticket-granting server (TGS, see below). Kerberos returns (2) a "puzzle" encrypted with the client's key containing a session key and the requested ticket, provided the user was found in the Kerberos database. The session key is a random number which is valid only for the current session. The returned ticket-granting ticket (TGT) consists of the client's name, the name of the TGS, current time, a lifetime for the ticket, the client's IP address, and the session key. The TGT is encrypted by a key only known to Kerberos TGS. The users themselves cannot do anything with it but to convey it to the server, the TGS in this case. All encryption is based on DES.

A service (if it supports the Kerberos authentication scheme) can only be

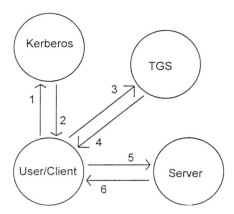

FIGURE 8   Kerberos authentication and authorization.

accessed by showing a service-specific ticket (ST). Such tickets can be retrieved from TGS (3) using the earlier received TGT. TGS is a special service which is responsible for providing access permissions (tickets) to all requesting client programs. TGS keeps a database of users and Kerberos based services. If the request is valid, an ST is returned (4). The ST consists of the client's name, the server name, the current time, the client's IP address, and a new (server specific) session key. The lifetime of the ticket is limited. ST is encrypted with the user's session key, so no new input of the user password is required.

A service request can be made (5) by issuing an authenticator and the received ST to the requested service. The authenticator is built from the client's name and IP address and the current time. It is encrypted in the session key received from TGS. The server checks the information in the authenticator and the ticket (ST) and checks for the IP address the request came from. If both match, the service request is allowed to proceed.

Other Authentication Schemes

Several enhancements to Kerberos and to DCE have been proposed. Most of them are concerned with improving the authentication scheme by using public key techniques.

- In Ref. 38, an authentication model and ticket-granting service (called privilege attribute service) based on the ECMA security framework (ECMA TR/46) is proposed. The model makes use of asymmetric encryption schemes. The authentication server does not use the user's password for encryption, which in Kerberos may be used for password attacks. Also, a very general mechanism for privilege transfer between clients and servers is proposed, allowing the representation of a wide variety of access privileges.
- In Ref. 39, a protocol is proposed which supports the authentication scheme over a set of realms of trust. A realm of trust can basically be

defined as the realm of a TGS. In some cases, it may be necessary to cross several realms because a specific service is not available on the realm of trust of the running user program.

- In Ref. 40, a portable, self-contained implementation of a distributed authentication service intended for open (TCP/IP) network environments is presented (SPX). An update of SPX, the Distributed Authentication Security Service (DASS), has been presented to the Internet standards body and to ECMA (41). It is designed to deal with distributed management of trust relationships in arbitrarily large networks with multiple, mutually suspicious jurisdictional authorities. DASS shares many concepts and data structures with ISO/CCITT X.509 Directory Authentication (ISO/IEC 9594-8) and Internet Privacy Enhanced Mail (RFCs 1421-1424).

DISTRIBUTED SYSTEM SECURITY: A SUMMARY

The above discussion shows that security issues today are influencing all relevant standardization efforts in the area of distributed computer systems. Different approaches are taken, dependent on the standards and/or user community.

With respect to security in operating systems, the basic mechanisms seem to be available. POSIX 1003.6 seems to be mostly involved in standardizing on data structures and algorithms for operating-system security mechanisms. The evaluation of systems is driven by government agencies (DoD, European agencies).

In the distributed area, two approaches are taken. In Internet-oriented user groups specific mechanisms and implementations are discussed (CIPSO, DNSIX). In many cases, projects initially were driven by DoD requirements (e.g., SDNS). Within ISO and other standardization bodies such as ECMA and ITU, a top-down approach is taken starting from security architectures, models, and frameworks.

In financial and electronic data interchange (EDI) application areas work is getting up to speed.

Future Work

Although considerable progress has been made in recent years (42), many issues remain to be solved. The following examples show some important areas, which will need to be covered if secure open systems are to be widely accepted in the user community.

1. Cryptographic techniques (such as symmetric and/or asymmetric ciphers) are proposed for assuring secure international data exchange and transfer. Whereas in specific areas corresponding regulations exist (finance), a wider application of encryption algorithms needs to be addressed by international agreements.
2. Security services (e.g., notarization, key control) are required for a wide acceptance of computer systems for trusted use. These services need to be based on underlying security mechanisms. Only if they can be based on standardized system mechanisms are new higher level services likely to be developed.

3. Widely accepted security application interfaces need to be defined for the portability of secure applications.
4. Secure systems will only be accepted if standards and their implementations are made transparent and understood by the user community. Users' security needs need to be identified by adequate risk management tools and methods. Security features themselves as well as the available evaluation criteria need to be comparable.
5. Differing definitions of security models and policies limit the possibilities to exchange and map security data representations to each other. As an example, in X.400 Mail privacy marks such as "in confidence" and "in strictest confidence" are used as extensions to the security classification ("unclassified," etc.). These marks are not represented in the Bell–LaPadula model, which forms the basis for most mandatory security policies in operating systems.

In the course of the last decades, security has become an essential aspect of Information Technology. It sill has to become accepted as an integral part of every IT system development and application. This also needs to be reflected in the associated standards work.

REFERENCES

Overview References

Security in Computing by Charles P. Pfleeger, Prentice-Hall, Englewood Cliffs, NJ, 1989

Security in Computing is a comprehensive overview over security risks and countermeasures in the computing environment. It can serve as an introduction for the interested reader, who is searching for general advice on what to watch out for when installing and running computer systems. After having read the book, the reader should have developed an understanding for the problems involved and what can be done. The book is also useful for the computer security student with exercises and references to original papers for further study. In each chapter, the important aspects are summarized at the end and specific bibliographic notes are provided.

The book starts with the question, "Is there a security problem in computing?" Although this question has become rhetorical in recent years, the text shows the multidimensional issues associated with computer security such as hardware, software, the people involved, and the computing environment.

In Chapters 2, 3, and 4, encryption is discussed in a broad sense. After a general introduction to encryption and decryption, secure encryption systems are specified, before showing their use in protocols for securing the communication between several partners or for authentication. RSA (asymmetric cipher) and DES (symmetric cipher) are discussed in detail, adequate to their wide use.

The issues related to application programs running in a multiuser, multiprocessing environment are discussed in Chapter 4-6. It is important to note that not only technical security aspects are presented but a holistic approach is taken, which takes program development and administrative tasks into account also. In Chapter

6, well-known security models for operating systems such as information flow models or lattice models are discussed together with proven design approaches. The issues of security evaluations or evaluation methods (43) are only briefly addressed.

Chapters 8–11 explore security-related issues in the areas of database systems, personal computing, computer networks, and communication systems. Each area is covered in sufficient detail to understand the issues as well as available counter measures. For example, in the database area, the problem of information inference by exploiting statistical properties of the data stored in database records is described. Potential controls consist of information suppression, tracking of user knowledge, and data disguise.

Last but no least, physical protection, risk analysis, and security planning, as well as legal and ethical issues in computer security are discussed together with their impacts on organization and professional behavior. Because very limited technical solutions to the mentioned issues are available, computer security must be taken into account throughout the whole computer system life cycle. Organizational aspects play an important role either to complement technical provisions or for covering specific areas such as copyrights and patents.

Information Security Handbook by William Caelli, Dennis Longley, and Michael Shain, Macmillan Publishers Ltd., London, 1991

The *Information Security Handbook* is exactly what the title says: an in-depth handbook covering computer security aspects in the widest sense. The book can be split into two parts. In a first part (Chaps. 2–6) organizational aspects of computer security are discussed. The second part (Chaps. 7–11) shows the more technical-oriented approach to addressing computer security. Both aspects are necessary for assuring the security of computer systems in their application environments. Of course, an introduction to the security problem is given (Chap. 1) as well as a comprehensive index at the end of the book. References at the end of each chapter help the reader to find additional literature on a problem-specific level.

The organizational part starts with management aspects of an organization or company, which are important to address when security is an issue. Examples are responsibility, segregation of duties, or management controls. Chapter 3 describes potential computer security risks and how they can be identified and covered. Methods and tools for risk analysis are introduced. Contingency planning and damage avoidance are dealt with in Chapter 4. Such heterogeneous aspects as insurance, action plans in case of damage, or backup policies are discussed. Chapter 5 gives an overview of legal aspects of computing such as intellectual property laws, hardware and software contracts and personnel and liability issues. Finally, Chapter 6 discussed monitoring and auditing of EDP installations and organizations.

The more technical-oriented part of the *Information Security Handbook* starts with an introduction to applications and theory of cryptography. The applications sections consider aspects such as privacy, integrity, authentication, and key management, whereas the theory sections give the reader an overview of different types of ciphers (classical ciphers, stream ciphers, symmetric block ciphers, and public key ciphers) and the underlying mathematical models. In Chapter 8, the controls of access to computer systems and data are discussed, giving the reader an in-depth view of user identification and authentication techniques and devices. Operating system access controls are shown based on examples, one of them the UNIX operating system. In the chapter entitled "Security of Stored Data and Programs" database security and malicious code such as viruses and worms are covered. Chapter 10 gives an overview of security aspects in (tele)communication systems. Finally, models of computer security and their use for the security evaluation of computer systems are presented in Chapter 11.

ACKNOWLEDGMENT

The use of names or product designations, and so forth in this document do not constitute a general authorization to use such names or designations. In many cases they are legally or contractually protected names or designations even if they are not marked as such.

REFERENCES

1. V. L. Voydock and S. T. Kent, "Security Mechanisms in High-Level Network Protocols; *Computing Surveys, 15*(2), 135–171 (1983).
2. E. J. Humphreys, "Taxonomy for Security Standardisation, Version 2.0," ITAEGV Document N69, XISEC Consultants Ltd., Ipswich U.K. (April 1992).
3. J. P. L. Woodward, "Security Requirements for System High and Compartmented Mode Workstation," MITRE Corp., Bedford, MA, Report MTR 9992, Rev. 1, November 1987 (= DRS-2600-5502-87, Defense Intelligence Agency).
4. "Trusted Network Interpretation of the Trusted Computer System Evaluation Criteria," NCSC-TG-005, NCSC, Fort Meade, MD (July 1987).
5. "Trusted Database Management System Interpretation (of the Trusted Computer System Evaluation Criteria," NCSC-TG-021, Version-1, NCSC, Fort Meade, MD (April 1991).
6. *IT Evaluationshandbuch; 1. Fassung vom 22. Februar 1990*, German Information Security Agency Bundesanzeiger Verlagsgesellschaft mbH., Köln, Germany, 1990.
7. *Information Technology Security Evaluation Criteria (ITSEC) – Provisional Harmonized Criteria, Version 1.2*, Commission of the European Communities, Brussels, 1991.
8. *Minimum Security Functionality Requirements for Multiuser Operating Systems; Issue 1, January 16, 1992*, National Institute of Standards and Technology, Gaithersburg, MD, 1992.
9. *Federal Criteria for Information Technology Security, Vols. I/II, Version 1.0*, NIST/NSA, Gaithersburg, MD, 1992.
10. C. Corbett, "ITSEC in Operation – An Evaluation Experience", *Proceedings of 1992 Annual Canadian Computer Security Conference.*
11. *UNIX System Security*, UNIX System Laboratories, Summit NJ, 1990.
12. P. H. Wood and S. G. Kochan, *UNIX System Security*, Hayden Books, Indianapolis, IN, 1985.
13. M. Reitenspiess and G. Spies, "SINIX Security – Today and the Future," in *Proceedings of Italian UNIX Users Group Conference*, May 1991.
14. R. Elliott, "POSIX Security Interfaces," in *Proceedings of Technologie Transparent – Sicherheit in Rechnersystemen*, December 1989.
15. Draft Security Interface for the Portable Operating System Interface for Computer Environments; P1003.6 Draft 11 = ISO/IEC JTC1/SC22 WG15 NO46R1; IEEE, New York, May 1991.

16. *X/Open Security Guide*, Prentice-Hall, Inc., Englewood Cliffs, NJ, 1988.
17. *X/OPEN Guide: Defining and Buying Secure Open Systems* X/Open Ltd, U.K., 1992
18. J. L. Berger, J. Picciotto, H. P. L. Woodward, P. T. Cummings, "Compartmented Mode Workstation: Prototype Highlights", *IEEE Trans. Software Eng. 16*(6), 608–618 (1990).
19. P. T. Cummings, D. A. Fullam, M. J. Goldstein, M. J. Gosselin, and J. Picciotto, "Compartmented Mode Workstation: Results Through Prototyping," in *Proceedings of 1987 IEEE Symposium on Security and Privacy*, 1987, pp. 2–12.
20. J. P. L. Woodward, "Exploiting the Dual Nature of Sensitivity Labels," in *Proceedings of 1987 IEEE Symposium on Security and Privacy*, 1987, pp. 23–31.
21. S. G. Kochan and P. H. Wood, *UNIX Networking*, Hayden Books, Carmel, IN, 1989.
22. S. Kent, "DoD Security Options for the Internet Protocol," RFC 1108 (December 1990).
23. M. St. Johns, "Draft Revised IP Security Option," RFC 1038 (January 1988).
24. R. L. Sharp and B. K. Yasaki, "A Multi-Level Secure TCP/IP", AT&T Bell Laboratories, Whippany, NJ (1990).
25. SecureWare, Inc., *MaxSix: The Trusted Network Component of Project Max*, SecureWare Inc., Atlanta, GA, 1990.
26. SecureWare Inc., *DNSIX, MaxSix, and Trusted Sockets, Rev. B*, SecureWare Inc., Atlanta, GA, 1991.
27. L. J. LaPadula, J. E. LeMoine, D. F. Vukelich, and J. P. L. Woodward, "DNSIX Detailed Design Specification, Version 2," MTR 10704 MITRE, Bedford, MA (April 1990).
28. Defense Intelligence Agency, *DNSIX Detailed Design Specification Version 2.1 (Final)*, Defense Intelligence Agency, Washington, DC, 1991.
29. L. J. LaPadula, J. E. LeMoine, D. F. Vukelich, J. L. Berger, and J. P. L. Woodward, "DNSIX Detailed Interface Specifications, Version 2," MITRE, Bedford, MA (April 1990).
30. Defense Intelligence Agency, *DNSIX Interface Specifications Version 2.1* (Final), Defense Intelligence Agency, Washington, DC, 1991.
31. J. Linn, "Generic Security Service Application Program Interface", Internet Draft; Common Authentication Technology WG (June 1991).
32. *X/Open Preliminary Specification: Generic Security Service API (GSS-API) Base*, X/Open Ltd, U.K., 1994.
33. *X/Open Snapshot: Generic Security Services API (GSS-API) Security Attributed and Delegation Extensions*, X/Open Ltd, U.K., 1994.
34. W. Fumy and H. P. Riess, "Network Security Management," in *Proceedings of IWACA'92*, 1992, pp. 139–146.
35. K. L. Barker and K. E. Kirkpatrick, "The SILS Model for LAN Security," in *Proceedings of 12th National Computer Security Conference*, 1989, pp. 267–276.
36. J. G. Steiner, C. Neuman, and J. I. Schiller, "Kerberos: An Authentication Service for Open Network Systems," in *Proceedings of the Winter USENIX Conference*, 1988.
37. E. Balkovich, S. R. Lerman, and R. P. Parmelee, "Computing in Higher Education: The Athena Experience," *Commun. ACM, 28*(11), 1214–1224 (1985).
38. T. A. Parker, "A Secure European System for Applications in a Multi-vendor Environment (The SESAME Project)", in *Proceedings of 1991 National Computer Security Conference*, October 1991.
39. J. N. Pato, "DCE Authorization Services, Privilege Server," OSF DCE Specifications, 1990.
40. J. J. Tardo and K. Alagappan, "SPX: Global Authentication Using Public Key Certificates," in *Proceedings of 1991 IEEE Symposium on Security and Privacy*, 1991.
41. Ch. Kaufman, "DASS—Distributed Authentication Security Service," Internet Draft, Networking Group (October 1991).

42. M. Reitenspiess, "Open System Security Standards," *Computers & Security, 12*, 341–361 (1993).

43. *Information Technology Security Evaluation Manual (ITSEM)*, Commission of the European Communities, Brussels, 1993.

References to Standards Documents

ANSI X3.106-1983: Modes of Operation for the Data Encryption Algorithm, 1983.

CCITT X.400 Series of Recommendations: Message Handling Systems, 1988.

CCITT X.500 Series of Recommendations: The Directory, 1990 (= ISO/IEC 9594).

DoD 5200.28-Std: DoD Trusted Computer System Evaluation Criteria (Orange Book), 1985.

ECMA TR/46: Security in Open Systems — A Security Framework, 1988.

ECMA-138: Security in Open Systems — Data Elements and Service Definitions, 1989.

FIPS Publication 46: Data Encryption Standard (DES), 1977.

FIPS Publication 81: DES Modes of Operation, 1980.

FIPS Publication 180: Secure Hash Standard (SHS), 1993.

FIPS Publication 185: Escrowed Encryption Standard (EES), 1994.

FIPS Publication 186: Digital Signature Standard (DSS), 1994.

IEEE 802.10: Interoperable Local Area Network (LAN) Security (SILS)

> Part A — Overview and Model; Draft.
> Part B — Secure Data Exchange Protocol (SDE); IEEE Press, 1992.
> Part C — Key Management Protocol; Draft.
> Part D — Security Management; Draft.
> Part E — Secure Data Exchange of Ethernet V2.0 in 802 LANs; Draft Standard, 1993.
> Part F — Secure Data Exchange (SDE) Sublayer Management; Draft Standard, 1993.

ISO/IEC 7498: Open Systems Interconnection — Basic Reference Model, 1983.

ISO/IEC 7498-2: Open Systems Interconnection — Basic Reference Model — Part 2: Security Architecture, 1988.

ISO/IEC 8073: Open Systems Interconnection — Transport Protocol Definition, 1992.

ISO/IEC 8372: Modes of Operation for a 64-Bit Block Cipher Algorithm, 1987.

ISO/IEC 8473: Open Systems Interconnection — Protocol for Providing the Connectionless-mode Network Service, 1992 (= ITU-T Recommendation X.233).

ISO/IEC 9594-1: Open Systems Interconnection — The Directory — Models, 1990 (= CCITT Recommendation X.501).

ISO/IEC 9594-8: Open Systems Interconnection — The Directory — Authentication Framework, 1990 (= CCITT Recommendation X.509).

ISO/IEC 9796: Digital signature scheme giving message recovery, 1991.

ISO/IEC 9797: Data integrity mechanism using a cryptographic check function employing a block cipher algorithm, 1994.

ISO/IEC 9798-1: Entity authentication — Part 1: General model, 1991.

ISO/IEC 9798-2: Entity authentication — Part 2: Mechanisms using symmetric encipherment algorithms, 1994.

ISO/IEC 9798-3: Entity authentication—Part 3: Entity authentication using a public key algorithm, 1993.

ISO/IEC DIS 9798-4: Entity authentication—Part 4: Mechanisms using a cryptographic check function, 1994.

ISO/IEC 9979: Procedures for the registration of cryptographic algorithms, 1991.

ISO/IEC 10116: Modes of operation for an n-bit block cipher algorithm, 1991.

ISO/IEC 10118-1: Hash-functions—Part 1: General, 1994.

ISO/IEC 10118-2: Hash-functions—Part 2: Hash-functions using an n-bit block cipher algorithm, 1994.

ISO/IEC 10164-7: OSI systems management—Part 7: Security alarm reporting function, 1992.

ISO/IEC 10164-8: OSI systems management—Part 8: Security audit trail function, 1993.

ISO/IEC DIS 10164-9: OSI systems management—Part 9: Objects and attributes for access control, 1993.

ISO/IEC 10165-2: Structure of Management Information, 1992.

ISO/IEC CD 10181-1: Security Frameworks in Open Systems—Part 1: Security Frameworks Overview, 1994.

ISO/IEC DIS 10181-2: Security Frameworks in Open Systems—Part 2: Authentication Framework, 1993.

ISO/IEC DIS 10181-3: Security Frameworks in Open Systems—Part 3: Access Control Framework, 1994.

ISO/IEC DIS 10181-4: Security Frameworks in Open Systems—Part 4: Non-Repudiation Framework, 1994.

ISO/IEC CD 10181-5: Security Frameworks in Open Systems—Part 5: Confidentiality Framework, 1993.

ISO/IEC CD 10181-6: Security Frameworks in Open Systems—Part 6: Integrity Framework, 1993.

ISO/IEC CD 10181-7: Security Frameworks in Open Systems—Part 7: Security Audit Framework, 1993.

ISO/IEC 10736: Transport Layer Security Protocol, 1994 (= ITU-T Recommendation X.274).

ISO/IEC 10745: Upper Layers Security Model, 1993 (= ITU-T Recommendation X.803).

ISO/IEC 11577: Network Layer Security Protocol, 1994 (= ITU-T Recommendation X.273).

ISO/IEC DIS 11586-1: Generic Upper Layers Security—Part 1: Overview, Models and Notation, 1993.

ISO/IEC DIS 11586-2: Generic Upper Layers Security—Part 2: Security Exchange Service Element Service Definition, 1993.

ISO/IEC DIS 11586-3: Generic Upper Layers Security—Part 3: Security Exchange Service Element Protocol Specification, 1993.

ISO/IEC DIS 11586-4: Generic Upper Layers Security—Part 4: Protecting Transfer Syntax Specification, 1993.

ISO/IEC CD 11770-1: Key management—Part 1: Key management framework, 1994.

ISO/IEC CD 11770-2: Key management—Part 2: Mechanisms using symmetric techniques, 1994.

ISO/IEC 11770-3: Key management — Part 3: Mechanisms using asymmetric techniques, 1994.

ISO/IEC TR 13594: Lower Layers Security Model, 1994 (= ITU-T Recommendation X.802).

ISO/IEC CD 13888-2: Non-repudiation — Part 2: Using symmetric encipherment algorithms, 1994.

RFC 1411: Telnet Authentication: Kerberos Version 4.

RFC 1416: Telnet Authentication Option.

RFC 1421: Privacy Enhancement for Internet Electronic Mail; Part I: Message Encryption and Authentication Procedures.

RFC 1422: Privacy Enhancement for Internet Electronic Mail; Part II: Certificate-Based Key Management.

RFC 1423: Privacy Enhancement for Internet Electronic Mail; Part III: Algorithms, Modes and Identifiers.

RFC 1424: Privacy Enhancement for Internet Electronic Mail; Part IV: Key Certification and Related Services.

RFC 1508: Generic Security Service, Application Program Interface.

RFC 1509: Generic Security Service, API: C-bindings.

RFC 1510: The Kerberos Network Authentication Service.

SDNS SDN.301: Security Protocol 3 (SP3), 1989.

SDNS SDN.401: Security Protocol 4 (SP4), 1989.

SDNS SDN.601: Key Management Profile — Communication Protocol Requirements for Support of the SDNS Key Management Protocol, 1989.

SDNS SDN.701: Message Security Protocol, 1989.

SDNS SDN.702: SDNS Directory Specifications for Utilization with the SDNS Message Security Protocol, 1989.

SDNS SDN.801: Access Control Concepts Document, 1989.

SDNS SDN.802: Access Control Specification, 1989.

SDNS SDN.902: Key Management Protocol — Definition of Services Provided by the Key Management Application Service Element, 1989.

SDNS SDN.903: Key Management Protocol — Specification of the Protocol for Services Provided by the Key Management Application Service Element, 1989.

SDNS SDN.906: Key Management Protocol — SDNS Traffic Key Attribute Negotiation, 1989.

XP63: Portability Guide, Issue 3, X/Open Publication T921, 1989.

XP64: Five Volume Set, X/Open Publications, T906, 1992.

WALTER FUMY

MANFRED REITENSPIESS

PARALLEL RENDERING

INTRODUCTION

In computer graphics, *rendering* is the process by which an abstract description of a scene is converted to an image. Figure 1 illustrates the basic problem. For purposes of this discussion, a scene is a collection of geometrically defined objects in three-dimensional *object space*, with associated lighting and viewing parameters. The rendering operation illuminates the objects and projects them into two-dimensional *image space*, where color intensities of individual pixels are computed to yield a final image.

For complex scenes or high-quality images, the rendering process is computationally intensive, requiring millions or billions of floating-point and integer operations for each image. The need for interactive or real-time response in many applications places additional demands on processing power. The only practical way to obtain the needed computational power is to exploit multiple processing units to speed up the rendering task, a concept which has become known as *parallel rendering*.

Historical Perspective

The incorporation of parallelism into rendering systems has been an evolutionary process, with its origins in the early days of computer graphics. The pioneering Graphic 1 display system developed at Bell Telephone Laboratories in the early 1960s used its own internal processor to drive the display and handle user interactions, allowing it to operate independently of its mainframe host (1). In 1968, Myer and Sutherland (2) examined the allocation of graphics functionality in a multiprocessor configuration composed of a host computer, display processor, and display channel.* They discussed the advantages and disadvantages of using shared memory to communicate between the central processor and the display subsystem, and they noted a trend toward increasingly complex display architectures.

During this same time period, more sophisticated graphics hardware began to appear, incorporating multiple function units and low-level parallelism in the form of simultaneous logic operations. Sproull and Sutherland's classic "clipping divider" provides a modest example (3). The demands and budgets of real-time flight simulation prompted more ambitious designs, including one by Schumacker et al. for the U.S. Air Force (4). That architecture included multiple processors and a variety of

---

*The concept of *channels* was common in mainframe systems from the 1960s and 1970s. Channels are essentially specialized coprocessors used to offload I/O tasks from the central processing unit.

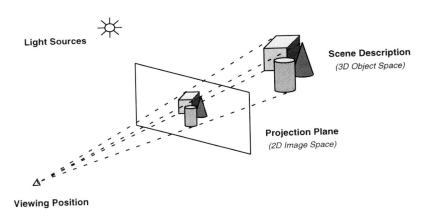

Light Sources

Scene Description
(3D Object Space)

Projection Plane
(2D Image Space)

Viewing Position

FIGURE 1   The generic rendering problem. A three-dimensional scene is projected onto an image plane, taking into account viewing parameters and light sources.

specialized function units organized into three distinct rendering subsystems, one for terrain, one for objects, and a third for point source lights.

During the 1970s, real-time flight simulation continued as a primary driver of high-performance graphics systems. By the end of the decade, these systems routinely incorporated modest levels of parallelism (5), but they were highly specialized and very expensive, making them ill-suited for more general rendering tasks.

The introduction of very large scale integrated circuits (VLSI) in the late 1970s and early 1980s marked an important turning point in the development of computer graphics architectures. The availability of compact, low-cost processors and high-capacity memory chips made high-performance systems practical for general-purpose use. The relative simplicity of constructing systems by replicating off-the-shelf components encouraged additional experimentation with parallel architectures. Early designs based on this new hardware paradigm included z-buffered scan conversion systems by Fuchs and Johnson (6,7) and Parke (8), and a pipelined polygon rendering architecture by Clark (9,10).

During the 1980s, the use of multiple special-purpose hardware units became the standard approach for achieving high rendering rates in graphics accelerators, graphics workstations, and specialized graphics computers. The advent of "massively" parallel computer systems, containing from tens to thousands of generic processing elements, added a new dimension to parallel rendering, promising added flexibility, but raising numerous algorithmic and efficiency issues for software-based parallel renderers.

Organization

In the remainder of our discussion, we assume a passing familiarity with the basic principles and terminology of computer graphics. Parallel processing concepts are presented at a somewhat more introductory level. We begin our examination of parallel rendering in the second section with a brief overview of the applications to which it has most commonly been applied. Specific application areas will be addressed in more detail in the context of subsequent sections. The third section explores different types of parallelism and how they relate to the rendering problem. The fourth section introduces a number of concepts which are central to an understanding of parallel rendering algorithms. Building on this base, the fifth section considers design and implementation issues for parallel renderers, with an emphasis on architectural considerations and application requirements. Throughout the third, fourth, and fifth sections, we illustrate our discussion with examples from the parallel rendering literature, encompassing both hardware and software systems. The last section completes our survey of parallel rendering systems with an examination of several parallel hardware architectures as well as radiosity and terrain rendering methods.

APPLICATIONS OF PARALLEL RENDERING

Parallel techniques are appropriate whenever rendering performance is an issue. Demanding applications such as real-time simulation, animation, virtual reality, photo-realistic imaging, and scientific visualization all benefit from the use of parallelism to increase rendering performance. Indeed, these applications have been primary motivators in the development of parallel rendering methods. Parallel rendering has been applied to virtually every image-generation technique used in computer graphics, including surface and polygon rendering, terrain rendering, volume rendering, ray tracing, and radiosity. Although the requirements and approaches vary for each of these cases, there are a number of concepts which are important in understanding how parallelism applies to the generic rendering problem. We consider these in the third and fourth sections.

PARALLELISM IN THE RENDERING PROCESS

Several different types of parallelism can be applied in the rendering process. These include *functional parallelism*, *data parallelism*, and *temporal parallelism*. Some are more appropriate to specific applications or specific rendering methods, whereas others have broader applicability. The basic types can also be combined into hybrid systems which exploit multiple forms of parallelism. Each of these options is discussed below.

Functional Parallelism

One way to obtain parallelism is to split the rendering process into several distinct functions which can be applied in series to individual data items. If a processing unit is assigned to each function (or group of functions) and a data path is provided from one unit to the next, a rendering *pipeline* is formed (Fig. 2). As a processing unit completes work on one data item, it forwards it to the next unit and receives a new item from its upstream neighbor. Once the pipeline is filled, the degree of parallelism achieved is proportional to the number of functional units.

 The functional approach works especially well for polygon and surface rendering applications, where three-dimensional (3D) geometric primitives are fed into the beginning of the pipe, and final pixel values are produced at the end. This approach

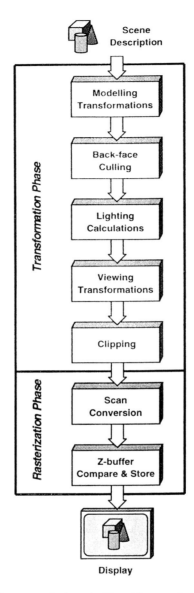

FIGURE 2   A typical polygon rendering pipeline. The number of function units and their order varies depending on details of the implementation.

has been mapped very successfully into the special-purpose rendering hardware used in a variety of commercial computer graphics workstations produced during the 1980s and 1990s. The archetypal example is Clark's Geometry System (9,10), which replicated a custom VLSI geometry processor in a 12-stage pipeline to perform transformation and clipping operations in two and three dimensions.

Despite its success, the functional approach has two significant limitations.

First, the overall speed of the pipeline is limited by its slowest stage, so functional units must be designed carefully to avoid bottlenecks. More importantly, the available parallelism is limited to the number of stages in the pipeline. To achieve higher levels of performance, an alternate strategy is needed.

Data Parallelism

Instead of performing a sequence of rendering functions on a single data stream, it may be preferable to split the data into multiple streams and operate on several items simultaneously by replicating a number of identical rendering units (Fig. 3). The parallelism achievable with this approach is not limited by the number of stages in the rendering pipeline, but rather by economic and technical constraints on the number of processing units which can be incorporated into a single system. Of particular importance is the communication network which routes data among the processing units. As we will see in subsequent sections, the characteristics of the communication network have a significant influence on the choice of rendering algorithms, and vice versa.

Because the data-parallel approach can take advantage of larger numbers of processors, it has been adopted in one form or another by most of the software renderers which have been developed for general-purpose "massively parallel" systems. Data parallelism also lends itself to scalable implementations, allowing the number of processing elements to be varied depending on factors such as scene complexity, image resolution, or desired performance levels.

Two principal classes of data parallelism can be identified in the rendering process. *Object parallelism* refers to operations which are performed independently on the geometric primitives which comprise objects in a scene. These operations constitute the first few stages of the rendering pipeline (Fig. 2), including modeling and viewing transformations, lighting computations, and clipping. *Image parallelism* occurs in the later stages of the rendering pipeline and includes the operations used to compute individual pixel values. Pixel computations vary depending on the rendering method in use but may include illumination, interpolation, composition, and visibility determination. Collectively, we call the object-level stages of the pipeline the *transformation phase*; the image-level stages are grouped together to form the *rasterization phase*.

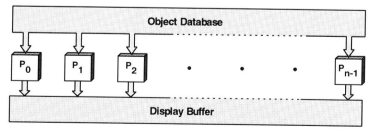

FIGURE 3   A data-parallel rendering system. Multiple data items are processed simultaneously and the results are merged to create the final image.

Potential levels of data parallelism can be quite high. The number of geometric primitives in a scene typically ranges from a few hundred to a few million. The number of pixel values to be computed may range from thousands to hundreds of millions, depending on image resolution, sampling frequency, and depth complexity of the scene. In practice, geometric primitives and pixels are usually processed in groups to take advantage of more efficient algorithms and to reduce communication requirements, but the available parallelism normally exceeds the number of processing elements by a large factor.

To avoid bottlenecks, most data-parallel rendering systems must exploit both object and image parallelism. Obtaining the proper balance between these two phases of the computation is difficult, as the workloads involved at each level are highly dependent on factors such as the scene complexity, average screen area of transformed geometric primitives, sampling ratio, and image resolution. One approach is to define performance targets for each phase and construct the system to meet those goals. This approach is generally preferred when separate hardware will be dedicated to object and image computations. In systems where the object and image computations are performed using the same processing units, performance targets must be based on the combined workloads. In either case, load balancing is important in assuring efficient utilization of the hardware.

Temporal Parallelism

In animation applications, where hundreds or thousands of high-quality images must be produced for subsequent playback, the time to render individual frames may not be as important as the overall time required to render all of them. In this case, parallelism may be obtained by decomposing the problem in the time domain. The fundamental unit of work is a complete image, and each processor is assigned a number of frames to render, along with the data needed to produce those frames.

Hybrid Approaches

It is certainly possible to incorporate multiple forms of parallelism in a single system. For example, the functional- and data-parallel approaches may be combined by replicating all or part of the rendering pipeline (Fig. 4). An early example of this approach is the LINKS-1 system (11), which contained 64 identical microcomputers which could be dynamically reconfigured into multiple pipelines of varying depth. A more recent example is Silicon Graphics' RealityEngine (12), which uses multiple transformation and rasterization units in a highly pipelined architecture to achieve rendering rates on the order of one million polygons per second. In similar fashion, temporal parallelism may be combined with the other strategies to produce systems with the potential for extremely high aggregate performance.

ALGORITHMIC CONCEPTS

The design of effective parallel rendering algorithms can be a challenging task. In some cases, existing sequential algorithms have straightforward parallel decompositions. In other cases, new algorithms must be developed from scratch. Whatever their origin, most parallel algorithms introduce overheads which are not present in

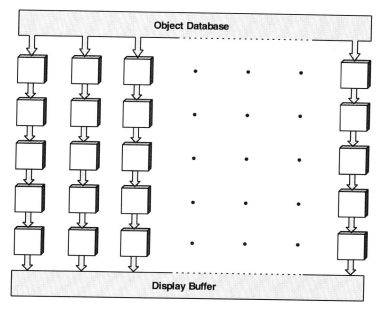

FIGURE 4 A hybrid rendering architecture. Functional parallelism and data parallelism are both exploited to achieve higher performance.

their sequential counterparts. These overheads may result from some or all of the following:

- Communication among tasks or processors
- Delays due to uneven workloads
- Additional or redundant computations
- Increased storage requirements for replicated or auxiliary data structures

To understand how these overheads arise in parallel rendering algorithms, we need to examine several key concepts. Some of these concepts (task and data decomposition, granularity, scalability, and load balancing) are common to most parallel algorithms, whereas others (coherence and object-space to image-space data mapping) are specific to the rendering problem. Each of these topics is considered in detail in the remainder of this section.

Embarrassingly Parallel Algorithms

Some problems can be parallelized trivially, requiring little or no interprocessor communication, and with no significant computational overheads attributable to the parallel algorithm. Such applications are said to be *embarrassingly parallel*, and efficient operation can be expected on a variety of platforms, ranging from networks of personal computers or graphics workstations up to massively parallel supercomputers. Rendering algorithms which exploit temporal parallelism typically fall into this category.

Rendering methods based on ray casting (such as ray tracing and direct volume rendering) also have embarrassingly parallel implementations in certain circumstances. Because pixel values are computed by shooting rays from each pixel into the scene, image-parallel task decompositions are very natural for these problems. If every processor has fast access to the entire object database, then each ray can be processed independently with no interprocessor communication required. This approach is practical for shared-memory architectures and also performs well on distributed-memory systems when sufficient memory is available to replicate the object database on every processor.

Coherence

In computer graphics, *coherence* refers to the tendency for features which are nearby in space or time to have similar properties (13). Many fundamental algorithms in the field rely on coherence in one form or another to reduce computational requirements. Coherence is important to parallel rendering in two ways. First, parallel algorithms which fail to preserve coherence will incur computational overheads which may not be present in equivalent sequential algorithms. Second, parallel algorithms may be able to exploit coherence to reduce communication costs or improve load balance.

Several types of coherence are important in parallel rendering. *Frame coherence* is the tendency of objects, and hence resulting pixel values, to move or change shape or color slowly from one image to the next in a related sequence of frames. This property can be used to advantage in load balancing and image display, as we will discuss in subsequent sections.

Scanline coherence refers to the similarity of pixel values from one scanline to the next in the vertical direction. The corresponding property in the horizontal direction is called *span coherence*, which refers to the similarity of nearby pixel values within a scanline (Fig. 5). Sequential rasterization algorithms rely on these

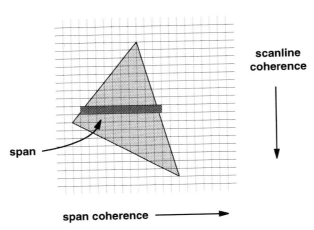

FIGURE 5   Spatial coherence in image space. Pixel values tend to be similar from one scanline to the next, and from pixel within spans. Sequential rendering algorithms exploit this property to reduce computation costs during scan conversion.

two forms of *spatial coherence* for efficient interpolation of pixel values between the vertices of geometric primitives. When an image is partitioned to exploit image parallelism, coherence may be lost at partition boundaries, resulting in computational overheads. The probability that a primitive will intersect a boundary depends on the size, shape, and number of image partitions (14,15), and hence is an important consideration in the design of parallel polygon renderers (16).

A related notion in ray-casting renderers* is *data* or *ray coherence*. This is the tendency for rays cast through nearby pixels to intersect the same objects in a scene. Ray coherence has been exploited in conjunction with data-caching schemes to reduce communication loads in parallel volume rendering and ray-tracing algorithms (17,18).

Task and Data Decomposition

Data-parallel rendering algorithms may be further distinguished based on the way in which the problem is decomposed into individual workloads or tasks. As work is essentially defined as "operations on data," the choice of task decomposition has a direct impact on data access patterns. On distributed-memory architectures, where remote memory references are usually much more expensive than local memory references, the issues of task decomposition and data distribution are inseparable. Shared-memory systems offer more flexibility, because all processors have equal access to the data. Although data locality is still important in achieving good caching performance, the penalties for global memory references tend to be less severe, and static assignment of data to processors is not generally required.

There are two main strategies for task decomposition. In an *object-parallel* approach, tasks are formed by partitioning either the geometric description of the scene or the associated object space. Rendering operations are then applied in parallel to subsets of the geometric data, producing pixel values which must then be integrated into a final image. In contrast, *image-parallel* algorithms reverse this mapping. Tasks are formed by partitioning the image space, and each task renders the geometric primitives which contribute to the pixels which it has been assigned.

The choice of image-parallel versus object-parallel algorithms is not clear-cut. Object-parallel algorithms tend to distribute object computations evenly among processors, but because geometric primitives usually vary in size, rasterization loads may be uneven. Furthermore, primitives assigned to different processors may map to the same location in the image, requiring the individual contributions to be integrated to produce the final image. With large numbers of processors, this integration step can place heavy bandwidth demands on memory buses or communication networks.

Image-parallel algorithms avoid the integration step but have another problem: Portions of a single geometric primitive may map to several different regions in the image space. This requires that primitives, or portions of them, be communicated to multiple processors, and the corresponding loss of spatial coherence results

---

*We use the term *ray casting* to include all rendering methods which project rays from the viewpoint through screen pixels into the scene. This encompasses both traditional ray-tracing algorithms as well as a large class of volume rendering methods.

in additional or redundant computations which are not present in equivalent sequential algorithms.

To achieve a better balance among the various overheads, some algorithms adopt a hybrid approach, incorporating features of both object- and image-parallel methods (16,19–21). These techniques partition both the object and image spaces, breaking the rendering pipeline in the middle and communicating intermediate results from object rendering tasks to image rendering tasks.

Granularity

Related to the concept of task and data decomposition is the notion of *granularity*. Granularity refers to the amount of computation in a basic unit of work. This workload unit may be defined to be an entire task, or perhaps some smaller quantum, such as the number of instructions executed between communication events. A computation is *fine grained* if workload units are small, or *coarse grained* if they involve substantial processing. Granularity may also refer to data decompositions. A fine-grained decomposition includes one or a few data items in each partition, whereas a coarse-grained decomposition uses larger blocks of data. In a rendering context, a fine-grained task might compute the value of a single pixel, whereas a coarse-grained task might compute an entire frame in an animation sequence.

Granularity often has a direct bearing on the efficiency of a parallel computation. Fine-grained computations generally incur more overhead for task scheduling and communication but offer the possibility of more precise load balancing. Coarse-grained computations tend to minimize communication and scheduling overheads, but they are more susceptible to load imbalances and impose tighter limits on the amount of available parallelism.

Granularity considerations are inseparably linked to performance parameters of the target architecture. For example, fine-grained algorithms are not well suited to systems which have high overheads for task scheduling and communication, such as workstation networks. On the other hand, a coarse-grained algorithm could not be expected to map well onto a Single Instruction Multiple Data (SIMD) architecture composed of thousands of simple processing elements. A further discussion of SIMD versus MIMD (Multiple Instruction Multiple Data) architectures can be found in the fifth section.

Scalability

Scalability of a parallel system refers to the ability to provide additional capacity by increasing the number of processing elements. Two distinct types of scalability are important in parallel rendering. *Performance scalability* is the ability to achieve higher levels of performance on a fixed-size problem. *Data scalability* is the ability to accommodate larger problem sizes, for example, more complex scenes or higher image resolutions.

Scalability considerations apply to both hardware architectures and software rendering algorithms. Either may have bottlenecks which limit the performance levels which can be achieved or the problem sizes which can be addressed. An important consideration in designing a parallel renderer is to ensure that the architecture and algorithms will scale to the levels desired.

Although traditional shared-memory systems offer the potential for low-overhead parallel rendering, their performance scalability is limited by contention on the buses or switch networks which connect processors to memory. Adding processors does not increase the memory bandwidth, so at some point the paths to memory become saturated, and performance stalls. For this reason, most parallel architectures which are intended to scale to hundreds or thousands of processing elements employ a distributed-memory model, in which each processor is tightly coupled to a local memory. The combined processor/memory elements are then interconnected by a relatively scalable network or switch. The advantage is that processing power and aggregate local memory bandwidth scale linearly with the number of hardware units in the system. The disadvantage is that references to nonlocal data may be several orders of magnitude slower than references to local data.

A number of recent systems combine elements of both architectures, using physically distributed memories which are mapped into a global shared address space (22–24). The shared address space permits the use of concise shared-memory programming paradigms and is amenable to hardware support for remote memory references. The result is that communication overheads can be significantly lower than those found in traditional message-passing systems, allowing algorithms with fine-grained communication requirements to scale to larger numbers of processors.

Load Balancing

In any parallel computing system, effective processor utilization depends on distributing the workload evenly across the system. In parallel rendering, there are many factors which make this goal difficult to achieve. Consider a data-parallel polygon renderer which attempts to balance workloads by distributing geometric primitives evenly among all of the processors. First, polygons may have varying numbers of vertices, resulting in differing operation counts for illumination and transformation operations. If back-face culling is enabled, different processors may discard different numbers of polygons, and the subsequent clipping step may introduce further variations. The sizes of the transformed screen primitives will also vary, resulting in differing operation counts in the rasterization routines. Depending on the method being used, hidden surface elimination will also produce variations in the number of polygons to be rasterized or the number of pixels to be stored in the frame buffer.

Although this list may seem intimidating, we observe that if the number of input primitives is large (as it usually is) and the primitives are randomly assigned to processors, the workload variations described above will tend to even out. Unfortunately, a much more serious source of load imbalance arises due to another factor: In real scenes, the distribution of primitives in image space is not uniform but tends to cluster in areas of detail. Thus, processors responsible for rasterizing dense regions of the image will have significantly more work to do than other processors which may end up with nothing more than background pixels. To make matters worse, the mapping from object space to image space is view dependent, which means the distribution of primitives in the image is subject to change from one frame to the next, especially in interactive applications.

Static Schemes

Strategies for dealing with this image-space load imbalance may be classified as either *static* or *dynamic*. Static load balancing techniques rely on a fixed data partitioning to distribute local variations across large numbers of processors. Figure 6 shows several different image partitioning strategies with different load balancing characteristics. Large blocks of contiguous pixels (Fig. 6a) usually result in poor load balancing, whereas fine-grained partitioning schemes (Fig. 6 c,d) distribute the load better. However, fine-grained schemes are subject to computational overheads due to loss of spatial coherence, as discussed above. Analytical and experimental results (15,25) indicate that square regions (Fig. 6b) minimize the loss of coherence because they have the smallest perimeter-to-area ratio of any rectangular subdivision scheme.

Dynamic Schemes

Dynamic load balancing schemes try to improve on static techniques by providing more flexibility in assigning workloads to processors. There are two principal strategies. The *demand-driven* approach decomposes the problem into a large number of independent tasks, which are then assigned to processors one-at-a-time or in small groups. When a processor completes one task, it receives another, and the process continues until all of the tasks are complete. If tasks exhibit large variations in run time, the most expensive ones must be started early so that they will have time to complete while other processors are still busy with shorter tasks. Failure to observe this rule results in poor load balancing as processors become idle waiting for long tasks to complete. Run-time estimates for tasks are usually computed heuristically in a preprocessing step, which introduces a computational overhead. The alternative is to use large numbers of fine-grained tasks in order to minimize potential varia-

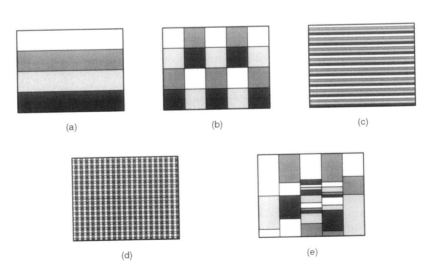

FIGURE 6   Image partitioning strategies. Shading indicates the assignment of image regions to four processors. (a) Blocks of contiguous scanlines; (b) square regions; (c) interleaved scanlines; (d) pixel interleaving in two dimensions; (e) adaptive partitioning (loosely based on Ref. 26).

tions, but this approach suffers increased overheads due to loss of coherence and more frequent task assignment operations.

The alternate *adaptive* strategy tries to minimize preprocessing overheads by deferring task partitioning decisions until one or more processors becomes idle, at which time the remaining workloads of busy processors are split and reassigned to idle processors. The result is that data partitioning is not predetermined, but instead adapts to the computational load (Fig. 6e). A good example is Whitman's image-parallel polygon renderer for the BBN TC2000 (26). Whitman's renderer initially partitions the image space into a relatively small number of coarse-grained tasks, which are then assigned to processors using the demand-driven model. When a processor becomes idle and no more tasks are available from the initial pool, it searches for the processor with the largest remaining workload and "steals" half of its work. The principal overheads in the adaptive approach arise in maintaining and retrieving nonlocal status information, partitioning tasks, and migrating data.

Although dynamic schemes offer the potential for more precise load balancing than static schemes, they are successful only when the improvements in processor utilization exceed the overhead costs. For this reason, dynamic schemes are easiest to implement on architectures which provide low-latency access to shared memory. In message-passing systems, the high cost of remote memory references makes dynamic task assignment, data migration, and maintenance of global status information more expensive, especially for fine-grained tasks. Ellsworth (16) attempted to overcome this limitation by employing an *interframe* load balancing scheme on Intel's Touchstone Delta system. Rather than trying to balance the load within a single frame of an image sequence (the *intraframe* approach), his renderer uses the workload distribution from one frame to reassign image regions for the next frame. This strategy assumes that the distribution of geometric primitives will be similar in consecutive images, an example of frame coherence. The advantage of this approach is that load balancing is performed at a higher level of granularity, with less overhead. Nonetheless, Ellsworth's experiments indicate that this technique was only partially successful, encountering scalability problems in obtaining global workload information for large numbers of processors.

Load Balancing for Ray-Casting Renderers

Although the above discussion is set in the context of polygon rendering algorithms, similar considerations apply for other rendering techniques. In ray-cast volume rendering, for example, the viewing angle, distribution of features within the volume, and optimizations such as early ray termination all contribute to workload imbalances. Nieh and Levoy use a demand-driven scheme in an image-parallel volume renderer for the Stanford DASH Multiprocessor (27). Their strategy uses an initial coarse-grained static partitioning of the image, with dynamic reassignment of subtasks based on a finer-grained second-level partitioning.

In ray tracing, the majority of the execution time is used to compute the intersections of rays with objects in the scene. Load imbalances arise because the cost of calculating ray–object intersections and evaluating secondary rays varies depending on the type and distribution of objects within the scene. Caspary and Scherson (28) and Salmon and Goldsmith (20) independently developed an innovative load balancing scheme for ray tracing on distributed-memory MIMD architectures. The method begins by organizing the object data as a hierarchical tree of bounding volumes, a well-known technique employed by sequential ray tracers to reduce the search space for intersection testing. The basic idea in the parallel implementation is to cut the tree at particular locations to produce a two-level object-space partitioning (Fig. 7). The upper portion of the tree (and its associated object data, which tends to be small) is replicated on every processor, whereas the subtrees below the cuts (which comprise the bulk of the data) are distributed among the processors. Two distinct types of tasks are spawned on each processor, one which performs intersection calculations in the upper tree, and another which performs the same calculations for local subtrees. Because the upper-level tree is available everywhere, any processor in the system can perform the initial intersection tests on any ray, effectively decoupling the image-space and object-space partitionings.

The upper-level task operates on one ray at a time, checking it for intersections against the volume extents in the upper portion of the tree. When an intersection test descends to the level of a cut, a ray message is sent to the subtree task on the appropriate processor, which completes the intersection calculations for that subtree and returns the result to the processor which originated the request. Rather than waiting for the result to come back, the upper-level task tries to stay busy by processing additional rays.

Caspary and Scherson's method differs from Salmon and Goldsmith's primarily in the way in which load balancing is achieved. Salmon and Goldsmith adopt a static approach, partitioning the image space among the processors and allocating subtrees to processors based on workload estimates derived from a preprocessing step. Caspary and Scherson use a simpler random allocation strategy for subtrees,

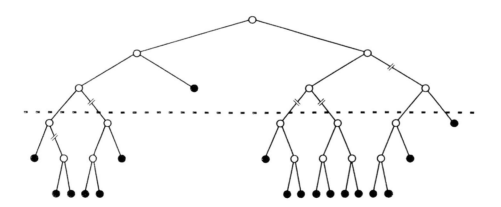

- - -   fixed-level cuts

//   cuts based on workload estimates

FIGURE 7   Hierarchical tree of bounding volumes. Subtrees are pruned out and distributed among processors. The upper portion of the tree is replicated on every processor. Cuts may be made at a fixed level in the tree (28) or at varying levels based on estimates of the subtree workloads (20).

major data structures, simplifies processor coordination, and maximizes the range of practical algorithms. The chief disadvantage is limited architectural scalability, which results in high memory latencies and contention for shared resources as the number of processors increases. To minimize these problems, good shared-memory algorithms must decompose the problem into tasks which avoid memory hot spots and keep critical sections and synchronization operations to a minimum. As most shared-memory systems are augmented with processor caches and/or local memories, algorithms intended for these platforms must also be structured to achieve good locality in their memory reference patterns.

Distributed-memory systems offer improved architectural scalability, but often with higher costs for remote memory references. For this class of machines, managing communication is a primary consideration. Because the rendering process tends to generate large volumes of intermediate data which must be dynamically mapped from object space to image space, parallel renderers must pay special attention to this issue. In the absence of special hardware support, global operations and synchronization may be particularly expensive, and the higher cost of data migration may favor static assignment of tasks and data.

SIMD Versus MIMD

In 1966, Flynn (45) proposed a taxonomy of computer architectures based on the number of instruction and data streams in the system. General-purpose parallel architectures fall into one of two categories: Single Instruction Multiple Data (SIMD) or Multiple Instruction Multiple Data (MIMD). In a pure SIMD architecture, every processor executes the same instruction at every clock cycle, in lock step. Conditionals are implemented by setting local mask bits which disable individual processors while some set of instructions is executed. Systems in this class typically provide large numbers of simple processors and instruction-level support for moving data on- and off-processor through the interconnection network. Examples of commercial SIMD systems include Thinking Machines' CM-2 and CM-200 and MasPar's MP-1 and MP-2.

By contrast, each processor in a MIMD architecture executes its own instruction stream, independently of every other processor. Processors are free to take divergent paths through a program, or even to execute completely different programs. Synchronization operations must be accomplished explicitly under software control. Recent systems in this class include the Intel Paragon, nCUBE3, Meiko C5-2, Thinking Machines CM-5, IBM SP2, and Cray Research T3D, among others.

Because they allow processors to respond to local differences in workload, MIMD architectures would appear to be a good match for the highly variable operation counts and data access patterns which characterize the rendering process (see subsection on Load Balancing). Furthermore, the MIMD environment lends itself to demand-driven and adaptive load balancing schemes, where processors work independently on relatively coarse-grained tasks. Numerous MIMD renderers have been implemented on a variety of hardware platforms. They encompass all of the major rendering methods, including polygon rendering (16,19,26), volume rendering (17,21,27,35,46,47), terrain rendering (48), ray tracing (18,20,49,50), and radiosity (51–54).

Despite the apparent mismatch between the variability of the rendering process and the tight synchronization of SIMD architectures, a number of parallel renderers have demonstrated good performance on SIMD systems (33,55–57). There are several reasons for this. First, the flexibility of MIMD systems imposes a burden on applications and operating systems, which must be able to cope with the arrival of data from remote sources at unpredictable intervals and in arbitrary order. This often results in complex communication and buffering protocols, particularly on distributed-memory message-passing systems. The lock-step operation of SIMD systems virtually eliminates these software overheads, resulting in communication costs which are much closer to the actual hardware speeds.

Second, it is often possible to structure algorithms as several distinct phases, each of which operates on a uniform data type. The rendering pipeline maps naturally onto this structure, and the regularity of the data structures within each phase leads to uniform operations, providing a good fit with the SIMD programming paradigm.

Finally, SIMD architectures usually contains thousands of simple processing elements. Because of their sheer numbers, good performance can often be achieved even though processors may not be fully utilized.

A data-parallel polygon renderer developed by Ortega et al. for the CM-200 and CM-5* illustrates these principles (33). Instead of the single remapping step used by most algorithms (see the subsection Object-Space to Image-Space Mapping), their algorithm breaks the rendering pipeline into three phases. A simplified schematic of the data flow is shown in Fig. 8. The first phase transforms and illuminates polygons, interpolating in the vertical direction to produce spans (Fig. 5). The spans are then reassigned to processors in order to level the load prior to the horizontal scan-conversion phase, and the resulting pixels are routed to their final destinations during the z-buffering phase. This multiphase approach provides uniform data structures at each stage of the pipeline, and efficient communication reduces the impact of the extra remapping step. The algorithm also takes advantage of low-overhead global summations to evaluate processor workloads at each iteration within the scan-conversion phase, an operation which would be prohibitively expensive on most large MIMD systems. The workload information is used to adaptively repartition span data when the imbalance becomes large enough to justify the expense. Despite these efforts, large disparities in polygon size degrade performance, and the algorithm works best for scenes composed of large numbers of small polygons, where variations in rasterization time are more tightly bounded.

SIMD architectures have also been used extensively for volume rendering. Hsu (56) developed an object-parallel volume renderer which employs a three-phase algorithm to regularize the data structures. His approach requires a single communication step for mapping partial ray segments to their image-space destinations for final compositing. Other researchers have adopted image-parallel approaches, holding the image data fixed and communicating object data instead (58–60).

---

*Although the CM-5 is a MIMD system, it has a number of hardware and software features which allow it to support SIMD-style programs efficiently.

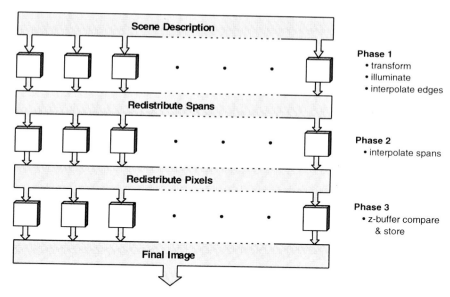

Phase 1
• transform
• illuminate
• interpolate edges

Phase 2
• interpolate spans

Phase 3
• z-buffer compare
& store

Scene Description

Redistribute Spans

Redistribute Pixels

Final Image

FIGURE 8   A three-phase rendering pipeline with two data redistribution steps. The extra communication step provides better load balancing and allows a SIMD implementation to operate on uniform data structures within each phase. (Based on Ref. 33.)

Communication

For renderers which exploit both image and object parallelism, a high volume of interprocessor communication is inherent in the process (see the subsection Object-Space to Image-Space Mapping). Managing this communication is a central issue in renderer design, and the choice of algorithm can have a significant impact on the timing, volume, and patterns of communication (14,21,61). There are three main factors which need to be considered: *latency, bandwidth,* and *contention.* Latency is the time required to set up a communication operation, irrespective of the amount of data to be transmitted. Bandwidth is simply the amount of data which can be communicated over a channel per unit time. If a renderer tries to inject more data into a network than the network can absorb, delays will result and performance will suffer. Contention occurs when multiple processors are trying to route data through the same segment of the network simultaneously and there is insufficient bandwidth to support the aggregate demand.

   The time for one processor to send data to another can be expressed by the following simple formula:

$$t_{comm} = t_{latency} + t_{transfer} + t_{delay},$$

where the total communication time, t_{comm}, is the sum of the latency ($t_{latency}$), data transfer time ($t_{transfer}$), and contention delay (t_{delay}). The transfer time is simply the volume of data to be sent divided by the channel bandwidth. Latency can be better understood as the sum of three components:

$$t_{latency} = t_{send} + t_{route} + t_{recv},$$

where t_{send} is the time to initiate a transfer, t_{route} is the latency through the network, and t_{recv} is the time to receive the data at the other end.

The values of these variables differ widely depending on the system in use. Hardware latencies for sending, receiving, and routing messages are in the submicrosecond range on many systems. However, software layers can boost these times considerably—measured send and receive latencies on message-passing systems often exceed the hardware times by a few orders of magnitude. Bandwidths exhibit similar variations, ranging from hundreds of kilobytes/second on workstation networks up to several gigabytes/second in dedicated graphics hardware. Although latencies and bandwidths can usually be determined with reasonable precision, contention delays are more difficult to characterize because they depend on dynamic traffic patterns which tend to be scene and view dependent.

A number of algorithmic techniques have been developed for coping with communication overheads in parallel renderers. A simple way to reduce latency is to accumulate short messages into large buffers before sending them, thereby amortizing the cost over many data items. Unfortunately, this technique does not scale well for the common case of object- to image-space sorting because the communication pattern is generally many–to–many (16,19). This implies that the number of messages generated per processor is $O(p)$, where p is the number of processors in the system. Assuming a fixed scene and image resolution and a p-way partitioning of the object and image data, the number of data items per processor is proportional to $1/p$, and the number of data items per message decreases as $1/p^2$. Hence, overheads due to latency increase linearly with the number of processors, and amortization of these overheads becomes increasingly ineffective.

One solution is to reduce the algorithmic complexity of the communication by using a multistep delivery scheme, as proposed by Ellsworth (16). With this method, the processors are divided into approximately $\sqrt{p}$ groups, each containing roughly $\sqrt{p}$ processors. Data items intended for any of the processors within a remote group are accumulated in a buffer and transmitted together as a single large message to a forwarding processor within the destination group. The forwarding processor copies the incoming data items into a second set of buffers on the basis of their final destinations, merging them with contributions from each of the other groups. The sorted buffers are then routed to their final destinations within the local group. Figure 9 illustrates this process. The net effect is that the number of messages generated per processor is reduced to $O(\sqrt{p})$ and message lengths decline more slowly (proportional to $1/p^{3/2}$ rather than $1/p^2$), allowing latencies to be amortized more effectively. The algorithm does require the bulk of the data to be examined, copied, and transmitted a second time, so the benefits are only realized when latency is sufficiently high. Nonetheless, Ellsworth found the technique to be effective when rendering small datasets with large numbers of processors.

Although helpful in reducing latency, large message buffers can contribute to contention delays when network bandwidth is insufficient, as Crockett and Orloff discovered in their experiments on an Intel iPSC/860 (19). The problem arises when a large volume of data is injected into the network within a short period of time. If the traffic fails to clear rapidly enough, processors must wait for data to arrive, and performance suffers. The problem is most pronounced when workloads are evenly balanced, as processors tend to be communicating at about the same time. By using a series of intermediate-sized messages and asynchronous communication protocols,

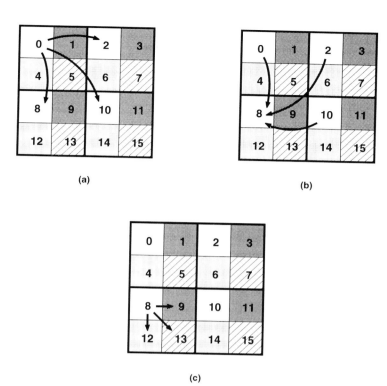

FIGURE 9   Two-step data redistribution. The image is partitioned into square regions which are assigned to 16 processors. Shading indicates sets of communicating processors for the first step. Data originating on processors 0, 2, or 10 which is destined for processors 9, 12, or 13 will pass through processor 8 first. (a) Step 1: destinations of processor 0; (b) step 1: sources for processors 8; (c) step 2: final destinations of processor 8. (Based on Ref. 16.)

the load on the network can be spread out over time, and data transfer can be overlapped with useful computation.

Memory Constraints

Memory consumption is another issue which must be considered when designing parallel renderers. Rendering is a memory-intensive application, especially with complex scenes and high-resolution images. As a baseline, a full-screen (1280 × 1024), full-color (24 bits/pixel), z-buffered image requires on the order of 10 MB of memory for the image data structures alone. The addition of features such as transparency and antialiasing can push memory demands into the hundreds of megabytes, a regime in which parallel systems or high-end graphics workstations are mandatory.

The structure of a parallel renderer can have a major impact on memory requirements, either facilitating memory-intensive rendering by providing data scalability (see subsection on Scalability), or exacerbating the problem by requiring

replicated or auxiliary data structures. Sort-middle polygon rendering is one example of an approach which exhibits good data scalability, because object and image
data structures can be partitioned uniformly among the processing elements. The
cost of image memory in these systems is essentially fixed. By contrast, some sort-
last algorithms require the entire image memory to be replicated on every processor,
increasing the cost in direct proportion to the number of processing elements in the
system.

The issue of memory consumption involves many trade-offs, and system designers must balance application requirements, performance goals, and system cost.
For example, replicating object data in an image-parallel renderer can reduce or
eliminate overheads for interprocessor communication, a strategy which may work
well for rendering moderately complex scenes in low-bandwidth, high-latency environments, such as workstation networks. On the other hand, rendering algorithms
which are embedded in memory-intensive applications must be careful to limit their
own resource requirements to avoid undue interference with the application (34).
In this case, data scalability may be a more important consideration than absolute
performance.

As another example, message-passing renderers can often achieve performance improvements by aggregating data items into large buffers before sending
them, as discussed in the subsection on Communication. With fixed-length buffers
and direct communication, the total space needed for message buffers increases in
proportion to p^2, where p is the number of processors in the system. But as we
observed in the previous section, the average amount of data to be communicated
from each processor to every other processor decreases by the same factor, so a
more intelligent strategy would scale the size of individual buffers by $1/p^2$, thereby
holding the systemwide buffer space to a constant. However, latency amortization
may dictate that buffer sizes should not be allowed to drop below some efficiency
threshold, so beyond a certain number of processors, the buffer space would begin
to grow again. If Ellsworth's two-step sending method (16) is used instead, the total
number of buffers needed in the system is reduced to $p^{3/2}$, allowing this crossover
point to be deferred to larger system sizes.

Some renderers operate in distinct phases, requiring each phase to complete
before the next phase begins. This implies that intermediate results produced by
each phase must be stored, rather than being passed along for immediate consumption. The amount of intermediate storage needed for each phase depends on the
particular data items being produced, but in general is a function of the scene
complexity. For complex scenes, the memory overheads may be substantial, but
they do exhibit data scalability, assuming the object data are partitioned initially.

Image Assembly and Display

High-performance rendering systems generate prodigious quantities of output in
the form of an image stream. For full-screen, full-color animation (1280×1024
resolution, 24 bits/pixel, 30 frames/sec), a display bandwidth of 120 MB/sec is
required. Because most parallel renderers either partition or replicate the image
space, the challenge is to combine pixel values from multiple sources at high frame
rates. Failure to do so will create a bottleneck at the display stage of the rendering
pipeline, limiting the amount of parallelism which can be effectively utilized.

Hardware Solutions

The display problem is best addressed at the architectural level, and hardware rendering systems have adopted several different techniques. One approach is to integrate the frame buffer memory directly with the pixel-generation processors (12,62,63). Highly parallel, multiported buses or other specialized hardware mechanisms are then used to interface the distributed frame buffer to the video-generation subsystem. Alternatively, the rasterization engines and frame buffer may be distinct entities, with pixel data being communicated from one to the other via a high-speed communication channel. One example is the Pixel-Planes 5 system (64), which uses a 640 MB/sec token ring network to interconnect system components, including the pixel renderers and frame buffer. The PixelFlow system (31) pushes transfer rates a step further, using a pipelined image composition network with an effective interstage bandwidth in excess of 4 GB/sec. The frame buffer resides at the terminus of the pipeline, acting as a sink for the final composited pixel values.

Considerations for General-Purpose Systems

Sustaining high frame rates with general-purpose parallel computers is problematic, as these systems typically lack specialized features for image integration and display. There are two principal issues: assembling finished images from distributed components and moving them out of the system and onto a display. The bandwidth of the interprocessor communication network is an important consideration for the image assembly phase, because high frame rates cannot be sustained unless image components can be retrieved rapidly from individual processor memories. Several current systems, including the Intel Paragon and Cray T3D, provide networks with transfer rates exceeding 100 MB/sec, which is more than adequate for interactive graphics. The challenge on these systems is to orchestrate the image retrieval and assembly process so that the desired frame rates can be achieved. In the absence of multiported frame buffers, the image stream must be serialized, perhaps with some ordering imposed, and forwarded to an external device interface.

Assuming that the internal image assembly rate is satisfactory, the next bottleneck is the I/O interface to the display. The typical configuration on current systems uses a HIPPI interface (65) attached to an external frame buffer device. Although many of the existing implementations fail to sustain the 100 MB/sec transfer rate of the HIPPI specification, the technology is improving, and either HIPPI or emerging technologies such as ATM (66) are likely to provide sufficient external bandwidth in the near future.

Algorithmic Approaches

Most software-based parallel renderers either partition the image memory across processors, or replicate it everywhere. In the first scenario, the image partitions must be assembled to produce a complete image. This may be done either internally on the parallel machine or externally in the display system. *Internal assembly* implies that memory for a complete image must be allocated somewhere in the system, a requirement which is potentially at odds with the desire for data scalability. *External assembly* can occur in any of several places, including a host or front-end computer, an addressable external frame buffer, or on secondary storage.

For renderers which replicate the image memory on every processor, generating the finished product usually requires the individual contributions to be z-buffered or composited with a sort-last communication phase. As noted in the subsection on Sorting Classifications, this works best on architectures with high-bandwidth internal networks. The issue of memory allocation for the final result is moot, because renderers which adopt this strategy have already incurred this cost many times over (once on each processor).

Several algorithmic strategies are available for image assembly and composition. The naive approach is to have a designated processor or host accept the contributions from all of the other processors, performing the appropriate z-buffering or compositing operations for each contribution. Although this may be acceptable with small numbers of processors, it results in poor utilization and does not scale well, because the receiving processor is a serial bottleneck. An obvious improvement is to merge image components in a tree-structured fashion, combining contributions at each level in the tree. This results in somewhat better utilization of both processors and the communication network, and runs in $O(\log p)$ time. Ma et al. (35) observed that even with the tree-merging approach, processors are underutilized, and those at higher levels of the tree tend to have disproportionately high workloads. They devised an alternate scheme for compositing images which also runs in logarithmic time but keeps most or all of the processors busy at every stage. The key idea in their *binary-swap* compositing method is to split the image at each step, with pairs of processors operating on different subimages. At the end of the process, the image is partitioned among all of the processors, requiring a final image assembly step to retrieve all of the pieces. Figure 10 illustrates this procedure with four processors.

The pipelined compositing strategy used in the PixelFlow system (31) can also be implemented in software. Silva and Kaufman (67) adopt this approach in a distributed-memory volume renderer for the Intel iPSC/860 and Paragon systems. In order to improve processor utilization, several frames of animation are active in the system simultaneously (an example of temporal parallelism), with processors alternating between rendering and compositing tasks. A potential difficulty with pipelined image composition is high end-to-end latency as the system scales up and the length of the pipeline increases. Applications which require rapid response times, such as virtual reality and real-time simulation, may prefer to use a logarithmic image assembly method.

Remote Image Display

The utility of directly-attached frame buffers in conjunction with large-scale parallel systems is limited, as users are often located at geographically remote sites. This has prompted a number of researchers to examine the potential for transmitting images across local-area and wide-area networks. One example is the display system used in the PGL graphics library (34). PGL partitions its image memory, assigning scanlines to processors in interleaved fashion (Fig. 6c). Image assembly occurs externally on the receiving workstation, eliminating the need for a complete image buffer to be allocated within the parallel system. To reduce the volume of output to a manageable level, each processor compresses its local scanlines by determining which pixels have changed since the previous frame, and then run-length encoding the differences. The resulting contributions from each processor are merged into large packets which are sent across the network to a remote workstation for decom-

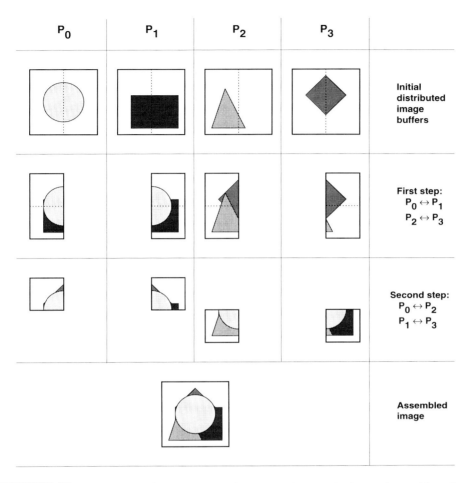

FIGURE 10 Binary-swap image compositing. At each step, the image is partitioned and every processor is responsible for compositing two image segments. (Based on Ref. 35.)

pression, image assembly, and display. Although straightforward, this technique has several advantages, including exploitation of both temporal and spatial image coherence, lossless encoding, embarrassingly parallel image compression, and rapid sequential decompression. Although performance depends heavily on factors such as network traffic and image resolution and content, this technique can provide up to a few frames per second across Ethernet (68) and FDDI (69) networks.

EXAMPLES OF PARALLEL RENDERING SYSTEMS

As we noted earlier, virtually all current graphics systems incorporate parallelism in one form or another. We have illustrated the preceding discussion with a number of examples. In this section, we round out our survey by examining some additional representative systems, running the gamut from specialized graphics computers to software-based terrain and radiosity renderers. Our coverage is by no means complete — many more examples can be found in the literature. Readers are encouraged to explore the References and the Bibliography at the end of this article for more information.

Polygon Rendering and Multipurpose Architectures

One of the earliest graphics architectures to exploit large-scale data parallelism was Fuchs and Poulton's classic Pixel-Planes system (62). Pixel-Planes parallelized the rasterization and z-buffering stages of the polygon rendering pipeline by augmenting each pixel with a simple bit-serial processor which was capable of computing color and depth values from the plane equations which described each polygon. The pixel array operated in SIMD fashion, taking as input a serial stream of transformed screen-space polygons generated by a conventional front-end processor. Although Pixel-Planes provided massive image parallelism, it suffered from poor processor utilization, because only those processors which fell within the bounds of a polygon were active at any given time. The serial front-end processor also proved to be a bottleneck as rasterization performance and scene complexities increased in subsequent generations of the architecture.

The Pixel-Planes 5 architecture (64) rectifies these deficiencies. Instead of a single large array of image processors, it incorporates several smaller ones which can be dynamically reassigned to screen regions in a demand-driven fashion. The serial front-end is replaced by a collection of general purpose transformation processors which operate in MIMD mode. The transformation and rasterization units are connected by a high-speed ring network, allowing data to flow in both directions. In addition to improved load balance and higher performance, the flexibility of the architecture allows it to be applied to a broader range of applications, including volume rendering and radiosity techniques. These architectural improvements are not without cost, however. The dynamic assignment of rasterization units to screen space requires the front-end processors to sort geometric primitives by screen region before initiating the rasterization phase. This implies both a computational overhead and a memory penalty for storing the sorted primitives.

Pixel-Planes 5 is a classic example of a sort-middle architecture, with global communication occurring at the break between the transformation and rasterization phases. By contrast, the newer PixelFlow design (31) implements a sort-last architecture, in which each processing node incorporates a full graphics pipeline. Object parallelism is achieved by distributing primitives across the nodes; pixel parallelism is provided by a Pixel-Planes-style SIMD rasterizer on each node. The sort-last strategy necessitates a bandwidth-intensive image composition step to integrate the partial images from each rasterizer, but this is accomplished using unidirectional nearest-neighbor communication in a 256-bit-wide pipelined interconnect (see the subsection on Hardware Solutions).

AT&T's Pixel Machine (63) combines pipelined parallelism with data parallelism in a programmable MIMD architecture. The system includes one or two 9-stage pipelines for object-level processing and an array of up to 64 pixel processors for image-level operations. Like Pixel-Planes, the frame buffer is integrated with the pixel processors, but in the Pixel Machine each processor is responsible for multiple pixels, distributed in a two-dimensional interleaved fashion. Each processing element is independently programmable and capable of floating-point operations, resulting in an architecture which is adaptable to a variety of rendering and image-processing tasks. As with Pixel-Planes, the limited parallelism provided by the front-end pipelines has proven to be a bottleneck when rendering small primitives.

Volume Rendering and Ray-Tracing Architectures

Graphics architectures have also been developed specifically for volume rendering and ray-tracing applications. In volume rendering, one of the keys to performance is providing high-bandwidth, conflict-free access to the volume data. This has prompted the development of specialized volume memory structures which allow simultaneous access to multiple data values. Kaufman and Bakalash's Cube system (70) introduced an innovative 3D voxel buffer which facilitates parallel access to cubes of volumetric data. A linear array of simple SIMD comparators simultaneously evaluates a complete shaft or "beam" of voxels oriented along any of the three principal axes (x, y, or z). The output of the comparator network is a single voxel chosen on the basis of transparency, color, or depth values. By iterating through the other two dimensions, the complete volume can be scanned at interactive rates. The most recent version of the Cube architecture, Cube-3 (71), supports a more general ray-casting model and incorporates additional parallel and pipelined hardware to support arbitrary viewing angles, perspective projections, and trilinear interpolation of ray samples.

Knittel and Straßer (72) adopt a somewhat different approach with a VLSI-based volume rendering architecture intended for desktop implementation. Memory is organized into eight banks in order to provide parallel access to the sets of neighboring voxels which are needed for trilinear interpolation and gradient computations at sample points along rays. The basic design consists of a volume memory plus four specialized VLSI function units arranged in a pipeline. One function unit performs ray casting and computes sample points along each ray, generating addresses into the volume memory. A second unit accepts the eight data values in the neighborhood of each sample and performs trilinear interpolation and gradient computations. A third unit computes color intensities for each sample point using a Phong illumination model, and the fourth unit composites the samples along each ray to produce a final pixel value. To obtain higher performance, the entire pipeline can be replicated, with subvolumes of the data being stored in each volume memory.

The SIGHT architecture (73) was designed specifically to support image-parallel ray tracing. The image space is partitioned across processors, with each processor responsible for tracing those rays which emanate from its local pixels. Interprocessor communication is largely avoided by replicating the object database in each processor's memory. An additional level of parallelism is achieved through the use of multiple floating-point arithmetic units in each processing element to speed up the ray intersection calculations.

Radiosity Renderers

Radiosity methods produce exceptionally realistic illumination of enclosed spaces by computing the transfer of light energy among all of the surfaces in the environment. Strictly speaking, radiosity is an illumination technique, rather than a complete rendering method. However, radiosity methods are among the most computationally intensive procedures in computer graphics, making them an obvious candidate for parallel processing.

Because the quality of a radiosity solution depends in part on the resolution used to compute energy transfers, the polygons which describe objects are typically subdivided into small patches. Energy transfers between patches are computed using geometric constructions known as *form factors*. In the basic radiosity method, form factors must be computed from every patch in the environment to every other patch. Because of this quadratic complexity, form-factor computations constitute the primary expense in radiosity methods. Hence, parallel implementations have focused on speeding up the generation of form factors.

Although radiosity solutions can be computed directly by solving the system of equations which describes the energy transfers between surfaces, all of the form factors must be generated first, resulting in lengthy solution times which preclude interactive use. For this reason, an alternate iterative approach known as *progressive refinement* (74) has become popular. In this technique, the patch with the highest energy level at each iteration is selected as the *shooting patch*, and energy is transferred from it to other patches in the environment. This process repeats until the maximum level of untransmitted energy drops below some specified threshold. In this way, an initial approximation of the global illumination can be computed relatively quickly, with subsequent refinements resulting in incremental improvements to the image quality.

Many of the parallel radiosity methods described in the literature attempt to speed up the progressive refinement process by computing energy transfers from several shooting patches in parallel (i.e., several iterations are performed simultaneously) (37,38,51–54). Because the time to complete an iteration can vary considerably depending on the geometric relationships among patches, load imbalance can seriously degrade overall performance. Several implementations compensate for this using a demand-driven strategy in which multiple worker processes independently compute form factors for different shooting patches (37,38,54). With this strategy, the complete patch database is usually replicated on every processor, and a separate master process picks shooting patches and completes the energy transfers using vectors of form factors generated by the workers. This approach has several drawbacks, including a lack of data scalability for complex scenes and the tendency for the master process to become a bottleneck as the number of workers increases.

The alternative is to distribute the patch database and radiosity computations across all of the processors. This strategy necessitates global communication in order to compute form factors and complete the energy transfers from shooting patches. Çapın et al. (53) use a simple ring network, circulating patch data and local results from processor to processor in a pipelined fashion to obtain global solutions. Because performance is limited at each step of the computation by the slowest processor, load imbalances can have a profound effect on overall performance. By ensuring that patches belonging to the same object are scattered across processors, variations in workload due to spatial locality are minimized, and a rough static load balance is maintained. Additional examples of radiosity renderers which use distributed databases can be found in Refs. 51 and 52.

The strategy of processing multiple shooting patches in parallel perturbs the order of execution found in the sequential version of the progressive refinement algorithm, and this can lead to slower convergence, partially offsetting the benefits of parallel execution. Although this effect is minimal when only a few shooting patches are active (75), it becomes more pronounced as the number of processors increases and the order of shooting patch selection deviates further from the optimum (53). In order to exploit massive parallelism, a different approach is needed.

In contrast to the previous examples, which all target MIMD systems with modest numbers of processors, Varshney and Prins describe a SIMD radiosity renderer implemented on a MasPar MP-1 with 4096 processing elements (76). As in Çapın et al.'s algorithm, patches are distributed uniformly among the processors. At each iteration, a global reduction operation is used to find the shooting patch with the highest energy, thus maintaining the convergence properties of the sequential algorithm. Once the shooting patch is selected, every other patch in the environment is projected onto the shooting patch's *single plane* (38), where it is scan-converted and z-buffered to determine visibility from the shooting patch. Form factors are obtained by accumulating contributions from the single-plane "pixels," and energy transfers are performed in parallel for each patch using the results from the form-factor computations. Although this algorithm is able to exploit the massive parallelism of its target architecture, load imbalances in the scan conversion phase are found to be significant, and further static or dynamic load balancing measures appear to be in order.

Terrain Rendering

In terrain rendering, the problem is to generate a plausible representation of a real or imaginary landscape as viewed from some point on or above the surface. Typically the viewpoint will change over time, often under interactive control, and in some applications additional objects such as vegetation, buildings, or vehicles must be included in the scene. Terrain rendering techniques have been widely applied in areas such as flight simulation, scientific data analysis and exploration, and creation of virtual landscapes for entertainment or artistic purposes. The need for high-quality images, high frame rates, rapid response to changes in viewpoint, and the ability to navigate through large datasets has stimulated the development of parallel terrain rendering techniques.

Although a variety of techniques can be used to render terrain, most of the parallel methods described in the literature begin with an aerial or satellite image of an actual planetary surface. This image is registered with a separate elevation dataset of the same region, typically represented by a two-dimensional grid with an associated height field. The problem, then, is to assign an elevation value to pixels in the input image and project them onto a display with hidden surfaces eliminated. This technique is known as *forward projection*, in contrast to ray-casting methods which begin at the eye point and project rays through display pixels into the scene. With the forward projection approach, care must be taken to account for the mismatch between input and output image projections, filling in gaps in the output image and compositing input pixels which map to the same location in screen space.

Kaba et al. (57,77) have developed data-parallel terrain rendering techniques for the Princeton Engine, a programmable SIMD system originally developed for real-time processing of digital video (78). Their methods utilize an object-parallel task decomposition, distributing the input image and elevation datasets among the

processors by assigning complete columns of pixels to processors. Before projecting
the data onto the display, it must be rotated and scaled to account for the viewing
direction and altitude. This is accomplished by decomposing the necessary transformations into a sequence of simple shear and shear–scale operations. To avoid costly
interprocessor communication, horizontal shears (along pixel rows) are decomposed into a transpose plus a vertical shear (which requires only local memory
references due to the columnwise data decomposition). The image transpose is
performed efficiently using the Princeton Engine's specialized output sequencer and
image feedback channel. Hidden surface elimination is accomplished by scanning
the transformed data from front to back, one horizontal scanline at a time. As each
scanline is processed, a horizon line is updated; only those pixels which lie above the
current horizon line will be visible. The vertical image partitioning assures that each
horizontal scan can be performed as a data-parallel operation. The system is capable
of rendering terrain fly-overs at 30 frames/sec using 512 × 512 resolution and 8-bit
color, or 15 frames/sec with 24-bit color.

At the Jet Propulsion Laboratory (JPL), Li and Curkendall (48) have developed techniques for rendering planetary surfaces using a variety of large-scale distributed-memory architectures, including Intel's iPSC/860, Delta, and Paragon systems, and Cray's T3D. Like Kaba, they use surface images registered with elevation
data and project object-space pixels into screen space. Whereas their initial methods
partitioned the input data by horizontal slices and assigned them to processors in
interleaved fashion, more recent implementations (79) decompose the data into
square regions which are randomly assigned to processors. The random assignment
provides a measure of stochastic load balancing, reducing sensitivity to hot spots in
the data which may occur when the view zooms in on small terrain regions.

For hidden surface elimination, Li and Curkendall use a standard z-buffer
technique, based on the distance from the view point to individual terrain pixels.
The output image memory is replicated on every processor, with each processor
projecting its local terrain pixels into its local output buffer. This necessitates a
sort-last image composition phase, which is performed using a logarithmic merge
similar to Ma et al.'s binary-swap method (see the subsection on Algorithmic Approaches). A final image assembly step is required to retrieve completed subimages
from each processor and route them to secondary storage or an external display.
JPL's parallel terrain renderers have been used to produce celebrated fly-overs of
Mars and Venus using data from NASA's planetary probes. Some of the datasets
involved are quite large (in excess of a gigabyte), making large-scale parallel systems
particularly attractive for this application.

Whereas the two previous examples both exploited data parallelism, other
approaches are certainly possible. Wright and Hsieh (80) describe a pipelined terrain rendering algorithm which has been implemented in hardware. As in the other
examples, a forward projection technique is used to map from object to image
space, but the surface data and objects in the scene are represented as specialized
volume elements (voxels). The architecture consists of two pipelines, one for voxel
processing and one for pixel processing. The output of the voxel pipeline feeds the
pixel pipeline, so conceptually the system can be viewed as one long pipeline. The
voxel pipeline scans through the database, generating columns of voxels which are
illuminated, transformed into viewing coordinates, and rasterized into pixels. The
pixel pipeline projects pixels from polar viewing coordinates into screen space,

performs haze, translucency, and z-buffering calculations, and normalizes pixel intensities. A variety of techniques are applied at different levels in the pipeline to reduce temporal and spatial aliasing. Objects in motion within the scene are rendered using additional passes through the pipeline. The hardware implementation is capable of rendering 10 frames/sec at 384 × 384 resolution, a speedup of more than three orders of magnitude over a software-based sequential implementation.

SUMMARY

As the above discussion illustrates, parallel processing techniques have been applied to virtually every computationally intensive task in computer graphics. Architectural platforms range from simple coprocessors to specialized VLSI circuitry to general-purpose parallel supercomputers. At every step, the algorithm or architecture designer is faced with a wide range of implementation strategies and a complex series of trade-offs. A successful parallel rendering design must take into account application requirements, architectural parameters, and algorithmic characteristics. As the rapidly growing power of rendering systems indicates, there have been numerous successes, but these are balanced by many other attempts which have stumbled. Many challenges remain, and the discipline of parallel rendering is likely to be an active one for years to come.

ACKNOWLEDGMENTS

This work was supported in part by the National Aeronautics and Space Administration under Contract No. NAS1-19480 while the author was in residence at the Institute for Computer Applications in Science and Engineering (ICASE), M/S 132C, NASA Langley Research Center, Hampton, VA.

The author would like to thank Tony Apodaca, Chuck Hansen, Scott Whitman, Craig Wittenbrink, Sam Uselton, and the staff of NASA Langley's Technical Library for their assistance in researching this article. David Banks and John van Rosendale provided valuable feedback on a draft of the manuscript.

REFERENCES

1. W. H. Ninke, "Graphic 1 — A Remote Graphical Display Console System," in *1965 Fall Joint Computer Conf.*, Vol. 27, Part 1, American Federation of Information Processing Societies, Washington, D.C., 1965, pp. 839–846.
2. T. H. Myer and I. E. Sutherland, "On the Design of Display Processors," *Commun. ACM, 11*(6), 410–414 (1968).
3. R. F. Sproull and I. E. Sutherland, "A Clipping Divider," in *1968 Fall Joint Computer Conf.*, Vol. 33, Part 1, American Federation of Information Processing Societies, Washington, D.C., 1968, pp. 765–775.
4. R. Schumacker, B. Brand, M. Gilliland, and W. Sharp, "Study for Applying Computer-Generated Images to Visual Simulation," Report AFHRL-TR-69-14, Air Force Human Resources Laboratory (Sept. 1969).
5. B. Schacter (ed.), *Computer Image Generation*, Wiley–Interscience, New York, 1983.

6. H. Fuchs, "Distributing A Visible Surface Algorithm Over Multiple Processors," in *Proc. ACM National Conf.*, 1977, pp. 449–451.

7. H. Fuchs and B. W. Johnson, "An Expandable Multiprocessor Architecture for Video Graphics," in *Proc. 6th Annual ACM–IEEE Symp. Computer Architecture*, 1979, pp. 58–67.

8. F. I. Parke, "Simulation and Expected Performance Analysis of Multiple Processor Z-Buffer Systems," *Computer Graphics, 14*(3), 48–56 (1980).

9. J. A. Clark, "A VLSI Geometry Processor for Graphics," *Computer, 13*(7), 59–68 (1980).

10. J. Clark, "The Geometry Engine: A VLSI Geometry System for Graphics," *Computer Graphics, 16*(3), 127–133 (1982).

11. H. Nishimura, H. Ohno, T. Kawata, I. Shirakawa, and K. Omura, "LINKS-1: A Parallel Pipelined Multicomputer System for Image Creation," in *Proc. 10th Annual Intl. Symp. Computer Architecture*, IEEE Computer Society Press, Los Alamitos, CA, 1983, pp. 387–394.

12. K. Akeley, "Reality Engine Graphics," in *Computer Graphics Proc., Annual Conf. Series, 1993*, ACM SIGGRAPH, 1993, pp. 109–116.

13. I. E. Sutherland, R. F. Sproull, and R. A. Schumacker, "A Characterization of Ten Hidden-Surface Algorithms," *Comput. Surveys, 6*(1), 1–55 (1974).

14. S. Molnar, M. Cox, D. Ellsworth, and H. Fuchs, "A Sorting Classification of Parallel Rendering," *IEEE Computer Graphics Appl., 14*(4), 23–32 (1994).

15. S. Whitman, *Multiprocessor Methods for Computer Graphics Rendering*, Jones and Bartlett, Boston, 1992.

16. D. Ellsworth, "A New Algorithm for Interactive Graphics on Multicomputers," *IEEE Computer Graphics Appl., 14*(4), 33–40 (1994).

17. P. Mackerras and B. Corrie, "Exploiting Data Coherence to Improve Parallel Volume Rendering," *IEEE Parallel Distrib. Technol. 2*(2), 8–16 (1994).

18. D. Badouel, K. Bouatouch, and T. Priol, "Distributing Data and Control for Ray Tracing in Parallel," *IEEE Computer Graphics Appl., 14*(4), 69–77 (1994).

19. T. W. Crockett and T. Orloff, "Parallel Polygon Rendering for Message-Passing Architectures," *IEEE Parallel Distrib. Technol., 2*(2), 17–28 (1994).

20. J. Salmon and J. Goldsmith, "A Hypercube Ray-tracer," in *Proc. Third Conf. Hypercube Concurrent Computers and Applications*, Vol. II, G. C. Fox, ed., ACM Press, New York, 1988, pp. 1194–1206.

21. U. Neumann, "Communication Costs for Parallel Volume-Rendering Algorithms," *IEEE Computer Graphics Appl., 14*(4), 49–58 (1994).

22. D. Lenoski, J. Laudon, K. Gharachorloo, W.-D. Weber, A. Gupta, J. Hennessy, M. Horowitz, and M. S. Lam, "The Stanford Dash Multiprocessor," *Computer, 25*(3), 63–79 (1992).

23. R. E. Kessler and J. L. Schwarzmeier, "Cray T3D: A New Dimension for Cray Research," in *Digest of Papers, COMPCON Spring '93*, IEEE Computer Society Press, Los Alamitos, CA, 1993, pp. 176–182.

24. Convex Computer Corporation, *Convex Exemplar System Overview*, Convex Computer Corporation, Richardson, TX, 1994.

25. D. S. Whelan, "Animac: A Multiprocessor Architecture for Real-Time Computer Animation," Ph.D. dissertation, California Institute of Technology (1985).

26. S. Whitman, "Dynamic Load Balancing for Parallel Polygon Rendering," *IEEE Computer Graphics Appl., 14*(4), 41–48 (1994).

27. J. Nieh and M. Levoy, "Volume Rendering on Scalable Shared-Memory MIMD Architectures," *Proc. 1992 Workshop on Volume Visualization*, ACM Press, New York, 1992, pp. 17–24.

28. E. Caspary and I. D. Scherson, "A Self-Balanced Parallel Ray-Tracing Algorithm," in

Parallel Processing for Computer Vision and Display, P. M. Dew, R. A. Earnshaw, and T. R. Heywood, eds., Addison-Wesley, Reading, MA, 1989, pp. 408–419.

29. Evans and Sutherland Computer Corporation, *Freedom Series Technical Report*, Evans and Sutherland Computer Corporation, Salt Lake City, 1992.

30. Cray Research, Inc., *Cray Animation Theater*, Cray Research, Inc., Eagan, MN, 1994.

31. S. Molnar, J. Eyles, and J. Poulton, "PixelFlow: High-Speed Rendering Using Image Composition," *Computer Graphics, 26*(2), 231–240 (1992).

32. M. Cox and P. Hanrahan, "A Distributed Snooping Algorithm for Pixel Merging," *IEEE Parallel Distrib. Technol., 2*(2), 30–36 (1994).

33. F. A. Ortega, C. D. Hansen, and J. P. Ahrens, "Fast Data Parallel Polygon Rendering," in *Proc. Supercomputing '93*, IEEE Computer Society Press, Los Alamitos, CA, 1993, pp. 709–718.

34. T. W. Crockett, "Design Considerations for Parallel Graphics Libraries," ICASE Report 94-49 (NASA CR-194935), Institute for Computer Applications in Science and Engineering (June 1994).

35. K.-L. Ma, J. S. Painter, C. D. Hansen, and M. F. Krogh, "Parallel Volume Rendering Using Binary-Swap Compositing," *IEEE Computer Graphics Appl., 14*(4), 59–68 (1994).

36. C. Giertsen and J. Petersen, "Parallel Volume Rendering on a Network of Workstations," *IEEE Computer Graphics Appl., 13*(6), 16–23 (1993).

37. C. Puech, F. Sillion, and C. Vedel, "Improving Interaction with Radiosity-based Lighting Simulation Programs," *Computer Graphics, 24*(2), 51–57 (1990).

38. R. J. Recker, D. W. George, and D. P. Greenberg, "Acceleration Techniques for Progressive Refinement Radiosity," *Computer Graphics, 24*(2), 59–66 (1990).

39. Pixar, *PhotoRealistic RenderMan Toolkit v3.5 Reference Manual*, Pixar, Richmond, CA, 1994.

40. T. Diede, C. Hagenmaier, G. Miranker, J. Rubinstein, and W. Worley, "The Titan Graphics Supercomputer Architecture," *Computer, 21*(9), 13–30 (1988).

41. B. Apgar, B. Bersack, and A. Mammem, "A Display System for the Stellar Graphics Supercomputer Model GS1000," *Computer Graphics, 22*(4), 255–262 (1988).

42. S. Dyer and S. Whitman, "A Vectorized Scan-Line Z-Buffer Rendering Algorithm," *IEEE Computer Graphics Appl., 7*(7), 34–45 (1987).

43. D. J. Plunkett and M. J. Bailey, "The Vectorization of a Ray-Tracing Algorithm for Improved Execution Speed," *IEEE Computer Graphics Appl., 5*(8), 52–60 (1985).

44. N. L. Max, "Vectorized Procedural Models for Natural Terrain: Waves and Islands in the Sunset," *Computer Graphics, 15*(3), 317–324 (1981).

45. M. J. Flynn, "Very High-Speed Computing Systems," *Proc. IEEE, 54*, 1901–1909 (1966).

46. J. Challinger, "Scalable Parallel Volume Raycasting for Nonrectilinear Computational Grids," in *Proc. 1993 Parallel Rendering Symp.*, ACM Press, New York, 1993, pp. 81–88.

47. E. Camahort and I. Chakravarty, "Integrating Volume Data Analysis and Rendering on Distributed Memory Architectures," *Proc. 1993 Parallel Rendering Symp.*, ACM Press, New York, 1993, pp. 89–96.

48. P. P. Li and D. W. Curkendall, "Parallel Three Dimensional Perspective Rendering," *Proc. Second European Workshop on Parallel Computing* (1992), pp. 320–331.

49. S. A. Green and D. J. Paddon, "A Highly Flexible Multiprocessor Solution for Ray Tracing," *Visual Computer, 6*(2), 62–73 (1990).

50. W. Lefer, "An Efficient Parallel Ray Tracing Scheme for Distributed Memory Parallel Computers," in *Proc. 1993 Parallel Rendering Symp.*, ACM Press, New York, 1993, pp. 77–80.

51. M. Feda and W. Purgathofer, "Progressive Refinement Radiosity on a Transputer

Network," in *Photorealistic Rendering in Computer Graphics: Proc. Second Eurographics Workshop on Rendering*, Springer-Verlag, Berlin, 1991, pp. 139–148.

52. A. G. Chalmers and D. J. Paddon, "Parallel Processing of Progressive Refinement Radiosity Methods," in *Photorealistic Rendering in Computer Graphics: Proc. Second Eurographics Workshop on Rendering*, Springer-Verlag, Berlin, 1991, pp. 149–159.

53. T. K. Çapın, C. Aykanat, B.Özgüç, "Progressive Refinement Radiosity on Ring-Connected Multicomputers," in *Proc. 1993 Parallel Rendering Symp.*, ACM Press, New York, 1993, pp. 71–76.

54. A. Ng and M. Slater, "A Multiprocessor Implementation of Radiosity," *Computer Graphics Forum, 12*(5), 329–342 (1993).

55. T. T. Y. Lin and M. Slater, "Stochastic Ray Tracing Using SIMD Processor Arrays," *Visual Computer, 7*(4), 187–199 (1991).

56. W. M. Hsu, "Segmented Ray Casting for Data Parallel Volume Rendering," in *Proc. 1993 Parallel Rendering Symp.*, ACM Press, New York, 1993, pp. 7–14.

57. J. Kaba, J. Matey, G. Stoll, H. Taylor, and P. Hanrahan, "Interactive Terrain Rendering and Volume Visualization on the Princeton Engine," in *Proc. Visualization '92*, IEEE Computer Society Press, Los Alamitos, CA, 1992, pp. 349–355.

58. G. Vézina, P. A. Fletcher, and P. K. Robertson, "Volume Rendering on the MasPar MP-1," in *Proc. 1992 Workshop on Volume Visualization*, ACM Press, New York, 1992, pp. 3–8.

59. P. Schröder and J. B. Salem, "Fast Rotation of Volume Data on Data Parallel Architectures," in *Proc. Visualization '91*, IEEE Computer Society Press, Los Alamitos, CA, 1991, pp. 50–57.

60. P. Schröder and G. Stoll, "Data Parallel Volume Rendering as Line Drawing," in *Proc. 1992 Workshop on Volume Visualization*, ACM Press, New York, 1992, pp. 25–31.

61. D. W. Jensen and D. A. Reed, "A Performance Analysis Exemplar: Parallel Ray Tracing," *Concurrency: Pract. Exp., 4*(2), 119–141 (1992).

62. H. Fuchs and J. Poulton, "Pixel-Planes: A VLSI-Oriented Design for a Raster Graphics Engine," *VLSI Design, Q3*, 20–28 (1981).

63. M. Potmesil and E. M. Hoffert, "The Pixel Machine: A Parallel Image Computer," *Computer Graphics, 23*(3), 69–78 (1989).

64. H. Fuchs, J. Poulton, J. Eyles, T. Greer, J. Goldfeather, D. Ellsworth, S. Molnar, G. Turk, B. Tebbs, and L. Israel, "Pixel-Planes 5: A Heterogeneous Multiprocessor Graphics System Using Processor-Enhanced Memories," *Computer Graphics, 23*(3), 79–88 (1989).

65. J. P. Hughes, "HIPPI," in *Proc. 17th Conf. Local Computer Networks*, IEEE Computer Society Press, Los Alamitos, CA, 1992, pp. 346–354.

66. R. J. Vetter, "ATM Concepts, Architectures, and Protocols," *Commun. ACM, 38*(2), 30–38 (1995).

67. C. T. Silva and A. E. Kaufman, "Parallel Performance Measures for Volume Ray Casting," in *Proc. Visualization '94*, IEEE Computer Society Press, Los Alamitos, CA, 1994, pp. 196–203.

68. J. F. Shoch, Y. K. Dalal, and D. D. Redell, "Evolution of the Ethernet Local Computer Network," *Computer, 15*(8), 10–27 (1982).

69. F. E. Ross, "An Overview of FDDI: The Fiber Distributed Data Interface," *IEEE J. Selected Areas Commun., 7*(7), 1043–1051 (1989).

70. A. Kaufman and R. Bakalash, "Memory and Processing Architecture for 3D Voxel-Based Imagery," *IEEE Computer Graphics Appl., 8*(6), 10–23 (1988).

71. H. Pfister, A. Kaufman, and T. Chiueh, "Cube-3: A Real-Time Architecture for High-Resolution Volume Visualization," in *Proc. 1994 Symp. Volume Visualization, ACM SIGGRAPH*, 1994, pp. 75–82.

72. G. Knittel and W. Straßer, "A Compact Volume Rendering Accelerator," in *Proc. 1994 Symp. Volume Visualization*, ACM SIGGRAPH, 1994, pp. 67–74.

73. T. Naruse, M. Yoshida, T. Takahashi, and S. Naito, "SIGHT—A Dedicated Computer Graphics Machine," *Computer Graphics Forum, 6*(4), 327–344 (1987).

74. M. F. Cohen, S. E. Chen, J. R. Wallace, and D. P. Greenberg, "A Progressive Refinement Approach to Fast Radiosity Image Generation," *Computer Graphics, 22*(4), 75–84 (1988).

75. D. R. Baum and J. M. Winget, "Real Time Radiosity Through Parallel Processing and Hardware Acceleration," *Computer Graphics, 24*(2), 67–75 (1990).

76. A. Varshney and J. F. Prins, "An Environment-Projection Approach to Radiosity for Mesh-Connected Computers," in *Proc. Third Eurographics Workshop on Rendering*, Springer-Verlag, Berlin, 1992, pp. 271–281.

77. J. Kaba and J. Peters, "A Pyramid-based Approach to Interactive Terrain Visualization," in *Proc. 1993 Parallel Rendering Symp.*, ACM Press, New York, 1993, pp. 67–70.

78. D. Chin, J. Passe, F. Bernard, H. Taylor, and S. Knight, "The Princeton Engine: A Real-Time Video System Simulator," *IEEE Trans. Consumer Electron., CE-34*(2), 285–297 (1988).

79. P. Li, D. Curkendall, W. Duquette, and H. Henry, "Interactive Scientific Visualization on Massively Parallel Processors," *CSCC Update, 13*(7), 4–6 (1994).

80. J. R. Wright and J. C. L. Hsieh, "A Voxel-Based, Forward Projection Algorithm for Rendering Surface and Volumetric Data," in *Proc. Visualization '92*, IEEE Computer Society Press, Los Alamitos, CA, 1992, pp. 340–348.

BIBLIOGRAPHY

Dew, P. M., R. A. Earnshaw, and T. R. Heywood (eds.), *Parallel Processing for Computer Vision and Display*, Addison-Wesley, Reading, MA, 1989.

S. Green, *Parallel Processing for Computer Graphics*. MIT Press, Cambridge, MA, 1991.

Hu, M.-C. and J. D. Foley, "Parallel Processing Approaches to Hidden-Surface Removal in Image Space," *Computer Graphics, 9*(3), 303–317 (1985).

M. Kaplan and D. P. Greenberg, "Parallel Processing Techniques for Hidden Surface Removal," *Computer Graphics, 13*(2), 300–307 (1979).

Kaufman, A., R. Bakalash, D. Cohen, and R. Yagel, "A Survey of Architectures for Volume Rendering," *IEEE Eng. Med. Biol., 9*(4), 8–23 (1990).

Lerner, E. J., "Fast Graphics Use Parallel Techniques," *IEEE Spectrum, 18*(3), 34–38 (1981).

Molnar, S. and H. Fuchs, "Advanced Raster Graphics Architecture," in *Computer Graphics: Principles and Practice*, 2nd ed., J. D. Foley, A. van Dam, S. K. Feiner, and J. F. Hughes (eds.), Addison-Wesley, Reading, MA, 1990, pp. 855–922.

Singh, J. P., A. Gupta, and M. Levoy, "Parallel Visualization Algorithms: Performance and Architectural Implications," *Computer, 27*(7), 45–55 (1994).

Theoharis, T., *Algorithms for Parallel Polygon Rendering*, G. Goos and J. Hartmanis (eds.), Lecture Notes in Computer Science Vol. 373, Springer-Verlag, Berlin, 1989.

THOMAS W. CROCKETT

AN UNDERGRADUATE COURSE-ADVISING EXPERT SYSTEM IN INDUSTRIAL ENGINEERING

INTRODUCTION

Background

The course-advising process for undergraduate students in industrial engineering at the University of Missouri–Columbia is usually time-consuming, both for the faculty advisors and the students. Each faculty member is assigned approximately 15 students, with the exception of the Director of Undergraduate Studies who advises approximately 45 students. During the weeks prior to registration, students must schedule appointments with their faculty advisors to complete a trial study form and an enrollment form.

The purpose of the trial study form is to ensure that the student is taking courses in the proper sequence and to eliminate scheduling conflicts. Once the faculty advisor has approved the schedule, the enrollment form is then completed. The advisor signs both forms, after which the student can then proceed with the rest of the registration process.

Problem

The difficulty with this advising process is that although it happens regularly, it happens at intervals that are too long. Students consult their faculty advisors for course advising only once a semester, and yet the faculty advisors are expected to recall all the necessary advising facts and relationships in those times. Once a semester, the faculty advisors must mentally update themselves on each of their students' files to see what courses have been taken, which prerequisites have been satisfied, and what courses should be taken next. The faculty advisors must also remain current with any curriculum changes. Although guidelines are available in an advising packet and an advisor's manual, the process is still time-consuming and sometimes involves special cases that are not always covered in the packet or the manual. The process is especially cumbersome for new faculty members.

Industrial engineering is a distinct engineering discipline which uses physical laws and principles of science and technology to design and develop systems for producing goods or providing services at higher quality and lower cost. Being in the business of making improvements, it made sense to find a more systematic way of handling the undergraduate course-advising process.

Objective

The objective of the project was to provide quality and consistent course advising for industrial engineering undergraduate students in an easily accessible and timely fashion. The student would still meet with the advisor, but only for final approval. Toward this end, we chose an expert system medium. Expert systems are used in a variety of applications, including equipment diagnostics, project scheduling, and process control. They are useful because they make expert knowledge accessible to all types of users. The industrial engineering course-advising expert system, named IEADVISE, should give important advising facts, ensure that the students are aware of degree requirements, list course descriptions and prerequisites, and ultimately assist in planning a course schedule.

Significance

The perceived benefits from using an expert system approach included the following:

1. A thorough analysis and understanding of the undergraduate advising process that would come about as a by-product of the expert system development
2. The permanent storage of course-advising information
3. The occurrence of preliminary course advising without the presence of a faculty advisor
4. The freeing up of time for faculty advisors that can be devoted to other tasks.

The primary significance of an expert system for industrial engineering undergraduate course advising would be the simplification of the process for both the student and the faculty advisor.

Often, a student merely wants to know the selection of courses that he or she will be eligible to take in the following semester. In this case, the student can consult IEADVISE by answering the questions posed by the expert system. Based on the answers provided by the student, and the course prerequisites, corequisites, current standing, and other information stored in the knowledge base, the expert system determines a set of eligible courses. Upon completion of the session, the student will be presented with a list of suitable courses. The student will then be able to plan a tentative schedule based on the generated list. Actual consultation with the faculty advisor will, therefore, be limited to seeking opinions on electives and course loads, as well as for final approval of the student's schedule.

RELATED LITERATURE ON EXPERT SYSTEMS IN ACADEMIC ADVISING

Expert Systems

Expert or inference systems have matured as a technology since first implemented in the late 1970s. Rees (1) described expert systems as a computer program which embodies expert knowledge and can offer intelligent advice. Expert systems can manipulate knowledge as well as data, are easy to modify and update, will tolerate uncertainty in the answers, and are able to explain their operation. These features are the primary differences between expert systems and traditional computer programs. Expert systems can also be incrementally produced, allowing for execution and testing before completion (2).

The knowledge storage (knowledge base) is quite separate from the reasoning mechanism (the inference engine) (1). The knowledge base of an expert system is a codified collection of expert-level knowledge which pertains to a specific domain and is available to assist a nonexpert in performing a task (3). The inference engine is the part of the expert system that interprets the knowledge and does the reasoning.

Many types of problems have been solved or have been modeled using an expert system approach. Some of the more common problems include analysis and interpretation of measurement data, error detection, design configuration, repair, planning, simulation, and maintenance (4). One reason for the success of expert systems is they do not solve problems solely by the use of facts and calculations, but they also incorporate heuristic and qualitative reasoning much like human experts. Before 1960, the concept of machines that could think was only speculation. After 1960, the scientists were too optimistic, predicting that machines comparable to human intelligence would be readily available within 10 years. It was not until the mid-1970s that machine intelligence would be primarily based on knowledge processing.

According to Paton (5), expert systems allow organizations to capture expert knowledge forever as human experts enter and leave the organization. Knowledge engineering will essentially replace traditional data processing. Today, expert systems are already accepted as computer tools for representing knowledge. Their embellishment using other emerging tools such as fuzzy logic, genetic algorithms, and neural nets will certainly enhance their capabilities.

Expert Systems in Academic Advising

The related literature on expert systems in academic advising is scant and fairly recent. In 1990, Hatfield (6) proposed a computerized system to replace the human teaching assistant (TA). Although the system was not specifically called an expert system, it did have the characteristics of an expert system. It used a knowledge-based format to store facts and procedures and was labeled an "expert teaching assistant." The intended benefits included the capability to generate unique assignments for each student from a general description of the assignment from the professor, assign open-ended problems, and grade the returned solutions. The Computer Teaching Assistant (CTA) was implemented in compiled BASIC at Northern Arizona University for electrical engineering and technology courses. The article reported that the implementation was in its early stages and that plans were underway to experimentally evaluate the benefits of the expert system in a beginning physics course.

Wood (7) reported on the development of a Trainee Teacher Support System (TTSS), an academic advisory system for providing expert guidance and feedback to trainee teachers on classroom dynamics. The article dealt primarily with the nature of the specific knowledge involved, such as the perceived causes of certain types of classroom behavior and the formalization of the knowledge in terms of rules and meta-rules. There was no mention in the article of the actual prototype or of the outcome of using such a system.

The only work reported in the open literature that was close in relation to our project was a technical note describing Advice, an expert system for evaluating study plans of systems and industrial engineering graduate students at the University of Arizona in Tucson by Shen and Bahill (8). Advice was designed to check for inconsistencies in graduate student study plans prior to graduation. It was written in M.1, a backward-chaining expert system shell, with knowledge obtained from professors, a department handbook, and the university catalog. It reported success in detecting mostly minor mistakes and a few serious mistakes. The testing was based on 7 student plans evaluated by Advice and later reviewed by the graduate committee chairman, and 14 study plans previously approved by human advisors and the graduate committee and later evaluated by Advice. The description was scant and did not provide much information about the nature of the knowledge, the knowledge representation, or the interface mechanism between the study plan and the expert system.

IEADVISE (9), the subject of this article, is also an academic advisory system. However, it differs from Advice and the other systems by the nature of the knowledge involved, the representation scheme, and the extent to which its evaluation has been carried out. IEADVISE actually specifies a set of eligible courses for the student to take, unlike Advice which did not specify courses but only checked for sufficiency within an aggregation of subject areas. The nature of the knowledge and the knowledge representation in IEADVISE are clearly described in this article. It has been implemented, and the resulting efficacy of its implementation in terms of accuracy and acceptance are evaluated and presented as an example of a working expert system application.

METHODOLOGY

This section will outline the approach taken in this study, including the data collection, model development, and model verification/validation. Tasks which require expert knowledge are well suited for implementation as an expert system (4). With human experts for industrial engineering undergraduate course advising available in the persons of the director of undergraduate studies, the associate dean for admissions, and the senior faculty members, an expert system approach was a feasible choice for solving the course-advising problem. The advising packet (10) and the advisor's manual (11) provided supplemental information in terms of documentation for well-established practices. As in all human undertakings, however, the process of undergraduate course advising involved some unwritten rules and practices for special cases that were only available from the human experts.

The first step in designing this system was to describe the types of information needed and the manner in which these types of information were used in advising students. To properly conduct a course-advising session, a faculty advisor must know a number of factors, including which courses have already been taken, what courses may have sequencing problems, and if the student needs to repeat any courses. Figure 1 summarizes the advising process. It generally involved an update of the previous advisor checklist against general items [nondegree courses, college-level examination program (CLEP) course waivers, sequencing problems, etc.], total hour requirements, specific degree items [minimum grade point average (GPA), minimum course grade, etc.], and technical elective items. Consequently, it

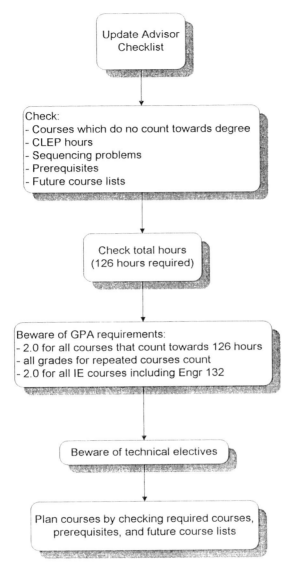

FIGURE 1 Traditional industrial engineering advising process. (Adapted with permission from Ref. 9.)

was possible to discern the set of eligible courses that the student would be eligible to take for the following semester.

IEADVISE was configured to advise students in a manner similar to a human advisor. The intent was to have IEADVISE handle routine course advising and reserve the faculty advisor consultation time for more individualized and more complicated problems. The general format was for the user to be asked a series of questions. Based on each response, a course of action would be initiated. Any vital information would be clearly represented on the screen. This format diminished the possibility of such information being overlooked, which was a problem in the pre-expert-system advising process.

The expert system shell used was the Expert System Environment or ESE (3). ESE facilitated the construction of expert system applications with a development environment (ESXD). The expert system would then be accessible to the user via a consultation environment (ESXC). Within the development environment, the rules and parameters (facts) related to the problem were first defined, and then placed in expert system format. This definition involved examining the relationships of all the variables that were active in the advising process. From this point, the model exhibited the antecedent–consequent form that would determine the conclusion for any combination of given conditions. The essential components of the above process is the same for other expert system shells besides ESE.

After the knowledge base had been put in place, it was verified for consistency, completeness, and correctness. Consistency ensures that the rules are in agreement and that one rule does not negate or conflict with any other rule. Completeness ensures that all possible situations and combinations are taken into account. Any user should be able to get comprehensive results from consulting the expert system. Correctness ensures the accuracy of the information in the parameters and rules.

Verification had two components: checking that the knowledge was consistent and complete, and verifying that the information was correctly applied (3). When transferring knowledge from an expert to a knowledge base, a variety of errors could occur. The built-in ESE editor was used to check for syntax errors upon data entry. The editor syntactically checked both parameter constraints and rule clauses. Inconsistencies and incompleteness, however, had to be checked manually because ESE did not do semantic checking between clauses in a rule, or between rules.

Then verification was done to ensure correct results would be given when consulted by a user. Various test consultations were run to see if the appropriate recommendations would be generated for different cases. When inaccurate results were obtained, the authors determined the source of the error with the use of the explanation facility and the *Find, Trace,* and *Rerun* commands. These latter features were special functions provided in the development environment to facilitate debugging of the expert system. They were conveniently accessible via function keys.

Following verification, the expert system was validated in two ways. First, previously completed trial study forms (prepared with the help of a faculty advisor) that were on file for each student in a sample population were compared against the results generated by the expert system. Second, currently enrolled students were asked to consult the expert system and to fill out a questionnaire for data analysis. IEADVISE took eight person-months to develop. Half of that period was spent on knowledge acquisition, organization, and representation. The other half of that period was spent on actual system coding, verification, and validation. The expert system, its operation and a sample session, and the verification and validation results will be described in the following sections.

SYSTEM DESCRIPTION

Expert System Shell Considerations

An expert system shell offers less flexibility of design and range of applications than programming languages (5). They do, however, offer an expert system structure, and an enquiry, storage, and rule-generating framework which allows the developer to focus on knowledge extraction and representation. A shell is essentially an expert system without the specific knowledge required for a particular application (12).

After careful consideration, the expert systems shell ESE was chosen as the development tool. ESE resides in the University of Missouri–Columbia mainframe computer, MIZZOU1, an IBM 3090 machine that runs under a VM/CMS operating system. MIZZOU1 is accessible 24 hours a day through hard-wired workstations in 11 sites, through gateway connections, and through dial-up modem service. Its accessibility made it an appropriate medium for building a course-advising expert system. From IEADVISE, students will receive a potential course schedule. Each student should be able to provide selective information on previous courses taken, grades received, and the semester for which they seek advising. The expert system will then take this information and advise the student on course selection based on knowledge-base rules.

Major System Components

In the development stage, the expert system developer takes the expert-level knowledge and develops a knowledge base. In the usage stage, the end user consults the knowledge base to obtain a course of action. An important step in developing the knowledge base was to define the parameters and the logical relationships between those parameters. A parameter is a domain fact, and in this application is either a string, number, or a Boolean. An example of a string parameter in IEADVISE is MATH. It contains a list of all the math courses an industrial engineering student is required to take, as well as precalculus courses that certain students may be required to take. Within the consultation environment, the student will be asked, "What is the last Math course you completed or are currently enrolled in with a grade of "C" or better?" The student will then be asked to mark the appropriate choice from a list of math courses, and IEADVISE will then store this information.

A number parameter is used when IEADVISE requires a numeric value to evaluate a student's status. For example, incoming freshmen are required to take math placement tests to determine the appropriate introductory math course. An example of a number parameter in IEADVISE is MMPT___SCORE, which is posed as, "What was your MMPT score? (Enter a number ≥ 0 and ≤ 40)," where MMPT refers to the Missouri Math Placement Test.

A Boolean parameter is used for logical questions in which the answer is either *yes* or *no*. For example, IEADVISE uses a Boolean parameter to qualify the type of student consulting the system. IEADVISE asks, "Are you an incoming freshman?" Based on the student's response, IEADVISE establishes one of two focus control blocks. A focus control block is a branching mechanism in ESE which will be described more fully in a subsequent section.

A rule defines the relationship between parameters. It is an IF–Then statement which consists of a premise clause(s) and an action clause(s). The action clause is acted upon if the premise clause statement is found to be true. For example, a rule utilizing the MATH string parameter is, If MATH = '80', then MAY___ TAKE___MATH = '175'. This means that if the student had marked '80' from the set of choices when asked about his or her current math level with a grade of C or better, this rule would set the MAY___TAKE___MATH parameter equal to

'175' for the student's schedule. Math 80 and Math 175 are course codes for certain levels of college mathematics courses.

An example of a rule utilizing the MMPT___SCORE and TRIG___SCORE (Trigonometry Placement Test) number parameters and the FRESHMAN___ GROUP___NUMBER string parameter is

If FRESHMAN___GROUP___NUMBER = 'I' or FRESHMAN___ GROUP___NUMBER = 'II'
    and MMPT___SCORE ≥ 30
    and TRIG___SCORE ≥ 16
    Then MAY___TAKE___MATH = '80'.

Note the combined use of AND and OR to represent logical conditions. Similar rules were written for each range of MMPT and TRIG scores that pertained to different calculus and precalculus courses.

An example of a rule utilizing a Boolean parameter in IEADVISE is If CHEMISTRY = False then MAY___TAKE___CHEMISTRY = '5'., where CHEMISTRY is the Boolean parameter and '5' corresponds to Chem 5, a college chemistry course. IEADVISE also suggests that completion of certain courses is advisable, such as taking college algebra before enrolling in Chemistry 5.

Additional parameters were defined for physics, English, basic engineering, industrial engineering, humanities, history, economics, and technical electives. Each of these parameters would elicit information from the student about previous courses. For each of these parameters, a corresponding MAY___TAKE parameter was defined to determine the courses for which a student would be eligible.

At least one rule for each course in the industrial engineering undergraduate curriculum was defined to cover the entire range of options available to the student. In total, 32 parameters and 75 rules were utilized in the design of IEADVISE. IEADVISE was also configured so that updating of parameters and rules would be easy. The primary difficulty in defining the rules was the oftentimes uncertain situation of the undergraduate student. Although a recommended curriculum was available, few students followed the suggested sequence exactly. Therefore, each rule was defined solely on the basis of the semester, course prerequisites, and a student's previous courses. The rule

If IE = 'Engr 132' and
    IE = '207' and
    SEMESTER = 'WINTER' and
    IE ≠ '239'
    Then MAY___TAKE___IE = '239'

is an example of a typical rule. If a student was currently enrolled in or had completed Engr 132 (Probabilistic Models) and IE 207 (Operations Research Models), and the student was enrolling for the winter semester, and the student had not yet completed IE 239 (Evaluation of Engineering Data), then IEADVISE would recommend that the student enroll in IE239.

Once all the parameters and rules were defined, they were entered into the knowledge base. To enter the parameter MATH, for example, the following steps were followed:

1. Type EDP MATH. This statements tells ESE that the builder is editing (ED) a parameter (P) with the name MATH. EDP was used to initially define as well as revise all parameters.

2. Define the parameter as either string, number, or Boolean.
3. Define other relevant properties. For example, LONG PROMPT is used to formulate the question as desired. SOURCING SEQUENCE indicates the source of the parameter value as one of the following:
   (a) User will input from the terminal
   (b) A rule consequent
   (c) A default value will be used.
4. Repeat steps 1–3 for each parameter.

Rules were entered similarly using the EDit Rule (EDR) command. Each parameter and rule must also be owned by a focus control block (FCB).

IEADVISE, by design, required three FCBs. FCBs are the primary building blocks for the ESE (3). Each FCB represents a single unit of work to be accomplished during problem solving. The root FCB of IEADVISE, also known as the Parent FCB, determined whether the student was an incoming freshman (*FCB: Freshman*) or a returning/transfer student (*FCB:All___Others*). Each FCB contains instructions on how to process the parameters and rules associated with the FCB. Figure 2 illustrates the IEADVISE FCB framework.

FCB:Student (the Parent FCB) is the parent FCB established whenever a consultation of IEADVISE is initiated. Within this FCB, a determination will be made whether the student is an incoming freshman or a returning/transfer student. If the student declares oneself as a freshman, then *FCB:Student* will establish *FCB: Freshman*. *FCB:Freshman* will then ask questions based on rules and parameters contained within its structure. If, however, the student declares oneself as a returning/transfer student, then *FCB:All___Others* will be established.

FCB:Freshman uses parameters and rules involving the Freshman Group Number, ACT (American College Testing) score, MMPT score, TRIG score, and ACT-Math composite score, if necessary, to determine an incoming freshman's recommended schedule, course load, and block courses, if any. After the student is issued a schedule, IEADVISE will allow the student to continue the consultation for an indefinite number of times.

FCB:All___Others uses parameters and rules involving the semester enrolled for, senior standing if applicable, and courses in math, chemistry, industrial engineering, basic engineering, physics, English, humanities/social science electives, history, economics, and technical electives. FCBs have editable properties which allow more specific instructions to be included. Every parameter or rule must be "owned" by an FCB. However, a parameter or rule cannot be owned by both *FCB: Freshman* and *FCB:All___Others* because of the mutually exclusive condition set at the parent FCB.

SYSTEM OPERATION AND SAMPLE SESSION

The parameters and rules formalized in IEADVISE represent a comprehensive collection of undergraduate degree requirements in the Department of Industrial Engineering at the University of Missouri–Columbia. Appendix A illustrates a sample session of IEADVISE for a return/transfer student.

The session begins with a general introduction, followed by the parent FCB

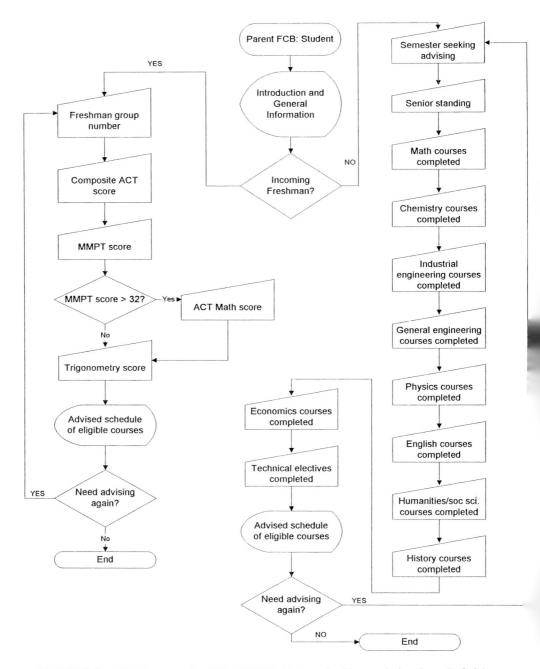

FIGURE 2   FCB framework of IEADVISE. (Adapted with permission from Ref. 9.)

query to classify either as a freshman or a return/transfer student. All of the questions in this FCB only require the user to mark with the **x** key the appropriate choice from a set of possible answers, regardless of whether the question is of a Boolean, string, or numeric type. If the user has a question about a course at any time during the consultation, a function key (PF4 key on an IBM 3270 terminal) can be pressed to get a complete course description. The user can also press another function key (PF10 key on an IBM 3270 terminal) at the final screen to see how IEADVISE arrived at the recommended schedule. IEADVISE will then show the rules enlisted and the current value of each parameter. These function key settings are listed within a small window that is always visible on the upper right-hand side of the screen during the session (not shown in the appendix). The final result consists of two parts: a feedback of the answers entered by the user (not shown in the appendix) and a set of courses which the student is eligible to register for the semester. The last screen asks the user if another advising session is desired. Aborting the session at any time and printing the session results are also a matter of pressing function keys (PF3 and PF5, respectively). An abbreviated user guide for IEADVISE is shown in Appendix B.

VERIFICATION AND VALIDATION

Initial Verification

The ESE development environment includes an interpreter which checks each knowledge-base object for syntactic correctness at the time it is entered. The interpreter also semantically checks parameter constraints and individual rule clauses. However, no semantic checking is done between clauses in a rule or between rules themselves. Therefore, it was possible for the knowledge base to contain both inconsistencies and incompleteness. Final checking was incumbent upon the authors, the expert system builders.

Three types of inconsistencies are possible: conflict, redundancy, and subsumption (3). Conflict occurs when two rules contain the same premise clauses but conclude different results. Redundancy refers to two rules containing the same premise clauses and concluding the same results. Subsumption means that two rules conclude the same results, but one rule contains additional clauses which place extra restrictions on when the rule will succeed. The less restrictive rule will always succeed whenever the more restrictive rule succeeds. These inconsistencies were manually checked by the authors during each phase of the development to ensure that they did not exist.

Incompleteness is caused by missing rules. A rule in ESE is considered missing if a desired conclusion has no rule associated with it. To check for incompleteness, the authors used flow diagrams and logic trees to search for missing rules.

Further Verification

Debugging of IEADVISE was done based on the undergraduate curriculum of the Department of Industrial Engineering. The authors consulted IEADVISE and answered the questions by entering the first semester of courses according to the curriculum sheet. The goal of this general checking was to see if IEADVISE would recommend the same courses that the curriculum sheet showed for the following semester and to see if IEADVISE would make any errors. An error was considered to be any recommendation by IEADVISE of a course that a student had already completed or was ineligible to take. Rules and parameters were then added or revised to rectify the errors.

Validation Using Current Student Files

The first validation procedure involved the use of existing student files. The authors obtained a list of all undergraduate students currently enrolled in the Department of Industrial Engineering. This list was divided into freshman, sophomore, junior, and senior categories. Eight students were randomly selected from each category. Information from their current transcript of courses were entered into the consultation environment in response to IEADVISE questions. The advising schedule generated by IEADVISE was then compared with the current trial study form (the actual schedule prepared with the help of a faculty advisor) of each student, to check for agreement between the course advising of the expert system and the human faculty advisor. The number of courses from IEADVISE that agreed with the trial study form was expressed as a percentage of correctness. Table 1 lists the result of this evaluation.

The average percentage from each student level ranged from a high of 96.87% correct (for freshmen) to a low of 70.50% correct (for seniors). The outcome was not surprising because IEADVISE's goal is to correctly advise students based on the prescribed curriculum. This task becomes more difficult as a student progresses to the senior year and has more options and electives from which to choose. In every case where there was a discrepancy, the reason why IEADVISE disagreed with a human advisor was due to one of the following reasons:

1. The student did not have all the necessary prerequisites according to the industrial engineering curriculum to enroll in the course the faculty advisor suggested (an error committed by the human advisor).

TABLE 1   Percentage Correct of IEADVISE Recommendations in Comparison with Human Advisor Recommendations

Number	Freshman	Sophomore	Junior	Senior
1	100.00	100.00	80.00	100.00
2	100.00	100.00	100.00	60.00
3	100.00	80.00	25.00	67.00
4	75.00	100.00	100.00	80.00
5	100.00	100.00	80.00	40.00
6	100.00	100.00	80.00	50.00
7	100.00	100.00	100.00	67.00
8	100.00	80.00	100.00	100.00
Average Percent				
Correct	96.87	95.00	83.13	70.50
Std. Deviation	8.84	9.26	25.49	21.77

Source: Adapted from Ref. 9, with permission.

2. The course was not required for a Bachelors of Science degree in industrial engineering.

An example of a difference was when a faculty advisor suggested that a student take an advanced English course. IEADVISE, on the other hand, was satisfied that the student had already completed the English requirement and suggested a different course that would fulfill a standing requirement in lieu of another English course. IEADVISE will suggest courses that will count toward the student's degree requirements and that will move the student closer to completion.

Note in Table 1 that for freshmen and sophomores, the average percentage correct was well above 90% with correspondingly low standard deviations. These students, being relatively new to the campus environment, typically require more advising than juniors and seniors. It was encouraging to observe that IEADVISE gave results that were very similar to a human advisor in this particular group. Juniors and seniors, on the other hand, have more flexibility and choices in their schedules. Thus, it was not surprising that the average percentage correct for their group was lower. However, with no average percentage correct below 70%, IEADVISE had achieved a fair degree of success in undergraduate course advising. Much like a human advisor, IEADVISE found it more difficult to advise the junior and senior students than the more structured freshmen and sophomore students.

Results for percentage correct that were lower than 100% did not reflect the courses suggested by IEADVISE that were not on the trial study form, rather the courses which were on the trial study form but were not suggested by IEADVISE. In this regard, IEADVISE is a more conservative course advisor. IEADVISE lists all the courses a student is eligible for, whereas a human advisor generally suggests courses within a 12–18 hour per semester range. IEADVISE is unable to distinguish between a student who may need a lighter load to boost his/her Grade Point Average (GPA) and an exceptional student who wishes to be challenged. Although more of an exception than the norm, this situation is perhaps where the personal touch of a human advisor may be more desirable than an impersonal computer program. Nonetheless, IEADVISE will save valuable time for the student and the faculty advisor by narrowing down the choices to a set of feasible courses.

Validation Using Student Evaluations

The second validation procedure involved recruiting 10 student volunteers from each industrial engineering year level, that is, freshman through senior, for a total of 40 students. Each student consulted IEADVISE, received an advising schedule, and filled out a short questionnaire. A sample questionnaire can be found in Appendix C. The objective of the evaluation was to elicit student reaction to a computerized course advisor. The questionnaire addressed six characteristics of interest, including the following:

1. Ease of use
2. Helpfulness of written and on-screen instructions
3. Timeliness
4. Accuracy of results
5. Probability of using IEADVISE again
6. Overall rating of IEADVISE

A scale of 1 to 5 was used, where 1 was Poor, and 5 was Excellent. For IEADVISE to be considered a viable alternative to the current advising process, it was decided that responses of 3 and above were acceptable values. Table 2 shows the result of this evaluation.

Although the total number of students who found IEADVISE at least acceptable in ease of use, helpfulness, timeliness, and accuracy (the first four characteristics) ranged in proportion from 0.86 to 0.95, only an average proportion of 0.65 indicated there was a chance or better that they would use IEADVISE again (the fifth characteristic). An average proportion of 0.68 rated IEADVISE as at least acceptable when compared to a human advisor (the sixth characteristic). The results seem to indicate that although IEADVISE is a fairly reliable and useful alternative for industrial engineering undergraduate course advising, students may be hesitant to give up the personal relationship they have developed with their human advisors.

For the individual student levels, the characteristics of ease of use, helpfulness, timeliness, and accuracy were consistently high, with proportion values all above 0.80 (except for Senior-Ease at 0.73). These numbers indicate that the value of IEADVISE itself is high across the board in the judgment of the students who were polled. The characteristics for probability of using again and overall comparison to human advisor collectively ranged from a low proportion of 0.40 (Sophomore-P-(Use Again)) to a high proportion of 0.80 (Freshman-P(Use Again)). The authors were at a loss to explain the low proportion of 0.40, other than to conjecture that the sophomore group may have misinterpreted the absence of the phrase "if it was made available to you" in the question to mean the probability of getting to use IEADVISE again. However, in each of the categories examined, the proportion of freshmen who rated IEADVISE with a 3 or higher was always above 0.70. Owing to the fact that freshmen generally require the most guidance of all the student levels, it was encouraging to note that this sector of the population felt confident about IEADVISE.

THE FUTURE OF COMPUTERIZED ACADEMIC COURSE ADVISING

This article described an undergraduate course-advising expert system in industrial engineering, including its knowledge base, structure, operation, verification, and validation. Based on the results of two validation procedures, a computerized course

TABLE 2   Proportion of Students Responding 3 or Higher to IEADVISE Questionnaire

Characteristic	Class				
	Freshman	Sophomore	Junior	Senior	Total
Ease	0.80	1.00	0.92	0.73	0.86
Helpfulness	0.90	1.00	1.00	0.91	0.95
Timeliness	0.90	0.90	1.00	0.91	0.93
Accuracy	1.00	0.80	1.00	0.82	0.91
P(Use Again)	0.80	0.40	0.67	0.73	0.65
Overall	0.70	0.70	0.75	0.55	0.68

Source: Adapted from Ref. 9, with permission.

adviser appears to be a viable supplement, if not an alternative, to a traditional faculty course adviser. A comparison with a sample of existing course schedules in the first validation showed IEADVISE accuracy to be high. A random sample population of students in the second validation found IEADVISE to be easy, helpful, timely, and accurate. These results were especially indicated for freshmen, a student level which needs the most guidance. Preference for it by the students compared to a faculty advisor interaction was not strongly supported in the second validation, for understandable reasons of familiarity with and the need for human interaction. Actually, an expert system for undergraduate course advising promotes the student exposure to and use of computers at an early stage. From the faculty viewpoint, the preliminary advising provided by the expert system is a definite time-saver and facilitator.

IEADVISE was implemented using a relatively simple and easy to learn, yet powerful, expert system shell (ESE). However, similar expert systems can be developed just as easily on other expert system shells on any platform. The application described here was directed only at the industrial engineering curriculum, but it can conceivably be expanded to include, or be adapted for, other disciplines. A possible extension will be to utilize external data routines to directly access a student's academic history, which already exists in the registrar's office as a restricted-access database, to save on the student having to reenter course history each time.

Today, there are many graphic user interfaces (GUIs) that make the computer interaction more appealing to the general user, and powerful modeling techniques such as object orientation which facilitate reliable reuse and organization of the course-advising process components to accommodate a broad spectrum of disciplines and environments. Ultimately, the future of computerized academic course advising will depend on the reliability and the ease of using and updating the course-advising software application.

APPENDIX A. IEADVISE SAMPLE SESSION FOR RETURN/TRANSFER STUDENTS

IEADVISE: An Expert System for Industrial Engineering Undergraduate Course Advising

by
Luis G. Occeña and Shannon L. Miller
Department of Industrial Engineering
University of Missouri–Columbia

This is an expert system that will help students to advise themselves on the courses that they are eligible to take in the upcoming semester before meeting with the faculty advisor. It is not designed to replace the faculty advisor but to serve only as an additional guide.

Before you begin the advising process, here are some general information for all students:

It is very important that each student register for Engr 132, IE 207, and IE 261 as soon as possible once he or she is eligible.

Courses which do not count towards the 126 hours necessary for a degree are:

Precalculus — Math 9, 10, 14 and 15
English 1
All Physical Education courses
All Music Theory courses and Marching Band
Military Courses (Exception: Last nine hours can count as technical electives if the student
needs technical electives. The student must receive a commission for these hours to count)

GPA Requirement:
A 2.0 for all courses that count toward the 126 hour degree. All grades count for repeated
courses.
A 2.0 for all Industrial Engineering courses. This includes Engr 132 and all courses taken in
the department.

Will you be an incoming freshman in the upcoming semester?
(Choose one of the following:)
_____ Yes
x _____ No

What semester are you seeking advising?
(Choose one of the following:)
x _____ FALL
_____ WINTER

Will you have senior standing in the semester for which you are being advised?
(Choose one of the following:)
_____ Yes
x _____ No

What is the highest level Math course you have completed or are currently enrolled in for
which you have received (or expecting to receive) a grade of "C" or higher?
(Choose one of the following:)

_____ none		_____ 201	
_____ 9		_____ 304	
_____ 10			
_____ 14			
_____ 15			
_____ 80			
x _____ 175			

Have you completed your chemistry requirement (Chemistry 5)?
(Choose one of the following:)
x _____ Yes
_____ No

What industrial engineering courses have you successfully completed (or are currently enrolled in)?
(Choose one of the following:)

_____ none	_____ 351	_____ 385
x _____ Engr 132	_____ 371	_____ 387
x _____ 207	_____ 372	_____ 388
_____ 239	_____ 381	_____ 397
x _____ 258	_____ 383	_____ 398
_____ 261	_____ 384	_____ all of the above
_____ 349		

What engineering courses are you currently enrolled in or have already completed?
(Choose one of the following:)

_____	none
x_____	20
x_____	30
_____	85
_____	124
_____	MAE OR CE 185
_____	195

What is the last Physics course you completed or are currently enrolled in (with a grade of "C" or higher)?
(Choose one of the following:)

_____	none
x_____	175
_____	176

What is the last English course you completed or are currently enrolled in?
(Choose one of the following:)

_____	none
_____	placement into 20
_____	placement into 20GH
_____	10
x_____	20
_____	20GH

Have you completed your humanities/social science electives (6–10 hours)? This includes 3 courses within a subgroup or cluster as determined by the College of Engineering. One of these courses must be numbered 100 or higher.
(Choose one of the following:)

_____	Yes
x_____	No

Have you fulfilled your history requirement? Typical courses that satisfy this requirement include History 3, 4, or 20; Political Science 1 or 11.
(Choose one of the following:)

x_____	Yes
_____	No

Have you fulfilled your economics requirement? Approved courses include Economics 1 or 2.
(Choose one of the following:)

_____	Yes
x_____	No

Have you completed all of your technical electives (5 hrs)?
(Choose one of the following:)

_____	Yes
x_____	No

The math courses you are eligible to take is 201.
The chemistry you may take is none required.
The physics course you are eligible to take is 176.
The English course you are eligible to take is none required.
The list of engineering courses you are eligible to take are

398
383
The electives you may take are
  economics requirement (3 hrs)
  humanities/social science electives (9 hrs)
  technical electives (5 hrs)

Do you want to go through the advising process again?
(Choose one of the following:)
_____   Yes
<u>x</u>___   No

Source: Reference 9.

APPENDIX B. INSTRUCTIONS FOR USING IEADVISE

Welcome to IEADVISE. IEADVISE is a resident expert system on the University of Missouri–Columbia mainframe MIZZOU1 for undergraduate course advising in Industrial Engineering. The goal of IEADVISE is to assist the Industrial Engineering undergraduate student in planning a next semester course schedule. Do this planning before meeting with your faculty advisor.

GENERAL HINTS BEFORE GETTING STARTED
Down or an arrow pointing down means there is more text on the next screen. *Press PF8 (or its equivalent key map) to scroll down.*
UP or an arrow pointing up means there is text on the previous screen. *Press PF7 (or its equivalent key map) to scroll up.*

PFKEYS:
PF1 Help — gives help information on ESE.
PF2 Toggle PF — toggles between 2 sets of PF key commands.
PF3 End — ends the consultation.
PF4 What — gives course descriptions.
PF5 Save — saves output in a print file.
PF6 Unknown — tells IEADVISE that the answer it is seeking is unknown to the user.
PF7 Up — scrolls upward.
PF8 Down — scrolls downward.
PF10 How — tells how IEADVISE arrived at a conclusion on the final screen.
PF12 Command — puts cursor on command line.

If you answer a question incorrectly and would like to go back to it, press PF2 to toggle to the other set of PF keys. Press PF10 Undo — to start going back to previous questions. Remember to press PF2 to toggle back when finished.

INSTRUCTIONS FOR USING IEADVISE
  1. Log onto the system using userid *ieadvise*.
  2. At the ready promplt, enter *setup ese*. IEADVISE is not case sensitive.
  3. To invoke the consultation environment, enter *esxc*.
  4. You may now either:
      a) enter *ieadvise* on the command line, or
      b) press the PF2 key. Move the cursor to IEADVISE and press the Enter key.
  5. To consult IEADVISE, enter *consult* on the command line.
  6. Answer the questions as prompted by IEADVISE, using any alphanumeric key.

7. To print the recommended schedule, press the PF5 key at the final screen. Follow site procedure for printing saved files.
8. To quit, press the PF3 key at any time.
9. Logoff.

APPENDIX C. IEADVISE VALIDATION QUESTIONNAIRE FOR USERS

Year in School
(Please Circle One)
FR   SO   JR   SR

Please circle the number that most closely represents your attitude about IEADVISE. Keep in mind that the purpose is to compare the computer expert to the human expert. Answer each questions based on your corresponding experience with your advisor.

How easy is IEADVISE to use?

1	2	3	4	5
Poor				Excellent

How helpful were the instructions (both written and on the screen)?

1	2	3	4	5
Poor				Excellent

How much time did it take to use IEADVISE compared to using an advisor?

1	2	3	4	5
Poor				Excellent

How accurate were the results? (Do you feel that you were advised to take the same courses that a human advisor would advise?)

1	2	3	4	5
Poor				Excellent

What is the probability that you would use IEADVISE again?

1	2	3	4	5
Poor				Excellent

Overall, how does IEADVISE compare to a human advisor?

1	2	3	4	5
Poor				Excellent

Source: Reference 9.

REFERENCES

1. P. L. Rees, "Practical Considerations Associated with Expert Systems," *Indus. Man. and Data Sys.*, Jan.–Feb. 3–6 (1988).
2. G. A. Finn, "Rules of Thumb for Implementing Expert Systems in Engineering," *In-Tech, 34*(4), 33–37 (1987).
3. IBM Corp., *Expert System Development Environment User Guide*, 2nd ed., IBM Corporation, Bethesda, MD, 1989.

4. E. Konrad, "Principles of Expert Systems," *Int. J. Appl. Eng. Ed., 6*(2), 113–117 (1990).
5. R. Paton, "Managing the Expert," *Indus. Man and Data Sys.*, April, 20–23 (1989).
6. J. M. Hatfield, "A Pseudo Expert Teaching Assistant," *Int. J. Appl. Eng. Ed., 6*(2), 265–268 (1990).
7. S. Wood, "The Trainee Teacher Support System: An Expert System for Advising Trainee Teachers on their Classroom Experience," *Expert Systems, 5*(4), 282–289 (1988).
8. Y. Shen and A. T. Bahill, "An In-Depth Study of An Expert System That Helps Evaluate Graduate Study Programs and a Statistical Summary of 25 Little Expert Systems," *Proc. IEEE Int. Conf. Systems, Man, Cybernet., SMC-2*, 249–251 (1988).
9. L. G. Occeña and S. L. Miller, "IEADVISE—An Undergraduate Course-Advising Expert System in Industrial Engineering," *Expert Systems, 10*(3), 139–149 (1993).
10. L. G. David, "Industrial Engineering Undergraduate Advising Packet," Department of Industrial Engineering, University of Missouri-Columbia, Columbia, MO (1990).
11. P. Braisted, "Engineering Advisor's Manual," College of Engineering, University of Missour-Columbia, Columbia, MO, 1990.
12. J. G. Burch and G. Grudnitski, *Information Systems: Theory and Practice*, John Wiley & Sons, New York, 1989.

BIBLIOGRAPHY

Adrion, W. R., M. A. Branstad, and J. C., Chernavsky, "Validation, Verification, and Testing of Computer Software," *ACM Comput. Surveys, 14*(2), 159–192 (1982).
Feigenbaum, E. A., and P. McCorduck, *The Fifth Generation*, Addison-Wesley, Reading, MA, 1983.
Gaschnig, J., P. Klahr, H. Pople, E. Shortliffe, and A. Terry, *Evaluation of Expert Systems: Issues and Case Studies in Building Expert Systems*, Addison-Wesley, Reading, MA, 1983.

LUIS G. OCCEÑA

SHANNON L. MILLER